The Phoenix Project

The Phoenix Project

A Novel About IT, DevOps,
and Helping Your Business Win

Gene Kim, Kevin Behr & George Spafford

25 NW 23rd Pl, Suite 6314
Portland, OR 97210

Third Edition
Printed in the United States of America
23 22 21 20 19 18   2 3 4 5 6 7 8 9 10

The Phoenix Project book design by Abbey Gaterud

ISBN: 978-1942788294
eBook ISBN: 978-1942788300
Kindle ISBN: 978-1942788324
Web PDF ISBN: 978-1942788317

The DevOps Handbook book design by Mammoth Collective

For information about special discounts for bulk purchases
or for information on booking authors for an event,
please visit our website at www.ITRevolution.com.

THE PHOENIX PROJECT, 5TH ANNIVERSARY EDITION

The Phoenix Project

PARTS UNLIMITED

Parts Unlimited: Business Executives

Steve Masters, CEO, acting CIO
Dick Landry, CFO
Sarah Moulton, SVP of Retail Operations
Maggie Lee, Senior Director of Retail Program Management
Bill Palmer, VP of IT Operations, former Director of Midrange
    Technology Operations
Wes Davis, Director of Distributed Technology Operations
Brent Geller, Lead Engineer
Patty McKee, Director of IT Service Support
John Pesche, Chief Information Security Officer (CISO)
Chris Allers, VP of Application Development

Parts Unlimited: Board

Bob Strauss, Lead Director, former Chairman, former CEO
Erik Reid, Board Candidate
Nancy Mailer, Chief Audit Executive

FOR IMMEDIATE RELEASE

Friday, August 29
Company: Parts Unlimited (PAUD)
Rating: SELL
Price Target: $8 (current $13)

Effective immediately, Parts Unlimited CEO, Steve Masters, is stepping down from his role as chairman after eight years of holding that position. Board Director Bob Strauss, who served as company chairman and CEO two decades ago, is returning from retirement to assume the role of chairman.

Parts Unlimited stock has tumbled 19 percent in the last 30 days under heavy trading, down 52 percent from its peak three years ago. The company continues to be outmaneuvered by its arch rival, famous for its ability to anticipate and instantly react to customer needs. Parts Unlimited now trails the competition in sales growth, inventory turns and profitability.

The company has long promised that its "Phoenix" program will restore profitability and close the gap by tightly integrating its retailing and e-commerce channels. Already years late, many expect the company to announce another program delay in its analyst earnings call next month.

We believe that institutional investors such as Wayne-Yokohama pressured Bob to reconfigure the board as the first of many actions to right the ship in Elkhart Grove. A growing number of investors are pushing for more significant leadership changes and strategic options, such as splitting up the company.

Despite Masters' past achievements that transformed Parts Unlimited into one of the top automotive parts manufacturers and retailers, we believe splitting up the chairman and CEO roles is long overdue. Parts Unlimited needs fresh leadership, either from the outside or from within. We believe Sarah Moulton, SVP of Retail Operations, and a rising star at the company, could just be what the company needs.

According to our sources, the board has given Strauss and Masters six months to make dramatic improvements. If they can't pull this off, expect more changes and turbulent times.

—Kelly Lawrence, Chief Industry Analyst, Nestor Meyers

###

Part 1

CHAPTER 1

• *Tuesday, September 2*

"Bill Palmer here," I say, answering my cell phone on the first ring.

I'm late, so I'm driving ten miles per hour over the speed limit, instead of my usual five. I spent the morning at the doctor's office with my three-year-old son, trying to keep the other toddlers from coughing on us, constantly being interrupted by my vibrating phone.

The problem of the day is intermittent network outages. As the Director of Midrange Technology Operations, I'm responsible for the availability and smooth functioning of a relatively small IT group at Parts Unlimited, a $4 billion per year manufacturing and retail company based in Elkhart Grove.

Even in the technology backwaters I've chosen to make my turf, I need to track network issues closely. Because these issues disrupt the services my group provides, people will blame the outages on me.

"Hi, Bill. This is Laura Beck, from Human Resources." She's not the person I usually deal with from HR, but her name and voice sound familiar…

Holy crap. I try not to swear out loud when I remember who she is. From the monthly company meetings. She's the VP in charge of HR.

"Good morning, Laura," I say with forced cheer. "What can I do for you?"

She responds, "When will you be in the office? I'd like to meet as soon as possible."

I hate vague requests to meet. I only do that when I'm trying to schedule a time to chew someone out. Or fire them.

Wait. Is Laura calling because someone wants to fire me? Was there an outage I didn't respond to quickly enough? As an IT Operations guy, the career-ending outage is the joke my peers and I tell one another daily.

We agree to meet at her desk in a half hour, but when she doesn't share any more details, I say in my most cajoling voice, "Laura, what's this all about? Is there a problem in my group? Or am I the one in trouble?" I laugh extra loudly, so she hears it over the phone.

"No, it's nothing like that," she says breezily. "You could even say this is good news. Thanks, Bill."

When she hangs up, I try to think of what good news would even look like these days. When I can't, I turn the radio back on and immediately hear a commercial from our largest retailing competitor. They're talking about their unparalleled customer service and a breathtaking new offering that allows people to customize their cars with their friends online.

The ad is brilliant. I'd use the service in a second, if I weren't such a loyal company man. How do they keep bringing such incredible new capabilities to market while we remain stuck in the mud?

I turn the radio off. Despite all our hard work and late nights, the competition keeps leapfrogging us. When our Marketing people hear this ad, they'll go ballistic. Because they're likely art or music majors, not people with a technology background, they'll publicly promise the impossible and IT will have to figure out how to deliver.

Each year, it gets harder. We have to do more with less, to simultaneously maintain competitiveness and reduce costs.

Some days, I think that it can't be done. Maybe I spent too much time as a sergeant in the Marines. You learn that you argue your case as best as you can with your officer, but sometimes you have to say, "Yes, sir," and then go take that hill.

I pull into the parking lot. Three years ago, finding an empty parking spot was impossible. Now, after all the layoffs, parking is rarely a problem.

When I walk into Building 5 where Laura and her staff reside, I immediately notice how nicely furnished it is. I can smell the new carpeting and there's even classy wood paneling on the walls. Suddenly, the paint and carpet in my building seem decades overdue for replacement.

That's IT's lot in life. At least we're not in a dingy, dimly lit dank basement, like in the British TV show, *The IT Crowd*.

When I get to Laura's office, she looks up and smiles. "Good seeing you again, Bill." She extends her hand, which I shake. "Have a seat while I see whether Steve Masters is available to meet."

Steve Masters? Our CEO?

She picks up and dials her phone while I sit down, looking around. The last time I was here was a couple of years ago when HR notified us that we needed to dedicate a room for nursing mothers. We were critically short of office and meeting space, and we had big project deadlines looming.

We merely wanted to use a conference room in a different building. However, Wes made it sound like we were a bunch of 1950s *Mad Men* Neanderthals. Shortly afterward, we were both summoned here for a half day of political rehabilitation and sensitivity training. Thanks, Wes.

Among other things, Wes is in charge of the networks, which is why I track network outages so closely.

Laura thanks the person on the other end of the phone and turns back to me. "Thanks for coming down on short notice. How is your family doing these days?" she asks.

My brow furrows. If I wanted to chitchat, there are many people I'd rather talk to than someone in HR. I force myself to banter about our families and kids, trying not to think about my other pressing commitments. Eventually I say, without much grace, "So, what can I do for you this morning?"

"Of course." She pauses, and then says, "Effective as of this morning, Luke and Damon are no longer with the company. This went all the way to the top, with Steve getting involved. He's chosen you to be the VP of IT Operations."

She smiles broadly, holding out her hand again, "You're our newest VP in the company, Bill. I think some congratulations are in order?"

Holy crap. I numbly shake her hand.

No, no, no. The last thing I want is a "promotion."

Luke was our CIO, or Chief Information Officer. Damon worked for him and was my boss, in charge of IT Operations across the entire company. Both gone, just like that.

I didn't see this coming. There wasn't any chatter on the subspace radio. Nothing.

For the last decade, like clockwork, new CIOS would come and go every two years. They stay just long enough to understand the acronyms, learn where the bathrooms are, implement a bunch of programs and initiatives to upset the apple cart, and then they're gone.

CIO stands for "Career Is Over." And VPs of IT Operations don't last much longer.

I've figured out that the trick to a long career in IT Operations management is to get enough seniority to get good things done but to keep your head low enough to avoid the political battles that make you inherently vulnerable. I have absolutely no interest in becoming one of the VPs who just give each other PowerPoints all day long.

Fishing for more information, I joke, "Two executives leaving at the same time? Were they stealing money from the stores late at night?"

She laughs, but quickly returns to her HR-trained deadpan, "They both chose to pursue other interests. More than that, you'll have to find out from them."

As the saying goes, if your colleague tells you they've decided to quit, it was voluntary. But when someone else tells you they've decided to quit, it was mandatory.

Ergo, my boss and his boss were just whacked.

This is exactly why I don't want a promotion. I'm extremely proud of the team I've built over the last ten years. It's not the largest group, but we're the most organized and dependable, by far. Especially compared to Wes.

I groan at the thought of managing Wes. He doesn't manage a team— he's barely one step ahead of a chaotic mob.

As I break out in a cold sweat, I know I will never accept this promotion.

All this time, Laura has been talking, and I haven't heard a single word. "—and so we'll obviously need to talk about how we're going to announce this transition. And Steve wants to see you as soon as possible."

"Look, thanks for the opportunity. I'm honored. But I don't want this role. Why would I? I love my current job, and there are tons of important things that still need to be done."

"I don't think this is optional," she says, looking sympathetic. "This came straight from Steve. He chose you personally, so you'll have to talk with him."

I stand up and reiterate firmly, "No, really. Thanks for thinking of me, but I've already got a great job. Good luck finding someone else."

Minutes later, Laura is walking me to Building 2, the tallest building on campus. I'm angry at myself for getting sucked into this insanity.

If I run now, I'm pretty sure she wouldn't be able to catch me, but then what? Steve would just send a whole squad of HR goons to fetch me.

I don't say anything, definitely not feeling like small talk anymore. Laura doesn't seem to care, walking briskly beside me, nose buried in her phone, occasionally gesturing directions.

She finds Steve's office without ever looking up, obviously having made this walk many times before.

This floor is warm and inviting, furnished just like it was in the 1920s, when the building was constructed. With dark hardwood floors and stained glass windows, it's from an era when everyone wore suits and smoked cigars in their offices. The company was booming then—Parts Unlimited made various widgets inside almost every make of automobile, when horses were being vanquished from daily life.

Steve has a corner office, where a no-nonsense woman is keeping guard. She's about forty, radiating cheerfulness and a sense of organization and order. Her desk is tidy, with Post-it notes everywhere on the wall. There's a coffee mug with the words "Don't Mess With Stacy" by her keyboard.

"Hi, Laura," she says, looking up from her computer. "Busy day, huh? So, this is Bill?"

"Yep. In the flesh," Laura replies, smiling.

To me she says, "Stacy keeps Steve in line. You'll grow to know her well, I suspect. You and I can finish up later." Then she leaves.

Stacy smiles at me. "Pleasure. I've heard a lot about you already. Steve is expecting you." She points to his door.

I immediately like her. And I think about what I've just learned. It's been a busy day for Laura. Stacy and Laura are on very familiar terms. Steve has HR on speed dial. Apparently, people who work for Steve don't last long.

Great.

Walking in, I'm a little surprised to find Steve's office looks just like

Laura's. It's the same size as my boss' office—or rather, my ex-boss' office—and potentially my new office if I'm stupid, which I am not.

Maybe I was expecting Persian rugs, water fountains, and large sculptures everywhere. Instead, there are photos on the wall of a small propeller airplane, his smiling family, and, to my surprise, one of him in a US Army uniform on a runway somewhere tropical. I note with surprise the insignia visible on his lapels.

So, Steve was a major.

He is sitting behind his desk, scrutinizing what appear to be paper spreadsheets. There's a laptop open behind him, displaying a browser full of stock graphs.

"Bill, good to see you again," he says, standing and shaking my hand. "It's been a long time. About five years, right? It was after you pulled off that amazing project to integrate one of the manufacturing acquisitions. I trust life has been treating you well?"

I'm surprised and a bit flattered that he remembered our brief interaction, especially when it was so long ago. I smile in return, saying, "Yes, very well, thank you. I'm amazed you remember something so far back."

"You think we give out awards like that to just anyone?" he says earnestly. "That was an important project. To make that acquisition pay off, we needed to nail it, which you and your team did superbly.

"I'm sure Laura has told you a bit about the organizational changes I've made. You know Luke and Damon are no longer with the company. I intend to fill the CIO position eventually, but in the meantime, all of IT will report to me."

He continues, brisk and businesslike, "However, with Damon's departure, I have an organizational hole I need to fill. Based on our research, you're clearly the best candidate to take over as VP of IT Operations."

As if he just remembered, he says, "You were a Marine. When and where?"

I announce automatically, "22nd Marine Expeditionary Unit. Sergeant. I was in for six years but never saw combat."

Remembering how I joined the Marines as a cocky eighteen-year-old, I say with a small smile, "The Corps really straightened me out—I owe them a lot, but I sure hope neither of my sons join under the same conditions I did."

"I bet," Steve laughs. "I was in the Army for eight years myself, slightly longer than I was obligated to. But I didn't mind. ROTC was the only way I could pay for college, and they treated me well."

He adds, "They didn't coddle us like they did you Marines, but I still can't complain."

I laugh, finding myself liking him. This is the longest interaction we've had. I suddenly wonder if this is what politicians are like.

I try to stay focused on why he summoned me here: He's going to ask me to undertake some kamikaze mission.

"Here's the situation," he says, motioning me to have a seat at his conference table. "As I'm sure you're aware, we must regain profitability. To do that, we need to increase our market share and average order sizes. Our retail competitors are kicking our ass. The whole world knows this, which is why our stock price is half what it was three years ago."

He continues, "Project Phoenix is essential to closing the gap with the competition, so we can finally do what the competition has been doing for years. Customers need to be able to buy from us from wherever they want, whether it's on the Internet or in our retail stores. Otherwise, we'll soon have no customers, at all."

I nod. I might be in the technology backwaters, but my team has been involved with Phoenix for years. Everyone knows how important it is.

"We're years late delivering," he continues. "Our investors and Wall Street are howling. And now, my board is losing confidence in our ability to hit our commitments.

"I'll be blunt," he says. "The way things are going, I'll be out of a job in six months. As of last week, Bob Strauss, my old boss, is the new chairman of the company. There's a vocal group of shareholders trying to split up the company, and I don't know how much longer we can fend them off. What's at stake here is not just my job, but the nearly four thousand employees who work here at Parts Unlimited."

Suddenly, Steve looks much older than the early fifties I had guessed him to be. Looking right at me, he says, "As acting CIO, Chris Allers, our VP of Application Development, will report to me. And so will you."

He stands up and starts to pace, "I need you to keep all the things that are supposed to be up, well, up. I need someone reliable, who isn't afraid to tell me bad news. Above all, I need someone I can trust to do the right thing. That integration project had many challenges, but you always kept a cool head. You've built a reputation as someone who is dependable, pragmatic, and willing to say what you really think."

He's been candid with me, so I reply with the same. "Sir, with all due respect, it seems very difficult for senior IT leadership to succeed here. Any request for budget or staff is always shot down, and executives are replaced so quickly, some never even get a chance to fully unpack."

With finality, I say, "Midrange Operations is critical to getting Phoenix done, too. I need to stay there to see those things through to completion. I appreciate you thinking of me, but I can't accept. However, I promise I'll keep my eyes open for any good candidates."

Steve looks at me appraisingly, his expression surprisingly grave. "We've had to cut budgets across the entire company. That edict came straight from my board. My hands were tied. I won't make promises I can't keep, but I can promise you I'll do whatever it takes to support you and your mission.

"Bill, I know you didn't ask for this job, but the company's survival is at stake here. I need you to help me save this great company. Can I count on you?"

Oh, come on.

Before I can politely decline again, I suddenly hear myself saying, "Yes, sir, you can count on me."

I panic, realizing that Steve somehow used some Jedi mind trick on me. I force myself to stop talking, before I make more dumb promises.

"Congratulations," Steve says, standing up and shaking my hand firmly. He clasps my shoulder. "I knew you'd do the right thing. On behalf of the entire executive team, we're grateful for you stepping up."

I look at his hand grasping mine, wondering if I can backpeddle my way out.

Not a chance in hell, I decide.

Swearing to myself, I say, "I'll do my best, sir. And could you at least explain why no one who accepts this position lasts very long? What do you want most from me? And what don't you want?"

With a resigned half smile, I add, "If I fail, I'll try to make sure it's in a new and novel way."

"I like that!" Steve says, laughing loudly. "What I want is for IT to keep the lights on. It should be like using the toilet. I use the toilet and, hell, I don't ever worry about it not working. What I don't want is to have the toilets back up and flood the entire building." He smiles broadly at his own joke.

Great. In his mind, I'm a glorified janitor.

He continues, "You have a reputation of running the tightest ship in the IT organization. So I'm giving you the entire fleet. I expect you to make them all run the same way.

"I need Chris focused on Phoenix execution. Anything in your area of responsibility that takes focus away from Phoenix is unacceptable. That applies not just to you and Chris, but everyone else in this company. Is that clear?"

"Absolutely," I say, nodding. "You want the IT systems to be reliable and available, and for the business to be able to depend upon them. You want disruptions to normal operations kept to an absolute minimum so that the business can focus on getting Phoenix done."

Looking surprised, Steve nods. "Exactly. Yes, well put. Whatever you said, that's exactly what I want."

He hands me an e-mail printout from Dick Landry, the CFO.

> From: Dick Landry
> To: Steve Masters
> Date: September 2, 8:27 AM
> Priority: Highest
> Subject: ACTION NEEDED: payroll run is failing
>
> Hey, Steve. We've got serious issues with this week's payroll. We're trying to figure out if the problem is with the numbers or in the payroll system. Either way, thousands of employees have paychecks stuck in system & are at risk of not getting paid. Seriously bad news.
>
> We must fix this before payroll window closes at 5 PM today. Please advise on how to escalate this, given the new IT org.
>
> Dick

I wince. Employees not getting paychecks means families not being able to pay their mortgages or put food on the table.

Suddenly, I realize that my family's mortgage payment is due in four days, and we could be one of the families affected. A late mortgage payment could screw up our credit rating even more, which we spent years repairing after we put Paige's student loans on my credit card.

"You want me to jump on this and manage the incident to conclusion?"

Steve nods, giving me the thumbs-up. "Keep me posted on the progress, please." His expression turns grave. "Every responsible company takes care of its employees. Many of our factory workers live from paycheck to paycheck. Do not create hardship for their families, you hear? This could get us in trouble with the union, maybe even triggering a work-stoppage, creating some very bad press for us."

I nod automatically. "Restore critical business operations and keep us out of the front-page news. Got it. Thanks."

Why, exactly, I'm thanking him is not clear.

CHAPTER 2

• *Tuesday, September 2*

"How'd it go in there?" Stacy asks kindly, looking up from her keyboard.

I just shake my head. "I can't believe it. He just talked me into taking a new job I don't want. How did that happen?"

"He can be very persuasive," she says. "For what it's worth, he's one-of-a-kind. I've worked for him for nearly ten years, and I'll follow him anywhere. Anything I can help with to make your job easier?"

Thinking for a moment, I ask, "There's an urgent payroll issue that needs to be fixed. Dick Landry is on floor three, right?"

"Here you go," she says, before I've finished asking my question, handing me a Post-it note with all of Dick's contact information. Office location, phone numbers, and everything.

Grateful, I smile at her. "Thanks a lot—you are fantastic!"

I dial Dick's cell phone on my way to the elevator. "Dick here," he answers gruffly, still typing in the background.

"This is Bill Palmer. Steve just made me the new VP of IT Operations, and he asked me to—"

"Congratulations," he interrupts. "Now look, my people found a huge payroll irregularity. When can you get to my office?"

"Right away," I reply. I hear the click of him ending the call. I've had warmer welcomes.

On the third floor, I walk through Finance and Accounting, surrounded by pinstriped shirts and starched collars. I find Dick at his desk, still on the phone with someone. When he sees me, he puts his hand over the mouthpiece. "You from IT?" he asks gruffly.

When I nod, he says into the phone, "Look, I gotta run. Someone who's supposedly going to help is finally here. I'll call you back." Without waiting for an answer, he hangs up the phone.

I've never actually seen someone who routinely hangs up on people. I brace myself for a conversation that is likely to be short on any comforting "let's get to know each other" foreplay.

As if in a hostage situation, I slowly raise my hands, showing Dick the printed e-mail. "Steve just told me about the payroll outage. What's the best way for me to get some situational awareness here?"

"We're in deep kimchi," Dick responds. "In yesterday's payroll run, all of the records for the hourly employees went missing. We're pretty sure it's an IT issue. This screwup is preventing us from paying our employees, violating countless state labor laws, and, no doubt, the union is going to scream bloody murder."

He mutters under his breath for a moment. "Let's go see Ann, my Operations Manager. She's been pulling her hair out since yesterday afternoon."

Walking quickly to keep up, I nearly run into him when he stops and peers through a conference room window. He opens the door. "How's it going in here, Ann?"

There are two well-dressed women in the room: one, around forty-five years old, studies the whiteboard, filled with flowcharts and a lot of tabulated numbers, and the other, in her early thirties, types on a laptop. Spreadsheets are strewn all over the large conference room table. The older woman gestures with an open marker at what appears to be a list of potential failure causes.

Something about the way they dress, and their concerned and irritated expressions, makes me think they were recruited from a local accounting firm. Ex-auditors. Good to have them on our side, I suppose.

Ann shakes her head in exhausted frustration. "Not much progress, I'm afraid. We're almost certain this is an IT systems failure in one of the upstream timekeeping systems. All of the hourly factory worker records got screwed up in the last upload—"

Dick interrupts her. "This is Bill from IT. He's been assigned to fix this mess or die trying, is what I think he said."

I say, "Hi, guys. I've just been made the new head of IT Operations. Can you start from the beginning and tell me what you know about the problem?"

Ann walks over to the flowchart on the whiteboard. "Let's start with the information flow. Our financial system gets payroll data from all our various divisions in different ways. We roll up all the numbers for salaried and hourly personnel, which includes wages and taxes. Sounds easy, but it's extremely complex, because each state has different tax tables, labor laws, and so forth.

"To make sure something doesn't get screwed up," she continues, "we make sure the summarized numbers match the detailed numbers from each division."

As I hurriedly jot down some notes, she continues, "It's a pretty clunky and manual process. It works most of the time, but yesterday we discovered that the general ledger upload for hourly production staff didn't come through. All of the hourlies had zeroes for their hours worked and amount due.

"We've had so many problems with this particular upload," she says, obviously frustrated, "that IT gave us a program that we use to do manual corrections, so we don't have to bother them anymore."

I wince. I don't like finance personnel manually changing payroll data outside the payroll application. It's error-prone and dangerous. Someone could copy that data onto a USB drive or e-mail it outside of the organization, which is how organizations lose sensitive data.

"Did you say all the numbers for salaried employees are okay?" I ask.

"That's right," she replies.

"But hourly employees are all zeroes," I confirm.

"Yep," she again replies.

Interesting. I ask, "Why do you think the payroll run failed when it was working before? Have you had problems like this in the past?"

She shrugs. "Nothing like this has happened before. I have no idea what could have caused it—no major changes were scheduled for this pay period. I've been asking the same questions, but until we hear from the IT guys, we're stuck dead in the water."

"What is our backup plan," I ask, "if things are so hosed that we can't get the hourly employee data in time?"

"For crying out loud," Dick says. "It's in that e-mail you're holding. The deadline for electronic payments is 5 p.m., today. If we can't hit that window, we may have to FedEx bales of paper checks to each of our facilities for them to distribute to employees!"

I frown at this scenario and so does the rest of the finance team.

"That won't work," Ann says, clicking a marker on her teeth. "We've outsourced our payroll processing. Each pay period, we upload the payroll data to them, which they then process. In the worst case, maybe we download the previous payroll run, modify it in a spreadsheet, and then re-upload it?

"But because we don't know how many hours each employee worked, we don't know how much to pay them!" she continues. "We don't want to overpay anyone, but that's better than accidentally underpaying them."

It's obvious that plan B is fraught with problems. We'd basically be guessing at people's paychecks, as well as paying people who were terminated, and not paying people who were newly hired.

To get Finance the data they need, we may have to cobble together some custom reports, which means bringing in the application developers or database people.

But that's like throwing gasoline on the fire. Developers are even worse than networking people. Show me a developer who isn't crashing production systems, and I'll show you one who can't fog a mirror. Or more likely, is on vacation.

Dick says, "These are two lousy options. We could delay our payroll run until we have the correct data. But we can't do this—even if we're only a day late, we'll have the union stepping in. So, that leaves Ann's proposal of paying our employees something, even if it's the incorrect amount. We'd have to adjust everyone's paycheck in the next pay period. But now we have a financial reporting error that we've got to go back and fix."

He pinches the bridge of his nose and continues to ramble. "We'll have a bunch of odd journal entries in our general ledger, just when our auditors are here for our SOX-404 audits. When they see this, they'll *never* leave.

"Oh, man. A financial reporting error?" Dick mutters. "We'll need approval from Steve. We're going to have auditors camped out here until the cows come home. No one'll ever get any real work done again."

SOX-404 is short for the Sarbanes-Oxley Act of 2002, which Congress enacted in response to the accounting failures at Enron, WorldCom, and Tyco. It means the CEO and CFO have to personally sign their names, attesting that their company's financial statements are accurate.

Everyone longs for the days when we didn't spend half our time talking to auditors, complying with each new regulatory requirement *du jour*.

I look at my notes and then at the clock. Time is running out.

"Dick, based on what I've heard, I recommend that you continue to plan for the worst and we fully document plan B, so we can pull it off without further complications. Furthermore, I request that we wait until 3 p.m. before making a decision. We may be still able to get all the systems and data back."

When Ann nods, Dick says, "Okay, you've got four hours."

I say, "Rest assured that we understand the urgency of the situation and that you'll be apprised of how it's going as soon as I find out myself."

"Thanks, Bill," Ann says. Dick remains silent as I turn around and walk out the door.

I feel better, now that I've seen the problem from the business perspective. It's now time to get under the covers and find out what broke the complex payroll machinery.

While walking down the stairs, I dig out my phone and scan my e-mails. My feeling of calm focus disappears when I see that Steve hasn't sent out an announcement of my promotion. Wes Davis and Patty McKee, who until today were my peers, still have no idea that I'm now their new boss.

Thanks, Steve.

When I enter Building 7, it hits me. Our building is the ghetto of the entire Parts Unlimited campus.

It was built in the 1950s, and last remodeled in the 1970s, obviously built for utility, not aesthetics. Building 7 used to be our large brake-pad manufacturing factory until it was converted into data center and office space. It looks old and neglected.

The security guard says cheerfully, "Hello, Mr. Palmer. How is the morning going so far?"

For a moment, I'm tempted to ask him to wish me luck, so he can get paid the correct amount this week. Of course, I merely return his friendly greeting.

I'm headed toward the Network Operations Center, or as we call it, the NOC, where Wes and Patty are most likely to be. They're now my two primary managers.

Wes is Director of Distributed Technology Operations. He has technical responsibility for over a thousand Windows servers, as well as the database and networking teams. Patty is the Director of IT Service Support. She owns all the level 1 and 2 help desk technicians who answer the phones around the clock, handling break-fix issues and support requests from the business. She also owns some of the key processes and tools that the entire IT Operations organization relies upon, like the trouble ticketing system, monitoring, and running the change management meetings.

I walk past rows upon rows of cubicles, the same as every other building. However, unlike Buildings 2 and 5, I see peeling paint and dark stains seeping through the carpet.

This part of the building was built on top of what used to be the main assembly floor. When they converted it, they couldn't get all the machine oil cleaned up. No matter how much sealant we put down to coat the floors, oil still has a tendency to seep through the carpet.

I make a note to put in a budget request to replace the carpets and paint the walls. In the Marines, keeping the barracks neat and tidy was not only for aesthetics but also for safety.

Old habits die hard.

I hear the NOC before I see it. It's a large bullpen area, with long tables set up along one wall, displaying the status of all the various IT services on large monitors. The level 1 and 2 help desk people sit at the three rows of workstations.

It's not exactly like mission control in *Apollo 13*, but that's how I explain it to my relatives.

When something hits the fan, you need all the various stakeholders and technology managers to communicate and coordinate until the problem is resolved. Like now. At the conference table, fifteen people are in the midst of a loud and heated discussion, huddled around one of the classic gray speakerphones that resembles a UFO.

Wes and Patty are sitting next to each other at the conference table, so I walk behind them to listen in. Wes leans back in his chair with his arms crossed over his stomach. They don't get all the way across. At six feet three inches tall and over 250 pounds, he casts a shadow on most people. He seems to be in constant motion and has a reputation of saying whatever is on his mind.

Patty is the complete opposite. Where Wes is loud, outspoken, and shoots from the hip, Patty is thoughtful, analytical, and a stickler for processes and procedures. Where Wes is large, combative, and sometimes even quarrelsome, Patty is elfin, logical, and levelheaded. She has a reputation for loving processes more than people and is often in the position of trying to impose order on the chaos in IT.

She's the face of the entire IT organization. When things go wrong in IT, people call Patty. She's our professional apologist, whether it's services crashing, web pages taking too long to load, or, as in today's case, missing or corrupted data.

They also call Patty when they need their work done—like upgrading a computer, changing a phone number, or deploying a new application. She does all of the scheduling, so people are always lobbying her to get their work done first. She'll then hand it off to people who do the work. For the most part, they live in either my old group or in Wes' group.

Wes pounds the table, saying, "Just get the vendor on the phone and tell them that unless they get a tech down here pronto, we're going to the competition. We're one of their largest customers! We should probably have abandoned that pile of crap by now, come to think of it."

He looks around and jokes, "You know the saying, right? The way you can tell a vendor is lying is when their lips are moving."

One of the engineers across from Wes says, "We have them on the phone right now. They say it'll be at least four hours before their SAN field engineer is on-site."

I frown. Why are they talking about the SAN? Storage area networks provide centralized storage to many of our most critical systems, so failures are typically global: It won't be just one server that goes down; it'll be hundreds of servers that go down all at once.

While Wes starts arguing with the engineer, I try to think. Nothing about this payroll run failure sounds like a SAN issue. Ann suggested that it was probably something in the timekeeping applications supporting each plant.

"But after we tried to rollback the SAN, it stopped serving data entirely," another engineer says. "Then the display started displaying everything in kanji! Well, we think it was kanji. Whatever it was, we couldn't make heads or tails of those little pictures. That's when we knew we needed to get the vendor involved."

Although I'm joining late, I'm convinced we're totally on the wrong track.

I lean in to whisper to Wes and Patty, "Can I get a minute with you guys in private?"

Wes turns and, without giving me his full attention, says loudly, "Can't it wait? In case you haven't noticed, we're in the middle of a huge issue here."

I put my hand firmly on his shoulder. "Wes, this is really important. It's about the payroll failure and concerns a conversation I just had with Steve Masters and Dick Landry."

He looks surprised. Patty is already out of her chair. "Let's use my office," she says, leading the way.

Following Patty into her office, I see a photo on her wall of her daughter, who I'd guess is eleven years old. I'm amazed at how much she looks like Patty—fearless, incredibly smart, and formidable—in a way that is a bit scary in such a cute little girl.

In a gruff voice, Wes says, "Okay, Bill, what's so important that you think is worth interrupting a Sev 1 outage in progress?"

That's not a bad question. Severity 1 outages are serious business-impacting incidents that are so disruptive, we typically drop everything to resolve them. I take a deep breath. "I don't know if you've heard, but Luke and Damon are no longer with the company. The official word is that they've decided to take some time off. More than that, I don't know."

The surprised expressions on their faces confirm my suspicions. They didn't know. I quickly relate the events of the morning. Patty shakes her head, uttering a tsk-tsk in disapproval.

Wes looks angry. He worked with Damon for many years. His face reddens. "So now we're supposed to take orders from you? Look, no offense, pal, but aren't you a little out of your league? You've managed the midrange systems, which are basically antiques, for years. You created a nice little cushy job for yourself up there. And you know what? You have absolutely no idea how to run modern distributed systems—to you, the 1990s is still the future!

"Quite frankly," he says, "I think your head would explode if you had to live with the relentless pace and complexity of what I deal with every day."

I exhale, while counting to three. "You want to talk to Steve about how you want my job? Be my guest. Let's get the business what they need first and make sure that everyone gets paid on time."

Patty responds quickly, "I know you weren't asking me, but I agree that the payroll incident needs to be our focus." She pauses and then says, "I think Steve made a good choice. Congratulations, Bill. When can we talk about a bigger budget?"

I flash her a small smile and a nod of thanks, returning my gaze to Wes.

A couple moments go by, and expressions I can't quite decipher cross his face. Finally he relents, "Yeah, fine. And I will take you up on your offer to talk to Steve. He's got a lot of explaining to do."

I nod. Thinking about my own experience with Steve, I genuinely wish Wes luck if he actually decides to have a showdown with him.

"Thank you for your support, guys. I appreciate it. Now, what do we know about the failure—or failures? What's all this about some SAN upgrade yesterday? Are they related?"

"We don't know," Wes shakes his head. "We were trying to figure that out when you walked in. We were in the middle of a SAN firmware upgrade yesterday when the payroll run failed. Brent thought the SAN was corrupting data, so he suggested we back out the changes. It made sense to me, but as you know, they ended up bricking it."

Up until now, I've only heard "bricking" something in reference to breaking something small, like when a cell phone update goes bad. Using it to refer to a million-dollar piece of equipment where all our irreplaceable corporate data are stored makes me feel physically ill.

Brent works for Wes. He's always in the middle of the important projects that IT is working on. I've worked with him many times. He's definitely a smart guy but can be intimidating because of how much he knows. What makes it worse is that he's right most of the time.

"You heard them," Wes says, gesturing toward the conference table where the outage meeting continues unabated. "The SAN won't boot, won't serve data, and our guys can't even read any of the error messages on the display because they're in some weird language. Now we've got a bunch of databases down, including, of course, payroll."

"To work the SAN issue, we had to pull Brent off of a Phoenix job we promised to get done for Sarah," Patty says ominously. "There's going to be hell to pay."

"Uh-oh. What exactly did we promise her?" I ask, alarmed.

Sarah is the SVP of Retail Operations, and she also works for Steve. She has an uncanny knack for blaming other people for her screwups, especially IT people. For years, she's been able to escape any sort of real accountability.

Although I've heard rumors that Steve is grooming her as his replacement, I've always discounted that as being totally impossible. I'm certain that Steve can't be blind to her machinations.

"Sarah heard from someone that we were late getting a bunch of virtual machines over to Chris," she replies. "We dropped everything to get on it. That is, until we had to drop everything to fix the SAN."

Chris Allers, our VP of Application Development, is responsible for developing the applications and code that the business needs, which then get turned over to us to operate and maintain. Chris' life is currently dominated by Phoenix.

I scratch my head. As a company, we've made a huge investment in virtualization. Although it looks uncannily like the mainframe operating environment from the 1960s, virtualization changed the game in Wes' world. Suddenly, you don't have to manage thousands of physical servers anymore. They're now logical instances inside of one big-iron server or maybe even residing somewhere in the cloud.

Building a new server is now a right-click inside of an application. Cabling? It's now a configuration setting. But despite the promise that virtualization was going to solve all our problems, here we are—still late in delivering a virtual machine to Chris.

"If we need Brent to work the SAN issue, keep him there. I'll handle Sarah," I say. "But if the payroll failure was caused by the SAN, why didn't we see more widespread outages and failures?"

"Sarah is definitely going to be one unhappy camper. You know, suddenly I don't want your job anymore," Wes says with a loud laugh. "Don't get yourself fired on your first day. They'll probably come for me next!"

Wes pauses to think. "You know, you have a good point about the SAN. Brent is working the issue right now. Let's go to his desk and see what he thinks."

Patty and I both nod. It's a good idea. We need to establish an accurate timeline of relevant events. And so far, we're basing everything on hearsay.

That doesn't work for solving crimes, and it definitely doesn't work for solving outages.

CHAPTER 3

• *Tuesday, September 2*

I follow Patty and Wes as they walk past the NOC, into the sea of cubicles. We end up in a giant workspace created by combining six cubicles. A large table sits against one wall with a keyboard and four LCD monitors, like a Wall Street trading desk. There are piles of servers everywhere, all with blinking lights. Each portion of the desk is covered by more monitors, showing graphs, login windows, code editors, Word documents, and countless applications I don't recognize.

Brent types away in a window, oblivious to everything around him. From his phone, I hear the NOC conference line. He obviously doesn't seem worried that the loud speakerphone might bother his neighbors.

"Hey, Brent. You got a minute?" Wes asks loudly, putting a hand on his shoulder.

"Can it wait?" Brent replies without even looking up. "I'm actually kind of busy right now. Working the SAN issue, you know?"

Wes grabs a chair. "Yeah, that's what we're here to talk about."

When Brent turns around, Wes continues, "Tell me again about last night. What made you conclude that the SAN upgrade caused the payroll run failure?"

Brent rolls his eyes, "I was helping one of the SAN engineers perform the firmware upgrade after everybody went home. It took way longer than we thought—nothing went according to the tech note. It got pretty hairy, but we finally finished around seven o'clock.

"We rebooted the SAN, but then all the self-tests started failing. We worked it for about fifteen minutes, trying to figure out what went wrong. That's when we got the e-mails about the payroll run failing. That's when I said, 'Game Over.'

"We were just too many versions behind. The SAN vendor probably never tested the upgrade path we were going down. I called you, telling you I wanted to pull the plug. When you gave me the nod, we started the rollback.

"That's when the SAN crashed," he says, slumping in his chair. "It not only took down payroll but a bunch of other servers, too."

"We've been meaning to upgrade the SAN firmware for years, but we never got around to it," Wes explains, turning to me. "We came close once, but then we couldn't get a big enough maintenance window. Performance has been getting worse and worse, to the point where a bunch of critical apps were being impacted. So finally, last night, we decided to just bite the bullet and do the upgrade."

I nod. Then, my phone rings.

It's Ann, so I put her on speakerphone.

"As you suggested, we looked at the data we pulled from the payroll database yesterday. The last pay period was fine. But for this pay period, all the Social Security numbers for the factory hourlies are complete gibberish. And all their hours worked and wage fields are zeroes, too. No one has ever seen anything like this before."

"Just one field is gibberish?" I ask, raising my eyebrows in surprise. "What do you mean by 'gibberish'? What's in the fields?"

She tries to describe what she's seeing on her screen. "Well, they're not numbers or letters. There's some hearts and spades and some squiggly characters… And there's a bunch of foreign characters with umlauts… And there are no spaces. Is that important?"

When Brent snickers as he hears Ann trying to read line noise aloud, I give him a stern glance. "I think we've got the picture," I say. "This is a very important clue. Can you send the spreadsheet with the corrupted data to me?"

She agrees. "By the way, are a bunch of databases down now? That's funny. They were up last night."

Wes mutters something under his breath, silencing Brent before he can say anything.

"Umm, yes. We're aware of the problem and we're working it, too," I deadpan.

When we hang up, I breathe a sigh of relief, taking a moment to thank whatever deity protects people who fight fires and fix outages.

"Only one field corrupted in the database? Come on, guys, that definitely doesn't sound like a SAN failure." I say. "Brent, what else was going on yesterday, besides the SAN upgrade, that could have caused the payroll run to fail?"

Brent slouches in his chair, spinning it around while he thinks. "Well, now that you mention it… A developer for the timekeeping application called me yesterday with a strange question about the database table structure. I was in the middle of working on that Phoenix test VM, so I gave him a really quick answer so I could get back to work. You don't suppose he did something to break the app, do you?"

Wes turns quickly to the speakerphone dialed into the NOC conference call that has been on this whole time and unmutes the phone. "Hey, guys, it's Wes here. I'm with Brent and Patty, as well as with our new boss, Bill Palmer. Steve Masters has put him charge of all of IT Ops. So listen up, guys."

My desire for an orderly announcement of my new role seems less and less likely.

Wes continues, "Does anyone know anything about a developer making any changes to the timekeeping application in the factories? Brent says he got a call from someone who asked about changing some database tables."

From the speakerphone, a voice pipes up, "Yeah, I was helping someone who was having some connectivity issues with the plants. I'm pretty sure he was a developer maintaining the timekeeping app. He was installing some security application that John needed to get up and running this week. I think his name was Max. I still have his contact information around here somewhere… He said he was going on vacation today, which is why the work was so urgent."

Now we're getting somewhere.

A developer jamming in an urgent change so he could go on vacation—possibly as part of some urgent project being driven by John Pesche, our Chief Information Security Officer.

Situations like this only reinforce my deep suspicion of developers: They're often carelessly breaking things and then disappearing, leaving Operations to clean up the mess.

The only thing more dangerous than a developer is a developer conspiring with Security. The two working together gives us means, motive, and opportunity.

I'm guessing our CISO probably strong-armed a Development manager to do something, which resulted in a developer doing something else, which broke the payroll run.

Information Security is always flashing their badges at people and making urgent demands, regardless of the consequences to the rest of the organization, which is why we don't invite them to many meetings. The best way to make sure something doesn't get done is to have them in the room.

They're always coming up with a million reasons why anything we do will create a security hole that alien space-hackers will exploit to pillage our entire organization and steal all our code, intellectual property, credit card numbers, and pictures of our loved ones. These are potentially valid risks, but I often can't connect the dots between their shrill, hysterical, and self-righteous demands and actually improving the defensibility of our environment.

"Okay, guys," I say decisively. "The payroll run failure is like a crime scene and we're Scotland Yard. The SAN is no longer a suspect, but unfortunately, we've accidentally maimed it during our investigation. Brent, you keep working on the injured SAN—obviously, we've got to get it up and running soon.

"Wes and Patty, our new persons of interest are Max and his manager," I say. "Do whatever it takes to find them, detain them, and figure out what they did. I don't care if Max is on vacation. I'm guessing he probably messed up something, and we need to fix it by 3 p.m."

I think for a moment. "I'm going to find John. Either of you want to join me?"

Wes and Patty argue over who will help interrogate John. Patty says adamantly, "It should be me. I've been trying to keep John's people in line for years. They never follow our process, and it always causes problems. I'd love to see Steve and Dick rake him over the coals for pulling a stunt like this."

It is apparently a convincing argument, as Wes says, "Okay, he's all yours. I almost feel sorry for him now."

I suddenly regret my choice of words. This isn't a witch hunt, and I'm not looking for retribution. We still need a timeline of all relevant events leading up to the failure.

Jumping to inappropriate conclusions caused the SAN failure last night. We won't make these kinds of mistakes again. Not on my watch.

As Patty and I call John, I squint at the phone number on Patty's screen, wondering if it's time to heed my wife's advice to get glasses. Yet another reminder that forty is just around the corner.

I dial the number, and a voice answers in one ring, "John here."

I quickly tell him about the payroll and SAN failure and then ask, "Did you make any changes to the timekeeping application yesterday?"

He says, "That sounds bad, but I can assure you that we didn't make any changes to your midrange systems. Sorry I can't be of more help."

I sigh. I thought that by now either Steve or Laura would have sent out the announcement of my promotion. I seem destined to explain my new role in every interaction I have.

I wonder if it would be easier if I just sent out the announcement myself.

I repeat the abridged story of my hasty promotion yet again. "Wes, Patty, and I heard that you were working with Max to deploy something urgent yesterday. What was it?"

"Luke and Damon are gone?" John sounds surprised. "I never thought that Steve would actually fire both of them over a compliance audit finding. But who knows? Maybe things are finally starting to change around here. Let this be a lesson to you, Bill. You Operations people can't keep dragging your feet on security issues anymore! Just some friendly advice…

"Speaking of which, I'm suspicious about how the competition keeps getting the jump on us," he continues. "As they say, once is coincidence. Twice is happenstance. Third must be enemy action. Maybe our salespeople's e-mail systems have been hacked. That would sure explain why we're losing so many deals."

John continues to talk, but my mind is still stuck at his suggestion that Luke and Damon may have been fired over something security related. It's possible—John routinely deals with some pretty powerful people, like Steve and the board as well as the internal and external auditors.

However, I'm certain Steve didn't mention either John or Information Security as reasons for their departure—only the need to focus on Phoenix.

I look at Patty questioningly. She just rolls her eyes and then twirls her finger around her ear. Clearly, she thinks John's theory is crazy.

"Has Steve given you any insights on the new org structure?" I ask out of genuine curiosity—John is always complaining that information security was always prioritized too low. He's been lobbying to become a peer of the CIO, saying it would resolve an inherent conflict of interest. To my knowledge, he hadn't succeeded.

It's no secret that Luke and Damon sidelined John as much as possible, so he couldn't interfere with people who did real work. John still managed to show up at meetings, despite their best efforts.

"What? I have no clue what's going on," he says in an aggrieved tone, my question apparently striking a nerve. "I'm being kept in the dark, like usual. I'll probably be the last to find out, too, if history is any guide. Until you told me, I thought I was still reporting to Luke. And now that he's gone, I don't know who I'm reporting to. You got a call from Steve?"

"This is all above my pay grade—I'm as much in the dark as you are," I respond, playing it dumb. Quickly changing the subject, I ask, "What can you tell us about the timekeeping app change?"

"I'll call Steve and find out what's going on. He's probably forgotten Information Security even exists," he continues, making me wonder whether we'll ever be able to talk about payroll.

To my relief, he finally says, "Okay, yeah, you were asking about Max. We had an urgent audit issue around storage of PII—that is, personally identifiable information like SSNs—that's Social Security numbers, obviously, birthdays, and so forth. European Union law and now many US state laws prohibit us from storing that kind of data. We got a huge audit finding around this. I knew it was up to my team to save this company from itself and prevent us from getting dinged again. That would be front-page news, you know?"

He continues, "We found a product that tokenized this information, so we no longer have to store the SSNs. It was supposed to be deployed almost a year ago, but it never got done, despite all my badgering. Now we're out of time. The Payment Card Industry auditors, that's PCI for short, are here later this month, so I fast-tracked the work with the time-keeping team to get it done."

I stare at my phone, speechless.

On the one hand, I'm ecstatic because we've found the smoking gun in John's hand. John's mention of the SSN field matches Ann's description of the corrupted data.

On the other hand: "Let me see if I've got this right..." I say slowly. "You deployed this tokenization application to fix an audit finding, which caused the payroll run failure, which has Dick and Steve climbing the walls?"

John responds hotly, "First, I am quite certain the tokenization security product didn't cause the issue. It's inconceivable. The vendor assured us that it's safe, and we checked all their references. Second, Dick and Steve have every reason to be climbing the walls: Compliance is not optional. It's the law. My job is to keep them out of orange jumpsuits, and so I did what I had to do."

"'Orange jumpsuits?'"

"Like what you wear in prison," he says. "My job is to keep management in compliance with all relevant laws, regulations, and contractual obligations. Luke and Damon were reckless. They cut corners that severely affected our audit and security posture. If it weren't for my actions, we'd probably all be in jail by now."

I thought we were talking about a payroll failure, not being thrown in jail by some imaginary police force.

"John, we have processes and procedures for how you introduce changes into production," Patty says. "You went around them, and, once again, you've caused a big problem that we're having to repair. Why didn't you follow the process?"

"Ha! Good one, Patty," John snorts. "I did follow the process. You know what your people told me? That the next possible deployment window was in four months. Hello? The auditors are on-site next week!"

He says adamantly, "Getting trapped in your bureaucratic process was simply not an option. If you were in my shoes, you'd do the same thing."

Patty reddens. I say calmly, "According to Dick, we have fewer than four hours to get the timekeeping app up. Now that we know there was a change that affected SSNs, I think we have what we need."

I continue, "Max, who helped with the deployment, is on vacation today. Wes or Brent will be contacting you to learn more about this tokenization product you deployed. I know you'll provide them with whatever help they need. This is important."

When John agrees, I thank him for his time. "Wait, one more question. Why do you believe that this product didn't cause the failure? Did you test the change?"

There's a short silence on the phone before John replies, "No, we couldn't test the change. There's no test environment. Apparently, you guys requested a budget years ago, but…"

I should have known.

"Well, that's good news," Patty says after John hangs up. "It may not be easy to fix, but at least we finally know what's going on."

"Was John's tokenization change in the change schedule?" I ask.

She laughs humorlessly. "That's what I've been trying to tell you. John rarely goes through our change process. Nor do most people, for that matter. It's like the Wild West out here. We're mostly shooting from the hip."

She says defensively. "We need more process around here and better support from the top, including IT process tooling and training. Everyone thinks that the real way to get work done is to just do it. That makes my job nearly impossible."

In my old group, we were always disciplined about doing changes. No one made changes without telling everyone else, and we'd bend over backward to make sure our changes wouldn't screw someone else up.

I'm not used to flying this blind.

"We don't have time to do interrogations every time something goes wrong," I say, exasperated. "Get me a list of all the changes made in the past, say, three days. Without an accurate timeline, we won't be able to establish cause and effect, and we'll probably end up causing another outage."

"Good idea," she nods. "If necessary, I'll e-mail everyone in IT to find out what they were doing, to catch things that weren't on our schedule."

"What do you mean, 'e-mail everyone?' There's no system where people put in their changes? What about our ticketing system or the change-authorization system?" I ask, stunned. This is like Scotland Yard e-mailing everyone in London to find out who was near the scene of a crime.

"Dream on," she says, looking at me like I'm a newbie, which I suppose I am. "For years, I've been trying to get people to use our change management process and tools. But just like John, no one uses it. Same with our ticketing system. It's pretty hit-or-miss, too."

Things are far worse than I thought.

"Okay, do what you need to do," I finally say, unable to hide my frustration. "Make sure you hit all the developers supporting the timekeeping system as well as all the system administrators and networking people. Call their managers, and tell them it's important that we know about any changes, regardless of how unimportant they may seem. Don't forget John's people, too."

When Patty nods, I say, "Look, you're the change manager. We've got to do better than this. We need better situational awareness, and that means we need some sort of functional change management process. Get everyone to bring in their changes so we can build a picture of what is actually going on out there."

To my surprise, Patty looks dejected. "Look, I've tried this before. I'll tell you what will happen. The Change Advisory Board, or CAB, will get together once or twice. And within a couple of weeks, people will stop attending, saying they're too busy. Or they'll just make the changes without waiting for authorization because of deadline pressures. Either way, it'll fizzle out within a month."

"Not this time," I say adamantly. "Send out a meeting notice to all the technology leads and announce that attendance is not optional. If they can't make it, they need to send a delegate. When is the next meeting?"

"Tomorrow," she says.

"Excellent," I say with genuine enthusiasm. "I'm looking forward to it."

When I finally get home, it's after midnight. After a long day of disappointments, I'm exhausted. Balloons are on the floor and a half-empty bottle of wine sits on the kitchen table. On the wall is a crayon poster saying, "Congratulations Daddy!"

When I called my wife, Paige, this afternoon telling her about my promotion, she was far happier than I was. She insisted on inviting the neighbors over to throw a little celebration. Coming home so late, I missed my own party.

At 2 p.m., Patty had successfully argued that of the twenty-seven changes made in the past three days, only John's tokenization change and the SAN upgrade could be reasonably linked to the payroll failure. However, Wes and his team were still unable to restore SAN operations.

At 3 p.m., I had to tell Ann and Dick the bad news that we had no choice but to execute plan B. Their frustration and disappointment were all too evident.

It wasn't until 7 p.m. when the timekeeping application was back up and 11 p.m. when the SAN was finally brought back online.

Not a great performance on my first day as VP of IT Operations.

Before I left work, I e-mailed Steve, Dick, and Ann a quick status report, promising to do whatever it takes to prevent this type of failure from happening again.

I go upstairs, finish brushing my teeth, and check my phone one last time before going to bed, being careful not to wake up Paige. I curse when I see an e-mail from our company PR manager, with a subject of "Bad news. We may be on the front page tomorrow…"

I sit on the bed, squinting to read the accompanying news story.

Elkhart Grove Herald Times

Parts Unlimited flubs paychecks, local union leader calls failure 'unconscionable'

Automotive parts supplier Parts Unlimited has failed to adequately compensate its workers, with some employees receiving no pay at all, according to a Parts Unlimited internal memo. The locally headquartered company admitted that it had failed to issue correct paychecks to some of its hourly factory workers and that others hadn't received any compensation for their work. Parts Unlimited denies that the issue is connected to cash flow problems and instead attributes the error to a payroll system failure.

The once high-flying $4 billion company has been plagued by flagging revenue and growing losses in recent quarters. These financial woes, which some blame on a failure of upper management, have led to rampant job insecurity among local workers struggling to support their families.

According to the memo, whatever the cause of the payroll failure, employees might have to wait days or weeks to be compensated.

"This is just the latest in a long string of management execution missteps taken by the company in recent years," according to Nestor Meyers Chief Industry Analyst Kelly Lawrence.

Parts Unlimited CFO Dick Landry did not return phone calls from the *Herald Times* requesting comment on the payroll issue, accounting errors and questions of managerial competency.

In a statement issued on behalf of Parts Unlimited, Landry expressed regret at the "glitch," and vowed that the mistake would not be repeated.

The *Herald Times* will continue to post updates as the story progresses.

Too tired to do anything more, I turn off the lights, making a mental note to myself to find Dick tomorrow to apologize in person. I close my eyes and try to sleep.

An hour later I'm still staring at the ceiling, very much awake.

CHAPTER 4

• *Wednesday, September 3*

I drink my coffee as I open up my laptop at 7:30 a.m., hoping to get through my e-mails and voicemails before my 8 a.m. meeting. I stare at the screen. In the twenty-two hours since I was promoted, 526 new e-mails have arrived in my inbox.

Holy crap.

I skip all the messages about yesterday's failure and am startled by all the congratulatory notes from vendors, wanting to meet for lunch. How did they find out? I'm pretty sure most of my organization still doesn't know.

I read an e-mail from Ellen, my former boss' assistant, who is now assigned to support me, congratulating me and asking when we can meet. I reply, telling her I'd like to take her out for coffee this morning. I send a note to the IT service desk, requesting that Ellen be granted access to my calendar.

A blinking red light on my desk phone catches my attention. It reads, "7:50 a.m. 62 new voicemails."

My jaw drops. It would take an hour I don't have just to listen to them. I e-mail Ellen again, asking her to go through all my voicemails, transcribing any that require action.

Before I hit send, I quickly add, "If there are any messages from Steve or Dick, please call me right away on my cell phone."

Grabbing my clipboard, I hurry toward my first meeting when my phone vibrates. It's an urgent e-mail:

From: Sarah Moulton
To: Bill Palmer
Cc: Steve Masters
Date: September 3, 7:58 AM
Priority: Highest
Subject: Latest Phoenix slip

Bill, as you know, Project Phoenix is the most important project this company is undertaking. I've heard disturbing rumors that you are holding up the release.

I don't need to remind you that our competition isn't standing still. Each day that goes by, our market share goes down. I need everyone to have a sense of urgency. Especially from you, Bill.

We have an emergency project management meeting at 10 AM today. Please join us, and be prepared to explain these unacceptable delays.

Steve, I know how important this project is for you, given the commitments you've made to the board. Please feel free to attend. We'd love your perspective.

Regards,

Sarah

Oh no.

I forward the e-mail to Wes and Patty, flagging it as high priority. Something seems wrong in a world where half the e-mail messages sent are urgent. Can everything really be that important?

I call Wes' cell phone. "I just got your e-mail from Sarah," he says. "What utter bullshit."

"What's this all this about?" I ask.

He says, "I'm pretty sure it's about Brent not finishing up that configuration work for the Phoenix developers. Everyone is chasing their tails because the developers can't actually tell us what the test environment should look like. We're doing our best, but every time we deliver something, they tell us we did it wrong."

"When did they tell us about it?" I ask.

"Two weeks ago. It's the typical bullshit with Development, but worse. They're so freaked out about hitting their deadlines, they're only now starting to think about how to test and deploy it. Apparently, they're making it our problem. I hope you're wearing your asbestos underwear like me. Sarah is going to be at that meeting with torches, wanting to throw us onto the bonfire."

It's amazing to me how handoffs between Development and IT Operations always get screwed up. But given the perpetual tribal warfare between the two groups, maybe I shouldn't be surprised.

I reply, "I get the picture. Look, make sure you dig into this Dev specification issue personally. We've got to get this nailed down—grab everyone involved, whether they're in Dev or Ops, and lock them in a room until they come up with a written specification. Phoenix is so important, we can't afford to screw this up."

Wes says he's on it, and I ask, "Is there anything else Sarah could pop on us?"

He pauses to think and finally says, "No, I don't think so. We have a pretty valid reason, with the payroll run failure, for why Brent wasn't able to complete his work."

I agree. Feeling like our asses are sufficiently covered, I say, "See you at ten."

Less than an hour later, I'm walking to Building 9 in the hot sunshine, where many of the Marketing folks call home. To my surprise, I join a small army of IT people walking the same way. Why?

Then it hits me. The majority of our marketing projects can't be done without IT. High touch marketing requires high tech. But if there's so many of us assigned to these Marketing projects, shouldn't they be coming to us?

I imagine that Sarah likes it this way, the spider sitting back, enjoying seeing all the company minions making their way to her lair.

I arrive and immediately see Kirsten Fingle, who runs the Project Management Office sitting at the head of the table. I am a big fan of hers. She is organized, levelheaded, and a stickler for accountability. When she first joined the company five years ago, she brought a whole new level of professionalism to our organization.

At her right, Sarah leans back in her chair, tapping away on her iPhone, oblivious to the rest of us.

Sarah is my age: thirty-nine. She's very guarded about her age, always saying things in a way that would lead one to conclude she's much older, but never actually lying.

Yet another maddening thing about Sarah.

There are about twenty-five people in the room. Many of the business line owners are here, some of whom work for Sarah. Chris Allers is also here. Chris is a little older than me and looks lean and fit. He'll just as often be seen joking with someone as kicking their ass about missing a deadline. He has a reputation as a capable and no-nonsense manager. With nearly two hundred developers working for him, he needs to be.

To help with Phoenix, his team has grown by fifty people in the last two years, many through offshore development shops. Chris is constantly asked to deliver more features and do it in less time, with less money.

Several of his managers are in the room, too. Wes is also here, sitting right next to Chris. As I start to look for an open chair, I note how everyone seems unusually tense. And then I see why.

There, sitting right next to the only open seat at the table, is Steve.

Everyone seems to be going to great lengths to not stare at him. As I casually take my seat next to Steve, my phone vibrates. It's a text message from Wes:

Shit. Steve has never attended a project management meeting. We are totally screwed.

Kirsten clears her throat. "First on our agenda is Phoenix. The news isn't good. This project went from yellow to red about four weeks ago, and it's my personal assessment that the deadline is in grave jeopardy."

She continues in her professional voice, "To refresh your memory, last week there were twelve tasks in the critical path of Phoenix Phase 1. Only three of those tasks were completed."

There is a collective groan in the room, and several people mutter to one another. Steve turns to look at me. "Well?"

I explain, "The critical resource in question is Brent, who has been one hundred percent utilized helping to recover from the payroll failure, which we all know about. This was a totally unforeseen emergency but obviously one that we had to handle. Everyone knows how important Phoenix is, and we are doing everything we can to make sure Brent can stay focused."

"Thanks for that super creative explanation, Bill," Sarah immediately responds. "The real issue here is that your people don't seem to grasp how important Phoenix is to the company. Our competition is killing us in the market. You've all seen and heard the commercials about their new services. They're beating us on innovation, both in the retail stores and online. They've already lured away some of our biggest partners, and our sales force is starting to panic. I'm not the type to say, 'I told you so,' but their latest product announcement shows why we can't be acting as if this is just business as usual."

She continues, "See, Bill, in order for us to increase market share, we must ship Phoenix. But for some reason, you and your team keep dragging your feet. Maybe you're not prioritizing correctly? Or maybe you're just not used to supporting a project this important?"

Despite all my mental preparation, I feel my face get hot with anger. Maybe it was the condescending way she was parroting Steve to me. Or how she wasn't even looking at me while she was addressing me, instead looking at Steve to see how he reacts. Or the way she basically called me out-of-touch and incompetent.

Everyone is silent as I force myself to take a deep breath.

My anger dissipates. This is all just corporate theater. I don't like it but accept it for what it is. I almost made the Marines my career when I was up for promotion to staff sergeant. You don't become a senior NCO in the Marines without being able to play politics.

"Interesting," I say to Sarah. "You tell me which is more important: getting our factory employees paid or getting the Phoenix tasks done? Steve told me to resolve the payroll failure. How would you have prioritized this differently than Steve?"

At my mention of Steve, Sarah's expression changes. "Well, maybe if IT didn't cause the failure in the first place, you wouldn't have blown your commitments to us. I don't think we can depend on you and your team."

I nod slowly, not taking the bait. "I look forward to any suggestions you have to offer, Sarah."

She looks at me, then at Steve. Apparently deciding there are no more points to be gained here, she rolls her eyes. I see Wes shaking his head in disbelief at this discussion, staying uncharacteristically quiet.

Sarah continues, "We've spent over $20 million on Phoenix, and we're nearly two years late. We must get to market." Looking over at Chris, she asks, "Given the delays from Bill's group, when is the soonest we can go live?"

Chris looks up from his papers. "I've looked into this since we talked last week. If we expedite some things and if the virtualized environments from Bill's team work as expected, we can go into production one week from Friday."

I gape at Chris. He just made up an arbitrary date to go into production, with complete disregard for all the things we need to do before deployment.

I have a sudden flashback. In the Marines, we had a ritual for all the senior NCOs. We'd hang out with beers and watch *Star Wars: Return of the Jedi*. Every time Admiral Ackbar would cry, "It's a trap!" we'd all laugh uproariously, yelling for a replay.

This time, I'm not laughing.

"Now just wait a minute here!" Wes interjects, pounding the table. "What the hell are you trying to pull? We just found out two weeks ago about the specifics of the Phoenix deployment. Your guys still haven't told us what sort of infrastructure we need, so we can't even order the necessary server and networking gear. And by the way, the vendors are already quoting us three-week delivery times!"

He is now facing Chris, pointing at him angrily. "Oh, and I've heard that the performance of your code is so shitty, we're going to need the hottest, fastest gear out there. You're supposed to support 250 transactions per second, and you're barely doing even four! We're going to need so much hardware that we'll need another chassis to put it all in and probably have to pay a custom-manufacturing fee to get it in time. God knows what this will do to the budget."

Chris wants to respond, but Wes is relentless. "We still don't have a concrete specification of how the production and test systems should be configured. Oh, do you guys not need a test environment anymore? You haven't even done any real testing of your code yet, because that fell off the schedule, too!"

My heart lurches as all the implications sink in. I've seen this movie before. The plot is simple: First, you take an urgent date-driven project, where the shipment date cannot be delayed because of external commitments made to Wall Street or customers. Then you add a bunch of developers who use up all the time in the schedule, leaving no time for testing or operations deployment. And because no one is willing to slip the deployment date, everyone after Development has to take outrageous and unacceptable shortcuts to hit the date.

The results are never pretty. Usually, the software product is so unstable and unusable that even the people who were screaming for it end up saying that it's not worth shipping. And it's always IT Operations who still has to stay up all night, rebooting servers hourly to compensate for crappy code, doing whatever heroics are required to hide from the rest of the world just how bad things really are.

"Guys, I understand the desire to get Phoenix into production as quickly as possible," I say to Steve and Chris as calmly as I can. "But based on what we've heard from Wes, I think it is incredibly premature to deploy. We still don't know what equipment we need to hit the performance objectives, nor have we done any capacity testing to confirm our guesses. It's unlikely we have adequate documentation to run this thing in production, let alone get everything monitored and backed up."

In my most persuasive voice, I continue, "I want Phoenix in the market as badly as anyone else, but if the user experience is bad enough, we'll end up driving our customers to the competition."

I turn to Chris. "You can't just throw the pig over the wall to us, and then high-five each other in the parking lot, congratulating yourselves on how you made the deadline. Wes is telling us that the pig will probably break its leg, and it'll be my guys who work all-nighters and weekends to keep that pig alive."

Chris replies hotly, "Don't give me that bullshit about 'throwing the pig over the wall.' We invited your people to our architecture and planning meetings, but I can count on one hand the number of times you guys actually showed up. We routinely have had to wait days or even weeks to get anything we need from you guys!"

Then he just holds up his hands, as if everything is outside of his control. "Look, I'd like more time, too. But from the very beginning, we all knew that this was a date-driven project. That was a business decision we all made."

"Exactly!" Sarah exclaims before I can respond. "This just shows how Bill and his team lack the necessary sense of urgency. Perfection is the enemy of good. Bill, we simply do not have the luxury of time to polish this to whatever gold standard you're proposing. We need to create positive cash flow, and we cannot do that without taking back market share. And to do that, we need to deploy Phoenix."

She looks over at Steve. "We understand risk, don't we, Steve? You've been doing an absolutely amazing job selling this to analysts and even the guys on CNBC—I don't think we want egg on our face by shipping even later than we already are."

Steve nods his head and rubs his chin, rocking back and forth in his chair as he thinks. "Agreed," he finally says, leaning forward. "We've made commitments to our investors and analysts that we were going to launch Phoenix this quarter."

My jaw drops. Sarah has blunted all my arguments, leading Steve down a reckless, destructive path.

Exasperated, I say, "Does anyone think this is really odd? I've been in this room when we discussed installing new water fountains in the front of every store. We gave that team nine months to plan the rollout. Nine months! And all of us agreed that was reasonable.

"Now we're talking about Phoenix, which impacts thousands of point of sale systems, and all of the back-office order entry systems. This is at least ten thousand times more complex than rolling out new water fountains, with way more risk to the business. And you're only giving us one week to plan and execute the rollout?"

I throw my hands up, imploring Steve, "Doesn't this seem a bit reckless and unfair?"

Kirsten nods, but Sarah says dismissively, "Bill, that's a touching story but we're not discussing water fountains, we're discussing Phoenix. Besides, I believe the decision has already been made."

Steve says, "Yes, it has. Thank you for sharing what you view as the risks, Bill." He turns to Sarah. "When is the launch date?"

Sarah replies quickly, "Marketing launch is next Saturday, September 13. Phoenix will deploy at 5 p.m. the previous day."

Steve writes the date in the back of his notebook and says, "Good. Keep me posted on progress, and let me know if there's anything I can do to help."

I look over at Wes, who mimes with his hands an airplane crashing into the table in front of him and bursting into flames.

In the hallway, Wes says, "I thought that went pretty well, boss."

I'm not laughing. "What the hell happened in there? How did we get into this position? Does anyone know what's required from us to support this launch?"

"No one has a clue," he says, shaking his head in disgust. "We haven't even agreed on how to do the handoff with Development. In the past, they've just pointed to a network folder and said, 'Deploy that.' There are newborn babies dropped off at church doorsteps with more operating instructions than what they're giving us."

I shake my head at his awful imagery, but he's right. We've got a serious problem here.

He continues, "We're going to have to assemble a huge team, including Chris' guys, to figure out how we're going to pull this off. We have problems at every layer: networking, servers, databases, operating systems, applications, Layer 7 switching—the whole wad of crap. It's going to be late nights for all of us for the next nine days."

I nod unhappily. This type of all-hands effort is just another part of life in IT, but it makes me angry when we need to make some heroic, diving catch because of someone else's lack of planning.

I say, "Get your team assembled, and ask Chris to assemble his respective team as well. Stop trying to do this by e-mail and in the ticketing system. We need everyone in the same room."

"Speaking of commitments," I say, "What was Chris referring to when he said that our guys never showed up to the Phoenix architecture and planning meetings? Is that true?"

Wes rolls his eyes in frustration. "Yeah, it's true that his people would invite us at the last minute. Seriously, who can clear their calendar on less than a day's notice?"

"Although, in fairness," he says, after a moment, "we did get ample notice on a couple of the big planning meetings. And one of the most critical people who needed to be there wasn't able to make it, due to escalations. You can probably guess who that is…"

I groan. "Brent?"

Wes nods, "Yep. He's the guy we need at those meetings to tell those idiotic developers how things work in the real world and what type of things keep breaking in production. The irony, of course, is that he can't tell the developers, because he's too busy repairing the things that are already broken."

He's right. Unless we can break this cycle, we'll stay in our terrible downward spiral. Brent needs to work with developers to fix issues at the source so we can stop fighting fires. But Brent can't attend, because he's too busy fighting fires.

I say, "We need our best minds to prepare for this deployment, so make sure Brent is there."

Wes looks sheepish for a moment. I ask him, "What?"

"I think he's working a network outage right now." he replies.

"Not anymore," I say. "They're going to have to fix it without him. If someone has a problem with that, send them to me."

"Okay, whatever you want, boss." he says, shrugging his shoulders.

After the project management meeting, I'm in no mood to talk to anyone. I sit at my desk and grumble when my laptop doesn't wake up. The disk drive light just keeps blinking. When nothing shows on the screen, I grab my empty mug that I keep on my desk by the picture of Paige and my two sons and walk to the coffee machine in the corner.

When I get back to my desk, a window on the screen tells me that it's going to install some critical new updates. I sit down, click "OK" and watch the status bar crawl across the screen. Suddenly, I see the dreaded "blue screen of death." My laptop is now completely locked up and unusable.

It happens again even after I reboot. I mutter in frustration, "You've got to be kidding me!"

Just then, Ellen, my new assistant, pokes her head around the corner. Holding out her hand she says, "Good morning. Congratulations on the promotion, Bill!" Noticing my blue-screened laptop, she says sympathetically, "Ooh, that doesn't look good."

"Umm, thanks." I say, reaching out to shake her hand. "Yeah, about this laptop, can you get a hold of someone in desktop support? There's some serious crap headed our way from Phoenix, and I'm going to need it."

"No problem," she says, nodding with a smile. "I'll tell them our new VP is hopping mad, demanding that his laptop get fixed. Of all people, you need a working computer, right?

"You know," she adds, "I've heard that a bunch of other people are having problems like this today. I'll make sure you get to the top of the list. You can't afford to wait in line."

More bricked laptops? This is surely evidence that the universe is out to get me today.

"By the way, I need some help coordinating some emergency Phoenix meetings. Has anyone granted you access to my calendar yet?" I ask.

She rolls her eyes. "No. That's actually why I came down here. I wanted to see if you could print out your next couple of days. Obviously, that's out of the question. I'll have the desktop support person do that while he's here. Sometimes it takes weeks for the e-mail administrators to get around to stuff like this."

Weeks? That's unacceptable. I quickly look at my watch and realize I'll have to tackle this later. I'm already late.

"Do your best," I say. "I'm off to Patty's enterprise change management meeting. Call me if you need anything, okay?"

Being ten minutes late to Patty's meeting, I hurry into the room, expecting to see either a bunch of people waiting for me impatiently or perhaps a meeting already underway.

Instead, I see only Patty sitting at the conference table, typing away on her laptop.

"Welcome to the CAB, Bill. I hope you can find an empty chair," she says.

"Where is everybody?" I ask.

I'm baffled. When I ran the midrange group, my team would never miss our change management meetings. It was where we coordinated and organized all our work to make sure we didn't shoot ourselves in the foot.

"I told you yesterday that change management around here is hit-or-miss," Patty says, sighing. "Some groups have their own local change-management process, like yours. But most groups do nothing at all. Yesterday's outage is just proof that we need to have something at the enterprise level. Right now, the left hand rarely knows what the right hand is doing."

"So, what's the problem?" I ask.

She purses her lip. "I don't know. We sent a bunch of people to ITIL training, so they could get up to speed on all the best practices. We brought in some consultants, who helped us replace our ticketing system with an ITIL-compliant change management tool. People were supposed to put change requests into it, where it would get routed for approvals. But, even after two years, all we have is a great process on paper that no one follows and a tool that no one uses. When I pester people to use them, all I get are complaints and excuses."

I nod. ITIL stands for IT Infrastructure Library, which documents many IT best practices and processes, and the ITIL program has had a reputation of spending years merely walking in circles.

I'm bothered that Wes isn't here. I know he's busy, but if he's not here, why would any of his people bother to show up? Efforts like this must start and be continually maintained from the top.

"Well, they can bring their complaints and excuses to me," I say adamantly. "We're rebooting the change management process. With my total support. Steve's told me to make sure people can stay focused on Phoenix. Screwups like the SAN failure made us miss a Phoenix deliverable, and now we're paying for it. If someone wants to skip a change management meeting, they obviously are in need of some special compassionate coaching. From me."

At Patty's puzzled expression at my Phoenix reference, I tell her about how Wes and I spent our morning being run over by the bus. Sarah and Chris were at the wheel, but Steve was in back, cheering them on to floor it.

"Not good," she says, disapprovingly. "They even ran over Kirsten, huh?"

I nod silently but refuse to say more. I always liked that phrase in *Saving Private Ryan*: "There's a chain of command: gripes go up, not down."

Instead, I ask her to walk me through the current change process and the way it's been automated in the tools. It all sounds good. But there's only one way to see if the process works.

I say, "Schedule another CAB meeting for the same time Friday. I'll send out an e-mail to all the CAB members letting them know that this is mandatory."

When I get back to my cubicle, Ellen is at my desk, bending over my laptop, writing a note.

"Everything working, I hope?" I ask.

She startles at the sound of my voice. "Oh, my God. You scared me," she says laughing. "Support left you a replacement laptop because they couldn't get your laptop to boot, even after a half hour of trying."

She points at the far side of my desk, and I do a double take.

My replacement laptop appears to be almost ten years old—it's twice as large as my old one and looks three times as heavy. The battery has been taped on, and half the keyboard lettering is worn off from heavy use.

For a moment, I wonder if this is a practical joke.

I sit down and bring up my e-mail, but everything is so slow that several times I thought it had locked up.

Ellen has a sympathetic expression on her face. "The support guy said that this is all they have available today. Over two hundred people are having similar problems, and many aren't getting replacements. Apparently, people with your laptop model also have had their's break because of some security patch."

I forgot. It's Patch Tuesday, when John and his team roll out all their security patches from our major vendors. Once again, John is causing huge issues and disruptions for my team and me.

I merely nod and thank her for the help. After she's gone, I sit down and type out an e-mail to all the CAB members, my keystrokes often taking ten seconds to show up on the screen.

> From: Bill Palmer
> To: Wes Davis, Patty McKee, IT Operations Management
> Date: September 3, 2:43 PM
> Priority: Highest
> Subject: Mandatory CAB meeting Friday, 2 PM
>
> Today, I attended the weekly CAB meeting. I was extremely disappointed that I was the only one there, besides Patty, especially given the totally avoidable, change-related failure yesterday.
>
> Effective immediately, managers (or their assigned delegates) are required to attend all scheduled CAB meetings and to perform their assigned duties. We are resurrecting the Parts Unlimited change management process and it will be followed to the letter.

Any person(s) caught circumventing change management will be subject to disciplinary action.

There will be a mandatory CAB meeting Friday at 2 PM. See you there.

Call me if you have any questions or concerns.

Thanks for your support,

Bill

I hit send, waiting fifteen seconds for the e-mail to finally leave my outbox. Almost immediately, my cell phone rings.

It's Wes. I say, "I was just about to call you about the laptops. We've got to get replacements to our managers and employees so they can do their jobs, you hear?"

"Yeah, we're on it. But I'm not calling about that. And I'm not calling about Phoenix, either," he says, sounding irritated. "Look, about your memo on change management: I know you're the boss, but you better know that the last time we did one of these change management kumbayas, we ran IT straight into the ground. No one, and I mean absolutely *no one*, could get a single thing done. Patty insisted on having everyone take a number and wait for her pointy-heads to authorize and schedule our changes. It was absolutely ridiculous and a total waste of time."

He's unstoppable: "That software application she made us use is a total piece of crap. It takes twenty minutes to fill out all those fields for a simple five-minute change! I don't know who designed the process, but I think they assumed that we all get paid by the hour and want to talk about doing work instead of actually doing work.

"Eventually, the Networking and Server Team staged a rebellion, refusing to use Patty's tool," he continues heatedly. "But John waved an audit finding around and went to Luke, our old CIO. And just like you did, Luke said that following policies was a condition of employment, threatening to fire anybody who didn't follow them.

"My guys were spending half their time doing paperwork and sitting in that damned CAB meeting," he continues. "Luckily, the effort finally died, and John was too clueless to catch on that no one was actually going to the meetings anymore. Even John hasn't gone to one of those meetings in over a year!"

Interesting.

"I hear you," I say. "We can't repeat that, but we also can't have another payroll disaster. Wes, I need you there, and I need you to help create the solution. Otherwise, you're part of the problem. Can I count on you?"

I hear him sigh loudly. "Yeah, sure. But you can also count on me calling 'bullshit' if I see Patty trying to create some sort of bureaucracy that sucks out everybody's will to live."

I sigh.

Before, I was merely worried that IT Operations was under attack by Development, Information Security, Audit, and the business. Now, I'm starting to realize that my primary managers seem to be at war with each other, as well.

What will it take for us to all get along?

CHAPTER 5

• *Thursday, September 4*

I wake up with a jolt when the alarm clock goes off at 6:15 a.m.. My jaw still hurts from clenching it all night. The dismal prospects of the up-coming Phoenix launch were never far from my mind.

As usual, before climbing out of bed, I quickly scan my phone for any bad news. Usually, I would spend about ten minutes replying to e-mails—it always feels good to lob a couple of balls off my side of the court.

I see something that makes me bolt upright so abruptly that I wake up Paige. "Oh, my God. What, what?" she asks frantically, not fully awake.

"It's another e-mail from Steve. Hang on, darling…" I say to her, while I squint to read it.

> From: Steve Masters
> To: Bill Palmer
> Cc: Nancy Mailer, Dick Landry
> Date: September 4, 6:05 AM
> Priority: Highest
> Subject: URGENT: SOX-404 IT Audit Findings Review

Bill, please look into this ASAP. I don't need to tell you how critical it is to have a clean SOX-404 audit.

Nancy, please work with Bill Palmer, who is now in charge of IT Operations.

Steve

>>> Begin forwarded message:

We just concluded our Q3 internal audit in preparation for the upcoming SOX-404 external audit. We discovered some very concerning deficiencies that we need to discuss with you. Due to the severity and urgency of the findings, we need to meet with IT this morning.

Nancy

Indeed, there's a two-hour meeting scheduled for 8 a.m. on my calendar, set up by Nancy Mailer, Chief Audit Executive.

Holy crap. She is incredibly smart and formidable. Years ago during the retail acquisition integration, I watched her grill a manager from the business we were acquiring. He was presenting their financial performance, when she started a rapid-fire interrogation, like a cross between Columbo, Matlock, and Scarface.

He quickly broke, admitting that he was exaggerating his division's performance.

Recalling that meeting, my armpits feel damp. I haven't done anything wrong. But given the tone of the e-mail, she is clearly hot on the trail of something important, and Steve just threw me in her path.

I've always run a very tight ship in my Midrange Technology group. This kept Audit from interfering too much. Sure, there would still be a lot of questions and documentation requests, requiring us to spend a few weeks collecting data and preparing responses. Occasionally, they would find something, but we would quickly fix it.

I like to think that we built a mutually respectful working relationship. However, this e-mail portends something more ominous.

I look at my watch. The meeting is in ninety minutes, and I don't have a clue about what she wants to talk about.

"Shit!" I exclaim, as I jostle Paige's shoulder. "Honey, can you drive the kids into school today? Something really bad just came up involving the Chief Audit Executive and Steve. I need to make some phone calls and get to the office right away."

Annoyed, she says, "For two years you've always taken the kids on Thursdays! I have an early start today, too!"

"I'm sorry, honey. This is really important. The CEO of the company asked me to handle this. Steve Masters. You know, the guy on TV and who gives the big speeches at the company holiday party? I can't drop another ball after a day like yesterday. And the newspaper headline the night before that—"

Without a word, she storms down the stairs.

When I finally find the conference room for the 8 a.m. meeting, I immediately notice how silent it is, devoid of the usual small talk that fills the time while attendees trickle in.

Nancy sits at the head of the table, with four other people sitting around her. Sitting next to her is John along with his ever-present, black three-ring binder. As always, I'm surprised by how young he is. He's probably in his mid-thirties with thick, curly black hair.

John has a haggard look about him, and like many college students, has continually gained weight in the three years he's been here at Parts Unlimited. Most likely from all the stress associated with his failing moral crusade.

John actually reminds me more of Brent than anyone else in the room. However, unlike Brent who normally wears a Linux T-shirt, John wears a starched, collared shirt that's slightly too large.

Wes is conspicuously underdressed compared to everyone in the room, but he obviously doesn't care. The last person in the room is a young man who I don't recognize, presumably the IT auditor.

Nancy begins, "We have just concluded our Q3 internal audit in preparation for the upcoming external SOX-404 audits. We have a grave situation. Tim, our IT auditor, found an eye-opening number of IT control issues. Worse, many are repeat findings going into the third year. Left unresolved, these findings may force us to conclude that the company no longer has sufficient controls to assert the accuracy of its financial statements. This could result in an adverse footnote from the external auditors in the company 10-K filings with the US Securities and Exchange Commission.

"Although these are only preliminary findings, due to the gravity of the situation, I have already verbally informed the audit committee."

I blanch. Although I don't understand all the audit jargon, I know enough that this could ruin Dick's day and mean potentially more bad front-page news.

Satisfied that I understand the severity of the situation, Nancy nods. "Tim, please walk us through your conclusions."

He takes out a huge stack of stapled papers, handing one out to everyone assembled. "We have just concluded our audit of the IT general controls at Parts Unlimited for all of the critical financial systems. It took a team of four people over eight weeks to create this consolidated report."

Holy crap. I lift the two-inch thick stack of papers in my hand. Where did they find a stapler this big?

It's a printed Excel spreadsheet, with twenty rows per page in tiny eight-point type. The last page is numbered page 189. "There must be a thousand issues here!" I say in disbelief.

"Unfortunately, yes," he responds, not entirely able to hide his smug satisfaction. "We found 952 IT general control deficiencies, of which sixteen are significant deficiencies and two are potential material weaknesses. Obviously, we're very alarmed. Given how soon the external audit starts, we need your remediation plan as soon as possible."

Wes is hunched over the table, one hand on his forehead, the other hand flipping through page after page. "What kind of horseshit is this?"

He holds up one page. "'Issue 127. Insecure Windows operating system MAX_SYN_COOKIE setting'? Is this a joke? In case you haven't heard, we've got a real business to run. Sorry if that interferes with this full-time audit employment racket you've got going on here."

Trust Wes to say what people are thinking but are too smart to actually say aloud.

Nancy responds gravely, "Unfortunately, at this point, the phase of control review and testing is over. What we require from you now is the 'management response letter.' You need to investigate each of these findings, confirm them, and then create a remediation plan. We'll review it and then present to the audit committee and the board of directors.

"Normally, you would have months to prepare your response letter and execute your remediation plan," she continues, suddenly looking apologetic. "Unfortunately, the way the audit testing calendar worked out, we only have three weeks until the external auditors arrive. That's regrettable. We'll make sure to give IT more time in the next audit cycle. But this time around, we require your response by…"

She looks at her calendar. "One week from Monday, at the very latest. Do you think you can make it?"

Oh, shit.

That's just six working days away. We'll need half that time just to read the entire document.

Our auditors, who I've long believed are a force for justice and objectivity, are crapping on me, too?

I pick up the huge stack of papers again and look at a couple of random pages. There are many entries like Wes read, but others have references to inadequate security settings, presence of ghost login accounts, change control issues, and segregation of duties issues.

John flips his three-ring binder open and says officiously, "Bill, I brought up many of the same issues with Wes and your predecessor. They convinced the CIO to sign a management waiver, stating that he accepted the risk, and do nothing. Given that some of these are now repeat audit findings, I don't think we'll be able to talk our way out of it this time."

He turns to Nancy. "During the previous management regime, IT controls clearly weren't a priority, but now that all the security chickens are coming home to roost, I'm sure Bill will be more prudent."

Wes looks at John with contempt. I can't believe John is grandstanding in front of the auditors. It's times like this that make me wonder whose side he's really on.

Oblivious to Wes and me, John says to Nancy, "My department has been remediating some other controls, which I think we should be given credit for. For starters, we've completed the tokenization of the PII on our critical financial systems, so at least we dodged that bullet. That finding is now closed."

Nancy says dryly, "Interesting. The presence of PII is not in the scope of the SOX-404 audit, so from that perspective, focusing on the IT general controls might have been a better use of time."

Wait. John's urgent tokenization change was for nothing?

If that's true, John and I need to talk. Later.

I say slowly, "Nancy, I genuinely don't know what we can get to you by Friday. We're buried in recovery work and are scrambling to support the upcoming Phoenix rollout. Which of these findings are the most important for us to respond to?"

Nancy nods to Tim, who says, "Certainly. The first issue is the potential material weakness, which is outlined on page seven. This finding states that an unauthorized or untested change to an application supporting financial reporting could have been put into production. This could potentially result in an undetected material error, due to fraud or otherwise. Management does not have any control that would prevent or detect such a change.

"Furthermore, your group was also unable to produce any change management meeting minutes, which is supposed to meet weekly, according to your policy."

I try not wince visibly, recalling that no one even showed up at the CAB meeting yesterday, and during the payroll incident, we were so oblivious to John's tokenization change that we ended up bricking the SAN.

If we were clueless about those changes, I sincerely doubt that we'd notice if someone disabled a control that would enable a minor, say, $100 million fraudulent transaction.

"Really? That's unbelievable! I'll look into that." I say with what I hope is the right amount of surprise and moral outrage. After I pretend to take detailed notes on my clipboard, circling and underlining random words, I nod, prompting Tim to continue.

"Next, we found numerous instances where developers have administrative access to production applications and databases. This violates the required segregation of duty required to prevent risk for fraud."

I look over to John. "Really? You don't say. Developers making changes to an application without an approved change order? That certainly sounds like a security risk. What would happen if someone coerced a developer, say Max, into doing something unauthorized? We've go to do something about that, right, John?"

John turns bright red, but says politely, "Yes, of course. I agree and would be happy to help."

Tim says, "Good. Let's move onto the sixteen significant deficiencies."

A half hour later, Tim is still droning on. I stare glumly at the huge stack of findings. Most of these issues are just like the huge, useless reports we get from Information Security, which is another reason why John has such a bad reputation.

It's the never-ending hamster wheel of pain: Information Security fills up people's inboxes with never-ending lists of critical security remediation work, quarter after quarter.

When Tim finally finishes, John volunteers, "We must get these vulnerable systems patched. My team has a lot of experience patching systems, if you require assistance. These audit findings are an awesome opportunity to close some big security holes."

"Look, both of you guys have no idea what you're asking for!" Wes says to John and Tim, clearly exasperated. "Some of the servers that those manufacturing ERP systems run on are over twenty years old. Half the company will grind to a halt if they go down, and the vendor went out of business decades ago! These things are so fragile that if you even look at them at the wrong time of day, they'll crash and require all sorts of voodoo to get them to successfully reboot. They'll never survive the changes you're proposing!"

He leans over the table, putting his finger in John's face. "You want to patch it yourself, fine. But I want a signed piece of paper from you saying that if you push the button and the entire business grinds to a halt, you'll fly around and grovel to all the plant managers, explaining to them why they didn't hit their production targets. Deal?"

My eyes widen with amazement when John actually leans forward into Wes' finger and says angrily, "Oh, yeah? How about when we're on the front page of the news because we lost consumer data that we're responsible for protecting? You'll personally apologize to the thousands or millions of families whose data are now being sold by the Russian Mafia?"

I say, "Settle down, everyone. We all want to do what's right for the company. The trick is figuring out what we have time to do and what systems can actually be patched."

I look at the stack of papers. Wes, Patty, and I can assign people the task of investigating each issue, but who will actually do the work? We're already buried with Phoenix, and I fear that this new massive project might be the straw that breaks the camel's back.

I say to Nancy, "I'll get with my team right away, and we'll come up with a plan. I can't promise you that we'll have our response letter completed by then, but I can promise you that we'll get you everything we can. Will that be adequate?"

"Quite so," Nancy says amicably. "Going through the preliminary audit findings and identifying next steps were the only objectives for this meeting."

As the meeting adjourns, I ask Wes to stay behind.

Noticing this, John remains behind, as well. "This is a disaster. All my objectives and bonuses are tied to getting a clean compliance report for the SOX-404 and PCI audits. I'm going to fail because you Ops guys can't get your shit together!"

"Join the club," I say.

To get him off my back, I say, "Sarah and Steve decided to move up the Phoenix deployment date to next Friday. They want to skip all the security reviews. You probably should talk to Chris and Sarah right away."

Predictably, John swears and storms out, slamming the door behind him.

Exhausted, I lean back in my chair and say to Wes, "This is just not our week."

Wes laughs humorlessly. "I told you that the pace of things around here would make your head explode."

I gesture at the audit findings. "We're supposed to protect all our key resources for Phoenix, but that's sucking in everybody. We don't have a bunch of people just sitting on the bench we can throw at the audit findings, right?"

Wes shakes his head, his face uncharacteristically pinched with tension.

He flips through his stack of papers again. "We're definitely going to need to bring the technology leads into this. But as you said, they're already assigned to the Phoenix team. Should we reassign them here?"

I honestly don't know. Wes stares at one of the pages for a moment. "By the way, I think a bunch of these will require Brent."

"Oh, come on." I mutter. "Brent. Brent, Brent, Brent! Can't we do anything without him? Look at us! We're trying to have a management discussion about commitments and resources, and all we do is talk about one guy! I don't care how talented he is. If you're telling me that our organization can't do anything without him, we've got a big problem."

Wes shrugs, slightly embarrassed. "He's undoubtedly one of our best guys. He's really smart, and he knows a lot about almost everything we have in this shop. He's one of the few people who really understand how all the applications talk together at an enterprise level. Heck, the guy may know more about how this company works than I do."

"You're a senior manager. This should be as unacceptable to you as it is to me!" I say firmly. "How many more Brents do you need? One, ten, or a hundred? I'm going to need Steve to prioritize all this work. What I need from you is what resources we need. If I ask Steve for more resources, I don't want to have to crawl back, begging for more later."

He rolls his eyes. "Look, I'll tell you right now what's going to happen. We'll go to management and present our case. Not only will they say no, they'll cut our budget by another five percent. That's what they've done for the past five years. In the meantime, everyone will continue to want everything at the same time, and keep adding to our list of things to do."

Exasperated, he continues, "And just so you know, I have tried to hire more Brents. Because I never got the budget, I eliminated a bunch of positions just so I could hire four more very senior engineers at the same level of experience as Brent. And you know what happened?"

I merely raise my eyebrows.

Wes says, "Half quit within a year, and I'm not getting anywhere near the productivity I need from the ones who stayed. Although I don't have data to prove it, I'm guessing Brent is even more behind than ever. He complains that he had to spend a bunch of time training and helping the new guys, and is now stretched thinner than ever. And he's still in the middle of everything."

I respond, "You said that people 'add stuff to our list.' What does the list look like right now? Where can I get a copy? Who owns the list?"

Wes replies slowly, "Well, there are the business projects and the various IT infrastructure projects. But a lot of the commitments just aren't written down."

"How many business projects? How many infrastructure projects?" I ask.

Wes shakes his head. "I don't know offhand. I can get the list of business projects from Kirsten, but I'm not sure if anyone knows the answer to your second question. Those don't go through the Project Management Office."

I have a sinking feeling in the pit of my stomach. How can we manage production if we don't know what the demand, priorities, status of work in process, and resource availability are? Suddenly, I'm kicking myself that I didn't ask these questions on my first day.

Finally, I'm thinking like a manager.

I call Patty. "Wes and I just got hammered by audit and they need a response one week from Monday. I need your help to figure what all our work commitments are, so I can have an intelligent discussion with Steve about resourcing. Can you talk?"

She says, "That's right up my alley. Come on over."

After Wes briefs Patty on the implications of the mammoth audit report that he thumped down on the table, she whistles.

"You know, I really wish you were at that meeting with the auditors," I say. "Most of the biggest issues were around the absence of a functional change management process. I think you could end up being the auditors' best friend."

"Auditors have friends?" she laughs.

"I need you to help Wes estimate the work to fix the audit findings by Monday," I say. "But right now, let's talk about a higher level issue. I'm trying to get the list of what all our commitments to the organization are. How big is that list and how do things get on it?"

After hearing what Wes told me, Patty replies, "Wes is right. Kirsten owns the official business project list, almost all of which have something that we're on the hook for. We have our own IT Operations projects, which are typically managed by the technology budget owner—there is no centralized list of those projects."

Patty continues, "We also have all the calls going into the service desk, whether it's requests for something new or asking to fix something. But that list will be incomplete, too, because so many people in the business just go to their favorite IT person. All that work is completely off the books."

I ask slowly, "So, you're saying that we have no idea what the list of our commitments is? Really?"

Wes says defensively, "Until now, no one ever asked. We've always hired smart people and tasked them with certain areas of responsibility. We've never had to manage things beyond that."

"Well, we need to start. We can't make new commitments to other people when we don't even know what our commitments are now!" I say. "At the very least, get me the work estimate to fix the audit findings. Then, for each of *those* resources, tell me what their *other* commitments are that we're going to be pulling them off of."

Thinking for a moment, I add, "For that matter, do the same thing for every person assigned to Phoenix. I'm guessing we're overloaded, so I want to know by how much. I want to proactively tell people whose projects have been bumped, so they're not surprised when we don't deliver what we promised."

Both Wes and Patty look surprised. Wes speaks up first, "But…but we'd have to talk with almost everyone! Patty may have fun grilling people on what changes they're making, but we can't go around wasting the time of our best people. They've got real work to do!"

"Yes, I know they have real work to do," I say adamantly. "I merely want a one-line description about what all that work is and how long they think it will take!"

Realizing how this might come across, I add, "Make sure you tell people that we're doing this so we can get more resources. I don't want anyone thinking that we're outsourcing or firing anyone, okay?"

Patty nods. "We should have done this a long time ago. We bump up the priorities of things all the time, but we never really know what just got bumped down. That is, until someone screams at us, demanding to know why we haven't delivered something."

She types on her laptop. "You just want a list of organizational commitments for our key resources, with a one-liner on what they're working on and how long it will take. We'll start with all Phoenix and audit remediation resources first, but will eventually cover the entire IT Operations organization. Do I have it right?"

I smile, genuinely happy that Patty has framed it so succinctly. I know she's going to do a great job. "Exactly. Bonus points if you and Wes can determine which resources are most overutilized and how many new resources we need. That would be the basis of an ask to Steve for more staffing."

Patty says to Wes, "This should be pretty straightforward. We can put together fifteen-minute interviews, pull data from our service desk and ticketing system, get Kirsten's project list…"

Surprisingly, Wes agrees, adding, "We could also look in our budgeting tools to see how we've coded personnel and hardware requests."

I stand up. "Great thinking, guys. Get a meeting set up for us to go over what you find, no later than Friday. I want to have a meeting with Steve on Monday, armed with some real data."

She gives me the thumbs-up. Now we're getting somewhere.

CHAPTER 6

• *Friday, September 5*

In another one of the endless Phoenix status meetings, I realize that the developers are even more behind than we feared. As Wes had predicted, more and more work is being deferred to the next release, including almost all of the testing.

This means that we'll be the ones finding the problems when they blow up in production, instead of the Quality Assurance (QA) Department.

Great.

During a lull in the discussion, I look down at my phone and see an e-mail from Patty. She wants to meet about resourcing, promising some eye-opening surprises.

I open the attached spreadsheet, seeing an encouraging level of detail, but on my minuscule phone screen, I can't make heads or tails of it. I reply to Patty that I'm on the way and ask her to have Wes meet me there.

When I arrive, I'm surprised to see that Wes has set up a projector, displaying a spreadsheet on the wall. I'm excited that we're meeting to analyze the situation, instead of just reacting to the daily fires.

I grab a seat. "Okay, whatcha got for me?"

Wes starts. "Patty did a great job putting this together. What we found was—well, it was interesting."

Patty explains, "We did our interviews, collected the data, and then did our analysis. Right now, these numbers are only for our key resources. We're already seeing something troubling."

She points at a row in the spreadsheet. "First, we have a lot of projects. Kirsten says she's officially managing about thirty-five major business projects, each of which we have commitments to. Internal to IT Operations, we've already identified over seventy projects, and that number keeps growing with each person we interview."

"Wait," I say, genuinely startled, sitting upright in my chair. "We have 150 IT Operations people, right? If you've already found over 105 projects, that's 1.5 people per project. Doesn't that seem like a lot to you?"

Wes replies, "Totally. And we know that the project count is low. So by the end, it'll probably be more like one person per project. That's insane."

I ask, "How big are these internal projects?"

Wes switches tabs on the spreadsheet, showing the list of projects they've inventoried, along with the estimated number of man-weeks. "Consolidate and upgrade e-mail server," "Upgrade thirty-five instances of Oracle databases," "Install supported Lemming database server," "Virtualize and migrate primary business applications," and so on.

I groan. While some projects are small, most seem like major undertakings, estimated at three man-years or more.

When Patty sees the expression on my face, she says, "That was my reaction, too. We're on the hook for a huge number of projects. So, let's look at what our capacity is. This is a little harder, since we can't just assign random people to any given project."

She continues, "When we looked at who was assigned to each project and what their other commitments and availability were, here's what we found."

When Wes flips to another spreadsheet tab, my heart drops.

"Grim, huh?" says Wes. "Most of our resources are going to Phoenix. And look at the next line: Compliance is the next largest project. And even if we only worked on compliance, it would consume most of our key resources for an entire year! And that includes Brent, by the way."

Incredulous, I say, "You're kidding. If we put all our projects on hold except for the audit findings, our key resources would be tied up for an entire year?"

"Yep," Patty says, nodding. "It's hard to believe, but it just shows you how much work is in that stack of audit findings."

I look down at the table, speechless.

If someone had shown me these figures during my first conversation with Steve, I would have run from the room, screaming like a little boy.

It's not too late, I think, smiling at the image.

With practiced calm, I say, "Okay, knowing is always better than not knowing. Keep going."

Wes looks back at the spreadsheet. "The third largest item is incident and break-fix work. Right now, it's probably consuming seventy-five percent of our staff's time. And because these often involve critical business systems, incidents will take priority over everything else, including Phoenix and fixing audit findings.

"By the way, did you know that yesterday, when we were talking with Brent, we had to reschedule the interview twice because he had to go help fix an outage? So there we were interrupting him from Phoenix work, only to be interrupted by an outage!" he says, laughing.

I start to laugh, but then stop abruptly. "Wait. What outage? Why didn't I hear about it? We can't keep running our organization like this!"

"Well, it was another SAN issue, but nothing critical," Wes replies. "A drive went bad a couple of months ago, so the SAN was running with no redundancy. When another drive failed, the entire volume went down. Brent had to help restore some of the databases when we got the SAN back up."

Exasperated, I shout, "Dang it, Wes. That was completely preventable! Get one of your junior guys to look at the logs every day for drive failures. Maybe even have him visually inspect the drives and count all the blinking lights. It's called preventive maintenance for a reason! We need Brent on Phoenix, not piddly crap like this!"

Wes says defensively, "Hey, it's actually a little more complicated than that. We put in the order for replacement drives, but they've been stuck in Procurement for weeks. We had to get one of our vendors to give it to us on credit. This wasn't our fault."

I lose my temper. "Wes, listen to me. I DON'T CARE! I don't care about Procurement. I don't care how nice your vendors are. I need you to do your job. Make sure this doesn't happen again!"

I take a deep breath. I realize my frustration is not because of the drive failure, but because we're continually unable to stay focused on the things that matter most to the company.

"Look, let's put this aside for now," I say, looking back at Wes. "I'm serious about getting someone to look at that SAN daily, though. Set up a meeting sometime next week for you, me, and Patty to get to the bottom of these outages. We've got to figure out how to bring down the amount of break-fix work so we can get project work done. If we can't get Phoenix work done, it's jeopardizing the company."

"Yeah, I got it. I'll try to get it in before the Phoenix rollout." Wes says, nodding sullenly. "And I'll get on that SAN issue this afternoon."

"Okay, back to the spreadsheet," I say.

Patty observes glumly, "You're right. The one consistent theme in the interviews was that everyone struggles to get their project work done. Even when they do have time, they struggle to prioritize all their commitments. People in the business constantly ask our staff to do things for them. Especially Marketing."

"Sarah?" I ask.

"Sure, but it's not only her," she replies. "Practically every executive in the company is guilty of going directly to their favorite IT person, either asking a favor or pressuring them to get something done."

"How do we change the game here and get resourced to do all these projects properly?" I ask. "What should we be asking Steve for?"

Wes scrolls down his spreadsheet. "Based on our rough numbers, we'll probably need to hire seven people: three database administrators, two server engineers, one network engineer, and one virtualization engineer. Of course, you know that it'll take time to find these people and then another six to twelve months before they're fully productive."

Of course, I knew that new hires aren't productive right away. But it was still dispiriting to hear Wes point out that real help was still a long way off, even if Steve approved the headcount.

Later that day, as I'm walking to our second CAB meeting, I feel hopeful. If we can get our old change process going, we might be able to quickly resolve one of the largest audit issues and get some operational wins, as well.

I'm also pleased at how well Patty and Wes are working together.

As I near the conference room, I hear loud voices arguing.

"—then Patty got that engineer fired for doing his job. He was one of our best networking people. That wasn't your call to make!"

No mistake. That's Wes hollering. Then I hear Patty reply heatedly, "What? You signed off on that termination! Why is this suddenly my fault?"

I knew it was too good to be true.

I then hear John say, "That was the right call. We're going into our third year of a repeat audit finding around change controls. That goes in front of the audit committee. Next time around, it probably won't be just an engineer getting fired, if you get my drift."

Wait. Who invited John to this meeting?

Before John can make things any worse, I quickly step through the door and say cheerfully, "Good afternoon, everyone! Are we ready to review some changes?"

Fourteen people turn to look at me. Most of the technical leads from the various groups are sitting at the table. Wes is standing up behind his chair, fuming, while Patty is standing in the front of the room, arms crossed.

John sits in the back of the room, with his three-ring binder open, very much an unwanted guest.

Using both hands, I set down my antique laptop. It hits the table with a thud and a clatter as the battery falls off, the tape no longer holding it in place, and then I hear a scratching sound as the disk drive spins down.

Wes' angry expression disappears momentarily. "Wow, boss, nice gear. What is that, a Kaypro II? I haven't seen one of those in about thirty years. Let me know if you need an 8-inch floppy to load CP/M on it—I've got one in my attic at home."

Two of the engineers snicker and point. I smile briefly at Wes, grateful for the comic relief.

Remaining standing, I say to everyone, "Let me tell you why I assembled all of you here. Given the urgency of Phoenix, you can bet your ass that I wouldn't waste your time if I didn't think this was important."

I continue, "First, the events that led to the SAN and payroll failure on Tuesday must not happen again. What started off as a medium-sized payroll failure snowballed into a massive friendly-fire SAN incident. Why? Because we are not talking to one another about what changes we're planning or implementing. This is not acceptable."

"Second, John is right. We spent yesterday morning with our auditors, discussing a bunch of deficiencies they found," I continue. "Dick Landry is already crapping bricks because it could impact our quarterly financial statements. We need to tighten up our change controls, and as managers and technical leads, we must figure out how we can create a sustainable process that will prevent friendly-fire incidents and get the auditors off our back, while still being able to get work done. We are not leaving this room until we've created a plan to get there. Understood?"

When I'm satisfied that everyone has been properly cowed, I open it up for discussion. "So what's preventing us from getting there?"

One of the technical leads quickly says, "I'll start. That change management tool is impossible to use. There's a million mandatory fields and most of the time, the drop down boxes for the 'applications affected' don't even have what I need. It's why I've stopped even putting in change requests."

Another lead hollers out, "He's not kidding. To follow Patty's rules, I have to manually type in hundreds of server names in one of the text boxes. Most of the time, there's not enough room in the field! A hundred server names are supposed to fit in a sixty-four-character text box? What idiot built that form?"

Again, more unkind laughter.

Patty is bright red. She shouts, "We need to use drop-down boxes so we can maintain data integrity! And I'd love to keep the application list up-to-date, but I don't have the resources. Who's going to keep the application catalog and change management database current? You think it just magically updates itself?"

"It's not just the tool, Patty. It's the entire broken process," Wes asserts. "When my guys put in change requests, they have to wait a lifetime to get approvals, let alone get on the schedule. We have the business breathing down our neck to get crap done. We can't wait for you to hem and haw, complaining that we didn't fill out the form right."

Patty snaps, "That's crap, and you know it. Your people routinely break the rules. Like, say, when everyone marks all their change requests as an 'urgent' or 'emergency change'. That field is only for actual emergencies!"

Wes retorts, "We have to do that, because marking them urgent is the only way to get your team to look at it! Who can wait three weeks for an approval?"

One of the lead engineers suggests, "Maybe we make another field called 'extremely urgent?'"

I wait until the uproar quiets down. At this rate, we're getting nowhere fast. Thinking furiously, I finally say, "Let's take a ten-minute break."

When we reconvene the meeting, I say, "We are not leaving this meeting without a list of authorized and scheduled changes that we're implementing in the next thirty days.

"As you can see, my assistant has brought in a pile of blank index cards. I want each group to write down every change they're planning, one change per index card. I want three pieces of information: who is planning the change, the system being changed, and a one-sentence summary.

"I've drawn a calendar on the whiteboard where we will eventually post approved changes according to their scheduled implementation," I continue. "Those are the rules. Short and simple."

Wes picks up a pack of cards, looking at them dubiously. "Really? Paper cards, in this day and age? How about we use that laptop of yours, which probably even predates paper?"

Everyone laughs, but not Patty. She looks angry, obviously not pleased with the direction things are going.

"This isn't like any change management process I've ever seen," John says. "But I'll put my changes on the board, like the upcoming firewall updates and monitoring changes that're scheduled for the next couple of days."

Surprisingly, John's willingness to jump in inspires others, who begin writing their planned changes on their cards.

Finally, Wes says, "Okay, let's try it. Anything is better than using that busted change management tool."

One of the leads holds up a handful of cards. "I'm done with all the database changes we're planning to make."

When I nod for him to proceed, he quickly reads one of the cards: "Execute the vendor-recommended database maintenance script on Octave server xz577 to fix retail store POS performance issues. This affects the order entry database and applications. We'd like to do this next Friday evening at 8:30 p.m."

I nod, pleased with the clarity of his proposed change. But Wes says,

"That's not a change! That's just running a database script. If you were changing the script, then we'd have something to talk about. Next."

The lead replies quickly, "No, it's definitely a change. It temporarily changes some database settings, and we don't know what production impact it could have. To me, it's just as risky as a database configuration change."

Is it a change or not? I can see both sides of the argument.

After thirty minutes of arguing, it's still not clear that we know the definition of what a "change" should be.

Was rebooting a server a change? Yes, because we don't want anyone rebooting servers willy-nilly, especially if it's running a critical service.

How about turning off a server? Yes, for the same reason.

How about turning on a server? No, we all thought. That is, until someone came up with the example of turning on a duplicate DHCP server, which screwed up the entire enterprise network for twenty-four hours.

A half hour later, we finally write on the whiteboard: "a 'change' is any activity that is physical, logical, or virtual to applications, databases, operating systems, networks, or hardware that could impact services being delivered."

I look at my watch, alarmed that we've been in the room for nearly ninety minutes, and we still haven't even approved our first change. I push us to move faster, but at the end of our two-hour meeting, we've only posted five changes on the whiteboard.

Surprisingly, no one else seems frustrated except me. Everyone is vigorously engaged in the discussion, even Patty. Everyone is discussing risks of the proposed changes, even discovering that one change wasn't necessary.

Encouraged, I say, "We'll pick this up on Monday. Get all your cards to Patty as soon as you can. Patty, what's the best way for us to process all the cards?"

She says tersely, "I'll set up a basket later today. In the meantime, pile them up at the front of the table."

When we adjourn, several people tell me on their way out, "Great meeting," and "I wish we had more time to discuss changes," and "I'm looking forward to Monday."

Only Patty has remained behind, arms crossed. "We spent a lot of blood, sweat, and tears creating our old change management policy, and everyone still blew it off. What makes you think this will be any different?"

I shrug. "I don't know. But we'll keep trying things until we have a system that works, and I'm going to make sure everyone keeps helping us get there. It's not just to satisfy the audit findings. We need some way to plan, communicate, and make our changes safely. I can guarantee you that if we don't change the way we work, I'll be soon out of a job."

Pointing at her old policy document, she says, "We shouldn't just throw all this work out the window. We spent weeks designing it and hundreds of thousands of dollars with consultants, changing our tools around."

She tears up slightly. I remind myself of how long she's been trying to get this process integrated into the organization.

"I know that there was a lot of good work put into all this process," I say sympathetically. "Let's face it, though. No one was actually following it, as the auditors pointed out. We also know that people were gaming the system, just trying to get their work done."

I say sincerely, "We may be starting over, but we need all your experience and skills to make this work. It's still your process, and I know this is absolutely critical to our success."

"Okay," she says, sighing in resignation. "I suppose I care more about our survival than whether we use our old process or not."

Her expression changes. "How about I write up the outputs of the meeting and the new instructions for submitting requests for changes?"

Later that afternoon, I'm back in the Phoenix war room when Patty calls. I run out to the hallway. "What's up?"

She sounds stressed. "We've got a problem. I was expecting we'd have fifty changes for us to review next week. But we're already up to 243 submitted changes. I keep getting e-mails from people saying to expect more cards over the weekend… I think we're looking at over four hundred changes being made next week!"

Holy crap. Four hundred? How many of these four hundred changes are high risk, potentially affecting Phoenix, the payroll application, or worse?

I suddenly remember Rangemaster duty in the Marines. As Rangemaster, I was responsible for the safety of everyone on the firing range. I have a horrifying vision of a mob of four hundred unsupervised eighteen-year-olds jumping out of trucks, running to the firing range, firing their rifles into the air, hooting and hollering…

"Umm, at least people are following the process," I say, laughing nervously.

I hear her laugh. "With all the change requests coming in, how are we going to get them all authorized by Monday? Should we put a temporary hold on changes until we get them all approved?"

"Absolutely not," I say immediately. "The best way to kill everyone's enthusiasm and support is to prevent them from doing what they need to do. I doubt we'll get a second chance to get this right.

"Send out an e-mail telling everyone to submit any change for next week by Monday. Monday's changes will not need to be authorized but changes for the remainder of the week will. No exceptions."

I can hear Patty typing over the phone. "Got it. I'll probably need to have some of my people help organize all of the change cards over the weekend. Frankly, I'm stunned by how many changes there are."

So am I.

"Excellent," I say, leaving my concerns unvoiced.

CHAPTER 7

• *Friday, September 5*

When I get back to my desk, I'm looking for the Advil I usually keep on my desk when my cell phone rings. "Palmer here," I say, rummaging through my drawers.

"Hi, Bill. It's Stacy—Steve's assistant. I'm glad I caught you. There's a potential new board member in town named Erik Reid who needs to talk with all the IT executives. He's wondering if you're available for an hour right now."

"Hang on a sec while I pull up my calendar," I reply.

The screen resolution on this old laptop is so low that the weekly view is unusable. I switch to the daily view, and the screen goes blank as the laptop chatters and whirs.

I give up waiting and say earnestly, "Look, I know this is important, but can't this wait until Monday? You would not believe the day I'm having."

She replies quickly, "I wish it could wait, but he's only in town today. And from what I've seen, Bob Strauss, you know, the new company chairman, and Steve are in a tizzy because they're worried that Erik may not accept our offer to join the board. He's apparently some technology hotshot, and Bob and Steve managed to get him in town to woo him. He insists on meeting the IT leadership team before he leaves."

"Okay, I'm in," I say, suppressing a sigh.

"Good. We have him set up in the conference room right by me. Come on over—there's a great coffee and doughnut spread here."

I laugh. "Well, that's the first good news I've had all day. I'm on my way."

As I walk into the conference room in Building 2, I wave to Stacy, pondering the strange world I've been pulled into. I'm not used to being thrown into the middle of board politics.

As promised, by the window is a large cart with four types of coffee and six boxes of Vandal Doughnuts, a place in town so famous, there's a long line at almost all hours of the day.

A man in wrinkled khaki pants and an untucked denim button-down shirt is kneeling in front of the cart, unpacking the doughnuts onto two platters. I had no idea Vandal Doughnuts delivered.

I pick up a cup and start filling it with coffee, eyeing all the doughnuts. I say, "You know, my wife and I are huge fans of you guys. Back when we were dating, almost every Friday night we'd wait in line for twenty minutes to get our fix. Now that we have kids, she just sends me out to get them for her. Maybe I'll take one home for her tonight."

I grab a huge chocolate doughnut covered with Froot Loops, as well as a giant frosted glazed doughnut with bacon on it and three more that look tasty.

The deliveryman stands up and looks at me, smiling. "Yeah, I can see why. I'm really enjoying these doughnuts. I've never had anything like them before. I've probably eaten five since I've been here. Not great for the low-carb diet I'm on, though…"

Holding out his hand, he says, "I'm Erik."

Holy crap.

I look down. In one hand I have a cup of coffee, and in the other hand I'm holding an overflowing plate.

"Oh, jeez," I say hurriedly. I put everything on the table behind me, turning around again to shake his hand. "Good to meet you. I'm Bill— Bill Palmer."

I look him over again. He has a mustache, is around six feet tall and a bit overweight, and has long graying hair that touches his shoulders. When standing, he looks even more like someone from a delivery company than a potential board member, let alone some "technology hotshot."

Taking another look at him, I correct myself—I'm pretty sure a delivery person would have less-wrinkled clothes.

"No worries," he says cheerily, grabbing another doughnut from the tray and gesturing toward the table. "Have a seat. I was hoping to talk with each of the IT leaders while I was in town. Of course, I had to talk with Steve and—umm—what's your CFO's name? Darren? Dale? Whatever—they seemed like nice enough fellows. Maybe a little blind, but…"

He gestures dismissively. "I talked with your Development guy, too. Umm, Cary? Calvin? And, I'll be talking with your Security guy next, Jimmy, and your Retailing person, Sylvia."

I try to hide my pained expression as he's managed to mangle everyone's name.

"I see… And what have your impressions been so far?" I ask carefully.

He stops chewing and brushes some crumbs off his mustache, pausing to think. "It looks like you're in a world of hurt. IT Operations seems to have lodged itself in every major flow of work, including the top company project. It has all the executives hopping mad, and they're turning the screws on your Development guy to do whatever it takes to get it into production."

He looks me in the eye. "You're having chronic IT availability issues, causing company executives to be splashed on the front-page news. And now, Audit is hot on your tail, meaning more possible front-page news, and maybe even an adverse footnote on the quarterly financial statement. And anyone who knows anything about Phoenix knows that there's a lot more bad news to come on that front…" Ha! Better clear your calendar for when that one lands…"

As he's talking, I feel my face flush red, whether in anger or embarrassment I'm not sure.

"Things don't look so good for you, pal," he says. "At least not to a prospective board member, who's supposed to oversee and assess your performance."

I purse my lips, resisting the urge to say something that sounds defensive. I say neutrally, "Steve asked me to take this job three days ago. Even though I kept saying no, he eventually convinced me to accept the position. There've sure been a lot of surprises…"

He looks at me for a moment, and then guffaws. "Yeah, I'll bet!" he says, disarmingly. "Ha-ha! Surprises. So, what's your game plan for righting the ship?"

I look up for a moment, trying to figure out how to describe the few corrective actions I've put in place after this week. I reply, "Honestly, I'm still trying to get some situational awareness. Mostly, I'm being whip-lashed from one emergency to another. I do know that we need more rigor and discipline in how we work. I'm trying to figure out what processes we rely on to get work done around here. Based on what I've seen, I know we need to improve them so we stop shooting ourselves in the foot."

I think for a moment. "That's just to get us out of firefighting mode. I'm still trying to figure out how to resource an audit remediation project that just fell out of the sky. Based on what I've seen, we're seriously behind on our commitments. We're obviously going to need more people or get a lot more efficient to get all our committed work done."

Erik frowns. "'Rigor and discipline,' huh? I'm guessing you were a non-commissioned officer in the military. An E-6. No, you're too young. An E-5, right?"

I blink in surprise. "That's right. E-5, US Marine Corp. How did you know?"

"Lucky guess," he says glibly. "For one thing, you sure don't look like a chemical engineer or an auditor."

"What?" I ask.

"You're right that you can't achieve the strategic until you've mastered the tactical," he says, ignoring my question. "But what worked for you in the Marines will never work here, considering how they run this circus. Instead of one general in your chain of command, you've got ten generals calling the shots here, and all of them have a direct line to each and every private in your company."

I say slowly, "Wait. You're saying rigor and discipline don't matter?"

"Of course they matter," he says sternly. "But you have a much bigger problem, and it has nothing to do with your argle-bargle of 'efficiencies' and 'process.' Your problem right now is that you obviously don't actually know what 'work' is."

I stare at him.

Who is this buffoon? For a moment, I wonder whether I can assign Wes or Patty to deal with this guy, but Steve obviously wanted me to handle this personally.

"I know what work is," I say slowly. "We do it every day. If we can't keep the lights on and finish the work that the business requires, I'm out of a job."

"What then, exactly, is your definition of 'work?'" he asks, with a genuinely curious expression on his face.

"Well, I can tell you that Steve has stated over and over to me in no uncertain terms that we need to get Phoenix out the door. That qualifies as work in my mind."

He looks up, appearing to have a conversation with himself. "Yes, that's certainly one type of work. But you're still missing the three other types of work that IT Operations is responsible for. To me, that's nowhere near the level of understanding of work you need in order to fix your problems around project deliverables, outages, and compliance."

He stands up. "Grab your stuff. We're going for a ride."

Confused and annoyed, I look at my watch. It's 4:17 p.m. I have too much to do to waste much more time with this guy.

Then he's gone. I look out in the hallway, but he's not there, either. I look at Stacy questioningly, and she points toward the elevators. I run to catch up with him.

He's walked into an elevator that just opened. When he turns around, he holds the door open for me. "You probably don't even see when work is committed to your organization. And if you can't see it, you can't manage it—let alone organize it, sequence it, and have any assurance that your resources can complete it."

I frown, recalling my last meeting with Wes and Patty when they struggled to come up with the list of all our commitments to the organization. I say, "What is this? Some kind of intelligence test?"

"Yes, you could say that," he replies. "But don't worry. It's not just you. Steve has to pass his intelligence test, too. And for that matter, Dick, as well."

I follow him to his blue subcompact rental car and we drive five minutes to MRP-8, one of our manufacturing plants. It's enormous, probably four times bigger than my building, but this one is in immaculate condition, with some obvious recent renovations and add-ons.

A security guard in her late fifties greets us, "Good afternoon, Dr. Reid. How nice to see you! How are you doing? It's been a long time."

Erik shakes her hand warmly, replying with a wink, "Great seeing you again, Dorothy. We're just here to get a birds-eye view of the plant floor. Can we still get on the catwalk?"

She replies with a flirtatious smile, "It's closed to most people, but for you, I think we can make an exception."

I look at Erik suspiciously. He supposedly couldn't get anyone's name right, and yet he apparently remembers the name of some security guard from years past. And no one ever mentioned anything about a *Dr. Reid*.

After climbing five flights of stairs, we're standing on a catwalk that overlooks the entire plant floor, looking like it goes on for at least two city blocks in every direction.

"Look down there," he says. "You can see loading docks on each side of the building. Raw materials are brought in on this side, and the finished goods leave out the other. Orders come off that printer down there. If you stand here long enough, you can actually see all the WIP, that's 'work in process' or 'inventory' for plant newbies, make its way toward the other side of the plant floor, where it's shipped to customers as finished goods."

"For decades at this plant," he continues, "there were piles of inventory everywhere. In many places, it was piled as high as you could stack them using those big forklifts over there. On some days, you couldn't even see the other side of the building. In hindsight, we now know that WIP is one of the root causes for chronic due-date problems, quality issues, and expediters having to rejuggle priorities every day. It's amazing that this business didn't go under as a result."

He gestures broadly with both arms outstretched, "In the 1980s, this plant was the beneficiary of three incredible scientifically-grounded management movements. You've probably heard of them: the Theory of Constraints, Lean production or the Toyota Production System, and Total Quality Management. Although each movement started in different places, they all agree on one thing: WIP is the silent killer. Therefore, one of the most critical mechanisms in the management of any plant is job and materials release. Without it, you can't control WIP."

He points at a desk near the loading docks closest to us. "See that desk over there?"

I nod but also look pointedly at my watch: 4:45 p.m.

Oblivious to my impatience, he says, "Let me tell you a story. Decades ago, there used to be a guy named Mark. He was the supervisor for that first work center, right down there by that desk. Those racks hold the folders for incoming jobs. Isn't it amazing that those folders look exactly like they did back then?

"At any rate," he continues, "one day I see Mark picking up a folder to start some job. I ask him, 'On what basis did you choose that job, versus any of the others?'

"And you know what he tells me? He says, 'It's a job that requires this work center first. And we're open.'"

He shakes his head incredulously. "I could hardly believe it. I tell him, 'Your station is just the first of twenty operations. You don't factor the availability of any of the other nineteen stations in your decision?' And he replies, 'Well, no. This is the way I've done it for twenty years.'"

He laughs. "I suppose to him, it sounds like a reasonable way to pick which job to perform. He's keeping the first station busy, and it's similar to first-in, first-out scheduling. But of course, now everyone knows that you don't release work based on the availability of the first station. Instead, it should be based on the tempo of how quickly the bottleneck resource can consume the work."

I just stare at him blankly.

He continues, "Because of how Mark was releasing work, inventory kept piling up in front of our bottleneck, and jobs were never finished on time. Every day was an emergency. For years, we were awarded Best Customer of the Year from our air freight shipment company, because we were overnighting thousands of pounds of finished goods to angry customers almost every week."

He pauses and then says emphatically, "Dr. Eliyahu M. Goldratt, who created the Theory of Constraints, showed us how any improvements made *anywhere besides the bottleneck* are an illusion. Astonishing, but true! Any improvement made after the bottleneck is useless, because it will always remain starved, waiting for work from the bottleneck. And any improvements made before the bottleneck merely results in more inventory piling up at the bottleneck."

He continues, "In our case, our bottleneck was a heat treat oven, just like in Goldratt's novel, *The Goal*. We also had paint-curing booths that later became constraints, too. By the time we froze the release of all new jobs, you couldn't even see the bottleneck work centers because they were surrounded by huge piles of inventory. Even from up here!"

Despite myself, I laugh with him. It's obvious in hindsight, but I can imagine that to Mark, it was anything but obvious. "Look, thanks for the history lesson. But I learned most of this already in business school. I don't see how this could possibly be relevant to managing IT Operations. IT is not like running a factory."

"Oh, really?" he turns to me, frowning intensely. "Let me guess. You're going to say that IT is pure knowledge work, and so therefore, all your work is like that of an artisan. Therefore, there's no place for standardization, documented work procedures, and all that high-falutin' 'rigor and discipline' that you claimed to hold so near and dear."

I frown. I can't figure out if he's trying to convince me of something I already believe or trying to get me to accept an absurd conclusion.

"If you think IT Operations has nothing to learn from Plant Operations, you're wrong. Dead wrong," he says. "Your job as VP of IT Operations is to ensure the fast, predictable, and uninterrupted flow of planned work that delivers value to the business while minimizing the impact and disruption of unplanned work, so you can provide stable, predictable, and secure IT service."

Listening to him, I wonder if I should be writing this down.

He studies me closely. "Well, I can see that we're not ready to have this discussion. Until you gain a better understanding of what work is, any conversation we have about controlling work will be totally lost on you. It would be like talking about acrobatics to someone who doesn't believe in gravity yet.

"Rest assured, though," he says, pointing at the job release desk, "in order to get to where you want to go, eventually you *will* need to figure out what your equivalent to that desk is. You must figure out how to control the release of work into IT Operations and, more importantly, ensure that your most constrained resources are doing only the work that serves the goal of the entire system, not just one silo.

"Once you figure this out, young Bill, you will be well on your way toward understanding the Three Ways," he says. "The First Way helps us understand how to create fast flow of work as it moves from Development into IT Operations, because that's what's between the business and the customer. The Second Way shows us how to shorten and amplify feedback loops, so we can fix quality at the source and avoid rework. And the Third Way shows us how to create a culture that simultaneously fosters experimentation, learning from failure, and understanding that repetition and practice are the prerequisites to mastery."

Although he now sounds oddly like Master Shifu in the movie *Kung*

Fu Panda, I'm listening intently. The need for rigor and discipline, and constantly practicing and honing our skills are important lessons I've kept with me from the Marines. The lives of my men depended upon it there, and my job depends upon it here. Creating that predictability is what I'm most intent on instilling in my IT Operations group.

Erik hands me a slip of paper with a phone number on it. "Remember, there are four types of work. You've named business project work as one. When you have the other three, give me a call."

He takes out his car keys from his pocket and asks, "Do you want a lift back to your office?"

It's 5:10 p.m. when I finally get back to my cubicle. I log back into my clunker laptop to reply to e-mails. But I can't concentrate.

The last hour with Erik was like being in a strange parallel universe. Or like being forced to watch a psychedelic movie made in a drug-induced haze.

What did Erik mean that there were four categories of work?

I think back to my meeting with Wes and Patty. Wes mentioned we have a separate list for IT infrastructure projects and business projects. Are infrastructure projects another type of work?

As I ponder this, an e-mail notification window pops up on my screen, indicating another e-mail expecting a response.

Are e-mails another type of work?

I doubt it. At the plant, Erik gestured to the entire plant floor. When he mentioned "work," he seemed to mean it at an organizational level not at the level of an individual contributor or manager.

I think about it some more. Then I shake my head and quickly e-mail Steve, letting them know that I connected with Erik. I'm certain that a decade from now, I'll be telling my friends about my brief encounter with the raving madman on the manufacturing plant floor.

I need to get moving. Paige will be seriously annoyed if I come home late on a Friday night. When I undock the laptop from the docking station, an incredibly loud alarm pierces the air.

"Holy crap!" I shout, realizing that the sound is coming from my laptop. Fumbling, I try to turn down the volume, to power it off, but nothing makes the sound stop.

Frantically, I flip the laptop over and try to take the battery out, but the tape keeps it attached. I grab a letter opener, finally managing to slash the tape and get the battery out.

The laptop finally goes silent.

CHAPTER 8

• *Monday, September 8*

I spent all weekend working on a PowerPoint slide deck for my meeting with Steve this morning. Despite all that work, I wish I could have done more to prepare.

I force myself to relax, visualizing having a healthy and vigorous business discussion with him, walking out with everything I ask for. I keep reminding myself how important this is for the company and my organization. Everyone worked so hard to prepare for this and now success or failure depends on how well I can communicate it all to Steve.

Stacy smiles when I arrive and says warmly, "Go on in. I'm sorry we could only get you thirty minutes."

I stop just inside the door, where Sarah is sitting with Steve at the table. Sarah is telling Steve, "—you did an amazing job telling the story of where we're going. These were some of the most skeptical analysts around, but they clearly got excited. You've also given them a reason for us to talk again when Phoenix goes live. They also seem pretty impressed with the Phoenix roadmap."

They're telling analysts about the Phoenix roadmap? With so many features being delayed to the next release, I question the wisdom of making insufficiently informed promises to the market.

Steve just nods and replies happily, "Let's see if it changes their impressions of us. Good job scheduling the call. Catch you later today for the next one."

Sarah gives me a smile and says, "Hey, Bill. You're up and at it early today, aren't you?"

Gritting my teeth, I just ignore her comment. "Good morning, everyone." Trying to show an interest, I say, "Sounds like you had a good call."

Sarah smiles even more broadly. "Yes, they're really excited about our vision and agree that it's going to be a real game changer for us. This is what we need to change how we're perceived by the broader market and Wall Street."

I look levelly at her, wondering whether these briefings that we give the outside world might be what is causing such pressure on Chris' team to release features so prematurely.

I grab a seat across from Steve. I can't quite turn my back on Sarah, but I do my best.

I don't want to give Steve my handouts until Sarah has left the room, but she continues to talk with Steve, recounting their meeting and how to change the talk track for their next analyst call.

As they talk, all I can think of is how she's eating into my time with Steve.

Eleven minutes later, Steve laughs at a joke from Sarah, and she finally leaves the office, closing the door behind her. Steve turns to me and says, "Sorry about going over—our next Phoenix analyst briefing is in twenty minutes. So, what's on your mind?"

"You've impressed upon me from the very beginning that I need to help maximize the probability of success of the Phoenix rollout," I start. "Based on my observations of the past week, we are stretched dangerously thin, to the point that I believe Phoenix is in considerable jeopardy.

"I've had my staff establish what our levels of demand and capacity truly are," I continue. "We've started to inventory everything we're being asked to do, regardless of how big or small. Based on the analysis so far, it's clear to me that the demand for IT work far exceeds our ability to deliver. I've asked them to make more visible what the pipeline of work looks like, so we can make more informed decisions about who should be working on what and when."

With as much gravitas as I can muster, I say, "One thing is very clear, though. We are definitely understaffed. There's no way that we can deliver everything we've promised. Either we need to cut down the project list, or we've got to staff up."

Trying to replicate the reasoned and logical argument I've spent all weekend rehearsing, I continue, "The other big problem is that we have too many different projects competing for our attention. You've been consistent and clear that Phoenix is the most important, but we can't seem to keep resources dedicated to it. For instance, last Thursday, internal audit delivered to us a set of findings that we must investigate and assemble a response letter for in one week. Doing so will impact Phoenix."

I've been watching Steve as I talked, and so far, he's remained expressionless. I look at him calmly and ask, "What I'd like to get out of our meeting is an understanding of the relative priority of Phoenix versus the audit findings and to talk about the number of projects and how to adequately staff them."

In my mind, I've done a good job of being the competent and passionate manager who is dispassionately struggling to decide how to best serve the business, without making moral judgments.

Steve replies in an exasperated voice, "What kind of bullshit prioritization question is this? If I went to my board and told them that I need to do either sales or marketing, and asked them which of those I should do, I'd be laughed out of the room. I need to do both, just like you need to do both! Life is tough. Phoenix is the top company priority, but that doesn't mean you get to hold the sox-404 audit hostage."

I count to three before saying, "Obviously, I'm not being clear. Both Phoenix and the compliance project share certain key resources, such as Brent. The compliance project *alone* would tie up these people for a year, but we need them focused on Phoenix. On top of that, our infrastructure is so fragile, that we have daily failures, which often require these same resources to restore normal operations. If a similar outage to the payroll run failure happened today, we'd likely have to pull Brent off both the Phoenix and compliance work to figure out what went wrong."

I look at him dead-on and say, "We've looked at different resourcing options, including hiring and moving people around, but none of them will have any effect fast enough to make a difference. If Phoenix is really the top priority, we need to put some of the compliance work on hold."

"Out of the question," he says, before I can even finish. "I've seen that big pile of audit findings, and we will be in very hot water if we don't get those issues fixed."

This is definitely not going according to plan. "Okay…" I say slowly. "We'll do our best, but let me state for the record that we're too understaffed to do a good job on either one, let alone both."

I wait for him to acknowledge my point. Seconds go by before he finally nods.

Realizing this is probably the best I'm going to get, I indicate to the first page of the handout I gave him. I say, "Let's zoom up and talk about project demand and capacity. We're currently supporting over thirty-five business projects through Kirsten's Project Management Office, and at current count, seventy-plus other smaller business projects and internal initiatives. And there are others out there that we just haven't counted yet. With our 143 IT Operations people, nothing is getting done as promised."

I point him to the second page of the handout, saying, "As you can see, my team and I have come up with a request for six additional resources that we're most short-handed on."

I go for the close, saying, "My goal is to increase our throughput so we won't be in this position again, and to get as many of these projects done as we can. I'd like your approval to get these openings immediately, so we can start our search. Talent like Brent is not easy to find, and we need to start sooner rather than later."

In my rehearsals, this is when Steve would run his finger down the figures, ask me some questions, and we'd have a meaningful discussion about how to make the best trade-offs. Maybe he'd even pat me on the back and compliment me on the quality of my analysis.

But Steve doesn't even pick up my handouts. Instead, he looks at me and says, "Bill, Phoenix is already $10 million over budget, and we must get cash-flow positive soon. You have some of the most expensive resources in the entire company. You have to use what you've got."

He crosses his arms and continues, "Last year, we had some IT analysts come in and benchmark our company against our peers. They told us that we're spending way more on IT than our competitors.

"You may think that with three thousand employees, six more employees won't make a difference. But, trust me, every expense is under scrutiny. If I can't close the profitability gap, I'll have to do another layoff. Your math of adding another $2 million in labor costs just doesn't work."

He continues in a more sympathetic voice. "My suggestion to you? Go to your peers and make your case to them. If your case is really valid, they should be willing to transfer some of their budget to you. But let me be clear: Any budget increases are out of the question. If anything, we may have to cut some heads in your area."

I spent hours role-playing worst-case scenarios over the weekend. Apparently, I'm going to have to practice being more pessimistic.

"Steve, I don't know how I can be more clear about this," I say, feeling a little desperate. "This stuff isn't magic. All this work being piled on us is done by real people. Commitments like the compliance work are made without any regard for what's already on people's plates, like Phoenix."

Realizing I have little to lose, but trying to shock some sense into him, I say, "If you really care about closing the gap with the competition by having Phoenix succeed, you sure aren't acting like it. To me, it seems like you're just being suckered to rush to the gunfight late, showing up with only a knife."

I expected some kind of reaction but he merely leans back, crossing his arms in front. "We're all doing our best. So you better go back and do the same."

Just then, the door opens as Sarah walks in. "Hi, Steve. Sorry to interrupt, but we have the next analyst call in two minutes. Shall I dial us in?"

Shit. I look down at my watch. 9:27.

She even robbed me of my last three minutes.

Utterly defeated, I finally say, "Okay, got it. Keep pushing. I'll keep you posted."

Steve nods in thanks, and then turns to Sarah as I close the door behind me. On my way out, I toss the presentation I had worked on all weekend into Stacy's recycling bin.

I try to wave away the stench of failure as I walk to the CAB meeting. I'm still thinking about how I'm going to break the bad news to Wes and Patty when I walk into the conference room that Patty has coined the Change Coordination Room.

All thoughts of Steve disappear when I see what's there.

Almost every area of the wall is now covered in whiteboards. Index cards cover nearly every inch of the whiteboards on two of the walls. It's not just one deep—in some places there are hooks attached to the board, with ten cards hanging off them.

On the conference room table are twenty, maybe even thirty, more piles of cards.

On the far side of the table, two guys who work for Patty have their backs to us, studying a card. After a moment, they tape it between two other cards in front of them.

"Holy crap," I say.

"We've got a problem." Patty says from behind me.

"Not enough space for more whiteboards?" I say, only half joking.

Before Patty answers, I hear Wes enter the room. "Holy shit!" he says. Where did all these cards come from? Are they all for this week?"

I turn to ask him, "Are you surprised? Most of these are coming from your group."

He looks around at all the boards and then at the cards on the table, "I knew that my guys were really busy, but, there must be a couple of hundred changes here."

Patty turns her laptop around to show us the spreadsheet she has open, "Since last Friday afternoon, there have been 437 changes submitted for this week."

Wes for once is speechless. He finally shakes his head and says, "And now we're supposed to go through and approve all of them? This meeting was only scheduled for an hour—we'd need days to go through all of these!"

He looks at me. "Mind you, I'm not saying that we shouldn't, but if we're going to do this every week…"

Again, Wes stops speaking, overwhelmed at the task in front of us.

Quite honestly, I feel the same way. Apparently, getting all the managers to submit their changes for the week was just the first step. I didn't expect that the process would fall apart as we went beyond collecting the data and actually set out to process and authorize the changes.

I force myself to say cheerfully, "This is a great start. Like most things, things get worse before they get better. We've got enthusiastic support from the technical managers, so now we've got to figure out how to get these changes scrutinized and scheduled on an on-going basis. Any ideas?"

Patty is first to speak up. "Well, no one says that we have to be the ones reviewing all the changes—maybe we can push down some of these to delegates."

I listen to Wes and Patty trade ideas back and forth before I say, "Let's go back to our goals: get the left and right hands to know what the other is doing, give us some situational awareness during outages, and give audit some evidence that we're addressing change control.

"We need to focus on the riskiest changes," I continue. "The 80/20 rule likely applies here: Twenty percent of the changes pose eighty percent of the risk."

I stare again at piles of cards in front of us and pick up a couple at random, searching for some inspiration.

Holding up a card that has a big frowny face drawn on it, I ask, "What's PUCCAR?"

"That worthless app," Wes says with disgust, "is the Parts Unlimited Check Clearing and Reconciliation application that someone implemented almost two decades ago. We call it 'pucker' because every time we change it, it blows up, and no one knows how to fix it. The vendor went out of business during the dot-com boom, but we've never gotten funding to replace it."

I ask, "If we know it's that prone to crashing, why do we need to change it?"

Wes says quickly, "We try not to. But sometimes the business rules change, and we also have to keep it patched. It's running an operating system that's out of maintenance, so it's always dicey…"

"Good! It's a risky change. What other types of changes are being submitted like PUCCAR?" I ask.

We make a pile of nearly fifty cards proposing changes to the Rainbow, Saturn, and Taser applications, and also changes to the network and certain shared databases, which could impact a significant portion, or even all, of the business.

"Even looking at those cards makes my heart palpitate," Wes says. "These are some of the dangerous changes we make around here."

He's right. I say, "Okay, let's mark all of these as 'fragile.' These are high risk and must be authorized by the CAB. Patty, changes like this should be at the top of the pile during our meetings."

Patty nods, taking notes saying, "Got it. We're predefining high-risk categories of change that not only must have change requests submitted, but must have authorization before being scheduled and implemented."

We quickly create a list of the top ten most fragile services, applications, and infrastructure. Any change request that could affect any of these will be immediately flagged for CAB scrutiny.

Patty adds, "We need to create some standard procedures around these changes—like when we'll want them implemented—and have key resources not only aware of them but also standing by, just in case things go wrong—even the vendors."

She adds with a half smile, "You know, like having firefighters and ambulances lined up on the runway, ready to spray safety foam when the airplane lands in flames."

Wes laughs and adds wryly, "Yeah, in the case of PUCCAR, have the coroner stock up on a bunch of body bags, too. And a PR person ready to handle the angry phone calls from the business, saying that some customers were allergic to the foam we used."

I laugh. "You know, that's an interesting idea. Let's let the business choose the foam. There's no reason why all the responsibility should rest on our shoulders. We can send an e-mail out to the business ahead of time and ask when the best implementation time would be. If we can give them data on the outcomes of previous changes, they may even withdraw the change."

Patty is typing away. "Got it. For these types of changes, I'll have my staff generate some reports on the changes' success rates and any associated downtime. This will help the business make more informed decisions around the changes."

I'm extremely pleased with Patty's idea and am confident that we're on the right track. "Okay, that still leaves four hundred cards to go. Any ideas?"

Wes has been going through the cards methodically, creating two big stacks of cards next to him. He picks a card from the bigger pile, "This pile has changes we do all the time. Like this one about the monthly tax table upload to the POS systems. I don't think we should suspend any of these changes.

"On the other hand, these changes are stuff like 'increasing the Java application server thread pool size,' 'installing the Kumquat vendor application hotfix to resolve performance issue,' and 'resetting the Kentucky data center load balancer to default duplex settings.'

"What the hell do I know about these things?" Wes says. "I just don't know enough about the context to have an actual opinion. I don't want to be like a seagull, flying in, crapping on people, and then flying away, you know?"

Excited, Patty says, "Excellent! The first ones are the low-risk changes that ITIL calls 'standard changes.' For changes we've done many times before successfully, we just preapprove. They still need to be submitted, but they can be scheduled without us."

When everyone nods, she continues, "That leaves about two hundred changes that are medium-risk changes that we still need to look at."

"I agree with Wes," I respond. "For these, we need to trust that the manager knows what he or she is doing. But I'd like Patty to verify that people have appropriately informed anyone they could affect, and gotten the 'okay to proceed' from all of them."

I think for a moment and say, "Take John's tokenization application. Before that change request would even come to us, I would expect him to get the nod from the application and database owners, and also the business. If he's done that, that's good enough for me. I view our role as making sure that he's dotted the i's and crossed the t's. At this level, I care more about the integrity of the process, not so much about the actual changes."

Patty is typing away. "Let me see if I've got this right: For the 'messy middle changes,' we're deciding that the change submitter has responsibility and accountability for consulting and getting approval from people potentially affected. Once they do that, they submit their change card for us to review and approve for scheduling."

I smile and say, "Yep. Work for you, Wes?"

At last, he says, "I think it'll work. Let's give it a shot."

"Good," I say. Then I say to Patty, "You can help make sure the change requesters are actually doing all the work beforehand?"

Patty smiles and says, "With pleasure."

She looks up at the board, tapping a pen on the table while she thinks. She says, "Today is Monday. We've already said today's changes are cleared for implementation. I propose we extend the amnesty period through tomorrow, and assemble a full CAB meeting for Wednesday, with the intent of scheduling the rest of the changes. That should give everyone enough time to prepare."

I look at Wes. He says, "This is good, but I'm already thinking about next week. We should tell everyone to keep the change requests coming in, and let's set up the weekly CAB meetings starting Friday the nineteenth."

Patty looks as pleased as I am that Wes is planning ahead to the following week, instead of griping. She says, "I'll have instructions sent to everyone in the next couple of hours."

After she finishes typing, she adds, "One last thing. I just want to point out that we're tying up two people, as well as myself, running this manual process. It's very labor intensive. Eventually, we're going to have to think about some way to automate this."

I nod. "No doubt that this isn't sustainable in its current form. But let's get a couple of CAB meetings under our belt and nail down what exactly the rules are. I promise you that we'll revisit this."

The meeting winds down and we all leave smiling. That's a first for my team.

CHAPTER 9

• Tuesday, September 9

I'm in the most ruthless budget meeting I've ever attended. Dick sits in the back of the room, listening attentively and occasionally officiating. We all defer to him, as he'll create the first cut of the annual plan. Sarah sits next to him, tapping away on her iPhone.

I finally pick up the phone. It must be a genuine emergency. It's been vibrating almost nonstop for the past minute.

I read, "Sev 1 incident: credit card processing systems down. All stores impacted."

Holy crap.

I know I've got to leave this meeting, despite knowing that everyone will try to steal my budget. I stand up, struggling with the large laptop, trying to keep more pieces from falling off. I almost make it out when Sarah says, "Another problem, Bill?"

I grimace. "Nothing that we can't handle."

In reality, any Sev 1 outage automatically qualifies as a very big problem, but I don't want to give her any ammunition.

When I get to the NOC, I grab the seat next to Patty, who is coordinating the call. "Everyone, Bill just joined us. To catch you up, we have confirmed that the order entry systems are down and we have declared a Sev 1 incident. We were just trying to establish what changed."

She pauses, looking at me. "And, I'm not confident we actually know."

I prompt everyone, "Patty asked a pretty simple question. So, what were all the changes made today that could have led to this outage?"

There is an awkward silence that stretches on as people either look down or look around at one another suspiciously. Everyone is avoiding eye contact.

I'm about to say something when I hear, "This is Chris. I told Patty this before, and I'm telling you again now, none of my developers changed anything. So cross us off your hit list. It was probably a database change."

Someone at the end of the table says angrily, "What? We didn't make any changes—well, not on anything that could have impacted the order entry systems. Are you sure it wasn't an operating system patch gone wrong again?"

Someone two seats over then sits up and says heatedly, "Absolutely not. We don't have any updates scheduled to hit those systems for another three weeks. I'd bet fifty bucks it was a networking change—their changes are always causing problems."

Slapping both hands over his eyes, Wes shouts, "For crying out loud, guys!"

Looking exasperated and resigned, he says to someone across the table, "You need to defend your honor, too? Everyone might as well have a turn."

Sure enough, the Networking lead across the table from him holds up both hands, looking hurt and aggrieved. "You know, it really isn't fair that Networking keeps getting blamed for outages. We didn't have any changes scheduled for today."

"Prove it," the database manager challenges.

The Networking lead turns bright red, his voice cracking. "This is bullshit! You're asking me to prove that we didn't do anything. How the hell do you prove a negative? Besides, I'm guessing the problem is a bad firewall change. Most of the outages in the last couple of weeks were caused by one of them."

I know I should probably put an end to this madness. Instead, I force myself to lean back in my chair and keep observing, one hand covering my mouth to hide my angry scowl and to keep me from saying something rash.

Patty looks exasperated and turns to me. "No one from John's team is present on the call. His team handles all the firewall changes. Let me try getting a hold of him."

I hear the sounds of loud tapping on a keyboard from the speakerphone, and then a voice says, "Umm, can someone try it now?"

There are sounds of multiple people typing on laptop keyboards, as they try to access the order entry systems.

"Hold it!" I say loudly, jumping halfway out of my chair, pointing at the speakerphone. "Who just said that?"

An awkward silence lengthens.

"It's me, Brent."

Oh, man.

I force myself to sit down again and take a long, deep breath. "Brent, thanks for the initiative, but, in a Sev 1 incident, we need to announce and discuss any actions before taking them. The last thing we want to do is to make things worse and complicate establishing root cause—"

Before I can finish, someone at the other end of the table interrupts from behind his laptop, "Hey, the systems are back up again. Good work, Brent."

Oh, come on.

I press my lips together in frustration.

Apparently, even undisciplined mobs can get lucky, too.

"Patty, wrap this up," I say. "I need to see you and Wes in your office immediately." I stand up and leave.

I remain standing in Patty's office until I have both of their attention. "Let me make myself clear. For Sev 1 incidents, we cannot fly by the seat of our pants. Patty, from now on, as the person leading a Sev 1 incident call, I need you to start the call presenting a timeline of all relevant events, especially changes.

"I'm holding you responsible for having that information close-at-hand, which should be easy since you also control the change process. That information comes from you, not all the yahoos on the conference call. Is that clear?"

Patty looks back at me, obviously frustrated. I resist the urge to soften my words. I know she's been working hard, and I've been piling even more onto her lately.

"Yeah, totally clear," she says wearily. "I'll work on documenting that process and will institute it as quickly as I can."

"Not good enough," I say. "I want you to host practice incident calls and fire drills every two weeks. We need to get everyone used to solving problems in a methodical way and to have the timeline available before we go into that meeting. If we can't do this during a prearranged drill, how can we expect people to do it during an emergency?"

Seeing the discouraged expression on her face, I put my hand on her shoulder. "Look, I appreciate all the work you're doing lately. It's important work, and I don't know what we'd do without you."

Next, I turn to Wes. "Impress upon Brent immediately that during emergencies, everyone must discuss changes they're thinking about, let alone the ones they actually implement. I can't prove it, but I'm guessing Brent caused the outage, and when he realized it, he undid the change."

Wes is about to respond, but I cut him off.

"Put a stop to this," I say forcefully, pointing at him. "No more unauthorized changes, and no more undisclosed changes during outages. Can you get your people under control or not?"

Wes looks surprised and studies my face for a moment. "Yeah, I'm on it, boss."

Wes and I spend nearly every waking hour late Tuesday and early Wednesday in the Phoenix war room. The deployment is only three days away. As each day goes by, the worse it looks.

It's a relief to head back to the Change Coordination Room.

As I walk in, most of the CAB is here. The messy pile of index cards is gone. Instead, they're either hanging on one of the whiteboards on the wall or neatly organized on the table in the front of the room, labeled "Pending Changes."

"Welcome to our change management meeting," Patty begins. "As you can see on the board, all of the standard changes have been scheduled. Today, we'll review and schedule all the high- and medium-risk changes. We'll then look at the change schedule to make any needed adjustments—I won't give away anything right now, but I think you'll see something that requires our attention."

She picks up the first pile of cards. "The first high-risk change is to a firewall, submitted by John, scheduled for Friday." She then reads out the people who have been consulted and signed off on the proposed change.

She prompts Wes and me, "Bill and Wes, do you approve this to go on the board as a Friday change?"

I'm satisfied that there have been enough eyes on this, so I nod.

Wes says, "Same for me. Hey, not bad. Twenty-three seconds to approve our first change. We beat our previous best time by fifty-nine minutes!"

There is scattered applause. Patty doesn't disappoint as she goes through the remaining eight high-risk changes, taking even less time for those. There is more applause, while one of her staff posts the cards on the board.

Patty picks up the medium-risk change stack. "There were 147 standard changes submitted. I want to commend everyone for following the process and talking with the people that needed to be consulted. Ninety of those changes are ready to be scheduled, and have been posted. I've printed them out for everyone to review."

Turning to Wes and me, she says, "I sampled ten percent of these, and, for the most part, they look good. I'll keep track of problem trends, just in case some of these need more scrutiny going forward. Unless there are any objections, I think we're done with the medium-risk changes. There's actually a more pressing problem that we need to address."

When Wes says, "No objections from me," I nod for Patty to proceed, who merely gestures to the boards.

I think I see what's wrong, but I stay quiet. One of the leads points to one of the boxes and says, "How many changes are scheduled for Friday?"

Bingo.

Patty flashes a small smile and says, "173."

On the board, it's now very obvious that nearly half the changes were scheduled for Friday. Of the remaining, half are scheduled for Thursday with the rest sprinkled earlier in the week.

She continues, "I'm not suggesting that 173 changes happening on Friday is bad, but I'm worried about change collisions and resource-availability conflicts. Friday is also the day Phoenix is being deployed.

"If I were air traffic control," she continues, "I'd say that the airspace is dangerously overcrowded. Anyone willing to change their flight plans?"

Someone says, "I've got three that I'd like to do today, if no one minds. I don't want to be anywhere near the airport when Phoenix comes in for a landing."

"Yeah, well, lucky you," Wes mutters. "Some of us have to be here on Friday. I can already see the flames pouring out of the wings…"

Two other engineers ask for their changes to be moved earlier in the week. Patty has them go to the board to move their change cards, verifying that it wouldn't interfere with other changes already scheduled.

Fifteen minutes later, the distribution of the cards on the change board is much more even. I'm less happy that everyone is moving their changes as far away from Friday as possible, like woodland creatures running away from a forest fire.

Watching the change cards being moved around, something else starts to bother me. It's not just the images of carnage and mayhem around Phoenix. Instead, it has something to do with Erik and the MRP-8 plant. I keep staring at the cards.

Patty interrupts my concentration. "—Bill, that concludes what we needed to get through. All the changes for the week are approved and scheduled."

As I try to reorient myself, Wes says, "You've done a really great job organizing this, Patty. You know I was one of your louder critics. But…" He gestures at the board, "All this is just terrific."

There is a murmur of agreement, and Patty flushes visibly. "Thanks. We're still in our first week of having a real change process, and this is the broadest participation we've ever had. But before we start patting ourselves on the back, how about we make it to a second week, okay?"

I say, "Absolutely. Thanks for all the time you're putting into this, Patty. Keep up the great work."

When the meeting adjourns, I stay behind, staring at the change board.

Several times during this meeting, something flickered at the edge of my mind. Was it something that Erik said that I dismissed earlier? Something to do with work?

Last Thursday, Wes and Patty did a manual inventory of all our projects, coming up with nearly a hundred projects. It was manually generated by interviewing all the line workers. Those projects certainly represent two categories of work: business projects and internal IT projects.

Looking at all the change cards on the wall, I realize that I'm looking at another collection of work that we once again manually generated. According to Patty, it's 437 discrete pieces of…work…that we're doing this week.

I realize that changes are the third category of work.

When Patty's people moved around the change cards, from Friday to earlier in the week, they were changing our *work schedule*. Each of those change cards defined the work that my team was going to be doing that day.

Sure, each of these changes is much smaller than an entire project, but it's still work. But what is the relationship between changes and projects? Are they equally important?

And can it really be that before today, none of these changes were being tracked somewhere, in some sort of system? For that matter, where did all these changes come from?

If changes are a type of work different than projects, does that mean that we're actually doing more than just the hundred projects? How many of these changes are to support one of the hundred projects? If it's not supporting one of those, should we really be working on it?

If we had exactly the amount of resources to take on all our project work, does this mean we might not have enough cycles to implement all these changes?

I debate with myself whether I'm on the verge of some large and meaningful insight. Erik asked me what my organization's equivalent to the job release desk on the plant floor. Does change management have anything to do with it?

Suddenly I laugh out loud at the absurd number of questions I've just asked myself. I feel like a one-man debate club. Or that Erik tricked me into doing some philosophical navel-gazing.

Thinking for a moment, I decide there's value in knowing that changes represent yet another category of work but don't know why.

I've now identified three of the four categories of work. For a brief moment, I wonder what the fourth category of work is.

CHAPTER 10

• *Thursday, September 11*

The next morning, bright and early, I'm back in the Phoenix war room. Kirsten gives us a rundown of the most critical Phoenix project tasks at the beginning of each day. Because the stakes are so high, committed tasks are usually reported by the responsible manager as "completed."

No one wants to get on Kirsten's bad side. Or Steve's, for that matter.

The bad news of the day comes from William Mason, Director of Quality Assurance, who works for Chris. Apparently, they're still finding twice as many broken features as are getting fixed.

It's never a good sign when pieces are falling off the car as it moves down the assembly line. No wonder all of us are dreading the deployment date.

I'm pondering how we can mitigate some of this risk when I hear Kirsten call Brent's name for the third time. And for the third time, Wes is having to explain why something didn't get done.

Sarah says from the back of the room, "Wes, once again we're getting bottlenecked by your people. Are there some personnel issues here that you need to be addressing?"

Wes turns bright red and is about to respond, when I quickly interject, "Kirsten, how many other tasks have been assigned to Brent?"

Kirsten quickly replies, "As of today, there are five outstanding tasks. Three were assigned last Wednesday, and two were assigned last Friday."

"Okay, I'm on it," I say. "As soon as we're done here, I'll look into what's going on. Expect a status report by noon today along with revised timelines for completion. I'll let you know if we require anything."

On my walk over to Brent's cube in Building 7, I remind myself that my goal is to observe and seek to understand. After all, this guy has come up in conversation every day since I accepted my new role.

Maybe Brent isn't actually as smart as we think. Or perhaps he *is* some technology Einstein and any attempt to find similarly skilled people will fail. Or maybe he's deliberately sabotaging our attempts to take work away from him.

But Brent seems professional and smart, not much different than many senior engineers I've worked with in the past.

As I approach his desk, I hear him on the phone and typing away on his keyboard. He's sitting down in front of his four monitors with a headset on, typing something into a terminal application.

I remain standing outside of his cube, discreetly listening in.

He says, "No, no, no. The database is up and running. Yeah, I know because it's right in front of me… Yes, I can do queries… Yes… Yes… No… I'm telling you, it has to be the application server… It's up? Okay, let me see… Wait, let me try doing a manual sync. Try it now…"

His cell phone rings. "Wait a second, I've got another call coming in. I'll call you right back."

He writes something down on a Post-it note, putting it on his monitor next to two other Post-it notes. Exasperated, he answers his cell phone, "Yeah, Brent here… The what service is down? Have you tried rebooting it? Look, I'm really slammed right now with Phoenix—I'll get back to you later today?"

I'm in the middle of silently congratulating him when I hear him say, "Uh-huh…I don't even know who that is. The VP of what? Okay, let me have a look."

I sigh, taking a seat in an empty cubicle to watch today's episode of A Day in The Life of Brent.

He's on the phone for another five minutes, hanging up only after some critical production database is back up and running.

I appreciate how Brent seems to genuinely care that everyone relying on IT systems can get their work done, but I'm dismayed that everyone seems to be using him as their free, personal Geek Squad. At the expense of Phoenix.

Brent grabs one of the Post-it notes off of his monitor and picks up his phone. Before he can dial, though, I stand up and say, "Hi, Brent."

"Agh!" he shouts, startled. "How long have you been there?"

"Only for a couple of minutes," I say, putting on my most friendly smile, grabbing a seat next to him. "Long enough to see you fix two people's problems. That's admirable, but I just came from Kirsten's daily Phoenix stand-up. There are five tasks that have been assigned to you, which are now late."

I show him the five tasks from the project management meeting. He says quickly, "I'm half-done with all of these already. I just need a couple of hours of quiet working time to get this done. I'd do this from home if I could, but the network connection is too slow."

"Who's been calling you, and what do they want?" I ask, frowning.

"Usually it's other IT people who are having problems fixing something," he replies, rolling his eyes. "When something goes down, I'm apparently the only person who knows where to go looking."

"I thought Wes hired a bunch of people to take over some of these escalations from you." I say.

Brent rolls his eyes again. "That was the idea. But most had other responsibilities and were never available when we needed them. Others were let go during the downsizings because they weren't busy enough. Trust me. That was no big loss. I ended up handling most of those issues anyway."

"How many calls are you getting each day? Are you logging these calls anywhere?" I ask.

"You mean, like in our ticketing system? No, because opening up a ticket for each of those calls would take longer than fixing the problem." Brent says dismissively. "The number of calls depends on the day. The last week has been worse than normal."

I get it now. I bet if anyone called right now and yelled loud enough or name-dropped someone scary enough, Brent could be dragged into fixing someone else's problem for hours on end.

"You tried to push back on the last person who called. What made you decide to work the issue, instead of telling them to go pound sand?" I ask.

He replies, "She told me that the VP of Logistics was screaming that replenishment orders weren't getting created, and that if it didn't get fixed right away, our stores were at risk of stocking out on fast-moving products. I didn't want to be the person being called out for single-handedly allowing stock-outs to happen in the stores."

I purse my lips. Company executives strong-arming my engineers into doing their bidding is total bullshit. But jeopardizing Phoenix is above their pay grade.

Standing up, I say, "Okay, from here on out, you're working only on Phoenix. Steve Masters has said that this is everyone's top priority. Now more than ever, the project needs you. I'm expecting you to reject any task that anyone tries to assign you."

Brent looks simultaneously relieved and concerned. Maybe he's thinking about that VP of Logistics.

I add, "If anyone contacts you about anything besides Phoenix, send them to Wes. Let him deal with all the jackasses."

He says skeptically, "Look, I appreciate this, but I really don't think this is going to work in the long run. Our guys around here just don't seem up-to-speed with how all our systems work. In the end, they keep coming to me."

"Well, they're going to have to learn. When they call, send them to Wes. If anyone's got a problem with that, then send them to me. In fact, put a vacation message on your e-mail, saying that you're not responding to anything except for Phoenix and to instead contact…"

At my prompting, Brent says with a small smile, "Wes."

"See? You're already getting the hang of it." I smile in return.

I point to his desk phone, "Do whatever it takes to break people of the habit of going directly to you. You've got my permission to turn off your phone ringer and change your voicemail greeting to say you're not available and to contact Wes instead. Whatever it takes."

Realizing that I'm distracting Brent from Phoenix by just standing here, I say quickly, "No, I'll have my assistant Ellen change your voice-mail greeting for you."

Brent smiles again, and says, "No, no, no. I can do that. Thanks for the offer, though."

I write my cell phone number on a Post-it note, and hand it to him, "Ellen will do it. We need you on those Phoenix tasks. Call if you need anything from me."

When he nods, I start heading back to Building 9, but then turn around to ask, "Hey, let me buy you a beer sometime next week?"

He agrees, his expression brightening.

As I leave the building, I immediately call Patty. When she picks up, I say, "Grab Wes and meet me outside the Phoenix war room. We need to change the way we're managing escalations to Brent. Right now."

We all sit down in the conference room across the hallway from the Phoenix war room.

"How'd it go with Brent?" Wes asks.

When I tell him that Brent wasn't able to work on Phoenix because of all the break-fix work, he blanches. "He's been in all these emergency meetings! How can he possibly think anything is more important than Phoenix!"

I say, "Good question. Why would Brent drop Phoenix to work on something else?"

Wes' bluster disappears for a couple of moments. "Probably because someone like me was screaming at him, saying that I absolutely needed his help to get my most important task done. And it's probably true: For way too many things, Brent seems to be the only one who knows how they actually work."

"If it were me, I'd try to justify it by saying that it would only take a couple of minutes…" Patty says. "Which could be true, but it's like death by a thousand cuts."

"Processes are supposed to protect people. We need to figure out how to protect Brent," I say. I then describe how I already told Brent to send everyone wanting anything to Wes.

"What? You want me to micromanage all of his time? I don't have time to be Brent's secretary or be some sort of help desk person!" he shouts.

"Okay, what's on your plate that's more important than making sure your resources are getting critical Phoenix work done?" I ask.

Wes looks back at me for several moments stonily and then laughs. "Okay, you got me. Look, Brent is a smart guy. But he's also one of the worst people I've ever met at writing anything down. Let me tell you a real story of how impossible this is going to be: Several months ago, we were three hours into a Sev 1 outage, and we bent over backward not to escalate to Brent. But eventually, we got to a point where we were just out of ideas, and we were starting to make things worse. So, we put Brent on the problem."

He shakes his head, recalling the memory, "He sat down at the keyboard, and it's like he went into this trance. Ten minutes later, the problem is fixed. Everyone is happy and relieved that the system came back up. But then someone asked, 'How did you do it?' And I swear to God, Brent just looked back at him blankly and said, 'I have no idea. I just did it.'"

Wes thumps the table and says, "And *that* is the problem with Brent. How the hell do you document that? 'Close your eyes and go into a trance'?"

Patty laughs, apparently recalling the story. She says, "I'm not suggesting Brent is doing this deliberately, but I wonder whether Brent views all his knowledge as a sort of power. Maybe some part of him is reluctant to give that up. It does put him in this position where he's virtually impossible to replace."

"Maybe. Maybe not," I say. "I'll tell you what I do know, though. Every time that we let Brent fix something that none of us can replicate, Brent gets a little smarter, and the entire system gets dumber. We've got to put an end to that.

"Maybe we create a resource pool of level 3 engineers to handle the escalations, but keep Brent out of that pool. The level 3s would be responsible for resolving all incidents to closure, and would be the only people who can get access to Brent—on one condition.

"If they want to talk with Brent, they must first get Wes' or my approval," I say. "They'd be responsible for documenting what they learned, and Brent would never be allowed to work on the same problem twice. I'd review each of the issues weekly, and if I find out that Brent worked a problem twice, there will be hell to pay. For both the level 3s and Brent."

I add, "Based on Wes' story, we shouldn't even let Brent touch the keyboard. He's allowed to tell people what to type and shoulder-surf, but under no condition will we allow him to do something that we can't document afterward. Is that clear?"

"That's great," Patty says. "At the end of each incident, we'll have one more article in our knowledge base of how to fix a hairy problem and a growing pool of people who can execute the fix."

Wes doesn't look completely convinced, but he eventually laughs. "I like it, too. We'll treat him like Hannibal Lecter—when we need him, we'll put him into a straightjacket, tie him to a wheelchair, and cart him out."

I laugh.

Patty adds, "To prevent another Brent escalation, we should log every keystroke and record the terminal session. Maybe even have someone follow him around with a video camera and turn on audit logging so we know exactly what he changed."

I like it, although it sounds a bit extreme. However, I suspect that it will take extreme measures to get us out of this situation.

I venture, "Maybe we take away his production access, so the only way the work can get done is him telling the level 3s what to do."

Wes guffaws. "He might quit if we did that right away."

"So, who do we have that's available to put into this level 3 resource pool?" I ask.

He hesitates. "Well, we have the two hires we made a year ago that were meant to help shore up Brent. One is working on creating server build standards, but we can take her off of that temporarily. There are two other engineers that we identified for cross-training years ago, but we never had the time to pursue it further. So, that's three people."

"I'll define the new Brent procedures," Patty says. "I like gating all access to him through you and Wes. But how will we discourage people like that VP of Logistics from going directly to Brent?"

I reply immediately, "We'll collect the names of the people who do, and I'll call each of their bosses to tell them to cease and desist. And then I'll let Steve know how they're disrupting Phoenix."

"Okay, let's give it a try," she says. "You know, we've got the 'stick' approach covered, but what about the 'carrot'? How can we motivate Brent and the engineers to follow this new process?"

"Maybe we send them to whatever conference or training they want. When senior engineers get to the level of Brent, or aspire to be Brent, they want to learn and share what they've done. As for Brent, how about we make him take a week off, completely free of any escalation duties?" Wes suggests.

"My God," Wes continues, shaking his head. "I don't think Brent's even been able to take a day off without a pager in about three years. You know, he'll burst into tears when we offer that to him."

"Make it so, guys," I say, smiling as I imagine that scene.

Before I forget, I add, "Wes, I want a timesheet from Brent every day, and I want every escalation Brent works in the ticketing system. We need that documented so we can analyze it later. Anyone using Brent's time will need to justify it to me. If it's not justified, I'll escalate it to Steve, and that person and his manager will have to explain to Steve why they think their project or task is so important."

"This is amazing," Patty says. "We've gotten more change, incident, and escalation processes going in the last week than we have in the last five years!"

"It's probably just in the nick of time," Wes says, sounding relieved. "Do me a favor, and don't tell anyone I said that. I've got a reputation to protect."

CHAPTER 11

• *Thursday, September 11*

Later that day during lunch, I curse loudly. I was trying to use my precious few unscheduled minutes during my break to get caught up on e-mails but forgot that my crappy laptop crashes if I turn it on while it's in the docking station. It's the third time I've done it this week.

I'm already eating late and half my lunch break will be gone by the time I can log on.

Looking around, I find a blank Post-it note on my desk and write in large letters, "DO NOT INSERT LAPTOP UNTIL POWERED ON!!!" and put it on the docking station to avert my next act of time-wasting stupidity.

I'm smiling at my countermeasure when Patty calls me on my cell phone. "You have a minute to talk? I'm seeing something very odd on the change calendar. You need to see this."

When I walk into the conference room, I see the now familiar change cards hanging on the wall. The inbox basket is full of cards and more are neatly stacked in piles on the table. Patty is scrutinizing something on her laptop, chewing a fingernail.

Looking exhausted, she says, "I'm starting to think this entire change process is a total waste of time. Organizing all these changes and managing all the stakeholder communication is taking up three people full-time. Based on what I'm seeing now, it may be useless."

To see her suddenly disparaging the processes she has championed for years is genuinely alarming.

"Whoa," I say, waving both my hands in front of her. "Catch me up, because I think you've done a fantastic job, and I don't want us to go back to the old ways. What has you so concerned?"

She points to the Monday and Tuesday change boxes. "At the end of each day, my people start closing out the scheduled changes. We wanted to make sure that any changes that weren't completed were flagged so they can be rescheduled and to make sure that our change calendar was tracking what was happening in reality."

She points to the corner of one card. "We put a check on the change cards that have been verified as completed and then indicate whether it caused a service incident or outage. Since last Friday, sixty percent of the scheduled changes didn't get implemented! Which means we're doing all this work to authorize and schedule these changes, only to find that they're not even getting done!"

I can see why Patty is alarmed.

"Why aren't they being completed? And what do you do with the incomplete change cards?" I ask.

She scratches her head. "I've called a bunch of the change requesters, and their reasons are all over the board. A couple people said that they couldn't get all the people they needed to start their change. Someone else discovered halfway through his change that the storage guys didn't finish expanding the SAN like they had promised, so he had to back out his change, two hours into the procedure."

I groan, thinking about the wasted time and effort. I keep listening as Patty continues, "Someone else said that she couldn't implement her change because there was an outage in progress. And a bunch of other people said, um…"

She looks uncomfortable, so I prompt her to continue. "Well, they said they needed Brent for a portion of their changes, and he wasn't available," she says reluctantly. "In some cases, Brent's involvement was planned. But in other cases, they discovered they needed his help only after they started implementing and had to abort when Brent wasn't available."

Before Patty is even finished speaking, I'm seeing red.

"*What?* Brent again? What is going on? Just how has Brent managed to wedge himself into everyone's path?

"Oh, shit!" I exclaim when it hits me what's happening. "Did we create this problem by focusing Brent solely on Phoenix? Is this new policy a mistake?"

She says after a moment, "You know, that's an interesting question. If you genuinely believe that Brent should only be working on the most important projects, then I think the new policy is correct, and we shouldn't change it back.

"I think it's also important to note that until recently, Brent was helping people implement their changes, without that dependency recorded anywhere. Or rather, he'd try to. But he'd invariably be too busy to help everyone, so many of these changes wouldn't have been completed, even in the old way."

I pick up my phone and speed-dial Wes, telling him to join us.

When he arrives a couple of moments later, he takes a seat and then looks at my old laptop, saying, "Jeez. You still carrying that thing around? I'm sure we have a couple of newer eight-year-old laptops that you could use."

Ignoring his comment, Patty quickly brings him up to speed. His reaction to her revelation isn't much different than mine.

"You've got to be kidding me!" he says angrily, slapping his palm on his forehead. "Maybe we should allow Brent to help people make changes?"

I quickly say, "No, that can't be the answer. I suggested that, too. But Patty pointed out that this would imply that the blocked changes are more important than Phoenix. Which they aren't."

I think aloud, "Somehow, just like we're breaking the habits of people asking Brent to help with break-fix work, we need to do the same with change implementation. We've got to get all this knowledge into the hands of people actually doing the work. If they can't grok it, then maybe we have a skills problem in those teams."

When no one says anything, I tentatively add, "How about we take those same level 3 engineers that are dedicated to protect Brent from break-fix to help with these change issues?"

Wes quickly responds, "Maybe. But it's not a long-term fix. We need the people doing the work to know what the hell they're doing, not enable more people to hoard knowledge."

I listen to Wes and Patty brainstorm ideas to reduce yet another dependency on Brent when something starts to bother me. Erik called WIP, or work in process, the "silent killer," and that inability to control WIP on the plant floor was one of the root causes for chronic due-date problems and quality issues.

We just discovered that sixty percent of our changes didn't complete as scheduled.

Erik had pointed to the ever-growing mountain of work on the plant floor as an indication that the plant floor managers had failed to control their work in process.

I look at the mountain of change cards piled up on today's date on the calendar, as if a giant snowplow had pushed them all forward. Suddenly, it's starting to seem like the picture Erik painted on the plant floor eerily describes the state of my organization.

Can IT work really be compared to work on a plant floor?

Patty interrupts my deep contemplation as she asks, "What do you think?"

I look back up at her. "For the last couple of days, only forty percent of the scheduled changes were completed. The rest are being carried forward. Let's assume that this continues for a bit longer, while we figure out how to disseminate all the Brent knowledge.

"We have 240 incomplete changes this week. If we have four hundred new changes coming in next week, we'll have 640 changes on the schedule next week!

"We're like the Bates Motel of changes," I say in disbelief. "Changes go in but never come out. Within a month, we'll have thousands of changes that we'll be carrying around, all competing to get implemented."

Patty nods, "That's *exactly* what's bothering me. We don't have to wait a month to see thousands of changes—we're already tracking 942 changes. We'll cross over one thousand pending changes sometime next week. We're running short of space to post and store these change cards. So why are we going through all this trouble if the changes aren't even going to get implemented!"

I stare at all the cards, willing them into giving me an answer.

An ever-growing pile of inventory trapped on the plant floor, as high as the forklifts could stack it.

An ever-growing pile of changes trapped inside of IT Operations, with us running out of space to post the change cards.

Work piling up in front of the heat treat oven, because of Mark sitting at the job release desk releasing work.

Work piling up in front of Brent, because of…

Because of what?

Okay, if Brent is our heat treat oven, then who is our Mark? Who authorized all this work to be put in the system?

Well, we did. Or rather, the CAB did.

Crap. Does that mean we did this to ourselves?

But changes need to get done, right? That's why they're changes. Besides, how do you say no to the onslaught of incoming work?

Looking at the cards piling up, can we afford not to?

But when was the question ever asked whether we should accept the work? And on what basis did we ever make that decision?

Again, I don't know the answer. But, worse, I have a feeling that Erik may not be a raving madman. Maybe he's right. Maybe there is some sort of link between plant floor management and IT Operations. Maybe plant floor management and IT Operations actually have similar challenges and problems.

I stand up and walk to the change board. I start thinking aloud, "Patty is alarmed that more than half our changes aren't completing as scheduled, to the extent that she's wondering whether this whole change process is worth the time we're investing in it.

"Furthermore," I continue, "she points out that a significant portion of the changes can't complete because Brent is somehow in the way, which is partially because we've directed Brent to reject all non-Phoenix work. We think that reversing this policy is the wrong thing to do."

I take a mental leap, following my intuition. "And I'd bet a million dollars that this is the exact wrong thing to do. It's because of this process that, for the first time, we're even aware of how much scheduled work isn't getting done! Getting rid of the process would just kill our situational awareness."

Feeling like I'm getting on a roll, I say adamantly, "Patty, we need a better understanding of what work is going to be heading Brent's way. We need to know which change cards involve Brent—maybe we even make that another piece of information required when people submit their cards. Or use a different color card—you figure it out. You need to inventory what changes need anything from Brent, and try to satisfy it instead with the level 3 engineers. Failing that, try to get them prioritized so we can triage them with Brent."

As I'm talking, I'm more confident that we're heading down the right path. At this point, we might not be fixing the problem, but at least we'll be getting some data.

Patty nods, her expression of concern and despair now gone. "You want me to get my arms around the changes that are heading to Brent, indicating them on the change cards and maybe even requiring this information on all new cards. And to get back to you when we know how many changes are Brent-bound, what the changes are, and so forth, along with a sense of what the priorities are. Did I get that right?"

I nod and smile.

She types away on her laptop. "Okay, I've got it. I'm not sure what we'll find out, but it's better than anything I came up with by a long shot."

I look over at Wes, "You look concerned—anything you want to share?"

"Uh…" Wes says eventually. "There's not much to share, really. Except that this is a very different way of working than anything I've seen in IT. No offense, but did you switch medication recently?"

I smile wanly, "No, but I did have a conversation with a raving madman on a catwalk overlooking the manufacturing plant floor."

But if Erik was right about WIP in IT Operations, what else was he right about?

CHAPTER 12

• *Friday, September 12*

It's 7:30 p.m. on Friday, two hours after the Phoenix deployment was scheduled to start. And things are not going well. I'm starting to associate the smell of pizza with the futility of a death march.

The entire IT Operations team was assembled in preparation for the deployment at 4 p.m. But there was nothing to do because we hadn't received anything from Chris' team; they were still making last minute changes.

It's not a good sign when they're still attaching parts to the space shuttle at liftoff time.

At 4:30 p.m., William had stormed into the Phoenix war room, livid and disgusted that no one could get all of the Phoenix code to run in the test environment. Worse, the few parts of Phoenix that were running were failing critical tests.

William started sending back critical bug reports to the developers, many of whom had already gone home for the day. Chris had to call them back in, and William's team had to wait for the developers to send them new versions.

My team wasn't just sitting around, twiddling our thumbs. Instead, we were frantically working with William's team to try to get all of

Phoenix to come up in the test environment. Because if they couldn't get things running in a test environment, we wouldn't have a prayer of being able to deploy and run it in production.

My gaze shifts from the clock to the conference table. Brent and three other engineers are huddling with their QA counterparts. They've been working frantically since 4 p.m., and they already look haggard. Many have laptops open to Google searches, and others are systematically fiddling with settings for the servers, operating systems, databases, and the Phoenix application, trying to figure out how to bring everything up, which the developers had assured them was possible.

One of the developers had actually walked in a couple of minutes ago and said, "Look, it's running on my laptop. How hard can it be?"

Wes started swearing, while two of our engineers and three of William's engineers started poring through the developer's laptop, trying to figure out what made it different from the test environment.

In another area of the room, an engineer is talking heatedly to somebody on the phone, "Yes, we copied the file that you gave us… Yes, it's version 1.0.13… What do you mean it's the wrong version… What? When did you change that?… Copy it now and try again… Okay, look, but I'm telling you this isn't going to work… I think it's a networking problem… What do you mean we need to open up a firewall port? Why the hell didn't you tell us this two hours ago?"

He then slams the phone down hard, and then pounds the table with his fist, yelling, "Idiots!"

Brent looks up from the developer laptop, rubbing his eyes with fatigue. "Let me guess. The front-end can't talk to the database server because someone didn't tell us we need to open a firewall port?"

The engineer nods with exhausted fury, and says, "I cannot freaking believe this. I was on the phone with that jackass for twenty minutes, and it never occurred to him that it wasn't a code problem. This is FUBAR."

I continue to listen quietly, but I'm nodding in agreement at his prognosis. In the Marines, we used the term FUBAR."

Watching tempers fray, I look at my watch: 7:37 p.m.

It's time to get a management gut check from my team. I round up Wes and Patty and look around for William. I find him staring over the shoulder of one of his engineers. I ask him to join us.

He looks puzzled for a moment, because we don't normally interact, but he nods and follows us to my office.

"Okay, guys, tell me what you think of this situation," I ask.

Wes speaks up first, "Those guys are right. This is FUBAR. We're still getting incomplete releases from the developers. In the past two hours, I've already seen two instances when they've forgotten to give us several critical files, which guaranteed that the code wouldn't run. And as you've seen, we still don't know how to configure the test environment so that Phoenix actually comes up cleanly."

He shakes his head again. "Based on what I've seen in the last half hour, I think we've actually moved backward."

Patty just shakes her head with disgust and waves her hand, adding nothing.

I say to William, "I know we haven't worked much together, but I'd really like to know what you think. How's it looking from your perspective?"

He looks down, exhaling slowly and then says, "I honestly have no idea. The code is changing so fast that we're having problems keeping up. If I were a betting man, I'd say Phoenix is going to blow up in production. I've talked with Chris a couple of times about stopping the release, but he and Sarah ran right over me."

I ask him, "What do you mean by you 'can't keep up'?"

"When we find problems in our testing, we send it back to Development to have them fix it," he explains. "Then they'll send back a new release. The problem is that it takes about a half hour to get everything set up and running, and then another three hours to execute the smoke test. In that time, we'll have probably gotten three more releases from Development."

I smirk at the reference to smoke tests, a term circuit designers use. The saying goes, "If you turn the circuit board on and no smoke comes out, it'll probably work."

He shakes his head and says, "We have yet to make it through the smoke test. I'm concerned that we no longer have sufficient version control—we've gotten so sloppy about keeping track of version numbers of the entire release. Each time they fix something, they're usually breaking something else. So, they're sending single files over instead of the entire package."

He continues, "It's so chaotic right now that even if by some miracle Phoenix does pass the smoke test, I'm pretty sure we wouldn't be able to replicate it, because there are too many moving parts."

Taking off his glasses, he says with finality, "This is probably going to be an all-nighter for everyone. I think there's genuine risk that we won't have anything up and running at 8 a.m. tomorrow, when the stores open. And that's a big problem."

That is a huge understatement. If the release isn't finished by 8 a.m., the point of sale systems in the stores used to check out customers won't work. And that means we won't be able to complete customer transactions.

Wes is nodding. "William is right. We're definitely going to be here all night. And performance is worse than even I thought it would be. We're going to need at least another twenty servers to spread the load, and I don't know where we can find so many on such short notice. I have some people scrambling to find any spare hardware. Maybe we'll even have to cannibalize servers in production."

"Is it too late to stop the deployment?" I ask. "When exactly is the point of no return?"

"That's a very good question." Wes answers slowly. "I'd have to check with Brent, but I think we could stop the deployment now with no issues. But when we start converting the database so it can take orders from both the in-store POS systems and Phoenix, we are committed. At this rate, I don't think that will be for a couple of hours yet."

I nod. I've heard what I've needed to hear.

"Guys, I'm going to send out an e-mail to Steve, Chris, and Sarah to see if I can delay the deployment. And then I'm going to find Steve. Maybe I can get us one more week. But, hell, even getting one more day would be a win. Any thoughts?"

Wes, Patty, and William all just shake their heads glumly, saying nothing.

I turn to Patty. "Go work with William to figure out how we can get some better traffic coordination in the releases. Get over to where the developers are and play air traffic controller, and make sure everything is labeled and versioned on their side. And then let Wes and team know what's coming over. We need better visibility and someone to keep people following process over there. I want a single entry point for code drops, controlled hourly releases, documentation… Get my drift?"

She says, "It would be my pleasure. I'll head up to the Phoenix war room for starters. I'll kick down the door if that's what it takes and say, 'We're here to help…'"

I give them all a nod of thanks and head to my laptop to write my e-mail.

> From: Bill Palmer
> To: Steve Masters
> Cc: Chris Anderson, Wes Davis, Patty McKee, Sarah Moulton, William Mason
> Date: September 12, 7:45 PM
> Priority: Highest
> Subject: URGENT: Phoenix deployment in major trouble—my recommendation: 1 week delay
>
> > Steve,
> > First off, let me state that I want Phoenix in production as much as anyone else. I understand how important it is to the company.
> > However, based on what I've seen, I believe we will not have Phoenix up by the tomorrow 8 AM deadline. There is SIGNIFICANT RISK that this may even impact the in-store POS systems.
> > After discussions with William I recommend that we delay the Phoenix launch by one week to increase the likelihood that Phoenix achieves its goals and avert what I believe will be a NEAR-CERTAIN disaster.
> > I think we're looking at problems on the scale of the "November 1999 Thanksgiving Toys R Us" train-wreck, meaning multiday outages and performance problems that potentially put customer and order data at risk.
> > Steve, I will be calling you in just a couple of minutes.
> > Regards,
> > Bill

I take a moment to collect my thoughts and call Steve, who answers on the first ring.

"Steve, it's Bill. I just sent out an e-mail to you, Sarah, and Chris. I cannot overstate how badly this rollout has gone so far. This is going to bite us in the ass. Even William agrees. My team is now extremely concerned that the rollout will not complete in time for the stores to open at 8 a.m. Eastern time tomorrow. That could disrupt the stores' ability to take sales, as well as probably cause multiday outages to the website.

"It's not too late to stop this train wreck," I implore. "Failure means that we'll have problems taking orders from anyone, whether they're in the stores or on the Internet. Failure could mean jeopardizing and screwing up order data and customer records, which means losing customers. Delaying by a week would just mean disappointing customers, but at least they'll come back!"

Steve breathes into the phone and then replies, "It sounds bad, but at this point, we don't have a choice. We have to keep going. Marketing already bought weekend newspaper ads announcing the availability of Phoenix. They're bought, paid for, and being delivered to homes across the country. Our partners are all lined up and ready to go."

Flabbergasted, I say, "Steve, just how bad does it have to be for you to delay this release? I'm telling you that we could be taking a reckless level of risk in this rollout!"

He pauses for several moments. "Tell you what. If you can convince Sarah to postpone the rollout, let's talk. Otherwise, keep pushing."

"Are you kidding me? She's the one who's created this kamikaze mess."

Before I can stop myself, I hang up on Steve. For a brief moment, I consider calling him back to apologize.

As much as I hate to, I feel like I owe the company one last try to stop this insanity. Which means talking to Sarah in person.

Back in the Phoenix war room it's stuffy and rank from too many people sweating from tension and fear. Sarah is sitting by herself, typing away on her laptop.

I call out to her, "Sarah, can we talk?"

She gestures to the chair next to her, saying, "Sure. What's up?"

When I say in a lowered voice, "Let's talk in the hallway."

As we walk out together in silence, I ask her, "From up here, how does it look like the release is going?"

She says noncommittally, "You know how these things go when we're trying to be nimble, right? There's always unforeseen things when it comes to technology. If you want to make omelets, you've got to be willing to break some eggs."

"I think it's a bit worse than your usual rollout. I trust you saw my e-mail, right?"

She merely says, "Yes, of course. And you saw my reply?"

Shit.

I say, "No. But, before you explain, I wanted to make sure you understood the implications and the risks we're posing to the business." And then I repeat almost word for word what I told Steve just minutes before.

Not surprisingly, Sarah is unimpressed. As soon as I stop talking, she says, "We've all been busting ass getting Phoenix this far. Marketing is ready, Development is ready. Everyone is ready but you. I've told you before, but apparently, you're not listening: Perfection is the enemy of good. We've got to keep going."

Marveling at this colossal waste of time, I just shake my head and say, "No, lack of competence is the enemy of good. Mark my words. We're going to be picking up the pieces for days, if not weeks, because of your dumb decisions."

As I storm back into the NOC, I read Sarah's e-mail, which makes me even more furious. I resist the urge to reply and add fuel to the fire. I also resist the emotional desire to delete it—I may need it to cover my ass later.

From: Sarah Moulton
To: Bill Palmer, Steve Masters
Cc: Chris Anderson, Wes Davis, Patty McKee, William Mason
Date: September 12, 8:15 PM
Priority: Highest
Subject: Re: URGENT: Phoenix deployment in major trouble—my recommendation: 1 week delay

Everyone is ready but you. Marketing, Dev, Project Management all have given this project their all. Now it's your turn.

WE MUST GO!

Sarah

Suddenly, I panic for a brief moment that I haven't told Paige anything for hours. I send her a quick text message:

Night keeps getting worse. Am here for at least a couple more hrs. Will catch u in am. Love you. Wish me luck, darling.

I feel a tap on my shoulder and turn around to see Wes. "Boss. We've got a very serious problem."

The expression on his face is enough to make me scared. I quickly stand up and follow him to the other side of the room.

"Remember when we hit the point of no return around 9 p.m.? I've been tracking the progress of the Phoenix database conversion, and it's thousands of times slower than we thought it would be. It was supposed to complete hours ago, but it's only ten percent complete. That means all the data won't be converted until Tuesday. We are totally screwed."

Maybe I'm more tired than I thought but I'm not following him. I say, "Why is this a problem?"

Wes tries again, "That script needs to complete before the POS systems can come up. We can't stop the script and we can't restart it. Apparently, there's nothing we can do to make it go faster. I think we can hack Phoenix so that it can run, but I don't know about the in-store POS systems—we don't have any to test with in the lab."

Holy crap.

I think twice before I ask, "Brent?"

He just shakes his head. "I had him look at it for a couple of minutes. He thinks that someone turned on database indexing too soon, which is slowing down the inserts. There's nothing we can do about it now, though, without screwing up data. I put him back on the Phoenix deployment."

"How is everything else going?" I ask, wanting a full assessment of the situation. "Any improvement on performance? Any update on the database maintenance tools?"

"Performance is still terrible," he says. "I think there's a huge memory leak, and that's even without any users on it. My guys suspect we're going to have to reboot a bunch of the servers every couple of hours just to keep it from blowing up. Damned developers…"

He continues, "We've scrounged up fifteen more servers, some of them new and some yanked from various corners of the company. And now, believe it or not, we don't have enough space in the data center racks to deploy them. We have to do a big recabling and racking job, moving crap around. Patty just put a call out and brought in a whole bunch of her people to help with that."

I feel my eyebrows hit my hairline in genuine surprise. And then I bend forward, laughing. I say, "Oh, dear God. We finally find servers to deploy, and now we can't find space to put them in. Amazing. We just can't get a break!"

Wes shakes his head. "You know, I've heard stories like this from my buddies. But this may turn out to be the mother of all deployment failures."

He continues, "Here's the most amazing part: We made a huge investment in virtualization, which was supposed to save us from things like this. But, when Development couldn't fix the performance problems, they blamed the virtualization. So we had to move everything back onto physical servers!"

And to think that Chris proposed this aggressive rollout date because virtualization would save our asses.

I wipe my eyes and force myself to stop laughing. "And how about the database support tools the developers promised us?"

Wes immediately stops smiling. "Absolute garbage. Our guys are going to have to manually edit the database to correct all the errors Phoenix is generating. And we're going to have to manually trigger replenishments. We're still learning about how much of this type of manual work Phoenix is going to require. It's going to be very error-prone and take a ton of people to do."

I wince, thinking about how this will tie up even more of our guys, doing menial work that the broken application should be doing. Nothing worries auditors more than direct edits of data without audit trails and proper controls.

"You're doing a great job here. Our top priority is finding out what the effect of the incomplete database conversion will be on the in-store POS system. Find someone who knows those things inside and out, and get their thoughts. If necessary, call someone on Sarah's team who handles day-to-day retail operations. Bonus points if you can get your hands on a POS device and server we can log into to see what the impact is ourselves."

"Got it," Wes says, nodding. "I know just the person to put on this."

I watch him head off and then look around, trying to figure out where I can be the most useful.

The morning light is starting to stream in from the windows, showing the accumulated mess of coffee cups, papers, and all sorts of other debris. In the corner, a developer is asleep under some chairs.

I had just run to the bathroom to wash my face and wipe the grime from my teeth. I feel a little fresher, but it's been years since I've pulled an all-nighter.

Maggie Lee is the Senior Director of Retail Program Management and works for Sarah. She is kicking off the 7 a.m. emergency meeting, and there are nearly thirty people packed into the room. In a tired voice, she says, "It's been a night of heroics, and I appreciate everyone doing what it takes to hit our Phoenix commitments.

"As you know, the reason for this emergency meeting is that something went wrong in the database conversion," she continues. "That means all the in-store POS systems will be down, which means that the stores will not have working cash registers. That means manual tills and manual card swipes."

She adds, "The good news is that the Phoenix website is up and running." She gestures at me and says, "My thanks to Bill and the entire IT Operations crew for making this happen."

Irritated, I say, "I'd far rather have those POS systems up instead of Phoenix. All hell is breaking loose in the NOC. All our phones have been lit up for the past hour, because people in the stores are all screaming that their systems aren't responding. It's like the Jerry Lewis Telethon down there. Like all of you, my voicemail has already filled up from the staff in our 120 stores. We're going to need to pull in more people just to man the phones."

A phone vibrates somewhere on the table, as if to punctuate my point.

"We need to get proactive here," I say to Sarah. "We need to send out a summary to everyone in the stores, as quickly as possible outlining what's happened and more specific instructions on how to conduct operations without the POS systems."

Sarah momentarily looks blank, and then says, "That's a good idea. How about you take a first cut at the e-mail, and we'll take it from there?"

Dumbfounded, I say, "What? I'm not a store manager! How about your group takes the first cut, and Chris and I can make sure it's accurate."

Chris nods.

Sarah looks around the room. "Okay. We'll get something together in the next couple of hours."

"Are you kidding me?" I shout. "Stores on the East Coast start opening in less than an hour—we need to get something out there now!"

"I'll take care of it," says Maggie, raising her hand. She immediately opens up her laptop and starts typing.

As I squeeze my head between my hands to see if I can make my headache hurt less, I wonder how much worse this rollout could get.

By 2 p.m. Saturday, it's pretty clear that the bottom is a lot further down than I thought possible.

All stores are now operating in total manual fallback mode. All sales are being processed by those manual credit card imprint machines, with the carbon paper imprints being stored in shoeboxes.

Store managers have had employees running to the local office supply stores to find more carbon paper slips for the card imprint machines, as well as to the bank, so they could give out correct change.

Customers using the Phoenix website are complaining about how it is either down or so slow as to be unusable. We have even managed to turn into a Twitter trending topic. All of our customers who had been excited to try our service started complaining about our big IT fail after seeing our TV and newspaper ads.

Those customers who were able to order online had a rude awakening when they went to the store to pick up their order. That's when we discovered that Phoenix seemed to be randomly losing transactions, and in other cases, it was double- or triple-charging our customers' credit cards.

Furious that we've potentially lost integrity of the sales order data, Ann from Finance drove in and her team has now set up *another* war room across the hallway, fielding calls from the stores to handle problem orders. By noon, there were piles of papers from hundreds of pissed off customers that were being faxed in from the stores.

To support Ann, Wes brought in even more engineers to create some tools for Ann's staff to use, in order to process the ever-growing backlog of screwed up transactions.

As I walk past the NOC table for the third time, I decide that I'm too exhausted to be of use to anyone. It's almost 2:30 p.m.

Wes is arguing with someone across the room, so I wait until he's done. I say to him, "Let's face up to the fact that this is going to be a multiday ordeal. How are you holding up?"

He yawns and replies, "I managed to get an hour of sleep. Wow, you look terrible. Go home and get a couple of hours yourself. I've got a handle on everything here. I'll call you if anything comes up."

Too tired to argue, I thank him and leave.

I wake with a start when I hear my cell phone ring. I bolt up and grab my phone. It's 4:30 p.m. Wes is calling.

I shake my head to gain some semblance of alertness and then answer, "What's up?"

I hear him say, "Bad news. In short, it's all over Twitter that the Phoenix website is leaking customer credit card numbers. They're even posting screenshots. Apparently, when you empty your shopping cart, the session crashes and displays the credit card number of the last successful order."

I've already jumped out of bed and am heading to the bathroom to get showered. "Call John. He's going to have kittens. There's probably some protocol for this, involving tons of paperwork and maybe even law enforcement. And probably lawyers, too."

Wes replies, "I already called him. He and his team are on the way in. And he is pissed. He sounded just like that dude from *Pulp Fiction*. He even quoted the line about the day of reckoning and striking people down with great vengeance and furious anger."

I laugh. I love that scene with John Travolta and Samuel L. Jackson. It's not how I would have typecast our mild-mannered CISO, but as they say, you always have to watch out for the quiet ones.

I take a quick shower. I run into the kitchen and grab a couple of sticks of the string cheese our son loves to eat. I take these with me in the car and start my drive back into the office.

When I get on the highway, I call Paige. She answers on the first ring, "Darling, where have you been? I'm at work and the kids are with my mom."

I say, "I was actually at home for an hour. I fell asleep the instant I crawled into bed, but Wes just called. Apparently, the Phoenix application started showing the entire world people's credit card numbers. It's a huge security breach, so I'm driving back in right now."

I hear her sigh disapprovingly. "You've been there for over ten years and you've never worked these kind of hours. I'm really not sure I like this promotion."

"You and me both, honey…" I say.

CHAPTER 13

• *Monday, September 15*

By Monday, the Phoenix crisis is a public fiasco. We made it onto the front-page news of all the technology sites. There are rumors that someone from *The Wall Street Journal* was trying to get Steve for an on-the-record interview.

I start with a jolt when I think I hear Steve mention my name.

Completely disoriented, I look around and realize that I'm at work and that I must have fallen asleep while waiting for the Phoenix status meeting to start. I sneak a peek at my watch. 11:04 a.m.

I have to look at my phone to figure out that it's Monday.

For a moment, I wonder where my Sunday went, but seeing Steve red-faced, and addressing the entire room makes me pay attention.

"—don't care one bit whose fault this is. You can bet your ass that this won't ever happen again on my watch. But right now, I don't give two shits about the future—we are massively screwing our customers and shareholders. All I want to hear about is how we're going to dig ourselves out of this hole and restore normal business operations."

He turns and points at Sarah saying, "And you are not off the hook until every one of your store managers says that they can transact normally. Manual card swipes? What are we, in some Third World country?"

Sarah replies calmly, "I totally understand how unacceptable this is. I'm making sure my entire staff knows that they are accountable and responsible."

"No," Steve responds quickly and gravely. "You are ultimately accountable and responsible. Do not forget that."

My heart actually lightens for a moment, as I wonder whether Steve has broken free of Sarah's spell.

Turning his attention back to the entire room he says gravely, "When the store managers say that we're no longer operating on life support, I need fifteen minutes from each and every person who had a hand in this. I expect you to clear your calendar. No excuses.

"That means you, Sarah, Chris, Bill, Kirsten, Ann. And even you, John," he says, pointing at people as he names them.

Way to go, John. You picked a great time to finally get noticed by Steve.

He continues, "I'll be back in two hours after I get on a phone call with another journalist because of this mess!"

His door slam shakes the walls.

Sarah breaks the silence. "Well, you all heard Steve. Not only do we need to get the POS systems up, but we must also get the Phoenix usability issues fixed. The press is having a heyday with the clunkiness of the ordering interface and everything timing out."

"Are you out of your mind?" I say, leaning forward. "We are keeping Phoenix alive by sheer heroics. Wes wasn't joking when he said that we're proactively rebooting all the front-end servers every hour. We can't introduce any more instabilities. I propose code rollouts only twice a day and restricting all code changes to those affecting performance."

To my surprise, Chris immediately chimes in, "I agree. William, what do you think?"

William nods. "Absolutely. I suggest we announce to the developers that all code commits must have a defect number that corresponds to a performance problem. Anything that doesn't will get rejected."

Chris says, "That good enough for you, Bill?"

Pleased with the solution, I say, "Perfect."

Although Wes and Patty seem simultaneously pleased and taken aback by this sudden cooperation from Development, Sarah is not pleased. She says, "I don't agree. We've got to be able to respond to the market, and the market is telling us that Phoenix is too hard to use. We can't afford to screw this up."

Chris replies, "Look, the time for usability testing and validation was months ago. If we didn't get it right the first time, we're not going to get it right without some real work. Have your product managers work on their revised mockups and proposals. We'll try to get it in as soon as we can after the crisis is over."

I affirm his position, saying, "I agree."

"You raise some good points. I approve," she says, apparently realizing that she wasn't going to win this argument.

I'm not sure Sarah is actually in a position to approve anything. But, luckily, the discussion turns quickly to how to regain POS functionality.

I revise my opinion of Chris upward a couple of notches. I still think he was a willing accomplice of Sarah's, but maybe I'll give him the benefit of the doubt.

Leaving the Phoenix war room, I see the room across the hallway where Ann and her team handle problem orders. I'm overcome by a sudden curiosity, genuinely wanting to see how they're doing.

I knock and walk in, still chewing a stale bagel from the meeting. Since Saturday, there has been an endless supply of pizzas, pastries, Jolt colas, and coffee to keep all the troops at their tasks.

Before me is a scene of frenetic activity: There are tables covered with piles of incoming faxes from the stores and twelve people walk from one to the next. Each fax is a problem order waiting to be routed to an army of finance and customer service representatives who have been press-ganged into service. Their job was to either deduplicate or reverse every one of these transactions.

In front of me, four finance people are sitting at another table, their fingers flying across ten-key calculators and open laptops. They're manually tabulating the orders, trying to calculate the scale of the disaster and doing reconciliations to catch any mistakes.

On the wall, they're keeping track of the totals. So far, five thousand customers have had either duplicate payments or missing orders, and there are an estimated twenty-five thousand more transactions that still need to be investigated.

I shake my head in disbelief. Steve is right. We massively screwed the customers this time. It's downright embarrassing.

On the other hand, I have to respect the operation the Finance people have put in place to handle the mess. It looks organized, with people doing what needs to get done.

A voice next to me says, "Another Phoenix trainwreck, huh?"

It's John, taking in the scene like me. He's not saying "I told you so," but almost. With him, of course, is his ever-present black three-ring binder.

John smacks his face with his palm. "If this were happening to our competitor, I'd be laughing my ass off. I told Chris over and over about this possibility, but he wouldn't listen. We're paying for it now."

He walks up to one of the tables and starts looking over people's shoulders. I see his body suddenly tense as he picks a pile of papers up. He flips through the papers, his face ashen.

He returns to where I'm standing, and whispers, "Bill, we've got a major problem. Outside. Now."

"Look at this order slip," he hisses as we stand outside. "Do you see the problem here?"

I look at the page. It's a scanned order slip, slanted and low-resolution. It's for a purchase of various auto parts, and the dollar amount seems reasonable at $53.

I say, "Why don't you just tell me?"

John points to a handwritten number scrawled by the scanned credit card and customer signature. "That three-digit number is the CVV2 code on the back of the credit card. That's there to prevent credit card fraud. Under the Payment Card Industry rules, we are not allowed to store or transmit anything on track 2 of the magnetic card stripe. Even possessing this is an automatic cardholder data breach and an automatic fine. Maybe even front-page news."

Oh, no. Not again.

He continues, as if reading my mind, "Yeah, but worse this time. Instead of just being on the local news, imagine Steve being splashed on the front page of every market where we have customers and stores. And then flying to DC to be grilled by senators, on behalf of all their outraged constituents."

He continues, "This is really serious. Bill, we've got to destroy all of this information immediately."

I shake my head, saying, "No way. We've got to process every one of those orders, so that we don't charge or even double-charge our customers. We're obligated to do this, otherwise we're taking money from them that we'll eventually need to return."

John puts his hand on my shoulder, "That may seem important, but that's only the tip of the iceberg. We're already in deep shit because Phoenix leaked cardholder data. This may be just as bad. We get fined according to the number of cardholders affected."

He gestures at all the papers, saying, "This could more than double our fines. And you think our audits are bad now? This will make them ten times more painful, because they'll classify us as a Level 1 merchant for the rest of eternity. They may even raise our transaction fees from three percent to—who knows how high? That could halve our retail store profit margins and—"

He stops mid-sentence and opens up his three-ring binder to a calendar. "Oh, shit! The PCI auditors are on-site *today* doing a business process walk-through. They're on the second floor, interviewing the order administration staff about our operations. They're even supposed to use this conference room!"

"You've got to be kidding me," I say as the feeling of panic starts to set in, which amazes me considering that it's been three days of constant adrenaline.

I turn to look through the window of the conference door and see very clearly all the finance people handling all the customer problem orders. Shit.

"Look," I say, "I know that sometimes people think you're not on our side, but I really need your help. You've got to keep the auditors off this floor. Maybe even out of this building. I'll put up some curtains on the windows, or maybe even barricade the door."

John looks at me and then nods. "Okay, I'll handle the auditors. But I still don't think you fully understand. As the custodians of cardholder data, we cannot allow hundreds of people to have access to it. The risk of theft and fraud is too high. We've got to destroy the data immediately."

I can't help but laugh for a moment at the endless stream of problems.

Forcing myself to focus, I say slowly, "Okay, I'll make sure the Finance people understand this and handle it. Maybe we can get them all scanned and shipped to an offshore firm for them to enter."

"No, no, no. That's even worse!" he says. "Remember, we're not allowed to transmit it, let alone send it to a third party. Understand? Look, just so we can claim plausible deniability, I'm going to pretend I didn't hear that just now. You've got to figure out how to destroy all this prohibited data!"

I get pissed off at John's mention of plausible deniability, regardless of whether it was well intentioned or not. I take a deep breath and say to him, "Keep those auditors off this floor, and I'll worry about the card imprints. Okay?"

He nods and says, "Roger. I'll call you when I park the auditors somewhere safe."

As I watch him walk quickly down the hallway to the stairway, I keep thinking to myself, "He's only doing his job. He's only doing his job."

I swear under my breath and turn back around to look back at the conference room. And now I see the big printed sign hanging on the door, proclaiming "Phoenix POS Recovery War Room."

Suddenly, I feel like I'm in the movie *Weekend at Bernie's*, where some teenage boys keep trying to hide or disguise a dead body from a hit man. Then I wonder if this is more like the massive around-the-clock shredding operation that allegedly happened at the offices of Arthur Andersen, the audit firm investigated after Enron failed. Am I complicit in destroying important evidence?

What a mess. I shake my head, and walk back into the conference room to deliver the bad news.

I finally get back down to the NOC at 2:30 p.m., and survey the carnage as I make my way to my office. Seven extra tables have been set up to make more meeting spaces, and there are people assembled around each of them. Empty pizza boxes are piled up on many of the tables and in one corner of the room.

I take a seat behind my desk, sighing in relief. I spent almost an hour with Ann's team on the cardholder data issue, and then another half hour arguing with them that this is really their problem, not mine. I told them that I could help, but that my team was too tied up trying to keep Phoenix running to take any more responsibility.

I realize with some amazement that this may have been the first time

I've been able to say no to anyone in the company since I started in this role. I wonder if I could have done it if we weren't the people almost single-handedly keeping our store order entry systems up.

As I ponder this, my phone rings. It's John. I answer quickly, wanting an update on the auditor issue. "Hey, John. How's it going?"

John replies, "Not terrible. I've got the auditors set up right next to me, here in Building 7. I've rearranged it so that all the interviews will be done here. They won't go anywhere near the Phoenix war room, and I've told the Building 9 security people explicitly not to let them past the front desk."

I chuckle at seeing John bend all the rules. "That's great. Thanks for pulling all that together. Also, I think Ann could use your help figuring what exactly it takes to stay in compliance with the cardholder data regulations. I helped as best I could, but…"

John says, "No problem. I'm happy to assist."

He hesitates for a couple of moments. "I hate to bring it up now, but you were supposed to give internal audit the sox-404 response letter today. How is that coming along?"

I burst out in laughter. "John, our plan was to get that report done over the weekend after the Phoenix deployment. But, as you know, things didn't quite go as planned. I doubt anyone has worked on it since Friday."

In a very concerned voice, John says, "You know that the entire audit committee looks at this, right? If we blow this deadline, it's like a red flag to everyone that we have severe control issues. This could drive up the length of the external audit, too."

I say as reasonably as I can, "Trust me, if there was anything I could do, I would. But right now, my entire team has been working around-the-clock to support the Phoenix recovery efforts. Even if they completed the report, and all I had to do was bend over and pick it up, I couldn't. We're that far underwater."

As I'm talking, I realize how liberating it is to state that my team is absolutely at capacity and that there aren't any calories left over for any new tasks, and people actually believe me.

I hear John say, "You know, I could free two engineers up. Maybe they could help do some of the legwork around estimating the remediation effort? Or if you need it, we could even put them into the technical resource pool to help with recovery. They're both very technical and experienced."

My ears perk up. We've got everyone deployed doing all sorts of things that this emergency requires and most have pulled at least one all-nighter. Some are monitoring fragile services and systems, others are helping field phone calls from the store managers, others are helping QA build systems and write tests, some are helping Development reproduce problems.

I say immediately, "That would be incredibly helpful. Send Wes an e-mail with a couple of bullet points on each of your engineers. If he doesn't have an urgent need for their skills, I'll task them on generating the remediation estimates, as long as it doesn't require interrupting anyone working Phoenix."

"Okay, great," John says. "I'll send the info to Wes later today, and I'll let you know what he and I decide to do."

He signs off, and I consider the potential stroke of good fortune that someone could be working on the audit response.

I then wonder if the fatigue is getting to me. Something is really screwy in the world when I'm finding reasons to thank Development *and* Security in the same day.

CHAPTER 14

By late Monday night, we had stabilized the situation. Working with Chris' team, the stores finally had working cash registers again, but everyone knows it's only a temporary fix. At least we don't need to keep sensitive cardholder data anymore, much to John's relief.

It's 10:37 a.m., and I'm standing outside of Steve's office with Chris. He's leaning against the wall, looking pensively at the floor. Ann, John, and Kirsten are also here, waiting for their turn, like penitent students waiting outside the principal's office in elementary school.

The door to Steve's office opens and Sarah walks out. She looks ashen faced and on the verge of tears. She was the first to go in, and her session didn't even take the whole ten minutes.

She closes the door behind her, blows out her breath, and says to Chris and me, "You're next."

"Here goes nothing…," I say, opening the door.

Steve stands by the window, looking out over the corporate campus. "Take a seat, gentlemen."

When we're sitting down, Steve starts to pace in front of us. "I've talked with Sarah. As the project leader, I'm holding her responsible for the success or failure of Phoenix. I have no idea if I have a leadership problem or if she just has the wrong people on the bus."

My jaw drops. Did Sarah somehow manage to weasel her way out of her part in this disaster? This whole thing is her fault!

Steve turns to Chris. "We put over $20 million into this project, and the lion's share went to your team. From where I'm standing, we'd be better off if we had nothing to show for it. Instead, I have half my company scrambling to pick up the wreckage from the damage you caused."

Turning back to both of us, he continues, "In the good years, we were a five percent net margin company. That meant to make $1 million, we had to sell $20 million in products. Who knows how many sales we lost over the weekend and how many loyal customers we've lost forever."

He starts pacing again. "We've done a terrible disservice to our customers. They're the people who need to fix their cars to get to work. They're fathers working on projects with their kids. We've also screwed some of our best suppliers and clients.

"To appease the people who actually used Phoenix, Marketing is now giving away $100 vouchers, which could cost us millions of dollars. Come on! We're supposed to take money from customers, not the other way around!"

As a former sergeant, I know there's a time and place for dressing someone down. But this is too much. "No offense, sir, but this is supposed to be news to me? I called you, explaining what would happen, asking you to delay the launch. You not only blew me off, you told me to try to convince Sarah. Where's your responsibility in all of this? Or have you outsourced all your thinking to her?"

As I'm talking, I realize I may be making a big mistake by saying what I really think. Maybe it's from weeks of crisis-fueled adrenaline, but it feels good rattling Steve's cage. Really good.

Steve stops pacing, pointing his finger at my forehead. "I know more about responsibility than you may learn in your entire lifetime. I'm tired of your Chicken Little routine, screaming that the sky is falling and then happily saying 'I told you so' afterward. I need you to come to me with some actual solutions."

Leaning into him, I say, "I told you *exactly* what was going to happen when your sidekick Sarah brought up this crazy plan almost two weeks ago. I proposed to you a timeline that would have prevented all this from happening. You tell me that I could have done better? I'm all ears." With exaggerated respect, I add, "*Sir.*"

"I'll tell you what I need from you," he replies calmly. "I need the business to tell me it's no longer being held hostage by you IT guys. This has been the running complaint the entire time I've been CEO. IT is in the way of every major initiative. Meanwhile, our competitors pull away from us, leaving us in the dust. Dammit, we can't even take a crap without IT being in the way."

He takes a deep breath. "None of this is why you're here today. I called you in to tell you two things. First, thanks to this latest IT screwup, the board has insisted that we investigate splitting up the company. They think the company is worth more sold off in pieces. I'm against this, but they've already got consultants in our panties investigating its feasibility. There's nothing I can do about that.

"Second, I'm done playing Russian roulette with IT. Phoenix just shows me that IT is a competency that we may not be able to develop here. Maybe it's not in our DNA. I've given Dick the green light to investigate outsourcing all of IT and asked him to select a vendor in ninety days."

Outsourcing all of IT. Holy shit.

That means everyone in my entire department may not have jobs anymore.

That means that I may not have a job anymore.

In a sudden and sobering instant, I realize that the feeling of elation and confidence I felt rattling Steve's cage was only an illusion. He has all the power. With a wave of his pen, he could outsource all of us to the lowest-cost bidder from some random corner of the planet.

I glance over at Chris, and he looks as shaken as I feel.

Steve continues, "I expect you'll give Dick all the help he requires. If you can pull off some sort of miracle during the next ninety days, we'll consider keeping IT in-house."

"Thank you, gentlemen. Please send in Kirsten," he says with finality.

"Sorry I'm late," I say, slumping down in the booth across from Chris.

Shell-shocked after our meeting with Steve, he and I decided to meet for lunch. In front of him is some sort of fruity drink with an umbrella.

I always figured him to be a blue-collar drinker—more like Pabst Blue Ribbon, not some bachelorette party mixed drink.

He laughs humorlessly. "Trust me. You showing up ten minutes late is the least of my problems. Get yourself a drink."

Paige tells me repeatedly that I shouldn't trust this guy. She has a great instinct for people, but when it comes to me, she's embarrassingly protective, which makes me laugh. I'm the ex-Marine, after all. She's just a "nice nurse."

"Any pilsner you have on tap, please," I say to the waitress. "And a scotch and water, too. It's been a rough day."

"That's what I heard. No problem at all, sweetie," she replies, laughing. To Chris, she asks, "Another mai tai for you?"

He nods, handing her his empty glass. So that's what a mai tai looks like. I've never tried one. We Marines are very self-conscious about what we're seen drinking.

Chris raises his water glass and says, "To having a common death sentence."

I smile wanly and raise my glass. Feeling obligated to inject some optimism, I say, "And here's to figuring out how we get a stay of execution from the governor."

We clink glasses.

"You know, I've been thinking," Chris says. "Maybe my group being outsourced wouldn't be the worst thing in the world. I've been in software development for virtually my entire career. I'm used to everyone demanding miracles, expecting the impossible, people changing requirements at the last minute, but, after living through this latest nightmare project, I wonder if it might be time for a change..."

I can't believe it. Chris has always been confident, even arrogant, seeming to really love doing what he does. "What kind of change? You thinking about opening a mai tai bar in Florida or something like that?"

Chris shrugs. When he looks down, I can see the huge bags underneath his eyes and the fatigue in his face. "I used to love this work, but it's gotten so much more difficult over the last ten years. Technology keeps changing faster and faster, and it's nearly impossible to keep up anymore."

The waitress comes back with our drinks. Part of me feels guilty about drinking during lunch on company time, but I figure I've earned it, having given enough of my personal time to the company over the last two weeks. Chris takes a long swig, and so do I.

He continues, "It's crazy what programmers, and even managers like me, have to learn every couple of years. Sometimes it's a totally new database technology, a new programming or project management method, or a new technology delivery model, like cloud computing.

"Just how many times can you throw out everything you know to keep up with the latest new-fangled trend? I look in the mirror every once in awhile, asking myself, 'Will this be the year that I give up? Will I spend the rest of my career doing COBOL maintenance or become just another has-been middle manager?'"

I laugh sympathetically. I chose to be in the technology backwaters. I was happy there. That is, until Steve threw me back into the big, shark-infested pool.

Shaking his head, he continues, "It's harder than ever to convince the business to do the right thing. They're like kids in a candy store. They read in an airline magazine that they can manage their whole supply chain in the cloud for $499 per year, and suddenly that's the main company initiative. When we tell them it's not actually that easy, and show them what it takes to do it right, they disappear. Where did they go? They're talking to their Cousin Vinnie or some outsourcing sales guy who promises they can do it in a tenth of the time and cost."

I laugh. "A couple of years ago, someone in Marketing asked my group to support a database reporting tool that one of their summer interns wrote. It was actually pretty brilliant, given that she only had a couple of months to work on it, and then it started being used in daily operations. How in the hell do you support and secure something that's written in Microsoft Access? When the auditors found out that we couldn't secure access to all the data, we spent weeks cobbling together something that satisfied them.

"It's like the free puppy," I continue. "It's not the upfront capital that kills you, it's the operations and maintenance on the back end."

Chris cracks up. "Yes, exactly! They'll say, 'The puppy can't quite do everything we need. Can you train it to fly airplanes? It's just a simple matter of coding, right?'"

After we order food, I tell him about how reluctant I was to accept my new role and my inability to get my arms around all the work that my group has committed to.

"Interesting," Chris says. "You know, we're struggling, too. We've never had so many problems hitting our ship dates. My engineers keep getting pulled off of feature development to handle escalations when things break. And deployments keep taking longer and longer. What used to take ten minutes to deploy starts taking an hour. Then a full day, then an entire weekend, then four days. I've even got some deployments that are now taking over a week to complete. Like Phoenix."

He continues, "What use is it having all these offshore developers building features if we aren't getting to market any faster? We keep lengthening the deployment intervals, so that we can get more features deployed in each batch."

He laughs. "I was in a meeting last week where the feature backlog was so long, the product managers were arguing about which features will get worked on three years from now! We can't even plan effectively for one year, let alone three years! What's the use?"

I listen intently. What's happening with Phoenix is a combination of the need to deliver needed features to market, forcing us to take short-cuts, which are causing ever-worsening deployments. He's put his finger on a very important downward spiral we need to break out of.

"Listen, Bill, I know it's a little late to say this, but better late than never. I'm really sorry about my part in this Phoenix fiasco. Sarah came to me a week before Kirsten's project management meeting, asking me all sorts of questions. She asked when would be the soonest that we could be code-complete. I had no idea she was going to interpret that as the go-live date, especially with Steve in the room. William predicted that it was going to be a disaster, and I should have listened to him, too. That was bad judgment on my part."

I look into his eyes for a couple of moments. I finally decide to believe him. I nod and say, "Thanks. Don't worry about it."

I add, "But don't do it again. If you do, I'll break both of your legs, and then I'll have Wes attend every one of your staff meetings. I'm not sure which is more motivating."

Chris smiles, raising his glass. "Here's to never letting this happen again, eh?"

A good thought. I smile and clink my glass against his.

I finish my second beer. "I'm really worried that Sarah is going to try to blame this whole thing on us, you know?"

Chris looks up from his glass and says, "She's like Teflon. Nothing sticks to her. We've got to stick together. I've got your back, and I'll give you a heads-up if I see her trying some weird political crap again."

"Likewise," I say emphatically.

I look at my watch. It's 1:20 p.m. It's time to head back, so I signal our waitress for the check. "This has been great. We need to do this more often. How about we meet once a week and figure out what we need to do to head off this boneheaded idea to outsource all of IT?"

"Absolutely," he says. "I don't know about you, but I'm not going to roll over on this. I'm going down swinging."

With that, we shake hands.

Even after eating some food, I feel buzzed. I wonder where I can find some breath mints so I won't smell like I spent the morning in a distillery.

I look at my schedule on my phone, and move all my meetings to later in the week. At 4 p.m., I'm still in my office when I get an e-mail from Chris.

> From: Chris Allers
> To: Bill Palmer
> Date: September 16, 4:07 PM
> Subject: Throwing a little post-Phoenix party
>
> Hey, Bill…
>
> It was good meeting for lunch—I had a great time.
>
> We're throwing a little impromptu party to celebrate the completion of Phoenix. It's nothing elaborate, but I've ordered a beer keg, some wine and food, and we're congregating right now in the Bldg 7 lunchroom.
>
> We'd love to have your folks join us. In my mind, it was one of the best team efforts I've seen in this company. I ordered enough booze for everyone on your team, too. :-)
>
> See you there,
> Chris

I genuinely appreciate Chris' gesture, and I think my team will, too. Especially Wes. I forward the e-mail to Wes and Patty, telling them to encourage everyone to make an appearance. They deserve it.

A couple of moments later my phone vibrates. I look down and read a reply from Wes:

From: Wes Davis
To: Bill Palmer, Patty McKee
Date: September 16, 4:09 PM
Subject: Re: Fwd: Throwing a little post-Phoenix party
    What a jackass. Most of my guys won't be able to make it. We're still busy fixing all the bad transaction data that their shitty code generated.
    Must be nice to have the luxury of celebrating. "Mission Accomplished" and all that, right?
    W

I groan. Although the crisis might be over for Chris' guys on the upper floors, the people like us in the basement are still bailing water.

Still, I think it's important that we get our guys to drop by the party. In order to succeed, we need to create these relationships with Chris' team. Even if it's only for a half hour.

I grit my teeth and call Wes. As Spock once said, "Only Nixon could go to China." And I guess I'm Nixon.

CHAPTER 15

Even though I can't take the entire day off, I take Paige out for break-fast. She's been holding things down on the home front single-handedly while I have spent every waking hour at work.

We're at Mother's, one of our favorite breakfast restaurants. We were here on their opening day almost eight years ago. The owner has since hit the big time. Not only has her restaurant become a local favorite, but she's written a cookbook, and we saw her all over TV during her book tour.

We are so happy to see her success. And I know Paige loves it when the owner recognizes us, even when it's crowded.

I look in Paige's eyes as she sits across from me at the table. The res-taurant is surprisingly crowded on a Wednesday morning. People hav-ing business meetings and local hipsters doing—well, whatever local hipsters do in the mornings. Working? Playing? I genuinely have no idea.

She says, holding the mimosa in her hands, "Thanks for taking some time off—are you sure you can't spend the rest of the day with me?"

At first, I almost didn't order one for myself, because I didn't want to have anything alcoholic on a workday. But, for the second day in a row,

I find myself saying, "Screw it."

Drinking my orange juice and champagne, I smile sadly, shaking my head. "I really wish I could, honey. If we were in Development, I'd give the entire team the day off like Chris did. But, in Operations, we're still finishing cleaning up from the Phoenix fiasco. I have no idea when life will be normal again."

She shakes her head slowly. "I can't believe that this is only your third week. You've changed. I'm not complaining, but I haven't seen you this stressed out since…"

She looks up for a moment, reviewing her memories. She looks back at me and says, "Ever! Half the time we're driving in the car, you have this distant look on your face. The rest of the time you're clenching your jaw, like you're reenacting some terrible meeting in your head. You never hear what I'm saying, because you're so preoccupied by work."

I start to apologize, but she cuts me off. "I'm not complaining. I don't want to wreck this nice moment while we're enjoying some time away from work and the kids. But, when I think about how happy you were before you accepted this role, I wonder why you're doing it."

I purse my lips together. Even with all the trauma in the past couple of weeks, I feel like the organization has been better off as a result of my contribution. And even with the imminent threat of being outsourced, I'm glad that I'm one of the people trying to fend them off.

And yet, for over five years, I was one of the very few people able to maintain any amount of work-life balance. And now that balance is completely gone.

A fellow NCO in the Marines once told me that his priorities were the following: provider, parent, spouse, and change agent. In that order.

I think about that. First and foremost, my most important responsibility is to be the provider for my family. My pay raise will help us get our debt paid down, and we can start saving money again for our children's college education like we always wanted to. It'd be difficult to give that up and go back to feeling like we're just treading water.

We both suspect that our house is now worth less than we paid for it. We tried to sell it a couple of years ago so we could move across town to be closer to her parents. But after nine months, we took it off the market.

With my promotion, we can pay off our second mortgage sooner. And maybe, just maybe, if things go well, in a few years Paige might be able to stop working.

But is it worth having to deal with Steve's raving demands for the impossible, day in and day out?

Even worse: having to deal with that nutcase, Sarah.

"See? You're doing it again. Let me guess," Paige says, interrupting my thoughts. "You're thinking about some meeting that you've had with Steve, and how he's turned into a total asshole that no one can reason with. Except for that nutcase, Sarah."

I laugh. "How did you know?"

She smiles. "It's so easy. You start looking off somewhere, and then your shoulders and jaw tense up, and your lips press together."

I laugh again.

Paige's expression turns sad. "I keep wishing that they picked someone else for this job. Steve knew exactly how to get you to say yes. He just made it sound like it was your duty to save his job and the company."

I nod slowly. "But, honey, now it's really true—if they outsource all of IT, almost two hundred people in my group could be out of a job or working for some faceless outsourcing firm. And another two hundred people in Chris' organization. I really feel like I can keep that from happening."

She looks dubious, saying, "You really think you and Chris can stop them? Based on what you've said, it sure sounds like they've already made up their mind."

After I drop off a subdued Paige at home, I take a moment in the driveway to look at my phone before driving into work.

I'm surprised when I see an upbeat e-mail from Wes.

> From: Wes Davis
> To: Bill Palmer, Patty McKee
> Date: September 19, 9:45 AM
> Subject: FW: Whew! A change management close call!
>
> Check this out, guys. One of the DBAs sent this out to all the other engineers this morning.
>
> >>> Begin forwarded message:
>
> Guys, the new change process saved our bacon this morning.

Today, we had two groups simultaneously making changes to the materials management database and application servers. Neither group knew about the other.

Rajiv spotted the potential collision on the change wall. We decided that my changes would go in first, and I'd call him when we were done.

We could have totally made a mess of things.

Keep those change cards coming, guys! It saved our butts today!

Thanks to Rajiv, Tom, Shelly, and Brent —

Robert

At last, some good news. One of the problems of prevention is that you rarely know about the disasters you averted.

But here we did. Nice.

And even better yet, it came from one of the engineers, not a manager.

When I get to my desk, I see the Post-it note on my docking station and smile. I carefully power on my laptop, wait patiently for two minutes for the login screen to come up before plugging it into the docking station.

No screaming alarm. Exactly as documented. Nice.

Someone knocks on my door.

It's Patty. "I'm glad I caught you. Do you have a minute? I think we have another problem."

"Sure," I say. "What's on your mind? Let me guess—more people complaining about change management?"

Patty shakes her head, looking grim. "A little more serious than that. Let's go to the Change Coordination Room?"

I groan. Every time Patty's summons me there, it's because of some new intractable problem. But problems, like dog poop left in the rain, rarely get better just by ignoring them.

I stand up and say, "Lead on."

When we get to the conference room, I look at the change board. Something looks very different. "Uh-oh," I say.

Patty looks at the board with me and says, "Uh-huh. Obvious, and yet, still kind of unexpected, right?"

I can only grunt in response.

On the board, up until last Thursday, it's pretty much as I remember it. On each day, there are somewhere between forty and fifty changes,

ed completed. But on the days following, there are barely any
posted at all. It's like someone just wiped all the cards clean off
the board.

"Where did they go?"

She points at another board on the side of the room that she's labeled, "Changes To Be Rescheduled." There's a basket underneath, overflowing with piles and piles of index cards.

Presumably, six hundred of them.

Understanding starting to dawn on me, I ask, "And the reason none of the changes got completed is…"

Patty rolls her eyes. "Phoenix happened, that's what. All scheduled work went out the window. We mobilized almost anyone who could type to help. And only now are they being released back to their normal duties. You can see on the board that today's the first day that scheduled changes are starting to happen as planned again."

This seems important for some reason.

And then it hits me.

I had called Erik briefly to tell him that I had discovered three of the four categories of work: business projects, internal projects, and changes. He merely said that there was one more type of work, maybe the most important type, because it's so destructive.

And in a searing moment of insight, I think I know what the fourth category of work is.

And then suddenly, I don't. My tenuous understanding flickers briefly, and then goes out entirely.

I say, "Damn!"

Patty looks at me questioningly, but I ignore her while I try to recapture that fleeting moment of clarity.

I look at the portion of the change board with no cards on it. It really is like some giant hand swept all those change cards aside that we had so meticulously scheduled and arranged on the board. And we know what swept it aside: It was Phoenix blowing up.

But Phoenix isn't the fourth category of work.

Maybe what I'm looking for is like dark matter. You can only see it by what it displaces or how it interacts with other matter that we can see.

Patty called it firefighting. That's work, too, I suppose. It certainly kept everyone up at all hours of the night. And it displaced all the planned changes.

I turn back to Patty and say slowly, "Let me guess. Brent didn't get any of his non-Phoenix change work completed either, right?"

"Of course not! You were there, right?" she says, looking at me like I had grown eight heads. "Brent was working around-the-clock on the recovery efforts, building all the new tooling to keep all the systems and data up. Everything else was put on the back-burner."

All the firefighting displaced all the planned work, both projects and changes.

Ah… Now I see it.

What can displace planned work?

Unplanned work.

Of course.

I laugh uproariously, which earns me a look of genuine concern from Patty, who even takes a step back from me.

That's why Erik called it the most destructive type of work. It's not really work at all, like the others. The others are what you planned on doing, allegedly because you needed to do it.

Unplanned work is what prevents you from doing it. Like matter and antimatter, in the presence of unplanned work, all planned work ignites with incandescent fury, incinerating everything around it. Like Phoenix.

So much of what I've been trying to do during my short tenure as VP of IT Operations is to prevent unplanned work from happening: coordinating changes better so they don't fail, ensuring the orderly handling of incidents and outages to prevent interrupting key resources, doing whatever it takes so that Brent won't be escalated to…

I've been doing it mostly by instinct. I knew it was what had to be done, because people were working on the wrong things. I tried to take all necessary steps to keep people from doing wrong work, or rather, unplanned work.

I say, cackling and pumping my arms as if I had just scored a game-winning, sixty-yard field goal, "Yes! I see it now! It really is unplanned work! The fourth category of work is unplanned work!"

My ebullient mood is tempered when I look at Patty, who looks puzzled and genuinely concerned.

"I promise to explain later," I say. "Just what is it that you wanted me to see on the change board?"

She's taken aback, but points again at the void of completed changes for the past week. "I know you were concerned about when sixty percent of the changes weren't getting completed. So, I thought you'd really flip your lid when one hundred percent of the changes didn't complete. Right?"

"Yep. This is great work, Patty. Keep it up!" I say agreeably.

And then I turn around and head out the door, reaching for my cell phone. There's someone I need to call.

"Hey!" Patty calls out. "Aren't you going to fill me in?"

I yell over my shoulder, "Later! I promise!"

Back at my desk I search everywhere for that slip of paper that Erik gave me. I'm pretty sure I didn't throw it away, but I honestly didn't think that I would ever use it.

I hear Ellen say from behind me, "Need help with anything?"

And soon, both of us are scrounging all over my desk to find that little piece of paper.

"Is this it?" she asks, holding up something that she retrieved from my inbox.

I look more closely, and yes! It's the crumpled two-inch strip of paper that Erik gave me. It looks like a gum wrapper.

Taking the piece of paper from her and holding it up, I say, "Great! Thank you so much for finding this—believe it or not, this may be the most important piece of paper I've gotten in years."

I decide to sit outside while I talk. In the bright autumn sunlight, I find a spot on a bench near the parking lot. As I sit down, there's not a cloud in the sky.

I call Erik, who answers on the first ring. "Hey, Bill. How are you guys doing after Phoenix crashed and burned so spectacularly?"

"Yeah, well… Things are improving," I say. "You may have heard that our POS systems went down, and we also had a small credit card number breach."

"Ha! 'Small credit card breach.' I like that. Like 'small nuclear reactor meltdown.' I've gotta write that one down," he says, snorting.

He's chuckling as though he predicted this level of calamity would occur, which, come to think of it, I suppose he did, in the conference room when I first met him. Something about "clearing the calendar."

Just like clearing the change board, I realize. I kick myself for not picking up on his clue sooner.

"I trust you can tell me now what the four categories of work are?" I hear him ask.

"Yes, I think I can," I say. "At the plant, I gave you one category, which was business projects, like Phoenix," I say. "Later, I realized that I didn't mention internal IT projects. A week after that, I realized that changes are another category of work. But it was only after the Phoenix fiasco that I saw the last one, because of how it prevented all other work from getting completed, and that's the last category, isn't it? Firefighting. Unplanned work."

"Precisely!" I hear Erik say. "You even used the term I like most for it: *unplanned work*. Firefighting is vividly descriptive, but 'unplanned work' is even better. It might even be better to call it 'anti-work,' since it further highlights its destructive and avoidable nature.

"Unlike the other categories of work, unplanned work is recovery work, which almost always takes you away from your goals. That's why it's so important to know where your unplanned work is coming from."

I smile as he acknowledges my correct answer, and am oddly pleased that he validated my antimatter notion of unplanned work, as well.

He says, "What is this change board that you mentioned?"

I tell him about my attempts to get some sort of change process going and my attempt to elevate the discussion above how many fields there were on the change form, which then resulted in getting people to put their intended changes on index cards and our need to juggle them on the board.

"Very good," he says. "You've put together tools to help with the visual management of work and pulling work through the system. This is a critical part of the First Way, which is creating fast flow of work through Development and IT Operations. Index cards on a *kanban* board is one of the best mechanisms to do this, because everyone can see WIP. Now you must continually eradicate your largest sources of unplanned work, per the Second Way."

Until now, having been so wrapped up in defining what work is, I had forgotten about Erik and his Three Ways. I dismissed them before, but I'm now listening closely to his every word.

And over the next forty-five minutes, I find myself telling him the entire tale of my short tenure. I'm interrupted only by Erik's loud laughs and guffaws as I describe the calamities and my attempts to curb the chaos.

When I'm finished, he says, "You've come much further than I thought: You've started to take steps to stabilize the operational environment, you've started to visually manage WIP within IT Operations, and you've started to protect your constraint, Brent. You've also reinforced a culture of operational rigor and discipline. Well done, Bill."

I furrow my brows and say, "Wait. Brent is my constraint? What do you mean?"

He replies, "Ah, well if we're going to talk about your next steps, you definitely need to know about constraints because you need to increase flow. Right now, nothing is more important."

Erik assumes a lecturing voice as he starts, "You say you learned about plant operations management when you were in business school. I hope as part of your curriculum, you read *The Goal* by Dr. Eli Goldratt. If you don't have a copy anymore, get another one. You're going to need it."

I think my copy of that book is in my office at home. As I jot a quick reminder to look for it, he continues, "Sensei Goldratt taught us that in most plants, there are a very small number of resources, whether it's men, machines, or materials, that dictates the output of the entire system. We call this the constraint—or bottleneck. Either term works. Whatever you call it, until you create a trusted system to manage the flow of work to the constraint, the constraint is constantly wasted, which means that the constraint is likely being drastically underutilized.

"That means you're not delivering to the business the full capacity available to you. It also likely means that you're not paying down technical debt, so your problems and amount of unplanned work continues to increase over time," he says.

He continues, "You've identified this Brent person as a constraint to restore service. Trust me, you'll find that he constrains many other important flows of work, as well."

I try to interrupt to ask a question, but he continues headlong, "There are five focusing steps which Sensei Goldratt describes in *The Goal*: Step 1 is to identify the constraint. You've done that, so congratulations. Keep challenging yourself to really make sure that's your organizational constraint, because if you're wrong, nothing you do will matter. Remember, any improvement not made at the constraint is just an illusion, yes?

"Step 2 is to exploit the constraint," he continues. "In other words, make sure that the constraint is not allowed to waste any time. Ever. It should never be waiting on any other resource for anything, and it should always be working on the highest priority commitment the IT Operations organization has made to the rest of the enterprise. Always."

I hear him say encouragingly, "You've done a good job exploiting the constraint on several fronts. You've reduced reliance on Brent for unplanned work and outages. You've even started to figure out how to exploit Brent better for the three other types of work: business and IT projects and changes. Remember, unplanned work kills your ability to do planned work, so you must always do whatever it takes to eradicate it. Murphy does exist, so you'll always have unplanned work, but it must be handled efficiently. You've still got a long way to go."

In a more stern voice, he says, "But you're ready to start thinking about Step 3, which is to subordinate the constraint. In the Theory of Constraints, this is typically implemented by something called Drum-Buffer-Rope. In *The Goal*, the main character, Alex, learns about this when he discovers that Herbie, the slowest Boy Scout in the troop, actually dictates the entire group's marching pace. Alex moved Herbie to the front of the line to prevent kids from going on too far ahead. Later at Alex's plant, he started to release all work in accordance to the rate it could be consumed by the heat treat ovens, which was his plant's bottleneck. That was his real-life Herbie."

"Fully two decades after *The Goal* was published," he continues, "Sensei David J. Anderson developed techniques of using a kanban board to release work and control WIP for Development and IT Operations. You may find that of interest. You and Penelope are close with your change board to a kanban board that can manage flow."

"So, here's your homework," he says. "Figure out how to set the tempo of work according to Brent. Once you make the appropriate mapping of IT Operations to work on the plant floor, it will be obvious. Call me when you've figured it out."

"Wait, wait," I say, hurriedly before he hangs up. "I'll do the homework, but aren't we missing the entire point here? What caused all the unplanned work is Phoenix. Why are we focusing on Brent right now? Don't we need to address all the issues with Phoenix inside of Development, where all the unplanned work actually came from?"

"Now you sound just like Jimmy, complaining about things you can't control," he sighs. "Of course Phoenix is causing all the problems. You get what you design for. Chester, your peer in Development, is spending all his cycles on features, instead of stability, security, scalability, manageability, operability, continuity, and all those other beautiful 'itties.

"On the other end of the assembly line, Jimmy keeps trying to retrofit production controls after the toothpaste is out of the tube," he says, scoffing. "Hopeless! Futile! It'll never work! You need to design these things, what some call 'nonfunctional requirements,' into the product. But your problem is that the person who knows the most about where your technical debt is and how to actually build code that is designed for Operations is too busy. You know who that person is, don't you?"

I groan. "Brent."

"Yep," he says. "Without solving your Brent problem, you'll just be inviting him to design and architecture meetings with Development, but he'll never show up because..."

Being prompted again, I respond, "Unplanned work."

"Good!" he says. "You're getting better at this. But before you get a big head, I'll tell you that there's still a big piece of the First Way that you're missing. Jimmy's problem with the auditors shows that he can't distinguish what work matters to the business versus what doesn't. And incidentally, you have the same problem, too. Remember, it goes beyond reducing WIP. Being able to take needless work out of the system is more important than being able to put more work into the system. To do that, you need to know what matters to the achievement of the business objectives, whether it's projects, operations, strategy, compliance with laws and regulations, security, or whatever."

He continues, "Remember, outcomes are what matter—not the process, not controls, or, for that matter, what work you complete."

I sigh. Just when I think I have a concrete enough understanding of constraints, once again Erik becomes illusive.

"Don't get distracted. Call me when you know how to throttle release of work to Brent," he says and hangs up.

I can't believe it. I try calling him back twice, but it rolls immediately to his voicemail.

Sitting down on the bench, I lean back, take a deep breath, and force myself to enjoy the warm morning. I hear birds chirping and the noise of traffic from the road.

Then, for the next ten minutes, I capture as much as I can remember on my clipboard, trying to piece together what Erik covered.

When I'm done, I head inside to call Wes and Patty. I know exactly what I need to do and am excited to get started.

CHAPTER 16

• *Thursday, September 18*

I'm at my desk, tying up some loose ends when Ellen runs up to me, holding an e-mail printout. It's from Dick, raising the alarm with all company executives that something has gone terribly wrong with the company invoicing systems. Earlier today, one of the clerks discovered that no customers had been invoiced for three days. Among other things, this means that customers haven't been paying on time, which means the company will have less cash in the bank at the end of the quarter than projected, which will raise all sorts of uncomfortable questions when the company earnings are announced.

It's clear from Dick's string of e-mails that he's livid, and apparently, his whole accounts receivable staff and controller have been chain smoking and doing damage control at all levels.

> From: Dick Landry
> To: Steve Masters
> Cc: Bill Palmer
> Date: September 18, 3:11 PM
> Priority: Highest
> Subject: ACTION NEEDED: Potential $50MM cash shortfall due to IT failure

ALL CUSTOMER INVOICES ARE STILL STUCK OR MISSING IN THE
SYSTEM. WE CAN'T EVEN RETRIEVE THEM TO MANUALLY SEND
INVOICES BY E-MAIL!

We're trying to figure out how we can resume normal business
operations. There's likely $50MM of receivables stuck in the system,
which will be missing from our cash account at end of quarter.

Get your IT guys to fix this. The hole this blows in our quarterly
numbers will be impossible to hide, and maybe even impossible to
explain away.

Call me, Steve. I'll be on the window ledge.

Dick

We're all gathered in the NOC conference room. I'm pleased that when Patty finishes describing the incident, she quickly presented all the relevant changes for the last seventy-two hours.

After she's done, I say firmly to the entire team, "First and foremost on my mind is the risk of losing transactions. Ladies and gentlemen, I need to be very clear about this: DO NOT TOUCH ANYTHING WITHOUT GETTING APPROVAL FROM ME. This is not an outage we're dealing with here. We're in a situation where we could accidentally lose order entry or accounts receivable data. This terrifies me. And *that* should absolutely terrify *you*.

"As Patty said, we need timelines and hypotheses for what might have caused the invoicing system to fail," I say. "This is our *Apollo 13* moment, and I'm Gene Kranz in Houston Mission Control. I don't want guesswork. I want hypotheses backed up with facts. So get back to your screens, assemble timelines and data, and I want to hear your best thinking on cause and effect. Failure is not an option."

By 6 p.m., Patty's team has documented over twenty different potential failure causes that have been proposed. After further investigation, eight remain as likely possibilities. An owner has been assigned to look into each.

Realizing that there's little more we can do as a group until they complete their research, we agree to reconvene at 10 p.m. tonight.

On the one hand, I'm frustrated that once again, we've been plunged into a crisis and our day is dominated by unplanned incident work. On the other hand, I feel a deep sense of satisfaction at the orderly nature of our incident investigation and quickly text Paige that I'll be joining the family for dinner shortly.

"Daddy," I hear, as I'm sitting in bed with Grant, trying to put him to sleep while keeping the thoughts of outages out of my head. "Why doesn't Thomas the Tank Engine have a tender car? Why?"

Smiling down at him, I marvel at the questions my three-year-old son comes up with. We're going through our nighttime ritual of reading books. I'm glad to be doing this again, which I do every night. Or did, that is, until the Phoenix recovery effort.

Most of the lights are off, but one lamp is still dimly lit. There is a pile of books on Grant's bed, and we're on the third one of the night.

I'm starting to get a little dry-mouthed from reading. The idea of taking a little break and doing some research on the Internet on train tender cars sounds pretty appealing.

I love how inquisitive my kids are and how much they love books, but there are nights when I'm so exhausted that I've actually fallen asleep during our nightly ritual. My wife will walk in, find me asleep with one of Grant's books lying on top of my face and Grant asleep beside me.

Despite how tired I am, I'm grateful to be at home early enough to resume my nighttime ritual with my older son.

"Yes, we need to find out, Daddy," Grant demands. I smile at him, and I dig my phone out from my pocket, intending to do a Google search for "tank engine tender car."

But first, I quickly scan my phone for any new updates on the customer invoicing problem. I'm amazed at the difference two weeks can make.

During the last Sev 1 incident that hit our credit card processing systems, the conference call was full of finger-pointing, denials, and, most importantly, wasted time when our customers couldn't give us money.

Afterward, we did the first of a series of ongoing blameless postmortems to figure out what really happened and come up with ideas on how to prevent it from happening again. Better yet, Patty led a series of mock incident calls with all hands on deck, to rehearse the new procedures.

It was terrific to watch. Even Wes saw the value.

I'm pleased to see all the e-mails indicating a lot of good information and effective discussion among the teams working the problem. They've kept the telephone conference bridge and a chat room open for people working the issue, and I plan on calling in at 10 p.m. to see how it's going.

That's forty-five minutes from now. Plenty of time to spend with Grant, who should be falling asleep soon.

He nudges me, obviously expecting more progress on the research front.

"Sorry, Granty. Daddy got distracted," I say as I open up the browser. I'm surprised by how many of the search results are all about Thomas the Tank Engine. It's the book series that spawned a multibillion dollar franchise of toy trains, clothing, videos, and coloring books. With two sons, we seem destined to own two of every item soon.

I'm reading a promising *Wikipedia* entry on trains when my phone starts vibrating and the screen displays "Call from Steve Masters."

I groan and double-check my watch. It's 9:15 p.m.

I've had way too many meetings and phone calls with Steve lately. In my head, I wonder how many of these meetings I can take.

On the other hand, after the Phoenix debacle, every outage and incident is trivial in comparison, right?

I say gently, "Hang on, Grant. Daddy has to take a phone call. I'll be right back." I jump out of his bed and walk into the dark hallway.

I'm glad I had just scanned through all the e-mail traffic on the outage just seconds before. I take a deep breath before I hit the button to answer the call.

I say, "Bill here."

Steve's loud voice booms in my ear. "Evening, Bill. I'm glad you're there. Of course you know about the customer invoicing problems from Dick?"

"Yes, of course," I reply, surprised at his tone. "My team declared a major incident early this afternoon and we've been working this issue ever since. I've been sending out status reports every hour. Dick and I spent twenty minutes on the phone earlier this evening. I know the problem is serious, and my team is following the process we've created after the payroll failure. I'm completely satisfied that the process is working."

"Well I just got off the phone with Dick, and he tells me that you're dragging your feet," says Steve, clearly very angry. "Obviously, I'm not calling you at night because I want to chitchat. Do you understand how intolerable this is? Yet another IT screwup jeopardizing everything. Cash is the lifeblood of the company, and if we can't invoice customers, we can't get paid!"

Falling back on old training on handling frustrated people, I calmly reiterate what I already stated. "As I said, I talked with Dick earlier today. He very much impressed upon me all the implications. We've activated our new incident process, and we're methodically looking into what could have caused the failure. They're doing exactly what I want them to, because with so many moving pieces, it's way too easy to make things worse by jumping to conclusions—"

"Are you in the office?" Steve demands, cutting me off before I could finish.

His question genuinely catches me off guard.

"Uh… No, I'm at home," I answer.

Is he worried that I've delegated the problem away? To reinforce my role in handling the crisis and what my expectations from my team are, I say, "I will be calling into the war bridge line at ten o'clock. As always, we have a duty officer on site, and those on my staff who need to be in the office are there already."

Finally, I ask bluntly, "Steve, want to tell me what's on your mind? I'm on top of this situation. What do you need that you aren't getting right now?"

He responds hotly, "What I need from you is some sense of urgency. Dick and his team are burning the midnight oil trying to figure out how our quarter will end up in six working days. But I think I already know what the answer will be."

He continues, "We'll probably miss almost every target that we've promised the board: revenue, cash, receivables—everything. In fact, every measure we've promised the board is going the wrong way! This screwup may confirm the board's suspicion that we've completely lost control of managing this company!"

Steve is almost snarling now as he says, "So, what I want from you, *Bill*, is to stay sufficiently on top of things, so that I don't have my CFO saying that you're dragging your feet. The house is burning down, and all I hear from you is about drawing pictures and timelines. What in the hell is wrong with you? You afraid to get people out of bed?"

I start again, "Steve, if I thought it would help, I'd have everyone pull all-nighters in the data center tonight. For Phoenix, some people didn't go home for nearly a week. Trust me, I know the house is on fire, but right now, more than anything, we need situational awareness. Before we send the teams crashing through the front door with fire hoses, we have to have someone at least quickly walk the perimeter of the yard—otherwise, we'll end up burning down the houses next door!"

I realize that I've raised my voice in the relative quiet of our house as we're trying to get the kids to sleep. I resume, more quietly, "And just in case you forgot, during the payroll outage, we made the outage worse by our own actions. We probably could have completed the payroll run during the business day if someone hadn't started screwing with the SAN. Because of that, we added another six hours to the outage, and we nearly lost payroll data!"

My hopes that the calm voice of reason is reaching him are dashed when I hear him say, "Oh, yeah? I don't think your team agrees with you. What was the name of that smart guy who you introduced me to? Bob? No, Brent. I talked with Brent earlier today, and he's very skeptical of your approach. He thinks what you're doing is separating people who actually do the work from what needs to get done. What is Brent doing right now?"

Shit.

I like transparency. I always try to make my team totally accessible to my boss and the business. But there's always risk in doing this.

Like having Brent spout off his crazy theories to the CEO.

"I hope Brent is at home, because that's exactly where he should be," I respond. "Until we know for sure exactly what went wrong, that's where I want him. Look, it's rocket scientists like him that often cause the problem in the first place. Every time we escalate to Brent, we perpetuate our reliance on him, and make it that much less likely we can fix things without him!"

Suspecting that I may be losing Steve, I start again. "The chaotic way we currently work, Brent is having to fix the punctured hulls almost every day. I'm pretty sure, though, that Brent is one of the main reasons the hull is punctured in the first place. It's not malicious, of course, but it's just a side effect of the way we work and fix outages here."

There is a pause. Then he says slowly and decisively, "I'm glad you're being so professorial about this, but we've got a wildfire that's out of control. Up until now, we've done it your way. And now we're going to do it my way.

"I want you to call Brent in, and I want him to roll up his sleeves and help fix this outage. And not just Brent. I want all eyeballs on screens and all hands on keyboards. I'm Captain Kirk. You're Scotty. And I need warp speed, so get your lazy engineers off their asses! Do you understand me?"

Steve is yelling so loudly by now that I'm holding the phone away from my ear.

Suddenly, I'm furious. Steve is going to screw this up again.

Recalling my days in the Marines, I finally say, "Permission to speak freely, sir?"

I hear Steve on the other end of the line snort dismissively in response. "Yes, dammit."

"You think I'm being overly cautious, and that I'm hesitating to do what needs to be done. But you are wrong. Dead wrong," I say adamantly. "If you do what I think you're suggesting, which is basically 'all hands on deck,' I predict that we're going to make things much worse."

I continue, "I tried to advise you of something very similar before the Phoenix launch. Up until now, we have not been sufficiently disciplined in how we work outages. Given all the complexity and moving pieces, there's too much likelihood of causing another problem. I may not know exactly what caused the customer invoicing issue, but I know enough to absolutely conclude that what you're proposing is a very bad idea. I recommend continuing along the lines I am currently prosecuting."

I hold my breath, waiting to hear how he reacts.

He says slowly, "I'm sorry you feel that way, Bill, but the drawers open on my side of the desk. I'm telling you that it's now DEFCON 1, so go get the smartest people working on this problem. And I want status updates on this IT failure every two hours until it's fixed. Understood?"

Before I can think about what to say, I find myself saying, "I don't know why you need me to do that. You're talking directly to my people, and you're calling all shots on the ground. Do it yourself. I can't be held responsible for the results of this FUBAR situation."

And before I hang up on him, I say with finality, "And expect my resignation in the morning."

I wipe the sweat off my forehead, and look up from my phone to see my wife Paige staring at me wide-eyed.

"Are you insane? You just quit? Just like that? How are we going to pay the bills now?" she asks, her voice rising.

I turn the ringer off on my phone and put it back in my pocket, saying, "Honey, I'm not sure how much of that conversation you heard, but let me explain…"

Part 2

CHAPTER 17

• Monday, September 22

In the four days since quitting, Paige has been fretting endlessly. On the other hand, I'm amazed at how much better I'm sleeping at night, as if some huge, hidden weight has been lifted from my shoulders.

Uninterrupted by e-mails or emergency pages, the weekend was incredibly peaceful. I was still receiving them on Thursday, but I just deleted the e-mail accounts and blocked the text messages.

It felt great.

I tell Paige not to take Grant to her mother's. Instead, I'm taking him on an adventure. Paige reacts with a bemused smile and helps me pack his Thomas the Tank Engine backpack.

By 8 a.m., we're out of the house and heading happily to the train station, where, for months, I've been promising to take him. For an hour we watch trains go by, and I'm continually amazed at Grant's unabashed joy. Despite the uncertainty around what I'll be doing next, I feel blessed that I can share this moment with Grant.

As I'm taking pictures of Grant screaming with delight and pointing at the diesel trains going by, I realize how few pictures I've taken of either of my kids in the last month.

We're still watching the trains when my phone rings. It's Wes. I let it roll to voicemail.

He calls several more times, and each time he leaves another voicemail.

Then Patty calls, which I let roll to voicemail, too. After three more calls, I mutter in exasperation, "Come on, guys…"

"Palmer," I answer the phone.

"Bill, we just heard the news from Steve," I hear Patty say, sounding like she's on a speakerphone. With surprising anger in her voice, she continues, "I've got Wes here, and we're both completely shocked. We knew something wasn't right when you didn't show up for our regular CAB meeting on Friday. I just can't believe you resigned during this outage—and after everything we've achieved!"

"Look, guys, it has nothing to do with you," I explain. "Steve and I just had some irreconcilable differences about how to resolve the big invoicing failure. I'm sure you guys will do fine without me."

As I say the last part, I feel slightly disingenuous.

"Well, we've pretty much screwed the pooch since you've left," Wes says, sounding genuinely abashed, confirming my worst fears. "Steve insisted that we bring in all the engineers, including Brent. He said he wanted a 'sense of urgency' and 'hands on keyboards, not people sitting on the bench.' Obviously, we didn't do a good enough job coordinating everyone's efforts, and…"

Wes doesn't finish his sentence. Patty picks up where he left off, "We don't know for sure, but at the very least, the inventory management systems are now completely down, too. No one can get inventory levels in the plants or warehouses, and they don't know which raw materials we need to replenish. All the finance guys are about to jump from window ledges, because they may not be able to close the books for the quarter on time. With all these systems down, no one has the data they need to compute cost of goods sold, gross profit, and net margin."

"Holy shit." Speechless for a moment, I finally say, "That's incredible."

Grant grabs at my phone, demanding my attention. I say, "Look, guys, I'm with my son, and we're in the middle of something important. I can't talk for very long. But rest assured that I'm really proud of everything that we've done together, and I know that you guys can get through this crisis without me."

"That's a load of junk, and you know it," Patty says. "How can you leave us in the lurch like this? We have so many things that we planned on fixing together, and you're leaving it all completely unfinished! I never figured you as someone who would quit like this!"

"I agree. Leaving now is pretty shitty, if you ask me," Wes says, chiming in.

I sigh. I'm never going to tell them about all the frustrating and absurd meetings I've had to put up with Steve. That's between him and me.

"I'm sorry to let you down, but it's something that I had to do," I say. "You'll do just fine. Just don't let Steve or anyone else micromanage you. No one knows the IT systems like you guys do, so don't let anyone try to call the shots, okay?"

I hear Wes mutter, "Too late for that."

By now, Grant is trying to hang up my phone. "Guys, I've got to run. We'll catch up later, okay? Over beers."

"Yeah, sure," Wes says.

"Gee, thanks for everything," Patty says. "Catch you around."

With that, the line disconnects.

I let out a long sigh. Then, looking at Grant, I put away my phone and give him my full attention again, intent on recapturing our moment of happiness before it was interrupted.

My phone rings again on our drive home. Grant is asleep in the backseat. This time, it's Steve.

Having no interest in talking with him just yet, I let it go to voicemail. Three times.

I pull into our garage and get out of the car, trying to get Grant out of his car seat without waking him up. As I walk through the house with him, I see Paige. I point to Grant, silently mouthing to her, "Asleep." I pad softly up the stairs, at last transferring him to his bed and taking off his shoes.

With a sigh of relief, I close the door behind me and walk back downstairs.

When Paige sees me, she says, "That bastard Steve called me this morning. I almost hung up on him, but he gave me a long story about doing all this soul-searching with some guy named Erik. He says he has a proposition for you. I told him I'd pass along the message."

When I roll my eyes, she says in a suddenly concerned voice, "Look, I know you resigned because you felt it was the right thing to do. But you know as well as I do that there aren't many other companies in town that pay as well as Parts Unlimited. Especially after your promotion. I don't want to move away from my family."

She looks levelly at me. "Honey, I know he's a bastard, but we both still need to earn a living. Promise me that you'll listen to what Steve has to say and keep an open mind, okay? Bill? Okay?"

I merely nod and step into the dining room, hitting the speed dial for Steve.

Steve answers his cell phone on the first ring. "Good afternoon, Bill. Thanks for calling me back. I had the pleasure of talking with your wife, telling her all about what a jackass I've been."

"Yeah, she said something to that effect," I respond. "She said that you really wanted to talk."

I hear him say, "Look, I wanted to apologize for the way I've behaved since you graciously accepted my request to become our VP of IT Operations. Dick thought I was crazy when I told him that I was going to have IT report to me. But I told him about how, when I first became a plant manager, many decades ago, I worked on the assembly line for a month, just to make sure that I understood the ins and outs of daily life of everyone who worked there.

"I promised Dick that I would get my hands dirty and not just delegate the problem away. I'm angry with myself that I haven't lived up to that promise. And delegating all the IT issues to Sarah was a total screwup.

"Listen, I know I haven't been fair to you, especially when you've fulfilled your end of the bargain. You've been a straight shooter, and you've genuinely tried to prevent bad things from happening."

He pauses for a couple of moments. "Look, I just got kicked in the ass by Erik and by the entire audit committee. He held my feet to the fire until I finally understood something. It made me realize that I've been doing something really wrong for many years, and I want to make it right.

"In short, I'd like you to resume your role as VP of IT Operations, effective immediately. I'd like to work with you, as Erik coined it, as the two sides of a dysfunctional marriage. Maybe the two of us together can figure out what is really going wrong with how IT is managed here at Parts Unlimited.

"I'm convinced that IT is a competency that we need to develop here. All I'm asking is that you spend ninety days with me and give it a try. And if at the end of the ninety days you still want to bail, then you can do so, with a one-year severance package."

Remembering my promise to Paige, I choose my words carefully. "You've been pretty consistent in being, as you say, a complete jackass for the past month. I've been very consistent in presenting to you my analyses and recommendations, over and over again. And each time, you've crapped on it. Why should I trust you now?"

Forty-five minutes later, after Steve continually tries to woo me back, I hang up the phone and go back into the kitchen where Paige is waiting to hear what happened.

CHAPTER 18

• *Tuesday, September 23*

The next morning, I'm driving into work at 6:30 a.m. for Steve's IT leadership off-site. He's calling it an off-site, even though the meeting is in Building 2.

Earlier this morning, I padded softly into Grant and Parker's rooms to say goodbye. Watching Parker sleep, I kissed him and whispered softly, "Sorry that daddy couldn't take you on an adventure today. It was your turn, but Daddy has to go back to work. This weekend, I promise."

This better be worth it, Steve.

The meeting is in the corporate boardroom. Walking onto the fifteenth floor, I still can't believe how different it is than all the other buildings.

Chris, Wes, and Patty are already here, all holding coffee cups and plates full of pastries.

Patty barely acknowledges my presence.

Wes greets me loudly, saying sarcastically, "Hey, Bill. Nice to see you. I hope you don't quit again today."

Thanks, Wes.

Chris acknowledges me with an understanding smile, rolling his eyes and making the motions of getting a beer. I nod and smile, and turn to the back of the room.

My mood brightens when I see the Vandal Doughnuts in back, and I start loading up my paper plate. As I'm trying to decide whether having six doughnuts on my plate is a breach of social protocol, I feel a hand clap me on my shoulder.

It's Steve. "Good to see you again, Bill. I'm glad you're here." Looking down at my overflowing plate, he laughs loudly. "Why not just take the entire platter with you?"

"Good idea. Glad to be here," I reply.

Erik takes a seat right across from me, saying, "Morning, Bill." Behind him is a large suitcase that he had lugged in.

I squint at the suitcase. The last time I saw a suitcase without wheels was in my mother's attic twenty years ago.

Erik's hair is dripping wet, soaking the shoulders of his denim shirt.

Was he running late this morning and had to run out of his hotel without drying his hair? Or does he look like this every morning?

Where exactly did Steve find this guy?

"Good morning," Steve says, addressing the room. "First, I appreciate everyone making it here so early. Especially since I know that you and your teams have been working incredibly long hours over the last two weeks."

"Ha!" Erik snorts. "That's probably the understatement of the century."

Everyone laughs nervously, going to extra lengths to not make eye contact with anyone else.

Steve smiles sadly. "I know that the last couple of weeks have been harrowing. I now realize just how much responsibility I bear for all of this. Not just for the Phoenix disaster, but everything leading up to the audit issues, the customer invoicing and inventory failures over the last couple of days, and the trouble we're having with the auditors."

He stops, obviously distraught and needing a moment to compose himself.

Is he tearing up?

Now here's a side of Steve you don't see every day. What the heck happened to Steve after I left?

He puts down an index card that he's been holding, shrugs his shoulders and gestures to Erik. "Erik described the relationship between a CEO and a CIO as a dysfunctional marriage. That both sides feel powerless and held hostage by the other."

His fingers worry at the card. "There are two things I've learned in the last month. One is that IT matters. IT is not just a department that I can delegate away. IT is smack in the middle of every major company effort we have and is critical to almost every aspect of daily operations."

He says, "I know that right now, nothing, absolutely nothing, is more important to the company's success than how this leadership team performs.

"The second thing I've learned is that my actions have made almost all our IT problems worse. I turned down Chris and Bill's requests for more budget, Bill's request for more time to do Phoenix right, and micromanaged things when I wasn't getting the results I wanted."

Steve then looks at me. "The person I wronged the most was Bill. He told me things that I didn't want to hear, and I shut him down. In hindsight, he was completely right, and I was completely wrong. And for that, Bill, I'm very sorry."

I see Wes' jaw drop open.

Completely embarrassed, I merely say, "All water under the bridge now. Like I said to you yesterday, Steve, apology not expected, but appreciated."

Steve nods and looks at his card for several moments. "The huge challenges ahead of us will require an outstanding team operating at their absolute best. Yet, we don't completely trust one another. I know that I am partially to blame, but that needs to end now.

"Over the weekend, I thought back on my career, which as you may know, could end at any moment, as my board has made clear. I know that my most rewarding times were always when I was part of a great team. That goes for both my professional and personal life.

"A great team doesn't mean that they had the smartest people. What made those teams great is that everyone trusted one another. It can be a powerful thing when that magic dynamic exists.

Steve continues, "One of my favorite books about team dynamics is *Five Dysfunctions of a Team*, by Patrick Lencioni. He writes that in order to have mutual trust, you need to be vulnerable. So, I'm going to tell you a little about myself and what makes me tick. And then I'm going to ask you to do the same.

"It may make you uncomfortable, but it's part of what I need from you as leaders. If you can't do it for yourself, do it for the livelihood of the nearly four thousand Parts Unlimited employees and their families. I don't take that responsibility lightly, and you shouldn't either."

Oh, shit. That's another part of "management off-sites" I forgot about. Touchy-feely crap.

Steve ignores the skyrocketing tension in the room as everyone, like me, puts up their deflector shields. "My family was dirt poor, but I'm extremely proud to be the first one to actually make it to college. No one before me made it out of high school. Growing up in rural Texas, my parents worked in a cotton mill. During the summers, my brothers and I were too young to work there, so we'd pick cotton in the fields."

People picked cotton in the last century? I quickly do the math in my head, wondering if this was possible.

"So there I am, on top of the world at the University of Arizona. My parents don't have money to pay tuition, so I find a job at a copper mine.

"I don't know if OSHA existed back then, but if they visited that mine, they would have shut it down. It was dangerous and filthy." He points at his left ear, saying, "I lost most of my hearing in this ear when some explosives went off too close to me.

"I finally get my first big break when I land a job at a pipe manufacturing plant, helping with equipment maintenance. This is the first job where I'm paid to think.

"I study management, and more than anything, I want to go into sales after college. From what I see at the plant, those sales guys have the best jobs in the world. They get paid to wine and dine clients, and they travel from city to city, seeing what all the best factories are doing."

Steve shakes his head ruefully. "But that's not how it turns out. To help pay for school, I join ROTC where I get my first glimpse of what kids from middle-class America are like. And it means that after college, instead of going to work in industry, I have to fulfill my obligations to the US Army, which is where I discover my love for logistics. I make sure materials get to where they need to. Soon, I have a reputation of being the go-to guy when you really need just about anything."

I'm riveted. Steve's a good storyteller.

"But it's hard being a poor country hick, surrounded by people from privileged families. I feel like I need to prove myself to everyone. I'm twenty-five years old, and I still have fellow officers constantly calling me dumb and slow because of my accent and upbringing…" he says, as his voice cracks slightly.

"It makes me even more determined to prove myself. After nine years, I'm ready to leave the Army after a distinguished career. Right before I'm discharged, my commanding officer tells me something that changes my life.

"He says that although I've gotten consistently high ratings over the years, without exception, none of the people who served under me would want to work with me again. He tells me that if there were an Asshole of the Decade Award, I'd win by a wide margin. And that if I want to make something of myself, I need to get this fixed."

In the corner of my eye, I see Wes roll his eyes at Chris, who pointedly ignores him.

"I know what you're thinking," Steve says, nodding at Wes. "But it's one of the most crushing moments of my life, and I realize that I've made a critical mistake in how I was living my life, betraying my own values.

"Over the next three decades, I became a constant student of building great teams that really trust one another. I did this first as a materials manager, then later as a plant manager, as head of Marketing, and later, as head of Sales Operations. Then twelve years ago, Bob Strauss, our CEO at the time, hired me to become the new COO."

Steve exhales slowly, rubbing his face, suddenly looking very tired and old. "Somehow, I've made the wrong turn again, just like I did in the Army. I've become that person I promised myself I'd never be again."

He stops talking and looks around the room. The silence goes on for a long time as we watch him stare out the window. The bright sun is starting to stream in through the conference room windows.

Steve says, "We have big problems in front of us that we need to fix. Erik is right. IT is not just a department. IT is a competency that we need to gain as an entire company. And I know that if we can reforge ourselves into a great team, where we can all trust one another, we can succeed."

He then says, "Are you guys willing to do what it takes to help create a team where we can all trust one another?"

Steve looks around the table. I see that everyone is looking back at him with rapt attention.

The silence lengthens uncomfortably.

Chris is the first to speak. "I'm in. Working in a screwed up team sucks, so if you're offering to help fix it, I'm all for it."

I see Patty and Wes also nodding, and then everyone turns to look at me.

CHAPTER 19

• *Tuesday, September 23*

At last, I nod, too.

Patty says, "You know, Bill, I think you've done a fantastic job in the past couple of weeks. And I'm sorry for how I reacted when you quit. I've seen such a difference in how the entire IT organization works. This is an organization that has resisted adopting any sort of process and had real problems with trust between departments. It's amazing to see, and I give most of the credit to you."

"I'm with her. I suppose I'm glad you're back, too, you big quitter," Wes laughs loudly. "Whatever I might have said on that first day, I don't want your job. We need you here."

Embarrassed, I just smile, acknowledging their remarks but not wanting them to blather on, saying, "Okay. Thanks, guys."

Steve nods, watching our interaction. At last, he says, "Let's go around the table and have each of you share something from your personal history. Where were you born? How many siblings did you have and where did you fit in? What childhood events helped form you as an adult?"

Steve continues, "The goal of this exercise is to get to know one another as people. You've learned a bit about me and my vulnerabilities.

But that's not enough. We need to know more about one another. And that creates the basis for trust."

He looks around. "Who wants to go first?"

Oh, shit.

Marines don't like this kind of touchy-feely stuff. I immediately avert my eyes, not wanting to be called on first.

Much to my relief, Chris volunteers.

He starts off, "I was born in Beirut as the youngest of three children. Before the age of eighteen, I had lived in eight different countries. As a result, I speak four languages."

Chris tells us about how he and his wife tried for five years to have children, the agony of having to administer the fertility treatment injections to her, and just not being able to go through it a third time.

Then he tells about the miracle of having identical twin boys, only to have complications, and having to stay with his wife in the intensive care unit for three months after they were born prematurely. And spending night after night, praying that they would be okay, and not wanting one twin to live his life without the other when they were destined to be able to understand each other in a way that no other person in the world could.

And how this experience taught him how selfish he was and his newfound desire to be unselfish.

To my surprise, I blink back tears, seeing Chris' earnest aspirations for his kids' future. I furtively notice others doing the same.

"Thank you for sharing, Chris," says Steve solemnly after a moment and then looks around the room. "Who's next?"

To my surprise and relief, Wes goes next.

I learn that he's been engaged three times in his life, and at the last minute, called off each one. And when he finally does get married, he quickly got divorced because she was tired of his maniacal car racing habit.

How can a guy who weighs nearly 250 pounds race cars?

Wes has four cars, and even if he weren't a Parts Unlimited employee, he would be one of our most fanatic customers. He spends most of his off-hours working on his Mazda Miata and old Audi that he races competitively almost every weekend. Apparently, he's struggled with a lifelong battle to lose weight, even as a young child. He talked about being the outcast.

He still battles his weight. Not to make friends or for his health, but to try to keep up with the skinny Asian teenage car racers half his age, even going to weight-loss camp. Twice.

There is a long silence.

I'm too nervous to laugh.

Steve finally says, "Thanks for sharing, Wes. Who's next?"

I purse my lips together and am again relieved when Patty raises her hand.

We learn that she was actually an art major. She's one of those people I've made fun of all my life? But she seems so reasonable!

She tells us what it's like growing up being the "smart girl with big boobs and glasses," trying to decide what to do in life. She switched majors five times in college, dropping out to become a singer-songwriter in Athens, Georgia, spending two years touring clubs around the country with her band. She went back to get her MFA but after confronting the potential poverty of making a living as an artist, applied to work at Parts Unlimited. She almost didn't get the job because of a civil disobedience arrest that was still on her record.

When Patty stops talking, Steve thanks her. And then smiling at my discomfort, he says, "Thank you. That leaves you, Bill…"

Even though I've known this moment is coming, the room seems to fade out.

I hate talking about myself. In the Marines, I was able to create a persona where I could just yell at people and tell them what needed to be done. I got paid to keep my people alive by being slightly smarter than they were and having great vocal cords.

I do not share my feelings with work colleagues.

Or with almost anyone, for that matter.

I look at the notepad in front of me, where I've been writing down ideas of what to share. All I see is nervous doodling.

The silence is nearly absolute, with everyone now looking at me expectantly. Not impatiently, I see. Instead, they seem patient and kind.

I see Patty's expression turn sympathetic.

I purse my lips together for a moment, and then just blurt out, "What influenced me most? When I realized that my mom did everything for us, and that my dad was completely undependable. He was an alcoholic and when things weren't going well, all my brothers and sisters hid from him. But it got to a point where I finally had enough and ran away. And I left them behind. And my youngest sister was only eight years old."

I keep going, "You know, getting arrested was one of the best things that ever happened to me. The alternative was having to go home. So instead, I joined the Marines. That introduced me to an entirely new world, where I learned that there was a totally different way of living your life. It taught me that you could be rewarded by doing things right and taking care of your fellow soldiers.

"What did I learn? That my main goal is to be a great father, not like the shitty father I had. I want to be the man that my sons deserve." I feel tears starting to fall down my cheeks, which I wipe away, angry that my body is betraying me.

"That good enough for you, Steve?" I say with a lot more anger than I had intended.

Steve nods with a half smile, saying slowly, "Thank you, Bill. I know that was as difficult for you as it was for all of us."

I exhale slowly. And breathe deeply one more time, trying to regain some equilibrium that I hadn't realized I'd lost.

The uncomfortable silence goes on.

"I know this isn't my place to say, Bill," Wes says slowly. "But, I'm pretty sure your dad would be incredibly proud of you. And he would realize what a total piece of shit he was, compared to you."

I hear laughter around the table, and Patty says quietly, "I agree with Wes. Those kids of yours are luckier than they'll ever know."

Wes grunts in agreement, and Chris nods at me. And I find myself crying for the first time in over thirty years.

Embarrassed, I pull myself together and look up at everyone.

I'm relieved to see everyone shifting mental gears and turning their attention back to Steve, who looks around the room.

"First, I'd like to thank all of you for giving of yourself and doing that exercise with me," he says. "Although it's nice to get to know each of you better, I wouldn't do this if I didn't think it was important. Solving any complex business problem requires teamwork, and teamwork requires trust. Lencioni teaches that showing vulnerability helps create a foundation for that.

"I know it's unrealistic to think we're going to leave this meeting knowing exactly what we need to do, with priorities and owners assigned," he continues. "But I would like to have a joint vision as we move toward a solution."

Steve puts both hands in front of him, and says, "Just to get the ball rolling, I'd like to propose that one of our main problems is that we blow every commitment and schedule that we make. People outside of IT are always grumbling that we miss whatever expectations we set. By a mile.

"Which makes me think," he says, looking around the room, "that we're probably not good at making internal commitments to one another here within IT. Thoughts?"

Uncomfortable silence.

"Look, I don't want to split hairs," Chris finally says defensively. "But if you look at the actual metrics, my group has delivered almost every major project on time. We make our dates."

"Yeah, just like you hit the Phoenix date, right?" Wes says, jeering. "Now that was a huge success. I heard Steve was really proud of your performance last week."

Chris turns red, raising both hands in front of him. "That's not what I meant." He thinks for a moment, adding, "It was a total disaster. But, technically, we did hit the date."

Interesting.

"If that's true," I say, digging in, "there's something really wrong with our definition of what a 'completed project' is. If it means 'Did Chris get all his Phoenix tasks done?' then it was a success. But if we wanted Phoenix in production that fulfilled the business goals, without setting the entire business on fire, we should call it a total failure."

"Let's stop pussyfooting here," Steve interrupts. "I've told Sarah that Phoenix was one of the worst executed projects in the history of our company. What's a better definition of success?"

Thinking for a moment, I finally say, "I don't know. But this is a recurring pattern. Chris' group never factors in all the work that Operations needs to do. And even when they do, they use up all the time in the schedule, leaving none for us. And we're always left cleaning up the mess, long afterward."

Chris nods understandingly. "Well, you and I are fixing some of this. Part of it is a planning and architecture issue, which you and I have talked about fixing. But you're underestimating how much of a bottleneck your group is. We've got a bunch of other applications that need to be deployed, but because your team is tied up, all the other deployments waiting in line get delayed as well."

He adds, "On any given week, we've got five or six application groups waiting in line for your group to deploy something or another. And when anything goes wrong, everything gets stacked up. No offense, but when you guys are late, it's like an airport that closes down. Before you know it, you have a bunch of airplanes circling, all waiting to land."

Wes grumbles loudly, "Yeah, well, that's what happens when the airplane you've built crash lands, totally destroying the runway."

Then Wes raises a placating hand. "Look, I'm not blaming you, Chris. I'm just stating a well-known fact. When deployments don't go as planned, whether the plan was written by your group or mine, it affects everybody else. That's all I'm saying."

I nod, agreeing with Wes' characterization. And surprisingly, Chris is nodding, as well.

I reply, "Erik has helped me understand that there are four types of IT Operations work: business projects, IT Operations projects, changes, and unplanned work. But, we're only talking about the first type of work, and the unplanned work that get's created when we do it wrong. We're only talking about half the work we do in IT Operations."

I turn to look at Steve, saying, "I showed you our project list. On top of the thirty-five business projects, we've got another seventy-five or so Ops projects we're working. We've got a backlog of thousands of changes that apparently all need to execute for some reason or another. On top of that, we have an ever increasing amount of unplanned work, mostly caused by all our fragile applications breaking, which includes Phoenix."

I say flatly, "We are way over capacity, given the amount of work in front of us. And we haven't even counted properly the big audit finding remediation project yet, which Steve says is still top-priority."

I see the understanding start to dawn on Steve and Chris.

Speaking of which…

I look around, puzzled. "Hey, where's John? If we're talking about compliance, shouldn't he be here, too? And isn't he a part of the IT leadership team as well?"

Wes groans softly, rolling his eyes, saying, "Oh, great, that's just who we need."

Steve looks startled. He looks at the index card he was holding earlier. Then he runs his finger down a printed calendar in front of him. "Shit. I forgot to invite him."

Chris mutters, "Well, we were getting so much done. It was probably a blessing in disguise, right?"

There's more uncomfortable laughter, but people seem embarrassed that we're making fun of John without him here.

"No, no, no, that's not what I meant," Steve says quickly, looking most embarrassed of all. "Bill is right—we need him here. Everyone, let's take a fifteen-minute break. I'm going to have Stacy track him down."

I decide to take a walk to clear my head.

When I return in ten minutes, I see the strewn remains of a corporate meeting in progress: Styrofoam cups half-filled with coffee, plates of leftover food, crumpled up napkins.

Across the room, Patty and Wes are having an animated discussion with Chris. At the other end of the table, Steve is talking on his cell phone with someone, while Erik looks at the pictures of automotive parts hanging on the wall.

I'm considering joining Patty and Wes when I see John walk in the room. Underneath his arm, of course, is the black three-ring binder.

"Stacy said you were looking for me, Steve?" he said. He makes a point of looking around slowly at the evidence of a meeting started without him long ago. "Did I miss a meeting notice? Or did I just get left out from yet another one?"

As almost everyone goes to extraordinary lengths to avoid eye contact with him, he says even more loudly, "Hey, it smells like people just had sex in here. Did I miss anything good?"

Chris, Patty, and Wes break off their conversation, and with exaggerated nonchalance, grab their original seats.

"Ah, good, you're here. I'm glad you could make it," says Steve, appearing completely unfazed. "Please grab a seat. Everyone, let's get started again."

"John, my apologies for not sending you an invite. It's completely my fault," Steve says, as he makes his way to the head of the table. "I organized this meeting yesterday at the last minute, right after the audit committee meeting. After recognizing my part in making all the IT problems worse, I wanted to assemble the IT leadership team to see if we could agree on a general direction of the solution to the issues we're having around projects, operational stability, and compliance."

John looks at me questioningly, lifting an eyebrow.

I'm curious at Steve's omission of the vulnerability exercise and all that. Probably he figured if he can't redo it, he might as well not even bring it up.

I nod reassuringly at John.

Steve turns to me. "Bill, please continue."

"When you brought up the word commitment, it reminded me of something Erik asked me last week that stuck with me," I say. "He asked on what basis do we decide whether we can accept a new project. When I said that I didn't know, he took me on another tour of MRP-8 manufacturing plant. He took me to Allie, the Manufacturing Resource Planning Coordinator, and asked her how she decides on whether to accept a new order."

I flip back to my notes. "She said that she would first look at the order and then look at the bill of materials and routings. Based on that, she would look at the loadings of the relevant work centers in the plant and then decide whether accepting the order would jeopardize any existing commitments.

"Erik asked me how we made the same type of decision in IT," I recall. "I told him then, and I'll tell you now, I don't know. I'm pretty sure we don't do any sort of analysis of capacity and demand before we accept work. Which means we're always scrambling, having to take shortcuts, which means more fragile applications in production. Which means more unplanned work and firefighting in the future. So, around and around we go."

To my surprise, Erik interrupts. "Well put, Bill. You've just described 'technical debt' that is not being paid down. It comes from taking shortcuts, which may make sense in the short-term. But like financial debt, the compounding interest costs grow over time. If an organization doesn't pay down its technical debt, every calorie in the organization can be spent just paying interest, in the form of unplanned work."

"As you know, unplanned work is not free," he continues. "Quite the opposite. It's very expensive, because unplanned work comes at the expense of…"

He looks around professorially for an answer.

Wes finally speaks up, "Planned work?"

"Precisely!" Erik says jovially. "Yes, that's exactly right, Chester. Bill mentioned the four types of work: business projects, IT Operations projects, changes, and unplanned work. Left unchecked, technical debt will ensure that the only work that gets done is unplanned work!"

"That sure sounds like us," Wes says nodding. He then looks firmly at Erik, saying, "And it's Wes, not Chester. I'm Wes."

"Yes, I'm sure you are," Erik says agreeably.

He addresses the rest of the room. "Unplanned work has another side effect. When you spend all your time firefighting, there's little time or energy left for planning. When all you do is react, there's not enough time to do the hard mental work of figuring out whether you can accept new work. So, more projects are crammed onto the plate, with fewer cycles available to each one, which means more bad multitasking, more escalations from poor code, which mean more shortcuts. As Bill said, 'around and around we go.' It's the IT capacity death spiral."

I smile to myself at Erik mangling Wes' name. I'm not sure what kind of mental game he's playing, but it's amusing to watch.

Uncertain, I ask Steve, "Are we even allowed to say no? Every time I've asked you to prioritize or defer work on a project, you've bitten my head off. When everyone is conditioned to believe that no isn't an acceptable answer, we all just became compliant order takers, blindly marching down a doomed path. I wonder if this is what happened to my predecessors, too."

Wes and Patty nod slightly.

Even Chris nods.

"Of course you can say no!" Steve replies heatedly, with a look of genuine irritation on his face. He then takes a deep breath before saying, "Let me be clear. I need you to say no! We cannot afford to have this leadership team be order takers. We pay you to *think*, not just *do!*"

Steve looks increasingly angry, saying, "What's at stake here is the survival of the company! The outcomes of these projects dictate whether this entire company succeeds or fails!"

He looks right at me. "If you, or for that matter, anyone knows that a project will fail, I need you to say so. And I need it backed up with data. Give me data like that plant coordinator showed you, so we can understand why. Sorry, Bill, I like you a lot, but saying no just based on your gut is not enough."

Erik snorts and mutters, "That's some pretty nice, soaring rhetoric, Steve. Very moving. But you know what your problem is? You guys in the business are punch drunk on projects, taking on new work that doesn't have a prayer of succeeding. Why? Because you have no idea what capacity you actually have. You're like the guy who is always writing checks that bounce, because you don't know how much money you have and never bother opening your mail.

"Let me tell you a story," he says. "Let me tell you about what that MRP-8 plant was like before I arrived. Those poor bastards would get these manila envelopes that would just show up, containing all sorts of crazy orders. The business would make absurd commitments to ship something at some impossible date, oblivious to all the work already in the system."

He continues, "It was a nightmare everyday. They had inventory piled up to the ceiling. And was there a systematic way to get WIP through the plant? Hell, no! What got worked on was based on who yelled the loudest or most often, who could engineer the best side deals with the expediters, or who could get the ear of the highest ranking executive."

Erik is as animated as I've ever seen him. "We started restoring sanity when we figured out where our constraint was. Then we protected it, making sure that time on the constraint was never wasted. And we did everything to make sure work flowed through it."

Erik then grows still and merely says, "To fix your problem, you need to do a lot more than just learning how to say no. That's the tip of the iceberg."

We all look at him, waiting for him to keep going. But instead, he stands up, walks to his suitcase, and opens it, revealing a jumble of clothes, a snorkel, a garbage bag, and boxer shorts.

He starts digging, takes out a granola bar, closes the suitcase, and returns to the table.

We all watch as he opens up the granola bar package and starts eating it.

Steve, looking as mystified as the rest of us, eventually says, "Erik, that's an intriguing story. Please keep going."

Erik sighs. "No, that's all I intended to say. If you can't figure out from that what you need to do, then there's really not much hope for any of you."

Steve slaps the table, exasperated.

But my mind is racing.

What we need to do isn't merely to prioritize better. I've already learned what the priorities are, however inconvenient: Phoenix. Making the audit findings go away. All while keeping everything running.

We think we know where the constraint is. It's Brent. Brent, Brent, Brent. And we've already taken steps to protect Brent from unplanned work.

I know I can't hire more resources.

I also know that the workload in my organization is totally out of control.

No amount of heroics on my part can make a big dent in the tidal wave of work that's been allowed to get into the system. Because no one ever said no.

Our mistakes were made long before it came to me. The mistakes were made by accepting the project and all the resulting shortcuts that Chris had to make before it reached me.

How can we reverse this insanity?

Then a strange idea hits me.

I think about it for another moment. It sounds utterly absurd, yet I can't find any flaws in the logic.

I say, "Steve, I have an idea. But please let me finish telling you the entire idea before you react."

And I tell them what I'm thinking.

Steve is the first to speak. "You must be out of your mind," Steve says, his initial disbelief turning into exasperation. "You want to just stop doing work? Who do you think we are? Subsidized potato farmers paid not to grow crops?"

But before I can respond, John speaks up. "I agree. Your idea seems like exactly the wrong thing to do. We've got a burning platform right now to finally do the right thing. We need to strike while the iron is hot. This is a perfect storm for us to finally get the budget we need to not only do the right things, but do the right things right."

He starts rattling off the points on his fingers, "We've got the audit finding that has board visibility, the high-visibility project that can't fail, and an operational failure that can't happen again, either. We should pour on the gas and put in the security controls we need, once and for all."

Wes interjects, chortling to John, "I'm stunned! I thought you would love Bill's idea. I mean, you love stopping things from getting done and saying no, right? This should be like a dream come true for you!"

John turns bright red, obviously preparing a scathing reply. But Wes puts his big, meaty hand on his shoulder, and says with a smile, "Hey, I'm just kidding, okay? Just making a joke."

Everyone starts talking at once when Erik suddenly stands up, crumples his granola bar wrapper, and throws it across the room into the wastebasket, missing it completely. He leans back in his chair, saying, "Bill, I think your proposal is very astute."

Looking at John, he continues, "Remember, Jimmy, the goal is to increase the throughput of the entire system, not just increase the number of tasks being done. And if you don't have a trustworthy system of work, why should I trust your system of security controls? Bah. A total waste of time."

John looks back at Erik, puzzled. "What?"

Erik sighs and rolls his eyes. Instead of responding to John, he turns his gaze to Steve. "You've been a plant manager. Think of it as freezing materials release until enough WIP completes and leaves the plant. In order to control this system, we need to reduce the number of moving parts."

When Steve doesn't appear convinced, Erik leans way forward in his chair and asks him pointedly, "Suppose you're managing the MRP-8 plant, and you have inventory piled to the ceiling. What would happen if you stopped releasing jobs and materials onto the plant floor?"

Surprised to be the target of the question, Steve considers it for a moment. "The amount of WIP in the plant goes down, because work will start leaving the plant as finished goods."

"Correct," Erik says, nodding approvingly. "And what will likely happen to due-date performance?"

"Due-date performance goes up, because WIP went down." Steve says, looking increasingly suspicious and reluctant about where Erik might be leading him.

"Yes, very good," Erik says encouragingly. "But on the other hand, what happens to inventory levels if you allow the plant to continue to accept orders and release new jobs?"

He says after a moment, "WIP goes up."

"Excellent," Erik says. "And what happens to due-date performance?"

Steve looks like he's just swallowed something that isn't agreeing with him, and he says eventually, "Everyone knows that in manufacturing, as WIP increases, due-date performance goes down.

"Wait a minute, here," he says, squinting at Erik. "You're not actually suggesting that this applies to IT, too? That by halting all work except for Phoenix, we'll reduce the amount of WIP in IT, and that this will somehow improve due-date performance? Is that seriously what you're suggesting?"

Erik leans back in his chair looking pleased with himself. "Yes."

Wes says, "Won't that leave most of us just twiddling our thumbs with nothing to do? That's 130 people in IT Operations just sitting around. Doesn't that sound a bit…wasteful?"

Erik scoffs and says, "I'll tell you about wasteful. How about over a thousand changes stuck in the system, with no apparent way of ever getting them completed?"

Wes frowns. Then he nods, saying, "That's true. The number of cards on Patty's change board keeps going up. If that's work in process, it's definitely spiraling out of control. We're probably only a couple weeks away from having those cards stacked to the ceiling, too."

I nod. He's right.

The idea is for IT Operations and Development to not accept any new projects for two weeks and to stop all work in IT Operations except for work related to Phoenix.

I look around. "If we single-task on the most important project for two weeks and still aren't able to make a big dent, then I think we should all find new day jobs."

Chris nods. "I think we should give it a shot. We'll keep working on the other active projects, but we'll freeze all deployment work except Phoenix. From Bill's perspective, it will look like that's the only thing we're working on. Make no mistake, Phoenix will be everyone's top priority."

Patty and Wes nod in agreement.

John crosses his arms. "I'm not sure if I can support this insane proposal. First, I've never seen any organization do anything even remotely like this before. Second, I'm very concerned that if we do this, we'll lose our shot at getting all the audit issues fixed. As Steve has already said, those audit findings could kill the company, too."

"You know what your problem is?" Erik says, pointing a finger at John. "You never see the end-to-end business process, so I guarantee you that many of the controls you want to put in aren't even necessary."

John says, "What?"

Again, Erik waves John's question away. "Don't worry about it for now. Let the inevitable happen, and we'll see what we can learn from it."

Steve turns to John. "I understand your concerns about security. But the biggest risk to the company is not the unresolved audit findings. The biggest risk to the company is that we don't survive. We need Phoenix to regain competitive parity."

He pauses and says, "Let's give this project freeze one week and see if it makes a difference in the Phoenix work. If we don't, we'll put the remediation work back on the front burner. Okay?"

John nods reluctantly. He then flips to a page in his three-ring binder, and makes some notes. He's probably recording Steve's promise.

"Steve, we definitely need your help to make this happen," I say. "My guys are routinely strong-armed into doing pet projects by almost every manager in this company. I think we need an e-mail from you to the entire company, not only explaining why you're doing this, but what the consequences will be if someone tries to put unauthorized work into the system."

Erik makes an encouraging noise.

"No problem," Steve quickly replies. "I'll send you all a draft after this meeting. Revise it and I'll send it out to all the company managers. Good enough for you?"

Trying to keep the disbelief out of my voice, I say, "Yes."

It's astonishing what we agree to in the next hour. IT Operations will freeze all non-Phoenix work. Development can't idle the twenty-plus non-Phoenix projects, but will freeze all deployments. In other words, no work will flow from Development to IT Operations for another two weeks.

Furthermore, we will identify the top areas of technical debt, which Development will tackle to decrease the unplanned work being created by problematic applications in production.

This will all make a huge difference in my team's workload.

Furthermore, Chris and Kirsten will review all Phoenix tasks not being worked, and steal resources from other projects to get them in work again.

Everyone seems energized and excited to put the plan into place—even John.

Before we all leave, Steve says, "Thank you all for your good thinking today and for sharing something about yourself. I feel like I know all of you better now. And, as unbelievable as I think Bill's crazy project freeze idea is, I think it could work. I look forward to this being the first of many great decisions this team will make.

"As I said, one of my goals is that we create a team where we can all trust one another," he continues. "Hopefully, we made a small step in that direction, and I encourage you to keep demanding honest and truthful communications between you."

He looks around the room and asks, "Is there anything that you guys need from me in the meantime?"

There are no requests, so we adjourn.

As we all get up to leave, Erik says loudly, "Great work, Bill. Couldn't have done it better myself."

CHAPTER 20

• *Friday, September 26*

Three days later, I'm at my desk, trying to read a report on Phoenix progress from Kirsten on my laptop. As it whirs and wheezes, I wonder how many weeks it's been since John's security patch bricked my laptop.

Getting replacement laptops is like a lottery. It's tempting to bribe one of the service desk people, as one of the Marketing managers suggested, but I refuse to jump the queue. I have to keep playing by the rules since I'm the person responsible for making and enforcing them. I make a note to talk with Patty about our urgent need to reduce lead times on these laptop replacements.

Finally, the e-mail comes up:

From: Kirsten Fingle
To: Steve Masters,
Cc: Bill Palmer, Chris Allers, Sarah Moulton
Date: September 26, 10:33 AM
Subject: Great news on project front!
    Steve,
    We are finally making headway. The project freeze and the resulting IT focus on Phoenix has broken the logjam. We've accomplished more

in the previous seven days that we typically get done in an entire month.

Kudos to everyone on the team!

On a side note: many project sponsors are very frustrated about their projects being put on hold. In particular, Sarah Moulton believes that her projects are exempt from the freeze. I referred her to you.

Attached is the formal status report. Please let me know if you have any questions.

Kirsten

Although the note about Sarah making trouble again makes my jaw clench, this is absolutely fantastic news.

We were expecting it, but the good news is welcome, nonetheless, especially after earlier in the week. We had a big setback because of a Sev 1 incident that took out all the internal phone and voicemail systems, bringing Sales and Manufacturing to its knees on the last day of the quarter.

Two hours into the outage, we discovered it was caused by one of our networking vendors who accidentally made a change to our production phone system instead of the hot spare.

The outage will impact our quarterly revenue, but we don't know how much yet. In order to prevent this from happening again, we're putting together a project to monitor our critical systems for unauthorized changes.

This monitoring project is what Wes, Patty, and John are talking about, huddled around Patty's conference table.

I say, "Sorry to interrupt, but I wanted to share the good news." I show them Kirsten's e-mail.

Wes leans back and says, "Well, that makes it official. Your project freeze is actually working."

Patty looks over at him, appearing surprised. "You actually doubted it? Come on, we've both been talking about how we've never seen people so focused before. It's amazing how the project freeze has reduced the priority conflicts and bad multitasking. We know it's made a huge difference in productivity."

Wes shrugs then smiles. "Until Kirsten gives us credit, it's all just in our heads."

He's got a point. It really is great to have Kirsten acknowledge the progress we're making.

"By the way," Patty says, "She's is not kidding about the business managers freaking out. I've had more and more VPs calling me, demanding a waiver for their various pet projects or asking to get some work done off the books. It's not just Sarah—she's just the most blatant and vocal."

I frown. "Okay, that's part of our job and we expected this. But, I don't want this kind of pressure being applied to any of our people. Wes?"

"I've told everyone on my team that they're to route any complaints to me. And trust me, I call each of those guys back and give them an earful," he says.

Patty says, "I'm already getting anxious about what we do after we lift the project freeze. Won't that be like opening up the floodgates?"

Once again, she has put her finger on something important. I say, "I'll call Erik, but before I do, how do we currently prioritize our work? When we commit to work on a project, a change, a service request, or anything else, how does anyone decide what to work on at any given time? What happens if there are competing priorities?"

"That happens every freaking day!" says Wes, looking incredulous. "That's what's so great about freezing all the projects except for one. No one has to decide what they're working on. No multitasking allowed."

"That's not my question," I say. "When we have multiple streams of work going on simultaneously, how does anyone decide what needs to get worked on at any given time?"

"Well," Wes says, "we trust them to make the right decision, based on the data they have. That's why we hire smart people."

This is not good.

Recalling my twenty minutes observing Brent before the project freeze, I ask, "And on what data do all our smart people base their prioritization decisions?"

Wes says defensively, "We all try to juggle the competing priorities as best as we can. That's life, right? Priorities change."

"Let's be honest," Patty says. "Priority 1 is whoever is yelling the loudest, with the tie-breaker being who can escalate to the most senior executive. Except when they're more subtle. I've seen a bunch of my staff always prioritizing a certain manager's requests, because he takes them out to lunch once a month."

Oh, great. In addition to some engineers being bullied, I have other engineers who are like Corporal Max Klinger from *M*A*S*H*, running their own black market of IT work.

"If this is true, there's no way we can lift the project freeze. Don't you see that we don't have any way of releasing work into IT and be able to trust that it will get worked on?"

Trying to keep the resignation out of my voice, I say, "Patty is right. We have a lot to figure out before the project freeze ends. Which is in exactly one week."

I decide to take a quick walk outside. I have thirty minutes before my next meeting, and I need to think.

I'm more unsettled than ever. When we have more than one project in the system at the same time, how do we protect the work from being interrupted or having its priority trumped by almost anyone in the business or someone else in IT?

The sun shines down on me. It's 11 a.m., and the air smells like autumn. The leaves on the trees are starting to turn orange and brown, and there are piles of them starting to form in the parking lot.

Despite my fretting, I realize how refreshing it is to be able to think about what work we need to be doing and how to prioritize and release it. For a moment, I marvel at the lack of constant firefighting that dominated so much of my career in IT.

The types of issues we're having to solve lately are so…cerebral.

It's what I thought management was all about when I got my MBA.

I'm convinced that if we do a good job thinking, we can make a real difference. In that moment, I decide to call Erik.

"Hello?" I hear him say.

"Hi, it's Bill. Do you have a couple of minutes to talk? I have some questions about the project freeze." I pause, and then add, "Or rather, what happens after we lift the project freeze."

"Well, it's about time. I was wondering when you'd figure out that you have a huge, new problem on your hands."

I quickly fill him in on the good news from Kirsten. I outline the problems we've stumbled upon while we consider the monitoring project and how we protect work in the system.

"Not bad, junior!" Erik says. "You've obviously put our discussion about constraints into practice and are doing everything you can to protect that constraint from being hit by unplanned work. You're asking some very important questions about the First Way and how you manage your flow of planned work. Until you can do that, you can't really manage much of anything, can you?

"You're confused because you're realizing you don't know how work is actually worked," he continues.

I suppress an irritated sigh.

"I think it's time for another trip to MRP-8. How soon can you get there?" he asks.

Surprised, I ask, "You're in town?"

"Yep" he says. "There's a meeting with the auditors and the finance guys this afternoon that I wouldn't miss for the world. Make sure you're there for it. We're going to make John's head fall off."

I tell him that I can be at MRP-8 in fifteen minutes.

Erik's in the middle of the lobby waiting for me.

I do a double take. He's wearing a faded T-shirt and a zippered, hooded sweatshirt with a faded union logo. He already has a visitor badge and is tapping his foot impatiently.

"I came as fast as I could." I say.

Erik merely grunts and gestures for me to follow him. Again, we climb the staircase and stand on the catwalk overlooking the plant floor.

"So tell me what you see," he says, gesturing toward the plant floor.

I look down, confused, not knowing what he wants to hear. Starting with the obvious, I say, "Like last time, I see raw materials coming in from the loading docks on the left. And on the right, I see finished goods leaving the other set of loading docks."

Surprisingly, Erik nods approvingly. "Good. And in between?"

I look down at the scene. Part of me feels foolish, afraid of looking like the Karate Kid being quizzed by Mr. Miyagi. But I asked for this meeting, so I just start talking. "I see materials and work in process, flowing from left to right—but, obviously, moving very slowly."

Erik peers over the catwalk, and says, "Oh, really? Like some sort of river?"

He turns to me, shaking his head with disgust, "What do you think this is, some sort of poetry reading class? Suddenly, WIP is like water running over smooth stones? Get serious. How would a plant manager answer the question? From where to where does the work go, and why?"

Trying again, I say, "Okay, okay. WIP goes from work center to work center, as dictated by the bill of materials and routings. And all that is in the job order, which was released at that desk over there."

"That's better," Erik says. "And can you find the work centers where the plant constraints are?"

I know that Erik had told me on that first odd trip to this plant.

"The heat treat ovens and paint curing booths," I say suddenly.

"There," I say, after scanning the plant floor and finally spotting a set of large machines by the far wall. "And there," I say, pointing at the large rooms with signs saying, "Paint Booth #30-A" and "Paint Booth #30-B."

"Good. Understanding the flow of work is key to achieving the First Way," Erik says, nodding. More sternly, he asks, "So now, tell me again which work centers you've determined to be the constraints in your organization?"

I smile, answering easily, "Brent. We talked about that before."

He scoffs, turning back to look at the plant floor.

"What?" I nearly shout. "How can it not be Brent? You even congratulated me when I told you it was Brent a couple of weeks ago!"

"Suddenly Brent is a robotic heat treat oven? You're telling me your equivalent of that paint curing booth down there is Brent?" he says with mock disbelief. "You know, that might be the dumbest thing I've ever heard."

He continues, "So, where would that leave your two managers, Chester and Penelope? Let me guess. Maybe they're equivalent to that drill press station and that stamping machine over there? Or maybe it's that metal grinder?"

Erik looks sternly at me, "Get serious. I asked you what work centers are your constraints. Think."

Completely confused, I look back down at the plant floor.

I know that part of the answer is Brent. But when I blurt it out so confidently, Erik all but smacks me on the head. Again.

Erik seems aggravated that I named an actual person, suggesting that Brent was a piece of equipment.

I look again at the heat treat oven. And then I see them. There are two people wearing coveralls, hard hats, and goggles. One is in front of a computer screen, punching in something, while the other is inspecting a pile of parts on a loading pallet, scanning something with his handheld computer.

"Oh," I say, thinking out loud. "The heat treat oven is a work center, which has workers associated with it. You asked what work centers are our constraints, and I told you that it was Brent, which can't be right, because Brent isn't a work center.

"Brent is a worker, not a work center," I say again. "And I'm betting that Brent is probably a worker supporting way too many work centers. Which is why he's a constraint."

"Now we're getting somewhere!" Erik says, smiling. Gesturing broadly at the plant floor below, he says, "Imagine if twenty-five percent of all the work centers down there could only be operated by one person named Brent. What would happen to the flow of work?"

I close my eyes to think.

"Work wouldn't complete on time, because Brent can only be at one work center at a time," I say. Enthusiastically, I continue, "That's exactly what's happening with us. I know that for a bunch of our planned changes, work can't even start if Brent isn't on hand. When that happens, we'll escalate to Brent, telling him to drop whatever he's doing, so some other work center can get going. We'll be lucky if he can stay there long enough for the change to be completely implemented before he's interrupted by someone else."

"Exactly!" he says.

I'm slightly dismayed at the warm feeling of approval that I feel in response.

"Obviously," he continues, "every work center is made up of four things: the machine, the man, the method, and the measures. Suppose for the machine, we select the heat treat oven. The men are the two people required to execute the predefined steps, and we obviously will need measures based on the outcomes of executing the steps in the method."

I frown. These factory terms are vaguely familiar from my MBA years. But I never thought they'd be relevant in the IT domain.

Looking for some way to write this down, I realize I left my clipboard in my car. I pat my pockets and find a small crumpled index card in my back pocket.

I hurriedly write down, "Work center: machine, man, method, measure."

Erik continues, "Of course, on this plant floor, you don't have one quarter of the work centers dependent upon one person. That would be absurd. Unfortunately for you, you do. That's why when Brent takes a vacation, all sorts of work will just grind to a halt, because only Brent knows how to complete certain steps—steps that probably only Brent even knew existed, right?"

I nod, unable to resist groaning. "You're right. I've heard my managers complain that if Brent were hit by the proverbial bus, we'd be completely up the creek. No one knows what's in Brent's head. Which is one of the reason I've created the level 3 escalation pool."

I quickly explain what I did to prevent escalations to Brent during outages to keep him from being interrupted by unplanned work and how I've attempted to do the same thing for planned changes.

"Good," he says. "You're standardizing Brent's work so that other people can execute it. And because you're finally getting those steps documented, you're able to enforce some level of consistency and quality, as well. You're not only reducing the number of work centers where Brent is required, you're generating documentation that will enable you to automate some of them."

He continues, "Incidentally, until you do this, no matter how many more Brents you hire, Brent will always remain your constraint. Anyone you hire will just end up standing around."

I nod in understanding. This is exactly as Wes described it. Even though he got the additional headcount to hire more Brents, we never were able to actually increase our throughput.

I feel a sudden sense of exhilaration as the pieces fall into place in my head. He's confirming some of my deeply held intuitions and providing an underpinning theory for why I believe them.

My elation is short-lived. He looks me over disapprovingly, "You're asking about how to lift the project freeze. Your problem is that you keep confusing two things. Until you can separate them in your head, you'll just walk around in circles."

He starts walking and I hurry after him. Soon, we're standing over the middle of the plant floor.

"You see that work center over there, with the yellow blinking light?" he asks, pointing.

When I nod, he says, "Tell me what you see."

Wondering what it would take to have a normal conversation with him, I resume my dumb trainee role. "Some piece of machinery is apparently down—that's what I'm guessing the blinking light indicates. There are five people huddled off to the side, including what looks like two managers. They all look concerned. There are three more people crouched down, looking into what I'm guessing is the machine inspection panel. They have flashlights and—yeah—they're also holding screwdrivers—definitely a machine down…"

"Good guess," he says. "That's probably a computerized grinder that is out of commission, and the maintenance team is working on getting it back online. What would happen if every piece of equipment down there needs Brent to fix it?"

I laugh. "Every outage escalated immediately to Brent."

"Yes." He continues, "Let's start with your first question. Which projects are safe to release when the project freeze is lifted? Knowing how work flows through certain work centers and how some work centers require Brent and some do not, what do you think the answer is?"

I slowly repeat what Erik just recited, trying to piece together the answer

"I got it," I say, smiling. "The candidate projects which are safe to release are those that don't require Brent."

I smile even wider when he says, "Bingo. Pretty simple, yes?"

My smile disappears as I think through the implications. "Wait, how do I know which projects don't require Brent? We never think we actually need Brent until we're halfway through the work!"

I immediately regret asking the question as Erik glares at me. "I'm supposed to give you the answer to everything that you're too disorganized to be able to figure out for yourself?"

"Sorry. I'll figure it out," I say quickly. "You know, I'll be so relieved when we finally know all the work that actually requires Brent."

"Damn right," he says. "What you're building is the bill of materials for all the work that you do in IT Operations. But instead of a list of parts and subassemblies, like moldings, screws, and casters, you're cataloging all the prerequisites of what you need before you can complete the work—like laptop model numbers, specifications of user information, the software and licenses needed, their configurations, version information, the security and capacity and continuity requirements, yada yada…"

He interrupts himself, saying, "Well, to be more accurate, you're actually building a bill of resources. That's the bill of materials along with the list of the required work centers and the routing. Once you have that, along with the work orders and your resources, you'll finally be able to get a handle on what your capacity and demand is. This is what will enable you to finally know whether you can accept new work and then actually be able to schedule the work."

Amazing. I think I almost get it.

I'm about ask some questions, but Erik says, "Your second question was whether it was safe to start your monitoring project. You already established it doesn't require Brent. Furthermore, you say that the goal of this project is to prevent outages, which prevents Brent escalations. More than that, when outages do occur, you'll need less of Brent's time to troubleshoot and fix. You've already identified the constraint, exploited it to squeeze the most out of it, and then you've subordinated the flow of work to the constraint. So, how important is this monitoring project?"

I think for a moment. And then groan at the obvious answer.

I run my fingers through my hair. "You said that we always need to be looking for ways to elevate the constraint, which means I need to do whatever is required to get more cycles from Brent. That's exactly what the monitoring project does!"

I say with some disbelief that I didn't see this before, "The monitoring project is probably the most important improvement project we have—we need to start this project right away."

"Precisely," Erik says. "Properly elevating preventive work is at the heart of programs like Total Productive Maintenance, which has been embraced by the Lean Community. TPM insists that we do whatever it takes to assure machine availability by elevating maintenance. As one of my senseis would say, 'Improving daily work is even more important than doing daily work.' The Third Way is all about ensuring that we're continually putting tension into the system, so that we're continually reinforcing habits and improving something. Resilience engineering tells us that we should routinely inject faults into the system, doing them frequently, to make them less painful.

"Sensei Mike Rother says that it almost doesn't matter what you improve, as long as you're improving something. Why? Because if you are not improving, entropy guarantees that you are actually getting worse, which ensures that there is no path to zero errors, zero work-related accidents, and zero loss."

Suddenly, it's so obvious and evident. I feel like I need to call Patty right away to tell her to start the monitoring project immediately.

Erik continues, "Sensei Rother calls this the Improvement Kata," he continues. "He used the word *kata*, because he understood that repetition creates habits, and habits are what enable mastery. Whether you're talking about sports training, learning a musical instrument, or training in the Special Forces, nothing is more to mastery than practice and drills. Studies have shown that practicing five minutes daily is better than practicing once a week for three hours. And if you want to create a genuine culture of improvement, you must create those habits."

Turning back to the plant floor, he continues, "Before we leave, turn your attention from the work centers to all the space *between* the work centers. Just as important as throttling the release of work is managing the handoffs. The wait time for a given resource is the percentage that resource is busy, divided by the percentage that resource is idle. So, if a resource is fifty percent utilized, the wait time is 50/50, or 1 unit. If the resource is ninety percent utilized, the wait time is 90/10, or nine times longer. And if the resource is ninety-nine percent utilized?"

Although I'm not quite understanding the relevance, I do the math in my head: 99/1. I say, "Ninety-nine."

"Correct," he says. "When a resource is ninety-nine percent utilized, you have to wait ninety-nine times as long as if that resource is fifty percent utilized."

He gestures expansively, "A critical part of the Second Way is making wait times visible, so you know when your work spends days sitting in someone's queue—or worse, when work has to go backward, because it doesn't have all the parts or requires rework.

"Remember that our goal is to maximize flow. Here at MRP-8, we had a situation many years ago where certain components were never showing up at final assembly on time. Was it because we didn't have enough resources or because certain tasks were taking too long?

"No! When we actually followed the parts around on the plant floor, we found that for the majority of time, the parts were just sitting in queues. In other words, the 'touch time' was a tiny fraction of 'total process time.' Our expediters had to search through mountains of work to find the parts and push them through the work center," he says incredulously.

"That's happening at your plant, too, so watch for it," he says.

I nod and say, "Erik, I'm still stuck on releasing the monitoring project. People always insist that their special project is urgent, and needs to be worked at the expense of everything else. Where do all the urgent audit and security remediation projects that John is screaming for fit in?"

Erik looks intently at my face and finally says, "Have you heard a single word I've been saying in the last two weeks?"

He looks at his watch and says, "Gotta go."

Startled, I watch him as he walks quickly to the catwalk exit. I have to run to catch him. He's a big guy, probably a little over fifty years old. Despite the extra pounds he's carrying, he moves fast.

When I catch up to him, I say, "Wait. Are you saying that audit issues aren't important enough to fix?"

"I *never* said that," he says, stopping in his tracks and turning to face me. "You screw up something that jeopardizes the business' ability to maintain compliance with relevant laws and regulations? You better fix it—or you should be fired."

He turns around and resumes his pace, saying over his shoulder, "Tell me. All those projects that Jimmy your CISO is pushing. Do they increase the flow of project work through the IT organization?"

"No," I quickly answer, rushing to catch up again.

"Do they increase operational stability or decrease the time required to detect and recover from outages or security breaches?"

I think a bit longer. "Probably not. A lot of it is just more busywork, and in most cases, the work they're asking for is risky and actually could cause outages."

"Do these projects increase Brent's capacity?"

I laugh humorlessly. "No, the opposite. The audit issues alone could tie up Brent for the next year."

"And what would doing all of Jimmy's projects do to WIP levels?" he asks, opening the door that takes us back into the stairwell.

Exasperated, I say as we descend the two sets of stairs, "It would go through the roof. Again."

When we reach the bottom, Erik suddenly stops and asks, "Okay. These 'security' projects decrease your project throughput, which is the constraint for the entire business. And swamp the most constrained resource in your organization. And they don't do squat for scalability, availability, survivability, sustainability, security, supportability, or the defensibility of the organization."

He asks deadpan, "So, genius: Do Jimmy's projects sound like a good use of time to you?"

As I start to answer, he just opens the exit door and walks through it. Apparently, it was a rhetorical question.

CHAPTER 21

• *Friday, September 26*

Despite breaking every speed limit on the way, I'm twenty minutes late to the audit meeting in Building 2. When I step into the conference room, I'm stunned at how packed it is.

It's immediately obvious that this is a high-stakes meeting, fraught with political nuance. Dick and our corporate counsel are at the head of the table.

Opposite them are the external auditors who are legally liable for finding financial reporting errors and fraud, and yet they still want to keep us as clients.

Dick and his team will try to show that everything the auditors have found is all a genuine misunderstanding. Their goal is to appear earnest, but indignant that their precious time is being wasted.

It's all political theater but high-stakes political theater that is definitely above my pay grade.

Ann and Nancy are also here along with Wes and some other folks who look familiar.

Then I see John and do a double take.

My God, he looks terrible—like someone on his third day of quitting an addiction. He looks as if he thinks that the entire room will turn on him at a moment's notice and tear him to shreds, which may not be that far from the truth.

Sitting next to John is Erik, who is the picture of composure.

How did he get here so quickly? And where did he change into those khaki pants and denim shirt? In the car? While he was walking?

As I sit down next to Wes, he leans toward me. He gestures at a stapled set of papers and whispers, "The agenda for this meeting is to go through these two material weaknesses and the sixteen significant deficiencies. There's John, looking like he's in front of the firing squad, waiting for the bullet."

I see the sweat stains under John's arms, and think to myself, *Good grief, John. Pull yourself together.* I'm the operational manager where all those IT deficiencies reside, so I'm actually the one on the firing line, not you.

But unlike John, I've had the benefit of having Erik's constant reassurances that everything will work out.

Then again, Erik doesn't have his ass on the line and for a brief moment, I wonder whether I should be as nervous as John.

Five hours later, the conference table is covered with marked-up papers and empty cups of coffee, the room smelling stale and rank from all the tension and heated arguments.

I look up at the sound of the audit partner closing his briefcase.

He says to Dick, "Given this new data, it does appear that for the two potential material weaknesses, the IT controls may indeed be out of scope and thus can be resolved very quickly. Thank you in advance for making yourselves available to get us the documentation we need to close out these issues as expeditiously as possible.

"We will take all this under advisement and send you something in the next day or two," he continues. "Most likely, we'll want to schedule further testing of these newly documented downstream controls to make sure they were in place and operating—to support the financial statement assertions you're making."

As he stands up, I stare in disbelief at the audit partner. We really dodged the bullet. Looking around the table, the Parts Unlimited team looks equally surprised.

One exception is Erik, who just nods approvingly, obviously irritated that it took so long to finally have the auditors on the run.

The other exception is John. He looks extremely distraught, sitting with his shoulders slumped over that I'm suddenly concerned about his well-being.

I'm about to get up to check on John when the audit partner shakes Dick's hand and, to my surprise, Erik gets up to give him a hug.

"Erik, it's been a long time since GAIT and Orlando," the audit partner says warmly. "I was sure our paths would cross again, but I never would have guessed it would be at a client engagement! What have you been up to lately?"

Erik laughs and says, "Mostly, happily sailing on my boat. A friend asked me to join the Parts Unlimited board, partly due to their external auditors making trouble with a bunch of young, bottom-up auditors who strayed off the reservation. I should have known you'd be involved."

The audit partner looks genuinely embarrassed, and they huddle together, whispering.

For the past five hours, John, Wes, and I sat on the sidelines while the business managers walked the auditors through a precise discussion about how the IT control issues simply couldn't lead to an undetected financial reporting error. They pulled out something called the "GAIT Principles" document and cited some of the enclosed flowcharts.

Like watching a tennis match, the ball went back and forth between our team and the auditors, using words like "linkage," "significance," and "controls reliance." On occasion, Dick would trot in a bunch of experts from the relevant business areas to show that even if someone malicious managed to cause a failure in the IT control, the fraud would still be caught by another control somewhere downstream.

Managers from Materials Management, Order Entry, Treasury, and Human Resources showed that even if the application, database, operating system, and firewall were riddled with security holes and thoroughly compromised, the fraudulent transaction would still be caught by some daily or weekly inventory reconciliation report.

Over and over again, they went through scenarios that assumed all the IT infrastructure was made of Swiss cheese, where any disgruntled or wrongdoing employee or external, malicious hacker could log in and commit fraud with impunity.

But they would still detect any material error in the financial statements.

Once, Dick pointed out that an entire department of twenty people is responsible for spotting erroneous, let alone fraudulent, orders. They, and not an IT control, served as the business safety net.

Each time, the auditors, often reluctantly, agreed that controls reliance was placed on finance doing reconciliations. And not on the IT systems or the IT controls within.

This was news to me. But I certainly wasn't going to disagree with them. In fact, if shutting up and staying silent would allow Parts Unlimited to escape all the audit findings, I'd be happy to drool and pretend to be unable to read.

"You have a minute to talk?" I hear John say beside me in a scratchy voice.

He's still slumped over, his head in his hands.

"Sure," I say, looking around at the nearly empty room. It's just John and me at the large conference table, while Erik continues his whispered powwow with the audit partner in the far corner.

John looks awful. If his shirt were just a little more wrinkled, and maybe had a stain or two in front, he could almost pass as a homeless person.

"John, are you coming down with something? You don't look so hot," I say.

His expression turns ugly, "Do you know how much political capital I've spent over the last two years, trying to get everyone to do the right thing? This organization has been kicking the information security can down the road for a decade. I put absolutely everything on the line. I told them the world would end if they didn't go beyond lip-service, and at least try to fix some of these systemic IT security issues… I mean, we need to at least pretend to care."

From the other side of the room, I see Erik turn to look at us. The audit partner doesn't seem to have heard John. Nevertheless, Erik puts his arm around him and collegially moves the conversation into the hallway, closing the door loudly behind him.

Oblivious, John continues, "You know, there are times when I think I'm the only person in this entire company that actually cares about the security of our systems and data. Do you know how it feels to have the entire Dev organization hiding their activities from me, and having to beg people to tell me where they're meeting? What is this, elementary school? I'm only trying to help them do their jobs!"

When I don't say anything, he just sneers at me. "Don't look at me like that. I know you look down at me, Bill."

I look at him with genuine surprise.

"I know you never read my e-mails. I have to call you to even get you to open them up—I know, because I get the read receipts while we're on the phone, you asshole."

Ah.

But I've read many of his e-mails without him having to call me first. However, before I can respond, he barrels forward, "You all look down on me. You know, I used to manage servers, just like you do. But I found my calling doing information security. I wanted to help catch bad guys. I wanted to help organizations protect themselves from people who were out to get them. It came out of a sense of duty and a desire to make the world a better place.

"But ever since I've been here, all I do is fight the corporate bureaucracy and the business, even though I'm trying to protect them from themselves." Laughing harshly he says, "The auditors were supposed to put the screws on us. They were supposed to punish us sinners for our ungodly ways. And you know what? All afternoon, we just watched the audit partner pamper us with kid gloves. What is the point of even having an information security program at all? Even the auditors don't care! Everything just got brushed under the rug for the cost of a golf game."

John is almost shouting, "Our auditors should be put on trial for incompetence! All those findings they dismissed were basic hygiene issues! We live in a churning cesspool of risk. I'm amazed this place doesn't just collapse under its own weight from lack of caring. I've waited for years for everything to come crashing down upon us."

He pauses, whispering, "And yet, here we still are…"

Just then, Erik enters the room again, slamming the door behind him. He grabs the seat closest to the door and looks sternly at John.

"You know what your problem is, Jimmy?" Erik says, pointing his finger at him. "You are like the political commissar who walks onto the plant floor, proudly flashing your badge at all the line workers, sadistically poking your nose in everybody's business and intimidating them into doing your bidding, just to increase your own puny sense of self-worth. Half the time, you break more than you fix. Worse, you screw up the work schedules of everyone who's actually doing important work."

This is going way overboard.

John sputters, "Who do you think you are? I'm trying to keep this organization secure and keep the auditors away! I'm—"

"Why, thank you for nothing, Mr. CISO," Erik says, interrupting him. "As you just observed, the organization can keep the auditors away without you having to do anything at all. You are like the plumber who doesn't even realize that you're servicing an airplane, let alone the route you're flying, or the business condition of the airline."

By now, John is white as a sheet, his jaw hanging open.

I'm about to intervene on his behalf, when Erik stands up and shouts to John, "I don't have anything further to say to you until you prove to me that you understand what just happened in this room. The business managed to dodge the SOX-404 audit bullet, without any help from your team. Until you figure out how and why, you don't have any business interfering with the daily operations of this organization. This should be your guiding principle: You win when you protect the organization without putting meaningless work into the IT system. And you win even more when you can take meaningless work out of the IT system."

He then turns to me and says, "Bill, you just may be right. You guys around here sure seem to have completely screwed up information security."

I never said any such thing. I turn to look at John, intending to convey that I have no idea what he's talking about, but John doesn't notice me. He's staring at Erik with an expression of intense hatred on his face.

Erik says to me, pointing his thumb at John, "This guy is like the QA manager who has his group writing millions of new tests for a product we don't even ship anymore and then files millions of bug reports for features that no longer exist. Obviously, he is making what you and I would call a 'scoping error.'"

John is shaking with outrage. He says, "How dare you! As a potential board director, I can't believe you're telling us to put our customer data and financial statements at risk!"

Erik looks calmly back at John. "You really don't get it, do you? The biggest risk to Parts Unlimited is going out of business. And you seem hell-bent on making it go out of business even faster, with all your ill-conceived, irrelevant technical minutia. No wonder you've been marginalized! Everyone else is at least *trying* to help the business survive. If this were an episode of *Survivor*, you'd have been voted off a long time ago!"

By now, Erik is standing over John. "Jimmy, Parts Unlimited has at least four of my family's credit card numbers in your systems. I need you to protect that data. But you'll *never* adequately protect it when the work product is already in production. You need to protect it in the processes that create the work product."

Putting his hands in his pockets, he says more softly, "You want a clue? Go to MRP-8 plant and find the plant safety officer. Go talk to her, find out what she's trying to accomplish and how she does it."

Erik's expression brightens slightly and he adds, "And please convey my regards to her. I'll be ready to talk with you again when Dick says he actually wants you around."

With that, he walks out the door.

John looks at me, "What the hell?"

Pulling myself out of my chair, I say, "Don't let it get to you. He says similar things to me. I'm exhausted and I'm going home. I suggest you do the same."

John stands up wordlessly. With the calm expression remaining on his face, he pushes the three-ring binder off the table. It hits the ground with a large thump, all the contents scattering everywhere. Hundreds of pages are now strewn across the floor.

He looks at me with a humorless smile and says, "I will. Go home, that is. I don't know if I'll be in tomorrow—or ever. What's the point, really?"

He then walks out of the room.

I stare at John's binder, not quite believing he discarded it so carelessly. He's been carrying it around for over two years. In front of where he was sitting is a single piece of paper, almost blank with a few lines scribbled on it. Wondering if it's a suicide note or a resignation letter, I sneak a quick peek at what appears to be a poem.

A haiku?

> Here I sit, hands tied
> Room angry, I could save them
> If only they knew

CHAPTER 22

• *Monday, September 29*

The Monday following the audit meeting, John disappeared. There is a betting pool in the NOC speculating whether he suffered a nervous breakdown, was fired, is just hiding, or worse.

I see Wes and some of his engineers, all laughing loudly, presumably at John's expense.

I clear my throat to get Wes' attention. When he walks over, I turn around so that my back is to the NOC, shielding everyone from hearing what I'm telling Wes. "Do me a favor? Don't fan the rumor mill about John. Remember what Steve was trying to impress upon us at the off-site? We need to build a mutually respectful and trusted working relationship with him."

Wes' smile disappears and after a moment, he finally says, "Yeah, I know. I'm just kidding, okay?"

"Good," I say, nodding. "Okay, enough of that. Follow me. I need to talk to you and Patty about the monitoring project." We go to her office, where she's sitting at her desk, typing away in a project management application, full of Gantt charts.

"Got a half hour?" I ask her.

When she nods, we gather around her conference table. I say, "I talked with Erik on Friday before the audit meeting. Here's what I learned."

I tell them how Erik validated that we can release the monitoring project and how important this project is to further elevate Brent. I then try to explain the thought process of how we can determine which projects we can safely release, based on whether they have any dependencies on Brent.

"Wait a second. Bill of resources and routings?" Wes says, suddenly looking very dubious. "Bill, I don't need to remind you that we're not running a factory here. This is IT work. We use our brains to get things done, not our hands. I know Erik has said a couple of smart things here and there, but come on… This sounds like some sort of consultant parlor trick."

"Look, I'm having trouble getting my head around this, too," I say. "But can you really say that the conclusions we're making based on his thinking are wrong? Do you think it's unsafe to release the monitoring project?"

Patty wrinkles her forehead. "We know that IT work can be projects or changes. And in many of the projects, there are many tasks or subprojects that show up over and over again. Like setting up a server. It's recurring work. I guess you could call that a subassembly."

She stands up, walks to the whiteboard, and draws some boxes. "Let's use the example of configuring a server. It involves procurement, installing the OS and applications on it according to some specification, and then getting it racked and stacked. Then we validate that it's been built correctly. Each of these steps are typically done by different people. Maybe each step is like a work center, each with its own machines, methods, men, and measures."

With less certainty, she continues, "But I'm not sure if I know what the machine would be."

I smile as Patty scrawls on the board. She's making some leaps that I haven't been able to make. I don't know where she'll end up, but I think she's on the right track.

"Maybe the machine," I speculate, "is the tools necessary to do the work? The virtualization management consoles, terminal sessions, and maybe the virtual disk space that we attach to it?"

Patty shakes her head. "Maybe. The consoles and terminals sound like they could be the machine. And I think disk space, the applications, license keys, and so forth are all actually inputs or the raw materials needed to create the outputs."

She stares at the whiteboard. At last, she says, "I suspect that until we do a couple of these, we'll just be stumbling in the dark. I'm starting to think that this whole work center notion actually describes IT work pretty well. For this server setup example, we know that it's a work center that gets hit by almost every business and IT project. If we nail this down, we'll actually be able to provide better estimates to Kirsten and all her project managers."

"Give me a break, guys," Wes says. "First, our work is not repetitive. Second, it requires a lot of knowledge, unlike the people who just assemble parts or tighten screws. We hire very smart people with experience. Trust me. We can't standardize our work like manufacturing does."

I consider Wes' point. "Last week, I think I would have agreed with you, Wes. But I watched one of the final assembly work centers on the manufacturing floor for fifteen minutes last week. I was overwhelmed with everything that was going on. Frankly, I could barely keep up with it. Despite trying to make everything repetitive and repeatable, they still had to do an incredible amount of improvisation and problem solving just to hit their daily production goals. They're doing a whole lot more than tightening screws. They're performing heroics every day, using every bit of experience and smarts they have."

I say adamantly, "They really earned my respect. If it weren't for them, we all wouldn't even have jobs. I think we have a lot to learn from plant floor management."

I pause. "Let's start the monitoring project as soon as we can. The sooner we start, the sooner we'll get the benefits. We need to protect each of our resources as if they were all Brents, so let's get this done."

"There's one more thing," Patty says. "I keep thinking about the lanes of work we're trying to create. I'd like to test some of these concepts with the incoming service requests, like account add/change/deletes, password resets, and—you know—laptop replacements."

She looks uncomfortably at my giant laptop, which is in even worse shape than when I first got it three weeks ago. I've had to put even more duct tape on it to keep it from falling apart, due to some further damage I caused when I used my car keys to pry it open. And now, half the paint on the screen lid has flaked off.

"Oh, for crying out loud," Wes groans, looking at it, genuinely embarrassed. "I can't believe we haven't gotten you a replacement. We don't suck *that* much. Patty, I'll find someone for you to dedicate to the laptop and desktop backlog."

"Fantastic," Patty replies. "I have a little experiment in mind that I'd like to try out."

Not wanting to get in the way, I say, "Make it so."

When I get to the office on the following Monday, Patty is waiting for me. "You have a second?" she asks, obviously eager to show me something.

Next thing I know, I'm standing in Patty's Change Coordination Room. I immediately spot on the back wall a new board. On it: index cards arranged in four rows.

The rows are labeled "Move worker office," "Add/change/delete account," "Provision new desktop/laptop," and "Reset password."

Each row has been divided up into three columns, labeled "Ready," "Doing," and "Done."

Interesting. This looks vaguely familiar. "What is this? Another change board?"

Patty breaks out into a grin and says, "It's a kanban board. After our last meeting, I went to MRP-8 myself. I was so curious about this work center notion that I had to see it in action. I managed to find one of the supervisors that I've worked with before, and he spent an hour with me showing how they managed the flow of work."

Patty explains that a kanban board, among many other things, is one of the primary ways our manufacturing plants schedule and pull work through the system. It makes demand and WIP visible, and is used to signal upstream and downstream stations.

"I'm experimenting with putting kanbans around our key resources. Any activities they work on must go through the kanban. Not by e-mail, instant message, telephone, or whatever.

"If it's not on the kanban board, it won't get done," she says. "And more importantly, if it is on the kanban board, it will get done quickly. You'd be amazed at how fast work is getting completed, because we're limiting the work in process. Based on our experiments so far, I think we're going to be able to predict lead times for work and get faster throughput than ever."

That Patty is now sounding a bit like Erik is both unsettling and exciting.

"What I've done," she continues, "is take some of our most frequent service requests, documented exactly what the steps are and what resources can execute them, and timed how long each operation takes. Here's the result."

She hands me a piece of paper proudly.

It's titled, "Laptop replacement queue." On it is a list of everyone who's requested either a new or replacement laptop or desktop along with when they submitted the request and the projected date they'll receive it. They're sorted by the oldest requests first.

I'm apparently fourteenth in line, with my laptop projected to arrive four days from now.

"You actually believe this schedule?" I say, trying to be skeptical. However, it really would be fantastic if we could actually publish this to everyone, and be able to hit those dates.

"We worked on this all weekend long," she replies. "Based on the trials we've done since Friday, we're pretty confident that we understand the time required go from start to finish. We've even figured out how to save a bunch of steps by changing where we're doing disk mirroring. Between you and me, based on the time savings we're generating, I think that we'll beat these dates."

She shakes her head. "You know, I did a quick poll of people we've issued laptops to. It usually takes fifteen turns to finally get them configured correctly. I'm tracking that now, and trying to drive this down to three. We're putting in checklists everywhere, especially when we do handoffs within the team. It's really making a difference. Error rates are way down."

I smile and say, "This is important. Getting executives and workers the tools they need to do their jobs is one of our primary responsibilities. I'm not saying I don't believe you, but let's keep these time estimates to ourselves for now. If you can generate a week's track record of hitting the dates, then let's start publishing this to all the requesters and their managers, okay?"

Patty smiles in return. "I was thinking the same thing. Imagine what this will do to user satisfaction if we could tell them when they make the request how long the queue is, tell them to the day when they'll get it, and actually hit the date, because we're not letting our workers multitask or get interrupted!

"My plant supervisor friend also told me about the Improvement Kata they've adopted. Believe it or not, Erik helped them institute it many years ago. They have continual two-week improvement cycles, each requiring them to implement one small Plan-Do-Check-Act project to keep them marching toward the goal. You don't mind that I've taken the liberty of adopting this practice in our group to keep us moving toward our own goals, right?"

Erik had mentioned this *kata* term and the continual two-week improvement cycles before. Once again, Patty is at least one step ahead of me.

"This is great work, Patty. Really, really well done."

"Thanks," she modestly responds, but she's grinning from ear to ear. "I'm really excited by what I'm learning. For the first time, I'm seeing how we should be managing our work, and even for these simpler service desk tasks, I know it's going to make a big difference."

She points at the change board at the front of the room. "What I'm really looking forward to is to start using these techniques for more complex work. Once we figure out what our most frequently recurring tasks are, we need to create work centers and lanes of work, just like I did for my service requests. Maybe we can even get rid of some of this scheduling, and create kanban boards instead. Our engineers could then take any card from the Ready column, move them to Doing, until they're Done!"

Unfortunately, I can't visualize it. "Keep going. Just make sure you're working with Wes on this, and that he's onboard, okay?"

"Already on it," she replies quickly. "In fact, I have a meeting with him later today to discuss putting a kanban around Brent, to further isolate him from our daily crises. I want to formalize how Brent gets work and increase our ability to standardize what he's working on. It'll give us a way to figure out where all of Brent's work comes from, both on the upstream and downstream sides. And of course, it will give us one more line of defense from people doing drive-bys on Brent."

I give her a thumbs-up, and get ready to leave. "Wait, the change board looks different. Why are the cards different colors?"

She looks at the board and says, "Oh, I haven't told you? We're color-coding the cards to help us get ready for when we lift the project freeze. We've got to have some way to make sure we're working on the most important things. So, the purple cards are the changes supporting one of the top five business projects, otherwise, they're yellow. The green cards are for internal IT improvement projects, and we're experimenting with allocating twenty percent of our cycles just for those, as Erik recommended we do. At a glance, we can confirm that there's the right balance of purple and green cards in work."

She continues, "The pink sticky notes indicate the cards that are blocked somehow, which we're therefore reviewing twice a day. We're also putting all these cards back into our change tracking tool, so we're putting the change IDs on each of the cards, too. It's a bit tedious, but at least now part of the tracking is automated."

"Wow, that's…incredible," I say, with genuine awe.

Later that day, I'm sitting down at another conference table with Wes and Patty to figure out how we're going to turn the project faucet back on slowly enough so we can drink but don't end up drowning.

"As Erik pointed out, we actually have two project queues that we need to sequence: business and internal projects," Patty says, pointing to the thin stapled set of papers in front of us. "Let's do the business projects first, because they're easier. We have the top five most important projects identified, as ranked by all the project sponsors. Four of these will require some work from Brent. When the freeze lifts, we propose that we only release these five projects."

"That was easy," Wes laughs. "I can't believe how much arguing, posturing, horse-trading, and backstabbing went on to get the top five projects identified. It was worse than Chicago politics!"

He's right. But in the end, we got our prioritized list.

"Now to the hard part. We're still struggling on how to prioritize our own seventy-three internal projects," she says, her expression turning glum. "There's still way too many. We've spent weeks with all the team leads trying to establish some sort of relative importance level, but that's all we've done. Argue."

She flips to the second page. "The projects seem to fall into the following categories: replacing fragile infrastructure, vendor upgrades, or supporting some internal business requirement. The rest are a hodge-podge of audit and security work, data center upgrade work, and so forth."

I look at the second list, scratching my head. Patty is right. How does one objectively decide whether "consolidating and upgrading e-mail server" is more or less important than "upgrading thirty-five instances of sql databases"?

I run my fingers down the page, trying to see if anything jumps out at me. It's the same list I saw during my first week on the job, and they still all look important.

Realizing that Wes and Patty have spent almost a week with this list, I try to elevate my thinking. There's got to be some simple way to prioritize this list that doesn't look like moving a bunch of boxes around.

Suddenly, I remember how Erik described the importance of preventive work, such as the monitoring project. I say, "I don't care how important everyone *thinks* their project is. We need to know whether it increases our capacity at our constraint, which is *still* Brent. Unless the project reduces his workload or enables someone else to take it over, maybe we shouldn't even be doing it. On the other hand, if a project doesn't even require Brent, there's no reason we shouldn't just do it."

I say assertively, "Give me three lists. One that requires Brent work, one that increases Brent's throughput, and the last one is everything else. Identify the top projects on each list. Don't spend too much time ordering them—I don't want us spending days arguing. The most important list is the second one. We need to keep Brent's capacity up by reducing the amount of unplanned work that hits him."

"That sounds familiar," Patty says. She digs up the list of fragile services that we created for the change management process. "We should make sure we have a project to replace or stabilize each one of these. And maybe we suspend indefinitely any infrastructure refresh project for anything that's not fragile."

"Now hang on a minute," Wes says. "Bill, you said it yourself. Preventive work is important, but it always gets deferred. We've been trying to do some of these projects for years! This is our chance to get caught up."

Patty says quickly, "Didn't you hear what Erik told Bill? Improving something anywhere not at the constraint is an illusion. You know, no offense, but you sort of sound like John right now."

Despite my best attempts, I still laugh.

Wes turns red for a moment, and then laughs loudly. "Ouch. Okay, you got me. But I'm just trying to do the right thing."

"Doh!" he says, interrupting himself. "I did it again."

We all laugh. It makes me wonder how John is doing. To the best of my knowledge, no one has seen him all day.

While Wes and Patty are scribbling notes, I scan the list of internal projects again. "Hey, why is there a project for upgrading the BART database even though it's going to be decommissioned next year?"

Patty peers down at her list and then looks embarrassed. "Oh, jeez. I didn't see that because we never reconciled the business and IT projects with each other. We're going to have to scrub the lists one more time to find dependencies like this. I'm sure there are others."

Patty thinks for a moment, "It's strange. Even though we have so much data on projects, changes, and tickets, we've never organized and linked them all together this way before.

"Here's another thing we can learn from manufacturing, I think," she continues. "We're doing what Manufacturing Production Control Departments do. They're the people that schedule and oversee all of production to ensure they can meet customer demand. When they accept an order, they confirm there's enough capacity and necessary inputs at each required work center, expediting work when necessary. They work with the sales manager and plant manager to build a production schedule so they can deliver on all their commitments."

Again, Patty is way ahead of me. This answers one of the first questions that Erik tasked me with before I quit. I make a note for us to visit MRP-8 to see their production control processes.

I get a creeping suspicion that "managing the IT Operations production schedule" should be somewhere in my job description.

Two days later, I'm surprised to see a new laptop in my office. My old laptop has been disconnected and moved to the side.

I look at my clipboard, flipping back to the laptop/desktop replacement schedule that Patty gave me earlier this week.

Holy crap.

Patty had promised laptop delivery for Friday, and I'm receiving it two days early.

I log on to make sure it's been configured properly. All the applications seem to be there, all my data have been transferred, e-mail is working, the network drives show up like before, and I can install new applications.

I feel tears of gratitude welling up when I see how fast my new laptop is. Grabbing Patty's schedule, I go next door. "I love the new laptop. Two days ahead of schedule, even. Everyone ahead of me got their systems, too, right?"

Patty grins. "Yep. Every single one of them. A couple of the early ones we delivered had a few configuration errors or were missing something. We've corrected it in the work instructions, and we seem to be batting one hundred percent delivering correct systems for the past two days."

"Great work, Patty!" I say, excitedly. "Go ahead and start publishing the schedule. I want to start showing this off!"

CHAPTER 23

• *Tuesday, October 7*

As I drive into work the following Tuesday morning, I get an urgent phone call from Kirsten. Apparently, Brent is now almost a week late delivering on another Phoenix task—allegedly something that Brent said would only take an hour to do. Once again, the entire Phoenix testing schedule is in jeopardy.

On top of that, several other of my group's critical tasks are late, putting even more pressure on the deadline. This is genuinely dispiriting to hear. I thought all our recent breakthroughs would solve these due-date performance issues.

How can we unfreeze more work if we can't even keep up now?

I leave Patty a voicemail. To my surprise, it takes her three hours to call me back. She tells me that something is going terribly wrong with our scheduling estimates and that we need to meet right away.

Once again, I'm in a conference room, with Patty at the whiteboard, and Wes scrutinizing the printouts she's taped up.

"Here's what I've learned so far," Patty says, pointing at one of the sheets of paper. "The task that Kirsten called about is delivering a test environment to QA. As she said, Brent estimated that it would take only forty-five minutes."

"Sounds about right," Wes says. "You just need to create a new virtualized server and then install the OS and a couple of packages on it. He probably even doubled the time estimate to be safe."

"That's what I thought, too," Patty said, but she's shaking her head. "Except it's not just one task. What Brent signed up for is more like a small project—there's over twenty steps involving at least six different teams! You need the OS and all the software packages, license keys, dedicated IP address, special user accounts set up, mount points configured, and then you need the IP addresses to be added to an ACL list on some file server. In this particular case, the requirements say that we need a physical server, so we also need a router port, cabling, and a server rack where we have enough space."

"Oh…," Wes says, sounding exasperated, reading what Patty is pointing at. He mumbles, "Physical servers are such a pain in the ass."

"You're missing the point. This would still be happening, even if it were virtualized," Patty says. "First, Brent's 'task' turns out to be considerably more than just a task. Second, we're finding that it's multiple tasks spanning multiple people, each of whom have their own urgent work to do. We're losing days at each handoff. At this rate, without some dramatic intervention, it'll be weeks before QA gets what they need."

"At least we don't need a firewall change," Wes says, snidely. "Last time we needed one of those, it took John's group almost a month. Four weeks for a thirty-second change!"

I nod, knowing exactly what Wes is referring to. The lead time for firewall changes has become legendary.

Wait. Didn't Erik mention something like this? For a firewall change, even though the work only required thirty seconds of touch time, it still took four weeks of clock time.

That's just a microcosm of what's happening with Brent. But what's happening to us right now is much, much worse, because there are handoffs.

With a groan, I put my head on the conference table.

"You okay?" Patty asks.

"Give me a second," I say. I walk up to the whiteboard and struggle to draw a graph with one of the markers. After a couple of tries, I end up with a graph that looks like this:

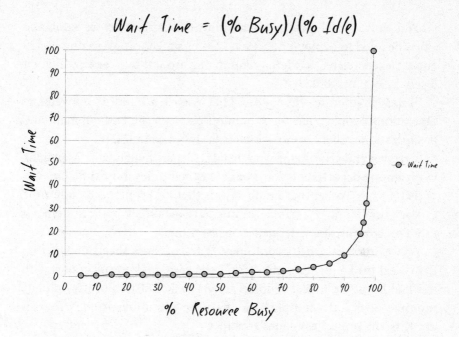

$$\text{Wait Time} = (\% \text{ Busy})/(\% \text{ Idle})$$

I tell them what Erik told me at MRP-8, about how wait times depend upon resource utilization. "The wait time is the 'percentage of time busy' divided by the 'percentage of time idle.' In other words, if a resource is fifty percent busy, then it's fifty percent idle. The wait time is fifty percent divided by fifty percent, so one unit of time. Let's call it one hour. So, on average, our task would wait in the queue for one hour before it gets worked.

"On the other hand, if a resource is ninety percent busy, the wait time is 'ninety percent divided by ten percent', or nine hours. In other words, our task would wait in queue nine times longer than if the resource were fifty percent idle."

I conclude, "So, for the Phoenix task, assuming we have seven hand-offs, and that each of those resources is busy ninety percent of the time, the tasks would spend in queue a total of nine hours times the seven steps…"

"What? Sixty-three hours, just in queue time?" Wes says, incredulously. "That's impossible!"

Patty says with a smirk, "Oh, of course. Because it's only thirty seconds of typing, right?"

"Oh, shit," Wes says, staring at the graph.

Suddenly, I recall my conversation with Wes right before Sarah and Chris decided to deploy Phoenix at Kirsten's meeting. Wes complained about tickets related to Phoenix bouncing around for weeks, which delayed the deployment.

It was happening then, too. That wasn't a handoff between IT Operations people. That was a handoff between the Development and IT Operations organization, which is far more complex.

Creating and prioritizing work inside a department is hard. Managing work among departments must be at least ten times more difficult.

Patty says, "What that graph says is that everyone needs idle time, or slack time. If no one has slack time, WIP gets stuck in the system. Or more specifically, stuck in queues, just waiting."

As we digest this, Patty continues. "Each of those sheets of paper on the board is like this Phoenix 'task,'" she says, making air quotes with her hands. "It looks like a single person task, but it's not. It's actually multiple steps with multiple handoffs among multiple people. No wonder Kirsten's project estimates are off.

"We need to correct this on Kirsten's schedule and her work breakdown structure, or WBS. Based on what I've seen, fully one-third of our commitments to Kirsten fall into this category."

"Just great," Wes says. "It's like *Gilligan's Island*. We keep sending people off on three-hour tours, and months later, we wonder why none of them come back."

Patty says, "I wonder if we could create a kanban lane for each of these 'tasks?'"

"Yes, that's it," I say. "Erik was right. You've just found a big pile of recurring work! If we can document and standardize this recurring work, and gain some mastery over it, just like you did with laptop replacement, I'm sure we can improve flow!"

I add, "You know, if we can standardize all our recurring deployment work, we'll finally be able to enforce uniformity of our production configurations. That would be our infrastructure snowflake problem—you know—no two alike. How Brent turned into Brent is that we allowed him to build infrastructure only he can understand. We can't let that happen again."

"Good point," Wes grunts. "You know, it's odd. So many of these problems we've been facing are caused by decisions we made. We have met the enemy. And he is us."

Patty says, "You know, deployments are like final assembly in a manufacturing plant. Every flow of work goes through it, and you can't ship the product without it. Suddenly, I know exactly what the kanban should look like."

Over the next forty-five minutes, we create our plan. Patty is going to work with Wes' team to assemble the top twenty most frequently recurring tasks.

She will also figure out how to better manage and control tasks when they are queued. Patty proposes a new role, a combination of a project manager and expediter. Instead of day-by-day oversight, they would provide minute-by-minute control. She says, "We need fast and effective handoffs of any completed work to the next work center. If necessary, this person will wait at the work center until the work is completed and carry to the next work center. We'll never let critical work get lost in a pile of tickets again."

"What? Someone assigned to carry around tasks from person to person, like a waiter?" Wes asks in disbelief.

"At MRP-8, they have a 'water spider' role that does exactly that," she counters. "Almost all of this latest Phoenix delay was due to tasks waiting in queues or handoffs. This will make sure it doesn't happen again.

"Eventually," she adds, "I'll want to move all the kanbans, so that we don't need a person acting as the signaling mechanism for work handoffs. Don't worry. I'll have it figured out in a couple of days."

Wes and I don't dare doubt her.

CHAPTER 24

• *Saturday, October 11*

The following Saturday was relatively peaceful. In fact, it's the most relaxing weekend my family has had since I took my new job. With Halloween a few weeks away, Paige insisted that we take the whole family out to the pumpkin patch.

It was a chilly Saturday morning, so we were exhausted just bundling up the kids and getting them in the car. When we arrived at the nearby farm, Paige and I laughed uncontrollably at Parker, who looked like a giant, angry sausage stuffed into his blue parka. She couldn't resist taking pictures while Grant orbited us in excitement, taking pictures with his own camera.

Afterward, we went to a local microbrewery, enjoying lunch on the patio in the warm afternoon sun.

"I'm so glad we could do this," Paige says. "It's really nice. You seem less stressed lately. I can really tell things are getting better."

She's right. It felt like we had turned a corner at work somehow. Just like how I wasn't wasting as much time fighting my ancient laptop, it seemed like my team was spending more and more of our time doing productive work and less and less firefighting.

Although I know getting a new laptop has absolutely nothing to do with our organizational performance, getting rid of that old clunker was like getting rid of a thousand-pound anchor that someone had tied around my neck while I was swimming across the ocean.

We're still grappling with gradually melting the project freeze. I'm guessing that we'll probably be able to unfreeze twenty-five percent of all the projects, along with a bunch of other new projects designed to further elevate Brent.

There were still so many uncertainties. But unlike before, our challenges feel within our ability to understand and conquer. Our goals finally seem achievable. I no longer feel like I am always on my heels, with more and more people piling on, trying to push me over.

With the business agreeing, with the exception of Sarah, on what the priorities are, my job actually seems fair. It feels like we have the initiative and are attacking the problem, instead of the other way around.

I like it.

I look up to see Paige smiling back at me and then yell out in panic as I see Parker knocking over her glass of beer.

The rest of the afternoon passes too quickly, but it's one of the best days I've had all year.

Later that evening, Paige is curled up with me on the couch. We're watching the Clint Eastwood movie *Pale Rider*. The kids have gone to sleep, and this is the first time we've actually watched a movie together in months.

I laugh uncontrollably watching the main character, "the Preacher" played by Eastwood, methodically pick off the gang of nine evil deputies. Paige looks at me with amused disapproval.

"What exactly is so funny about this?" she asks.

This makes me laugh harder. When another deputy gets shot in the background, I say, "Look at that! You know what's going to happen, but the marshal just stands there in the middle of the street, watching the carnage! Look at the way the wind rustles through his coat! And his gun isn't even drawn! I love it!"

"I'll never understand you," Paige says, shaking her head with a smile.

Just then, my cell phone rings. I instinctively reach for it.

Holy crap. It's John. No one has seen or heard from him since that audit meeting, over two weeks ago. We're pretty sure he hasn't been fired, but no one knows more than that. I've been meaning to check the local hospitals to make sure he's not convalescing alone somewhere.

As much as I want to talk with him, I don't want to leave Paige and the movie. I look at the clock, and see that there's probably only fifteen more minutes until the end. Not wanting to miss the final gunfight, I mute the phone. I'll call him back when the movie is over.

A couple of seconds later, my phone rings again, and I again hit the mute button.

My phone rings again. For the third time, I mute the phone, but quickly send him a text message: *Grt hearing from u. Can't talk right now. Will call u in 20m.*

Unbelievably, my phone buzzes again, so I turn the ringer off, putting my phone underneath some cushions on the couch.

Paige asks, "Who keeps calling?"

When I say, "John," she rolls her eyes, and we watch the remaining ten minutes of the movie.

"I can't believe I haven't seen that movie until tonight!" I say, giving Paige a squeeze. "That was such a great idea, darling!"

"It's been a great day. It's so nice having a normal life again," she says, returning my hug, and then with a smile, she gets up, taking the empty beer bottles with her.

I agree. I pick up my phone, my heart skipping a beat when I see "15 missed calls."

Suddenly afraid that I may have missed something truly disastrous, I quickly look to see who called. Every call was from John. I call him immediately.

"Billy, so good to hear your voice again—my friend—my dear, dear old—dear ol' friend," he slurs. Good Lord. He's completely drunk.

"Sorry I couldn't return your calls right away. I was out with Paige," I say, feeling guilty at my slight mistruth.

"No problem. Look, I just wanted to see you one—one lasht time before I left—be leaving," he says.

"Leaving? What do you mean 'leaving'? Where are you going?" I say with alarm, wondering how long he's been drinking. Maybe I should have called back sooner. I suddenly visualize him on the other end of the phone with an open bottle of sleeping pills in his hand, already half-empty.

I hear him laugh, maybe a bit hysterically. "Don't worry, Billy. I'm not going to kill myself. Haven't had enough to drink—yet. Har-har! I just wanted to see you before I left town tonight. Let me buy you one last drink."

"Uh, can't this wait until tomorrow? It's almost midnight," I say, slightly relieved.

He tells me that he'll be long gone by tomorrow and convinces me to join him at the Hammerhead Saloon downtown.

When I pull into the parking lot, I immediately spot John's Volvo station wagon. Hitched behind his car is a U-Haul trailer, and there's a pile of empty beer cans right outside the driver's side door.

I find him in a booth at the back of the crowded bar, and it's obvious he's been here all day. He doesn't seem to have bathed or changed his clothes since I last saw him. His hair is greasy and wildly askew as if he just woke up, his face is covered in stubble, and there are food stains on his shirt. His keys and wallet have been tossed carelessly next to the salt and pepper shakers.

John urgently waves over a waitress, taking a moment to rehearse his words, but still slurring as he says, "I'd like two double scotches, neat, for me and my friend here. And those yummy nachos... Please."

She looks over at me questioningly, obviously having already served him plenty. I nod, but say quietly, "Let's start with two cups of coffee, please. I'll take care of him." As I say it, I reach over and take his keys off the table.

For a moment, she looks dubious but gives me a small smile and walks away.

"Dude, you look like shit," I say candidly.

"Thanks, pal. So do you," he replies, before bursting out laughing.

"Nice. Where the hell have you been? Everyone has been looking for you," I say.

"I've been at home," he says, grabbing some popcorn from our table. "I've been mostly reading and watching TV. Whoa, there is some crazy shit on TV these days. Crazy! But then I started thinking it's time for me to move on, so I spent most of today packing. I just wanted to ask you one little question before I left."

"You mentioned that on the phone," I say, as the waitress arrives with two cups of coffee and the nachos. John looks with confusion at the mugs on the table, so I say, "Don't worry. Our drinks are on the way."

When I get him to take a sip of coffee, he asks, "Just tell me straight. Is it really true that I haven't done anything of value for you? In all the three years that we've worked together, I've never, ever been helpful?"

I take a deep breath, trying to decide what to tell him. A friend told me years ago, "To tell the truth is an act of love. To withhold the truth is an act of hate. Or worse, apathy."

I had laughed at those words at the time, but over the years, I've realized that having people give you honest feedback is a rare gift. Looking across at John, even though he looks like a completely broken man, I wonder whether the right thing to do is to just let him off easy and tell him what he wants to hear.

Finally, I say, "Look, John. You're a good guy, and I know your heart is in the right place, but up until you helped hide us from the PCI auditors during the Phoenix meltdown, I would have said no. I know that's not what you want to hear, but…I wanted to make sure that I wasn't feeding you a line of bullshit."

Amazingly, John looks even more crestfallen than before. "Where's that goddamned scotch?" he yells out. Turning back to look at me, he says, "Are you serious? After three whole goddamned years of working together, you're telling me that I haven't helped you, not even in the slightest bit?"

"Well, for most of those years, I was in charge of the midrange group, which you didn't get too involved with," I explain calmly. "We found our own security guidance on the web. When we did interact, you just tried to dump a bunch of work on me. Look, I care about security, and we always look for risks to our systems and data, but we're always up to our eyeballs in urgent work, trying to keep our heads above water. And in my new role, I'm just trying to help the company survive."

John says, "But don't you see, that's what I'm trying to do, too! I'm just trying to help you and the business survive!"

I reply, "I know. But, in my world, I'm responsible for keeping all our services up and running, and deploying new services like Phoenix. Security had to take a backseat. Trust me, I'm well aware of the risks of bad security, and I know it would be a career-ending move to have a large-scale security breach on my watch."

I shrug my shoulders. "I'm making the best possible decisions given my knowledge of the risks. I just don't think that all the stuff you wanted me to do would have helped the business as much as all the other things on my plate.

"Come on," I continue, "Does it bother you deep down that the business got through the SOX-404 audit without you? Does that make you question the importance and validity of your recommendations?"

John just stares back at me.

As if on cue, our waitress arrives with the two scotches. John picks his up, and finishes it in one gulp. "Another round, please."

When she looks at me, I shake my head and mouth the words, "Check, please? And call a cab?"

She nods and disappears. I take a sip of my scotch and look back at John. His head is now lolling backward and he's muttering something. By now, he's completely unintelligible.

I feel sorry for him.

I take his wallet off the table.

"Hey!" he says.

"Our waitress is tipping out, and I've got to pay her, but, I forgot my wallet at home," I say.

He laughs at me, looking at me blearily. "No problem, old pal. I'll get this one. I always get them, don't I?"

"Thanks," I say, and grab his driver's license. I wave over the waitress and point to his home address.

Returning John's wallet, I pull out my own and pay.

I help John up and pour him into the cab, making sure his wallet and keys are back in his pocket. Not wanting John to deal with the cabbie, I pay the cabbie, too.

Watching him leave, and then looking at his station wagon and U-Haul full of only a fraction of his worldly belongings, I just shake my head. I head back to my car, wondering when I'm going to see him next.

The next day, I call John a couple of times on his cell phone, but he never answers. I finally leave him a voicemail telling him that I hoped he got home okay, where his car was, and to give me a ring if he needs anything.

The rumor mill is abuzz. There's talk that he was hospitalized, arrested, abducted by aliens, or locked up in a mental institution.

I'm not sure how these rumors were starting, as I didn't tell anyone about my late-night meeting with him, nor was I ever going to.

I'm just finishing up putting Grant to bed on Monday night when I get a text message from John. I quickly read it: *Thanks for the lift home the other day. Been thinking. I told Dick that u'll be joining our 8AM mtg tomorrow. Should be interesting.*

What meeting with Dick?

I stare at my phone. On the one hand, John is alive and seems able to work. That's good.

On the other hand, John is now talking about meeting with Dick, the second most powerful executive in the company, tomorrow morning, potentially in some mentally unbalanced state and has already broadcast that I'm his coconspirator.

That's not so good. I quickly tap out my reply to him: *Good hearing from u. Hope you're doing ok? What is Dick meeting about? May not be able to make it.*

He responds immediately: *I've been arrogant. Realized yest that I don't actually know much about Dick. Must change that. Together.*

Worried that John may be completely off his rocker, I immediately call him. He answers on the first ring, sounding oddly cheery. I hear him say, "Good evening, Bill. Thanks again for Saturday night. What's up?"

"What exactly are you up to, John?" I say. "What's this meeting tomorrow with Dick about, and why are you dragging me into it?"

He replies, "I spent most of yesterday in bed, since I could barely get myself to the bathroom and back. My head felt like it was a lemon smashed by a brick. What drinks were you buying me that night?"

He doesn't wait for me to answer before continuing, "I kept thinking about our last conversation at the bar. I realized that if I haven't done anything useful for *you*, who I should have the *most* in common with, then it stands to reason that I haven't been useful to almost everyone else, who I have *nothing* in common with.

"That's got to change," he says adamantly.

I bite my tongue, wanting to hear John out before I recommend that he cancel tomorrow's meeting.

He continues, "I kept thinking about what Erik said, that he'd be ready to talk to me when Dick says he wants me around."

"Uh, I don't think a quick thirty-minute 'getting to know you' meeting is going to get you there," I say, seriously skeptical.

He responds with complete calm, "Wouldn't you agree, like so many things in life, that we must always start by at least gaining an understanding of the person we're dealing with? What could go wrong? I just want to learn more about his job."

In my head, I immediately envision John asking or saying something stupid, completely pissing Dick off, and Dick firing him on the spot, and then firing me, too, just to eliminate the contagion.

Yet I find myself saying, "Okay, I'll be there."

CHAPTER 25

• *Tuesday, October 14*

The next morning at 7:50 a.m., I'm heading toward Dick's office. As I round the corner, I see John already chatting amiably with Dick's assistant. My jaw drops. John's physical appearance has completely changed.

He's obviously showered and cleaned up. He's also shaved his head and appears to have lost fifteen pounds. He's wearing what I can only describe as a European styled shirt and a vest. Unlike the slightly baggy shirts he usually wears, the pink shirt he's wearing fits tightly on him. Combined with the vest, he looks like a…fashion model? London clubber? Las Vegas card dealer?

With the shaved head, his calm friendly smile and perfect posture, he looks like some sort of enlightened monk.

Most significantly, I notice that his three-ring binder is nowhere to be seen. Instead, he's carrying only a pristine black and white lab notebook and a pen.

"Good morning, Bill," John says with beatific calm.

"Hi," I finally say. "Uh, you're looking better than the last time I saw you."

He just smiles, and then says something quietly to Dick's assistant that makes her clap her hands over mouth and laugh loudly. She then gets up, walks over to Dick's door and gestures both of us to follow her, saying, "Let's see if we can start your meeting a little early. It'll give you more time with him."

I'm walking into Dick's office, trailing behind John.

"Nice haircut," Dick says to John with a smile, pointing at his own bald head. Then in a business-like tone, he says, "So what can I do for you? I have a commitment at 8:30, so let's not waste time."

John opens his notebook to the first page, which is completely blank. "Thanks for taking the time to meet with us on such short notice. I promise you that we won't waste your time. And to make sure I don't have any incorrect or preconceived notions, could you start by telling us what exactly you do here at Parts Unlimited? What is your exact role?"

My eyes widen in horror at John's question. This is what gets asked on Bring Your Kid To Work Day but not by company executives.

I quickly look over to gauge Dick's reaction. He looks surprised for a moment, but then blandly replies, "Interesting question."

He pauses briefly and then seems to just play along. "I started here at Parts Unlimited fifteen years ago as CFO, which, back then, was defined in a pretty traditional way. I was primarily responsible for managing the financial risks of the organization and leading the financial planning and operations processes. Even back then, we had a huge number of regulatory compliance issues, which I also owned.

"Shortly after Steve became CEO, he told me that we needed a senior executive to own planning and operations across the entire organization and then gave those responsibilities to me. To help ensure that the company achieves our goals, I set up the objectives and measurements program for the entire management team. I wanted to keep all our managers accountable, ensure that they have the skills necessary to succeed, and help make sure that complex initiatives always have the right stakeholders involved and so forth."

John looks up from furiously taking notes on the first page in his new notebook. "I've heard many people call you the 'de facto COO' around here, and that you're basically Steve's right-hand man."

Dick considers his comments for a moment, before saying, "My official title doesn't have 'operations' anywhere in it, but it's the part of my job that I love most. When a company is as big as we are, with so many business processes, so many managers and workers, almost everything is complex. As smart as Steve is, even he needs help making sure the company strategy and goals are realistic and making an objective assessment of what we're actually capable of."

With a very small smile, he adds, "Want to hear something funny? People say that I'm more approachable than Steve! Steve's incredibly charismatic, and let's face it, I'm an asshole. But when people have concerns, they don't want to have their minds changed. They want someone to listen to them and help make sure Steve gets the message."

I find myself leaning forward. I'm surprised to hear Dick giving John, and therefore me, such candid and informative answers.

"What differentiates a good day from a bad day for you?" John continues.

Momentarily taken aback, Dick laughs loudly. "I'll tell you what a good day feels like. It feels like the end of the year when we're beating the pants off the competition—when we haven't closed the books yet, but everyone knows that it's going to be a monster quarter. All the sales people would have hit quota, and the ones on top would have hit their accelerators. A good day feels like my staff panicking about the size of the commission checks we're going to be writing them.

"I'm not worried, because those big commission checks would mean the company is making money," he says, smiling even more broadly. "Steve would be excited to announce to Wall Street and the analysts how well the company is performing—all made possible because we had a winning strategy, and also because we had the right plan and the ability to operate and execute. It means that we got all the parts of this organization to click as a team and win.

"*That's* a fun day for me. We can plan and plan until the cows come home, but until we execute and achieve the goals, it's academic," he says. Then his smile disappears. "Of course, we haven't had a day like that in over four years…

"A bad day is like the one we had two weeks ago," he says, now looking frustrated and even angry. "We can't close the quarter because of some IT failure, we can't seem to execute on our most critical project to close the gap with the competition, we keep losing customers, the auditors are making noises about some restatement project, and the board of directors is debating whether to fire all of us because we're such screwups."

Dick shakes his head, with a wan, tired smile, "In those moments, you wonder whether the problem is the economy, our strategy, our management team, you IT guys, or, quite frankly, maybe the entire problem is me. Those are the days I just want to retire."

John looks down at his notes and then asks, "What are your goals, objectives, and measurements for this year?"

Dick gets up from the sitting area to walk to his desk, saying, "Here, I'll show you."

He picks up a thin, black three-ring binder that was open on his desk, sits back down across from us, and shows us the open binder. "Here are two slides I look at every day."

CFO GOALS
Health of company
Revenue
Market share
Average order size
Profitability
Return on assets
Health of Finance
Order to cash cycle
Accounts receivable
Accurate and timely financial reporting
Borrowing costs

"These are the company goals and the objectives I've set for finance," he explains. "I've learned that while the finance goals are important, they're not the most important. Finance can hit all our objectives, and the company still can fail. After all, the best accounts receivables team on the planet can't save us if we're in the wrong market with the wrong product strategy with an R&D team that can't deliver."

Startled, I realize he's talking about Erik's First Way. He's talking about systems thinking, always confirming that the entire organization achieves its goal, not just one part of it.

As I'm pondering this, Dick then points to the second slide, saying, "So that's what's on the second slide, which shows what I believe are the more important company goals. I look at this slide every day."

Are we competitive?

Understanding customer needs and wants: Do we know what to build?

Product portfolio: Do we have the right products?

R&D effectiveness: Can we build it effectively?

Time to market: Can we ship it soon enough to matter?

Sales pipeline: Can we convert products to interested prospects?

Are we effective?

Customer on-time delivery: Are customers getting what we promised them?

Customer retention: Are we gaining or losing customers?

Sales forecast accuracy: Can we factor this into our sales planning process?

John and I lean forward to study the slide. Usually company managers like me only see our departmental objectives. This slide shows the bigger picture.

As I'm thinking, John points at the slide and asks, "Which of these measurements are most at risk?"

Dick laughs humorlessly. "All of them! From a product portfolio perspective, the competition is killing us and taking market share away from us each day. We're $20 million and years into Project Phoenix, and we're still not competitive in the market yet. On the retailing and manufacturing side of the business, customer satisfaction is dropping, and we're losing customers, despite Sales' promise that we can win them back somehow."

John underlines some of his notes. "Can we have a copy of this? Bill and I would like to study this further and make sure our teams understand this, so we can ensure that everything we do helps advance these goals."

Dick thinks for a moment. "Sure. Can't hurt, I suppose. I'll have my assistant give you both a copy on your way out."

"One more thing," John says. "For each of these initiatives and measurements, who are the managers held responsible and accountable?"

Dick looks at John appraisingly, as do I. I've never seen this side of John before, either.

Dick says, "My assistant will get you the spreadsheet with those names on it, as well."

John thanks him and then looks at his watch. "We're almost out of time. This has been really terrific. Thank you for taking the time to tell us about your daily life. Is there anything that either of us can do for you?"

"Sure," he replies. "Stay focused and get Phoenix working. Without it, we are stuck in the mud."

I frown. I look at the second slide again. I feel like Phoenix is not what Dick should be asking me to focus on.

Unable to articulate why, I merely say, "Yes, sir. We'll surely have some good news to share by the end of the month." I'm not entirely sure what that good news will be, but I've learned that when dealing with senior officers, there's a time and a place for telling bad news. This is neither of them.

"Good," he says, giving us a tight-lipped smile.

We exchange parting pleasantries and head out of his office.

As the elevator doors open, John says to me, "You know, I think there's something very similar about us dodging the SOX-404 audit bullet and what's on Dick's second slide," he says. "I can't quite put my finger on it, but I think there's something here that we need to understand better."

"You're right," I say. "I don't think Dick realizes how much his measurements depend on IT. He asked me about Phoenix, but he should have asked me about all the objectives."

We both step into the elevator. I continue, "Are you available later today to meet? Let's see if we can connect all these dots. I suspect that we're sitting on the missing link that might explain both why the company keeps missing its goals as well as why IT keeps being undervalued."

"Absolutely," he says excitedly.

I can barely contain my sense of excitement. John's crazy meeting with Dick seems to have revealed something genuinely important.

I believe with utter certainty that whatever we're trying to figure out is critical to the First Way. He talked about the need to understand the true business context that IT resides in.

I'm pretty sure no one has linked Dick's top measurements to the prerequisite IT objectives.

No wonder Dick just has a vague sense that IT is screwing up—it's a dull, throbbing ache that he can't localize. Our next step is obvious: We must make those pains very specific and visible to convince Dick that IT is capable of not just screwing up less often but helping all of the business win.

This is too important and urgent to struggle blindly in the dark, and I need to call Erik for advice. Standing in the lobby of Building 2, I speed-dial him.

"Yeah?" I hear him answer.

I say, "Good morning, Erik. I've just had a remarkable meeting with Dick. Do you have some time to help me think this through?"

When he grunts, "Yes," I describe to him the meeting and how it came about and my certainty that it has uncovered something critical.

"Well, good for Jimmy. Or maybe I should call him 'John.' He finally got his head far enough out of his ass to begin to see," I hear Erik say as he laughs, not unkindly. "As part of the First Way, you must gain a true understanding of the business system that IT operates in. W. Edwards Deming called this 'appreciation for the system.' When it comes to IT, you face two difficulties: On the one hand, in Dick's second slide, you now see that there are organizational commitments that IT is responsible for helping uphold and protect that no one has verbalized precisely yet. On the other hand, John has discovered that some IT controls he holds near and dear aren't needed, because other parts of the organization are adequately mitigating those risks.

"This is all about scoping what really matters inside of IT. And like when Mr. Sphere told everyone in *Flatland*, you must leave the realm of IT to discover where the business relies on IT to achieve its goals." I hear him continue, "Your mission is twofold: You must find where you've under-scoped IT—where certain portions of the processes and technology you manage actively jeopardizes the achievement of business goals—as codified by Dick's measurements. And secondly, John must find where he's over-scoped IT, such as all those SOX-404 IT controls that weren't necessary to detect material errors in the financial statements.

"You may think that we're mixing apples and oranges, but I assure you that we are not," he continues. "Some of the wisest auditors say that there are only three internal control objectives: to gain assurance for reliability of financial reporting, compliance with laws and regulations, and efficiency and effectiveness of operations. That's it. What you and John are talking about are just different slides of what is called the 'coso Cube.'"

I force myself to keep listening, furiously taking notes so I can Google these terms later.

I hear him continue, "Here's what you and John need to do: Go talk to the business process owners for the objectives on Dick's second slide. Find out what their exact roles are, what business processes underpin their goals, and then get from them the top list of things that jeopardize those goals.

"You must understand the value chains required to achieve each of Dick's goals, including the ones that aren't so visible, like those in IT. For instance, if you were a cross-country freight shipping company that delivers packages using a fleet of one hundred trucks, one of your corporate goals would be customer satisfaction and on-time delivery."

I hear him continue, "Everybody knows that one factor jeopardizing on-time delivery is vehicle breakdowns. A key causal factor for vehicle breakdowns is failure to change the oil. So, to mitigate that risk, you'd create an SLA for vehicle operations to change the oil every five thousand miles."

Obviously enjoying himself, he keeps explaining, "Our organizational key performance indicator (KPI) is on-time delivery. So to achieve it, you would create a new forward-looking KPI of, say, the percentage of vehicles that have had their required oil changes performed.

"After all, if only fifty percent of our vehicles are complying with the required maintenance policies, it's a good bet that in the near future, our on-time delivery KPIs are going to take a dive, when trucks start getting stranded on the side of the road, along with all the packages they're carrying.

"People think that just because IT doesn't use motor oil and carry physical packages that it doesn't need preventive maintenance," Erik says, chuckling to himself. "That somehow, because the work and the cargo that IT carries are invisible, you just need to sprinkle more magic dust on the computers to get them running again.

"Metaphors like oil changes help people make that connection. Preventive oil changes and vehicle maintenance policies are like preventive vendor patches and change management policies. By showing how

IT risks jeopardize business performance measures, you can start making better business decisions.

"Okay, one last thing before I go," he says. "Make sure John fulfills his mission. He must talk with the finance side of the SOX-404 audit team. He must learn exactly how the business managed to dodge the last audit bullet and what the actual control environment looks like and where reliance is really placed. And he must then explain it to you.

"You'll be ready for your meeting with Dick when you've built out the value chains, linking his objectives to how IT jeopardizes it. Assembling concrete examples of how IT issues have jeopardized those goals in the past. Make sure you're prepared."

And with that, he says, "In fact, feel free to invite me to that meeting. I want to see Dick's face when you present what you learn," and he hangs up the phone.

CHAPTER 26

• *Friday, October 17*

When Patty enters the conference room, she gasps loudly when she sees John's transformed appearance. "Oh my God, John. You look fantastic!"

Surprisingly, when Wes arrives, he doesn't seem to notice anything different.

When everyone is here, I quickly share what I had learned from Erik. We decide that Patty and I will start the business process-owner interviews for "understanding customer needs and wants," "product portfolio," "time to market," and "sales pipeline," while John will research the business SOX-404 control environment, as directed by Erik.

It's Friday and we're scheduled to interview Ron Johnson, the VP of Manufacturing Sales. I worked with him years ago as part of the acquisition integration project and am surprised he's in town. He's usually out and about, traveling the world, helping to negotiate deals and save troubled accounts. He has a well-deserved reputation as one of the most fun people in the company to travel with. The size of his expense reports proves it.

Patty and I are sitting in front of his desk in Building 2. As we listen to him bellow at his colleagues on a conference call, I look at the many pictures of him on the wall: on golf courses, with his top sales people in exotic locales from decades of President's Clubs, and shaking hands with customers. In the corner is a fake potted tree, completely covered with hundreds of conference badges and lanyards.

This is definitely the office of someone who loves being in front of people. He's a large, gregarious guy with an even larger laugh.

Over many scotches with him one evening in Chicago, I was surprised to learn that much of his demeanor is a carefully crafted persona. While he's outwardly very loud and outspoken, he's actually an introvert by nature, very analytic and passionate about sales discipline. Hearing him chastise yet another person on the phone, I think about how odd it is that even a discipline like sales, known for its chaotic and unpredictable nature, is more predictable than IT.

There's at least a predictable funnel that comes from marketing campaigns, generating prospects, leads, qualified leads, and sales opportunities that leads to a sales pipeline. One sales person missing their number rarely jeopardizes the entire department.

On the other hand, any of my engineers can get me fired by making a seemingly small, harmless change that results in a crippling, enterprise-wide outage.

Ron slams down the phone. "Sorry, guys. Despite all the training I do, sometimes my team behaves like a bunch of wild animals," he says, still exasperated. He rips the stapled document he's holding in two, and then tosses it into his trash can.

"Oh man, Ron," I can't help but say. "Your recycling bin is right next to you!"

"I'll be dead long before the landfills are full!" he says with a large laugh.

He may be dead soon, but my kids won't be. As I explain to him why we're here, I reach under the desk to grab the papers from the wastebasket, putting them in the recycling bin. "You're listed as the owner of the 'sales pipeline' and 'sales forecast accuracy' measures on Dick's spreadsheet. What can you tell me about the challenges of hitting those numbers?"

"Look, I don't know much about IT. Someone on my staff might be better for you to talk to," he responds.

"Don't worry, I'm not asking about anything IT-related. Let's just talk about your measures," I assure him.

"Okay, it's your nickel…" he says. "If you want to talk about sales forecast accuracy, you first need to know why it's so inaccurate. It starts when Steve and Dick hand me a crazy revenue target, leaving me to figure out how to deliver on it. For years, I've had to assign way too much quota capacity to my team, so *of course* we keep missing our numbers! I tell Steve and Dick this, year after year, but they don't listen. Probably because they're having some arbitrary revenue target jammed down their throats by the board.

"It's a crappy way to run a company. It demoralizes my team, and my top performers are quitting in droves. Of course, we'll replace them, but it takes at least a year for replacements to perform at full quota capacity. Even in this lousy economy, it takes too long to find qualified sales people.

"You know what chaps my hide?" he continues. "Sarah promised that acquiring the retail stores would accelerate our sales. And has it happened? Hell, no!

"We're completely screwing up the execution. This morning, a district manager was screaming that they need truckloads of our new fuel injector kits because all his stores are completely stocked out. We're losing the easiest sales we can make! Our customers want to buy, but they're walking out empty-handed, probably buying something crappier from one of our competitors."

Ron says angrily, "We are clueless about what our customers want! We have too much product that will never sell and never enough of the ones that do."

His words sounding familiar, I look down at Dick's slide again. "You're saying that 'sales forecast accuracy' is being jeopardized by our poor grasp of 'understanding our customer needs and wants?' And that if we know what products were out of stock in the stores, we could increase sales?"

"You got it," he says. "With the traffic we get in the stores, that's the fastest and easiest way to increase revenue. It's a lot easier than dealing with the fickle whims of our large automotive buyers, that's for sure."

I make a note to myself to find out how stockout data are generated, and I see Patty furiously taking notes as well.

I ask Ron about the sales pipeline process and its challenges, and I get an earful. He tells us at length how difficult it is for his managers to get the reports they need out of our customer relationship management system (CRM) and the endless battle to make sure his entire sales force uses it in their daily work.

But the floodgates really open when I ask him what a bad day for him looks like.

"A bad day?" he repeats, staring at me disapprovingly. "Why, Bill, it's positively catastrophic when the MRP and phone systems that you manage go down like they did a few weeks ago. For just the MRP outage, we had customers screaming about delayed orders, and two of them canceled a quarter-million dollars of orders outright. We're scrambling to keep some of our best customers from putting $1.5 million of contracts up for rebid."

He leans across his desk. "And when the phones went down in the last few days of the quarter, and customers couldn't give us orders or make last-minute changes! That's delayed another $1.5 million of orders, and ten customers are reevaluating their contracts, putting another $5 million of contracts at risk."

"You're making my job much, much harder, pal," he says. "A lot of my sales people missed their quota by the tiniest fractions, due to things totally outside of their control. To keep morale up, I'm demanding Steve give quota credit for any order that was delayed because of our screwups."

I grimace. Steve's going to love that idea as much as he loved Sarah giving away vouchers to disgruntled Phoenix customers.

"I'm really sorry that happened on my watch. There's no excuse for it," I say sincerely. I tell him what happened with the vendor making the unauthorized change to the phone switch, and the steps we're taking to ensure that it doesn't happen again.

I explain, "We have change control policies, but as you know, training and trust only go so far—at some point, we need monitoring to enforce those policies. The trouble is, we need to expand the licensing beyond what Information Security has deployed, and emergency capital is hard to get these days. Especially for IT Operations."

Ron turns bright red. "Why? What are they saving it for? Probably another harebrained acquisition that Sarah is dreaming up." He laughs humorlessly. "How much money are we talking about?"

When I tell him, he looks disgusted. "We spend more money watering the lawns at the manufacturing plants every week! Dick is going to hear from me about this. If he's not willing to spend money, we may lose orders—even if your project is just insurance so we can collect on all the hard work my sales team does—it's a no-brainer!"

"We sure think so. Thanks for the support," I say. "We're about out of time. Are there any other challenges or impediments that we can help with?"

He looks at his watch for a moment. "No, just keep those vendors from crashing our phone systems again, you hear?"

Patty looks invigorated as she flips through all her notes by the elevator banks. She says, "Ron mentioned how critical the phones and the MRP systems are, but I'm sure there's more, like the inventory management systems. I'll work on creating the complete list of applications and infrastructure that support Ron. If any of them are fragile, we need to get them added to our replacement list. This is a great opportunity to be proactive."

"You read my mind," I say, smiling. "That preventive work supports the most important objectives of the company. How do we know? We started from the measures that Dick cares about most."

I'm pleased. Now I'm really looking forward to our next interview, which is with Maggie Lee, who sponsored Phoenix.

Patty and I meet with Maggie on the following Monday. Over the weekend, Sarah e-mailed me, demanding to know the agenda for the meeting, threatening to cancel it. When I start copying Dick and Steve on my replies, she relents, but warns me not to meddle with her department.

I'm not worried. Both Patty and I work with Maggie regularly. She's the business sponsor of over half the IT projects. Among other things, Maggie is responsible for making sure that the company has the best possible assortment of merchandise in each of our stores, and she owns the category and pricing roadmaps.

In describing her responsibilities, she summarizes, "Ultimately, the way I measure our understanding of customer needs and wants is whether customers would recommend us to their friends. Any way you cut it, our metrics aren't very good."

When I ask why, she sighs. "Most of the time, we're flying blind. Ideally, our sales data would tell us what customers want. You'd think that with all the data in our order entry and inventory management systems, we could do this. But we can't, because the data are almost always wrong."

Patty glances my way meaningfully as Maggie continues, "Our data quality is so bad that we can't rely on it to do any sort of forecasting. The best data that we have right now comes from interviewing our store managers every two months and the customer focus groups we do twice a year. You can't run a billion-dollar business this way and expect to succeed!

"At my last job, we received sales and stockout reports every day," she continues. "Here, we get them once a month from Finance, but they're full of errors. What do you expect? They're done by a bunch of college interns, copying and pasting numbers between a million spreadsheets."

"If you could wave a magic wand, what would you do instead?" I ask.

"How big of a magic wand?" she asks.

"It can do anything you want," I reply, smiling.

"That's a big magic wand," she says, laughing. "I want accurate and timely order information from our stores and online channels. I want to press a button and get it, instead of running it through the circus we've created. I'd use that data to create marketing campaigns that continually do A/B testing of offers, finding the ones that our customers jump at. When we find out what works, we'd replicate it across our entire customer list. By doing this, we'd be creating a huge and predictable sales funnel for Ron.

"I'd use that information to drive our production schedule, so we can manage our supply and demand curves. We'd keep the right products on the right store shelves and keep them stocked. Our revenue per customer would go through the roof. Our average order sizes would go up. We'd finally increase our market share and start beating the competition again."

As she's telling us this, she looks animated and excited. Then her exuberance disappears. Sounding defeated, she says, "But we're stuck with the systems we have, unfortunately."

"Wait a second. I thought Phoenix was supposed to fix all this?" I ask.

She snorts in disgust. "All we've gotten from Phoenix is a bunch of promises. It was supposed to do a lot of this reporting, but there's so much political pressure to ship something, they keep dropping features. And guess which feature they're delaying until sometime next year?" She rolls her eyes in disbelief.

"Reporting?" I guess, fearing the worst.

When Maggie nods, I try to stay upbeat. "For now, let's assume that the magic wand worked. We now have great data coming out of the stores. You're keeping the right products in the stores, and the campaigns you're dreaming up are succeeding beyond your wildest dreams. What then?"

"Life gets exciting, that's what!" she says, her eyes lighting up. "Last year, we shipped a custom fuel injection system for a new upcoming sports car. We had just six months to get this to market, from the drawing board to the shelves. We nailed it! The designers, R&D folks, and Marketing all kicked ass. We had the right product, right place, right brand, right price, and right quality. It was one of the best-selling products of the year.

"We took a risk and won big," she says. "If we had better visibility into our retail operations, with our amazing R&D and manufacturing capabilities, we could make fifty of those bets per year. I'd bet four of those would be runaway hits! We'd not only be profitable, we'd be insanely profitable."

Patty interjects, "What's an acceptable time to market for your products?"

She responds quickly, "These days? Products need to ship in six months. Nine months, tops. Otherwise, some Chinese company will steal our idea, have them on our competitors store shelves, and take the majority of the market.

"In these competitive times, the name of the game is quick time to market and to fail fast. We just can't have multiyear product development timelines, waiting until the end to figure out whether we have a winner or loser on our hands. We need short and quick cycle times to continually integrate feedback from the marketplace.

"But that's just half the picture," she continues. "The longer the product development cycle, the longer the company capital is locked up and not giving us a return. Dick expects that on average, our R&D investments return more than ten percent. That's the internal hurdle rate. If we don't beat the hurdle rate, the company capital would have been better spent being invested in the stock market or gambled on racehorses.

"When R&D capital is locked up as WIP for more than a year, not returning cash back to the business, it becomes almost impossible to pay back the business," she continues.

Holy crap. Maggie is starting to sound eerily like Erik, too. The need to continually reduce cycle times is part of the First Way. The need for amplification of feedback loops, ideally from the customer, is part of the Second Way.

But nine months to return cash back to the company, tops? We've been at Phoenix for nearly three years and it still hasn't created the desired business value.

I have a terrible feeling that we may be going about Phoenix entirely the wrong way…

Looking at my watch, I see that we're almost out of time. Putting the thoughts of Phoenix aside, I ask Maggie about other ways that IT is impeding the achievement of her goals.

Her expression darkens. "Well, there is one more thing…"

Maggie then describes the intense competition for IT project resources. "Our planning horizon is six to twelve months. How does anyone know what projects they should be working on three years from now?" she says angrily, suddenly reminding me of Ron.

Nothing unifies people better than complaining about IT.

"I completely understand your frustration," I say stoically. "You have any ideas on how to fix it?"

She shares a bunch of ideas about hiring more IT people, dedicating IT people to her group, putting more scrutiny on the projects that are clogging the IT project queue, and so forth.

Most of the ideas aren't new, and I merely raise my eyebrows at the notion of a larger IT budget. Steve and Dick will never go for that.

"Incredible!" Patty exclaims, as we leave Maggie's office. "I can't believe how frustrated Maggie and Ron are. Can you believe that unreliable data in the order entry and inventory management systems came up again? And I can't believe that Phoenix, as it's currently designed, won't actually fix the data quality problems!"

I nod and say decisively, "Get a meeting together with John and Wes. We'll show them what we've learned so far. Invite Chris, as well. This goes beyond just IT Operations. This may change how we prioritize and develop our applications, too."

As she leaves, I look at my Phoenix calculations again.

We've spent over $20 million on Phoenix over three years. With all that WIP and capital locked inside the project, it will likely never clear the ten percent internal hurdle rate. In other words, Phoenix should not have been approved.

CHAPTER 27

• *Tuesday, October 21*

I'm in a conference room with Patty, Wes, Chris, and John to share the progress Patty and I have made.

I begin by stating, "We interviewed Ron and Maggie, the business process owners on Dick's company measurements slide. I've spent some time thinking about what we've learned."

I dig out my notes and walk to the whiteboard, writing out, "Parts Unlimited desired business outcomes: increase revenue, increase market share, increase average order size, restore profitability, increase return on assets."

Then I draw the following table:

Performance Measures	Area of IT Reliance	Business Risk Due to IT	IT Controls Relied Upon
1. Understanding customer needs and wants	Order entry and inventory management systems	Data not accurate, reports not timely and require rework	
2. Product portfolio	Order entry systems	Data not accurate	
3. R&D effectiveness			
4. Time to market (R&D)	Phoenix	three-year cycle time & WIP makes clearing IRR hurdle rate unlikely	
5. Sales pipeline	CRM, marketing campaign, phone/ voicemail, MRP systems	Sales mgmt can't view/manage pipeline, customers can't add/change orders	
6. Customer on-time delivery	CRM, phone/ voicemail, MRP systems	Customers can't add/ change orders	
7. Customer retention	CRM, customer support systems	Sales cannot manage customer health	
8. Sales forecast accuracy	(same as #1)	(same as #1)	

Pointing at the whiteboard, I say, "The first column names the business capabilities and processes needed to achieve Dick's desired outcomes; the second column lists the IT systems that those business processes rely upon; the third column lists what can go wrong with either the IT systems or data; and in the fourth column, we'll write down the countermeasures to prevent those bad things from happening, or at a minimum, detect and respond."

For the next half hour, I walk them through the table and all the grievances. "Apparently, for the things that Dick cares about most, IT matters." I say, deadpan. Wes says, "Come on. I'm not the smartest guy in the room by any stretch. But, if we're so important, why are they trying to outsource all of us? Face it, we've been moved from one foster home to another for decades."

None of us have a good answer.

"You know, I really like Bill's third column: 'business risk due to IT,'"

John says. "By describing what could go wrong in IT that prevents the business outcome from being achieved, we're helping the business process owners get their bonuses. This should be *very* persuasive. We may even be thanked by the business for doing all this work, which would be a refreshing change."

"I agree. Nice job, Bill," Chris says, finally. "But what's the solution?"

I say, "Anyone have any ideas?"

Surprisingly, John speaks up first. "Seems pretty obvious to me. We need to come with the controls to mitigate the risks in your third column. We then show this table to Ron and Maggie, and make sure they believe that our countermeasures help them achieve their objectives. If they buy it, we work with them to integrate IT into their performance measures…

"That example Erik gave you is perfect. They integrated 'compliance with vehicle maintenance procedures' as a leading indicator for 'on-time delivery' and 'customer retention.' We need to do the same."

We roll up our sleeves and get to work.

For the phone and MRP systems, we quickly establish that the predictive measures include compliance with the change management process, supervision and review of production changes, completion of scheduled maintenance, and elimination of all known single points of failure.

When we tackle 'customer needs and wants," we get stuck.

It's John who gets us rolling again. "Here, the objective isn't system availability, it's the integrity of data, which, incidentally, form two of the three legs of the 'confidentiality, integrity, and availability triangle' or CIA." He asks Chris, "So, what's causing the data integrity issues?"

Chris snorts in disgust. "Phoenix fixes a bunch of them, but we still have issues. Most of them are caused upstream, because the Marketing people keep putting in malformed inventory SKUs. Marketing needs to get their crap together, too."

So for 'marketing needs and wants,' our proposed measurements include ability for Phoenix to support weekly and eventually daily reporting, percentage of valid SKUs created by Marketing, and so forth.

By the end of the day, we've generated a slide deck that Patty and I will take back to Ron and Maggie, which we'll then present to Dick.

"Now that, my friends, is a solid proposal," Wes says, proudly. With a loud laugh, he says, "Even a monkey could follow the dots we just connected!"

Over the next day, Patty and I get great feedback from Ron and Maggie, and they commit to supporting our proposal with Dick. When Ron learns that we still haven't been granted budget for our monitoring project, he calls up Dick right in front of us, leaving him a heated voice-mail, demanding to know why he's dragging his feet.

With all this enthusiastic support, I figure our Thursday meeting with Dick will be a slam dunk.

"All you've told me is that you're completely asleep at the wheel!" Dick says sternly, obviously unimpressed by what I've presented. Suddenly, I'm reminded of how Steve didn't even look at the spreadsheets I had prepared for him when I asked him to prioritize Phoenix and the audit finding work.

But Dick isn't being dismissive. He's actually angry. "You're telling me something a nutless monkey could have figured out. You didn't know these measurements were important? At every town hall meeting, Steve repeats them over and over. It's in our company newsletters, it's what Sarah talks about in every one of her strategy briefings. How could you all miss something so important?"

I see Chris and Patty fidget on either side of me as we sit across the table from Dick. Erik is standing by the window, leaning against the wall.

I have a flashback to when I was Marine sergeant, holding the flag on parade. Out of nowhere, a colonel appeared, growling at me in front of my entire unit, "That's an out of regulation watch band, Sergeant Palmer!" I could have died on the spot from embarrassment, because I knew I had screwed up.

But today, I'm certain I understand the mission, and for the company to succeed I need Dick to understand what I've just learned. But how?

Erik clears his throat, and says to Dick, "I agree a nutless monkey should have figured this out. So, Dick, explain why on that little mea-surement spreadsheet of yours, you list four levels of management for each of your measurements but nowhere are there any IT managers listed. Why?"

Not waiting for Dick to respond, he continues, "Every week, IT peo-ple get dragged into fire drills at the last minute by managers trying to achieve those measurements—just like Brent was pulled in to help launch Sarah's latest sales promotion." Erik pauses and says, "Quite frankly, I think you're just as much of a nutless monkey as Bill."

Dick grunts but doesn't seem perturbed. He finally says, "Maybe so, Erik. You know, five years ago, we used to have our CIO attend our quarterly business reviews, but he never opened his mouth except to tell us that everything we proposed was impossible. After a year of that, Steve stopped inviting him."

Dick turns back to me. "Bill, you're telling me that everyone could do everything right in the business, but because of these IT issues, we would all still miss these objectives?"

"Yes, sir," I say. "The operational risks posed by IT need to be managed just like any other business risk. In other words, they're not IT risks. They're business risks."

Again, Dick grunts. He slumps in his chair, rubbing his eyes. "Shit. How the hell are we supposed to write an IT outsourcing contract if we don't even know what the business needs?" he says, slamming his hand on the table.

He then asks, "Well, what's your proposal? You've got one, I presume?"

I sit upright and begin the pitch that I've rehearsed so many times with the team. "I'd like three weeks with each of the business process owners on that spreadsheet. We need to get the business risks posed by IT better defined and agreed upon and then propose to you a way to integrate those risks into leading indicators of performance. Our goal is not just to improve business performance but to get earlier indicators of whether we're going to achieve them or not, so we can take appropriate action.

"Furthermore," I continue. "I'd like to schedule a single topic meeting with you and Chris about Phoenix," then explaining my concerns how Phoenix as defined should not even have been approved.

I continue, "We're going way too slowly, with too much WIP and too many features in flight. We need to make our releases smaller and shorter and deliver cash back faster, so we can beat the internal hurdle rate. Chris and I have some ideas, but it will look very different than our current plan of record."

He remains silent. Then decisively, he declares, "Yes on both of your proposals. I'll assign Ann to help. You need the best talent in the company."

Out of the corner of my eye, I see Chris and Patty smile.

"Thank you, sir. We'll make it so," I say, standing up and pushing everyone out of the room, before Dick changes his mind.

As we walk out of his office, Erik claps his hand on my shoulder. "Not bad, kid. Congratulations on being well on your way to mastering the First Way. Now help John get there, because you're going to have your hands full tackling the Second Way."

Confused, I ask, "Why? What's going to happen?"

"You'll find out soon enough," Erik says with a chuckle.

On Friday, John convenes a meeting with Wes, Patty, and me, promising some fantastic news. He says effusively, "You guys did fantastic work linking IT to Dick's operational objectives. I've finally learned how we dodged the audit bullet, and I'm pretty sure we can do something equally fantastic to reduce our audit and compliance workload."

"Doing less audit work?" Wes says, looking up, putting his phone down. "I'm all ears!"

He has my attention, too. If there were some way to get audit off our backs without another Bataan Death March, it would be nothing short of a miracle.

He turns toward Wes and Patty. "I needed to figure out how we escaped all the findings from the internal and external auditors. At first, I thought it was just the audit partner bending over backward to retain us as a client. But that wasn't it at all…

"I got in front of everyone from the Parts Unlimited team who was at that meeting, trying to figure out who had the magic bullet. To my surprise, it wasn't Dick or our corporate counsel. Ten meetings later, I finally found Faye, a Financial Analyst who works for Ann in Finance.

"Faye has a technical background. She spent four years in IT," he says, as he hands out papers to each of us. "She created these SOX-404 control documents for the finance team. It shows the end-to-end information flow for the main business processes in each financially significant account. She documented where money or assets entered the system and traced it all the way to the general ledger.

"This is pretty standard, but she took it one step further: She didn't look at any of the IT systems until she understood exactly where in the process material errors could occur *and* where they would be detected. She found that most of the time, we would detect it in a manual reconciliation step where account balances and values from one source were compared to another, usually on a weekly basis.

"When this happens," he says, with awe and wonder in his voice, "she knew the upstream IT systems should be out of scope of the audit."

"Here's what she showed the auditors," John says, excitedly flipping to the second page. "Quote: 'The control being relied upon to detect material errors is the manual reconciliation step, not in the upstream IT systems.' I went through all of Faye's papers, and in every case, the auditors agreed, withdrawing their IT finding.

"That's why Erik called the pile of audit findings a 'scoping error.' He's right. If the audit test plan was scoped correctly in the beginning, there wouldn't have been any IT findings!" he concludes.

John looks around as Patty, Wes, and I stare blankly at him.

I say, "I'm not following. How does this relate to reducing the audit workload?"

"I'm rebuilding our compliance program from scratch, based upon our new understanding of precisely where we're relying our controls," John says. "That dictates what matters. It's like having a magic set of glasses that can differentiate what controls are earth-shattering important versus those that have no value at all."

"Yes!" I say. "Those 'magic glasses' helped us finally see what matters to Dick for company operations. It was right in front of us for years, but we never saw it."

John nods and smiles broadly. He flips to the last page of the handout. "I'm proposing five things that could reduce our security-related workload by seventy-five percent."

What he presents is breathtaking. His first proposal drastically reduces the scope of the SOX-404 compliance program. When he verbalizes so precisely why it's safe to do, I realize that John too is also mastering the First Way, having truly achieved a "profound appreciation of the system."

His second proposal requires that we find out how production vulnerabilities got there in the first place and that we ensure that they don't happen again by modifying our deployment processes.

His third proposal requires that we flag all the systems in the scope for compliance audits in Patty's change management process—so we can avoid changes that could jeopardize our audits—and that we create the on-going documentation that the auditors will ask for.

John looks around, seeing all of us staring at him in shocked silence. "Did I say something wrong?"

"No offense, John…" Wes says slowly. "But…uh… You feeling okay?"

I say, "John, I don't think you'll get any objections from my team on your proposals. I think they're great ideas." Wes and Patty vehemently nod in agreement.

Looking pleased, he continues, "My fourth proposal is to reduce the size of our PCI compliance program by getting rid of anything that stores or processes cardholder data, which is like toxic waste. Losing or mishandling it can be lethal, and it costs too much to protect.

"Let's start with the asinine cafeteria point of sale system. I never want to do another security review of that piece of crap. Frankly, I don't care who takes it, even if it's Sarah's cousin Vinnie. It's gotta go."

Patty has one hand covering her mouth, and even Wes' jaw is on the table. Has John completely lost his mind? This proposal seems…potentially reckless.

Wes thinks for a moment, and changes his mind. "I love it! I wish we could have gotten rid of it years ago. We've spent months securing that system for those audits. It even went into scope for the SOX-404 audits because it talked to the payroll systems!"

Patty eventually nods. "I suppose no one would argue that the cafeteria POS is a core competency. It doesn't help our business but can definitely hurt it. And it pulls scarce resources from Phoenix and our in-store POS systems, which are definitely part of our core competencies."

"Okay, John, let's do it. You're batting four out of four," I say, decisively. "But do you really think we can get rid of it in time to make a difference?"

"Yep," John says, smiling confidently. "I've already talked with Dick and the legal team. We just need to find a suitable outsourcer and convince ourselves that they can be trusted to maintain and secure the systems and data. We can outsource the work but not the responsibility."

Wes interjects hopefully, "Can you do something about getting Phoenix out of scope of the audits, too?"

"Over my dead body," John says flatly, crossing his arms. "My fifth and last proposal is that we pay down all the technical debt in Phoenix, using all the time we've saved from my previous proposals. We know there's a huge amount of risk in Phoenix: strategic risk, operational risk, huge security and compliance risk. Almost all of Dick's key measures hinge on it.

"As Patty said, our order entry and inventory management systems *are* a core competency. We're relying on it to give us a competitive edge, but with all the shortcuts we've taken with it, it's like a powder keg waiting to blow up."

Wes sighs, looking annoyed. *Bad old John is back*, his expression says.

I disagree. This John is far more complex and nuanced than the old John. In the span of a couple of minutes, he's been willing to take bigger, almost reckless, risks from outsourcing our cafeteria POS systems to his unyielding and categorical insistence that we secure and harden Phoenix.

I like this new John.

"You're absolutely right, John. We've got to pay down technical debt," I say firmly. "How do you propose we do it?"

We quickly agree to pair up people in Wes' and Chris' group with John's team, so that we can increase the bench of security expertise. By doing this, we will start integrating security into all of our daily work, no longer securing things after they're deployed.

John thanks everyone, indicating that we've covered everything on his agenda. I look at my watch. We're done thirty minutes early. This must be a new world record for the shortest time required to agree on anything security-related.

CHAPTER 28

• *Monday, October 27*

On my drive into work, I have to turn on my seat heaters months earlier than usual.

I hope this winter won't be as awful as last year. Paige's relatives, the most skeptical people I've ever met, have started wondering whether there actually might be something to this global climate change thing, after all.

When I get to my office, I take my laptop out of my bag, smiling at how quickly it powers on. As I write up a report for Steve on how far we've come in the last six weeks, I don't put in anything about my new laptop, but I want to.

To me, the laptop represents everything my team has achieved together. I'm incredibly proud of them. Life feels different now. The number of Sev 1 outages this month is down by more than two-thirds. Incident recovery time is down, too, probably by more than half.

The insight we've gained from that first strange meeting with Dick and John tells me that we're hot on the trail of understanding how we can really help the business win.

Opening up my e-mail, I see a note from Kirsten. All her project managers are gushing about how projects are flowing so much faster.

The number of tasks waiting for Brent and the rest of IT Operations is way down. In fact, if I'm reading the report correctly, Brent is almost caught up.

On the project front, we're in fantastic shape—especially with Phoenix.

There's another Phoenix deployment scheduled for Friday. It's only a bunch of defect fixes, with no major functionality added or changed, so it should be much better than last time. We've completed all of our deliverables on time, but as usual, there are still a million details that still need to be worked out.

I'm grateful that my team can stay so focused on Phoenix, because we've stabilized our infrastructure. When the inevitable outages and incidents do occur, we're operating like a well-oiled machine. We're building a body of tribal knowledge that's helping us fix things faster than ever, and, when we do need to escalate, it's controlled and orderly.

Because of our ever-improving production monitoring of the infrastructure and applications, more often than not, we know about the incidents before the business does.

Our project backlog has been cut way down, partially from eradicating dumb projects from our queue. And John has delivered. We've cut a bunch of unneeded security projects from our audit preparation and remediation work, replacing them with preventive security projects that my entire team is helping with. By modifying our development and deployment processes, we're hardening and securing both the applications and production infrastructure in a meaningful and systematic way. And we're gaining confidence that those defects will never happen again in the future.

Our change management meetings are going more smoothly and regularly than ever. We not only have visibility into what our teams are doing, but work is really flowing.

More than ever, people know exactly what they should be working on. People are getting satisfaction out of fixing things. I'm hearing that people are feeling happier and more upbeat, because they can actually do their jobs.

It's strange how much more clearly I see the IT world now and how differently it looks to me than even a couple of months ago.

Patty's experiments with establishing kanbans around Brent are a success. We're also finding instances of work going backward to Brent, because we didn't understand or didn't sufficiently specify some task or outcome, requiring Brent to translate or fix it.

When this happens now, we quickly jump on it to make sure that it doesn't happen again.

And it's not just Brent's work that we're improving. By reducing the number of projects in flight, we're keeping clear lanes of work, so work can go from one work center to the other quickly, getting completed in record time.

We've all but emptied our ticketing system of outdated work. In one case, we even found a ticket that Wes put in over ten years ago as a junior engineer, referring to some task for a machine that has been long since decommissioned. Now we have confidence that all work in the system is important and actually has a prayer of being completed.

We are no longer the Bates Motel of work.

Against my staff's expectations, we keep bumping up the number of projects we think we can handle concurrently. Because we have a better idea of what our flows of work are, and managing carefully which ones are allowed to go to Brent, we're finding that we can keep releasing more projects without impacting our existing commitments.

I no longer think of Erik as a raving madman, but he's eccentric, for sure. Now that I've seen the results with my own eyes in my own organization, I know that IT Operations work is very similar to plant work. Erik has stated repeatedly that our improvements to date are only the tip of the iceberg.

Erik says that we are starting to master the First Way: We're curbing the handoffs of defects to downstream work centers, managing the flow of work, setting the tempo by our constraints, and, based on our results from audit and from Dick, we're understanding better than we ever have what is important versus what is not.

At the end, I led the retrospective portion, where we self-assessed how we did and the areas that we should improve. When someone mentioned that we should start inviting people from Development when we do our outage postmortem root cause analysis meetings, I realized that we are now also well on our way to understanding Erik's Third Way, as well.

As Erik keeps reminding me, a great team performs best when they practice. Practice creates habits, and habits create mastery of any process or skill. Whether it's calisthenics, sports training, playing a musical instrument, or in my experience, the endless drilling we did in the Marines. Repetition, especially for things that require teamwork, creates trust and transparency.

Last week, as I sat through our latest biweekly outage drill, I was very impressed. We were getting very good at this.

I feel certain that if the payroll failure that happened on my first day of the job happened now, we could complete the entire payroll run—not just the salaried staff, but the hourly staff, as well.

John quickly got the approval from Dick and Steve to have an outsourcer to take over the cafeteria POS systems and replace it with something commercially supported.

It was a fascinating exercise for Wes, Patty, and me to work with John to put together the outsourcing requirements for the cafeteria POS systems. As part of the due diligence process, we were going to hear from all the prospective outsourcers all the dogmas we used to believe before all our interactions with Erik. It will be interesting to see if we can retrain them.

It seems to me that if anyone is managing IT without talking about the Three Ways, they are managing IT on dangerously faulty assumptions.

As I'm pondering this, my phone rings. It's John.

When I answer, he says, "My team discovered something troubling today. To prevent unauthorized black market IT activities from cropping up, we've started routinely reviewing all the proposed projects coming into Kirsten's Project Management Office. We also search all the corporate credit cards for recurring charges that might be for online or cloud services—which is just another form of unauthorized IT. Some people are going around the project freeze. You have time to talk?"

"Let's meet in ten minutes," I say. "Don't leave me hanging. Who's trying to backdoor the system?"

I hear John laugh on the other end of the line. "Sarah. Who else?"

I invite Wes and Patty to the impromptu meeting but only Patty can make it.

John starts presenting what he found. Sarah's group has four instances of using outside vendors and online services. Two are relatively innocuous but the others are more serious: she has contracted a vendor for a $200,000 project to do customer data mining and another vendor to plug into all our POS systems to get sales data for customer analytics.

"The first problem is that both projects violate the data privacy policy that we've given our customers," John says. "We repeatedly promise that we will not share data with partners. Whether we change that policy or not is, of course, a business decision. But make no mistake, if we go ahead with the customer data mining initiative, we're out of compliance with our own privacy policy. We may even be breaking several state privacy regulations that expose us to some liability."

This doesn't sound good, but John's tone of voice suggests there's worse to come. "The second problem is that Sarah's vendor uses the same database technology that we used for our cafeteria POS system, which we know is virtually impossible to secure and maintain support for in production, if and when it becomes a part of daily operations."

I feel my face get red hot. It's not just about another cafeteria POS system that we'll need to retrofit for production. It's because applications like this contribute to our inaccurate sales order entry and inventory management data. We have too many cooks in the kitchen and no one accountable for maintaining the integrity of the data.

"Look, I don't care about Sarah's project management and invoicing tools—if it makes them more productive, let them use it," I say. "It's probably safe as long as it doesn't interface with an existing business system, store confidential data, affect financial reporting, or whatever. But if it does, then we need to be involved and at least confirm that it doesn't impact any of our existing commitments."

"I agree," John says, "Want me to take the first stab at that outsourced IT service policy document?"

"Perfect," I say. But with less certainty, I continue, "Although, what's the right way to handle Sarah? I feel completely out of my league. Steve constantly protects her. How do we convey to him the potential mayhem she's causing with her unauthorized projects?"

Making sure John's office door is closed, I say to John and Patty "Guys, help me out. What does Steve see in her? How does she get away with so much crap? Over the past couple of weeks, I see how hard-nosed Steve can be, but Sarah routinely gets away with murder. Why?"

Patty snorts. "If Steve were a woman, I'd say that he's attracted to dangerous men. A bunch of us have speculated about this for years. I've had a theory, which I must say, was pretty much validated in our last off-site."

When she sees John and me both conspiratorially leaning forward, she smiles. "Steve prides himself on being an operations guy, and he's admitted several times in company meetings that he doesn't have a flair for strategy. I think that's why he loved working with his old boss and our new chairman Bob so much. For a decade, Bob was the strategy guy, and all Steve had to do was execute the vision.

"For years, Steve searched for a strategy person to be his right-hand man. He went through quite a few people, even setting a couple executives against each other in this awful, drawn out competition. Pretty Machiavellian," she continues. "And Sarah won. The word on the street was that there was a lot of backstabbing and underhanded tactics, but I suppose that's what it takes to come out on top. Evidently, she has mastered how to whisper the right things in his ear, reinforcing his paranoia and aspirations."

Patty's explanation is so much more sophisticated than anything I've come up with. In fact, it sounds strikingly similar to what Paige would speculate when I got that distant, angry look at dinnertime.

John says awkwardly, "Umm, you don't think there's anything between them, do you? Like, anything…untoward?"

I raise my eyebrows. I wondered about that, too.

Patty just bursts out laughing. "I'm a pretty good judge of people. Both my parents were psychologists. I'd eat both of their diplomas if that were true."

Seeing the expression on my face, she laughs even harder. "Look, not even Wes believes that, and there's no one better at manufacturing drama than him. Sarah's *scared to death* of Steve! You ever notice that when someone is talking, Sarah is always still looking at Steve, trying to gauge his reaction? It's freakish, actually."

She continues, "Steve has a blind spot for Sarah's shortcomings, because she has something he needs and admires, which is the ability to come up with creative strategies, regardless of whether the strategy is good or bad. On the other hand, because Sarah is so insecure, she'll do whatever it takes to not look bad.

"She simply doesn't care about the body count she leaves in her wake, because she wants to be the next CEO of Parts Unlimited." Patty says. "And apparently, Steve does too. He's been grooming her as his successor for years."

"What? She could be our next CEO?" I exclaim in shock, quickly wiping up the coffee I spit out onto John's conference table.

"Wow, boss. You don't hang out at the water cooler much, do you?" Patty says.

It's Phoenix deployment day, and I've missed Halloween with my kids.

It's already 11:40 p.m. As we're standing once again around the NOC conference table, I have an unsettling feeling of déjà vu. I count fifteen people here, including Chris and William.

Most people are tensely huddled around the table with laptops open, pizza boxes and candy wrappers piled behind them. Several other people are at the whiteboard, pointing at checklists or diagrams.

It took three hours longer than scheduled to migrate Phoenix into the QA test environment and get all the tests to pass. Although this is much better than the previous deployment, I thought we'd have fewer problems, given how hard we worked on improving the deployment process,

By 9:30 p.m., we were finally ready to do the migration into production. All the tests had finally passed, and Chris and William gave the thumbs-up to deploy. Wes, Patty, and I looked at the test reports, and gave the green light to start the deployment work.

Then all hell broke loose.

One of the critical database migration steps failed. We had only completed thirty percent of the deployment steps, and once again, we were dead in the water. Due to the database changes and the scripts already run, it wasn't possible to roll back in the time remaining before the stores opened tomorrow morning.

Once again, we had to fight our way forward, trying to get to the next step so the deployment could resume.

Leaning against the wall, I watch everyone work, arms crossed, trying not to pace. It's frustrating that once again we are grappling with another Phoenix deployment going bad, with potentially disastrous outcomes.

On the other hand, compared to last time, things are much calmer. While there is tension, and a lot of heated arguments, everyone is intensely focused on problem solving. We've already notified all the store managers about our progress, and they all have manual fallback procedures ready, just in case the POS systems are down when the stores open.

I see Wes say something to Brent, stand up to rub his forehead wearily, and then walk toward me. Chris and William also get up and follow him.

I meet them halfway. "Well?" I ask.

"Well," Wes replies when he's close enough to speak softly and be heard. "We've found our smoking gun. We just discovered that Brent made a change to the production database a couple of weeks ago to support a Phoenix business intelligence module. No one knew about it, let alone documented it. It conflicts with some of the Phoenix database changes, so Chris' guys are going to need to do some recoding."

"Shit," I say. "Wait. Which Phoenix module?"

"It's one of Sarah's projects that we released after the project freeze was lifted," he replies. "It was before we put the kanban around Brent. It was a database schema change that slipped through the cracks."

I swear under my breath. Sarah *again*?

Chris has a pinched expression on his face. "This is going to be tricky. We're going to have to rename a bunch of database columns, which will affect, who knows, maybe hundreds of files. And all the support scripts. This is going to be manual work and very error-prone."

He turns to William. "What can we do to at least get some basic testing performed before we continue the deployment?"

William looks vaguely ill, wiping sweat from his face with his hands. "This is very, very...dicey... We can test, but we still may not find the errors until we hit those lines of code. That means we're going to have failures in production, where the application just blows up. It may even take down the in-store POS systems, and that would be bad."

He looks at his watch. "We've only got six hours to complete the work. Because we don't have enough time to rerun all the tests, we're going to have to take some shortcuts."

We spend the next ten minutes sketching out a revised schedule that still completes by 6 a.m., enabling the stores to open normally with an hour to spare. As Chris and William head off to notify their teams, I indicate to Wes to remain behind.

"When we're out of the woods," I say, "we've got to figure out how to prevent this from happening again. There should be absolutely no way that the Dev and QA environments don't match the production environment."

"You're right," Wes says, shaking his head in disbelief. "I don't know how we're going to do it. But you've got no argument from me."

He looks behind him at Brent, incredulous. "Can you believe that Brent is at the center of all of this again?"

Much later, when the deployment is declared to be complete, everyone applauds. I look at my watch. It's 5:42 a.m. on Saturday morning. The team spent the entire night working, completing the deployment twenty minutes early. That is, twenty minutes early according to the emergency schedule we hammered out. According to the original schedule, we finished almost six hours late.

William has confirmed that the test POS systems are working, as well as the e-commerce website and all the associated Phoenix modules.

Patty has started sending out notifications to all the store managers that the deployment was "successful." She is attaching a list of known errors to look out for, an internal web page to get the latest Phoenix status, and instructions on how they can report any new problems. We're keeping all the service desk people on standby, and both Chris and my teams are on-call to provide early life support. Basically, we're all on standby to support the business.

With Wes and Patty handling the on-call schedule, I say "good job" to everyone and pack up my things. On my drive home, I wrack my brain, trying to think of how we can keep each Phoenix deployment from causing an emergency.

CHAPTER 29

• *Monday, November 3*

At 7:10 a.m. the following Monday, Chris, Wes, Patty, and John are again all seated with me in the boardroom. While we're waiting for Steve, we talk about the aftermath of the second Phoenix deployment.

Erik is in the back of the room. In front of him is a bowl, an emptied instant oatmeal packet, and a French press full of greenish water, with leaves floating in it.

Seeing my puzzled expression, he says, "Yerba maté. My favorite drink from South America. I never travel without it."

Steve walks through the door, still talking on his cell phone. "Look, Ron, for the last time, no! No more discounts—even if they were our last remaining customer. We've got to hold the line somewhere. Got it?"

He hangs up, exasperated, and finally sits down at the head of the table, muttering, "Sorry I'm late." He opens up his folder, taking a moment to study something inside it.

"Despite how the Phoenix deployment went over the weekend, I'm extremely proud of everything you've have done over the last couple of weeks. Many people have told me about how pleased they are with IT. Even Dick," he says incredulously. "He's told me about how you're helping to improve our key company performance measures, and he thinks it will be a game changer."

He smiles. "I am very proud to be a part of this team that is obviously working together better than ever, trusting one another, and getting incredible results."

He turns to John. "By the way, Dick has also told me that with your help, they've established that the financial restatement won't be material." Breaking into a smile, he says, "Thank God. I won't be on the cover of *Fortune* magazine wearing handcuffs, after all."

Just then, Sarah knocks on the door and enters the room.

"Good morning, Steve," she says, as she walks in primly, sitting down besides Erik. "I take it you wanted to see me about my new marketing initiatives?"

"You mean, the unauthorized shifts of work you're running inside the IT factory, like some unscrupulous Chinese plant manager?" Erik asks.

Sarah looks Erik up and down, obviously sizing him up.

Steve indicates to John to present his findings. When he concludes, Steve says sternly, "Sarah, I issued a clear statement. No one is allowed to start any new IT initiatives, internal or external, without my explicit approval. Please explain your actions."

Sarah picks up her iPhone and angrily taps away for a couple of moments. Putting it down, she says, "Our competitors are kicking our ass. We need every advantage we can get. To achieve the stated objectives that you've laid out, I can't wait for IT. I'm *sure* they're working very hard, doing their best with what they have and what they know—but it's not enough. We need to be nimble, and sometimes we need to buy instead of build."

Wes rolls his eyes.

I respond, "I know that IT hasn't always been able to deliver what you've needed in the past, and I know Marketing and Sales have gotten burned. We want the business to win as much as you do. The problem is that some of your creative initiatives are jeopardizing other important company commitments, such as complying with state laws and regulations on data privacy, as well as our need to stay focused on Phoenix.

"What you're proposing could lead to more data integrity problems in our order entry and inventory management system. Dick, Ron, and Maggie have made it clear that we must get this data cleaned up and keep it clean. Nothing is more important to understand customer needs and wants, have the right product portfolio, retain our customers, and ultimately increase our revenue and market share."

I add, "Supporting those projects also requires an incredible amount of work. We'd need to give your vendors access to our production databases, explain how we've set them up, do a bunch of firewall changes, and probably over a hundred other steps. It's not just as easy as signing an invoice."

She looks back at me scathingly. This is the most livid I've seen her.

Clearly, she doesn't like me quoting Dick's company objectives to her, using it to deny her what she wants.

It occurs to me that I might have just made a dangerous enemy.

She addresses the room, "Since Bill seems to understand the business so much better than I do, why doesn't he tell all of us what he proposes?"

"Sarah, no one understands better what your area of the business needs than you. You're absolutely entitled to go outside of the company to fulfill those needs if we can't deliver, as long as we make the decision understanding how it might jeopardize another part of the enterprise," I say as reasonably as I can. "How about you, Chris, and I meet regularly to see how we can help with your upcoming initiatives?"

"I'm very busy," she says. "I can't spend a whole day meeting with you and Chris. I've got an entire department to run, you know."

To my relief, Steve interjects. "Sarah, you will make the time. I look forward to hearing how those meetings go and how you resolve your two unauthorized IT initiatives. Are we clear?"

She says in a huff, "Yes. I'm just trying to do what's right for Parts Unlimited. I'll do the best with what I have, but I'm not optimistic about the outcome. You're really tying my hands here."

Sarah stands up. "By the way, I had a conversation with Bob Strauss yesterday. I don't think your leash is as long as you think it is. Bob says we need to be looking at strategic options, like splitting up the company. I think he's right."

As she leaves, slamming the door behind her, Erik says wryly, "Well, I'm sure we've seen the last of *her*…"

Steve looks at the door for a moment and then turns to me. "Let's go to the last item on today's agenda. Bill, you're concerned that we're going the wrong way with Phoenix—that not only are things going to get worse, but we may never achieve the desired business outcomes. That is extremely troubling."

I shrug my shoulders. "Now you know everything I know. I was actually hoping that Erik could give us some insights."

Erik looks up, wiping his mustache with a napkin. "Insights? To me, the answer to your problem is obvious. The First Way is all about controlling the flow of work from Development to IT Operations. You've improved flow by freezing and throttling the project releases, but your batch sizes are still way too large. The deployment failure on Friday is proof. You also have way too much WIP still trapped inside the plant, and the worst kind, too. Your deployments are causing unplanned recovery work downstream."

He continues, "Now you must prove that you can master the Second Way, creating constant feedback loops from IT Operations back into Development, designing quality into the product at the earliest stages. To do that, you can't have nine-month-long releases. You need much faster feedback.

"You'll never hit the target you're aiming at if you can fire the cannon only once every nine months. Stop thinking about Civil War era cannons. Think antiaircraft guns."

He stands up to throw his bowl of oatmeal in the wastebasket. Then he peers in the wastebasket and fishes his spoon back out.

Turning around, he says, "In any system of work, the theoretical ideal is single-piece flow, which maximizes throughput and minimizes variance. You get there by continually reducing batch sizes.

"You're doing the exact opposite by lengthening the Phoenix release intervals and increasing the number of features in each release. You've even lost the ability to control variance from one release to the next."

He pauses. "That's ridiculous, given all the investments you've made virtualizing your production systems. You still do deployments like they're physical servers. As Sensei Goldratt would say, you've deployed an amazing technology, but because you haven't changed the way you work, you haven't actually diminished a limitation."

I look around at everyone, confirming that no one understands what Erik is talking about, either. I say, "The last Phoenix release was caused by a production change to the database server that didn't get replicated in the upstream environments. I was about to agree with Chris. We should pause deployments until we can figure out how to keep all the environments synchronized. That means slowing down the releases, right?"

Remaining standing, Erik snorts. "Bill, that is simultaneously one of the smartest things I've heard all month—and one of the dumbest."

I don't react as Erik looks at one of the drawings on the boardroom wall. Pointing at it, he says, "Wilbur, what kind of engine is this?"

Wes grimaces and says, "That's a 1,300 CC engine for a 2007 Suzuki Hayabusa dragster motorcycle. And by the way, it's 'Wes.' Not 'Wilbur.' My name hasn't changed since last time."

"Yes, of course," Erik responds. "Dragster motorcycles are great fun to watch. This one probably goes over 230 miles per hour. How many gears does this racer have?"

Without pausing, Wes responds, "Six. Constant mesh, with a #532 chain drive."

"Does that include the reverse gear?" Erik asks.

"That model doesn't have a reverse gear," Wes replies quickly.

Erik nods as he looks more closely at the drawing on the wall, saying, "Interesting, isn't it? No reverse gear. So why should your flow of work have a reverse gear?"

The silence lengthens when Steve finally says, "Look, Erik. Can you just say what you're thinking? To you, this may be a fun game to play, but we've got a business to save."

Erik looks at Steve closely, studying him. "Think like a plant manager. When you see work going upstream, what does it mean to you?"

He quickly responds, "The flow of work should ideally go in one direction only: forward. When I see work going backward, I think 'waste.' It might be because of defects, lack of specification, or rework… Regardless, it's something we should fix."

Erik nods. "Excellent. I believe that, too."

He picks up his empty French press and spoon from the table, puts them into his suitcase and starts zipping it up. "The flow of work goes in one direction only: forward. Create a system of work in IT that does that. Remember, the goal is single-piece flow."

He turns to me. "Incidentally, this will also solve the problem that you've been fretting about with Dick. An inevitable consequence of long release cycles is that you'll never hit the internal rate of return targets, once you factor in the cost of labor. You must have faster cycle times. If Phoenix is preventing you from doing that, then figure out how to deliver the features some other way.

"Without being like Sarah, of course," he says with a small smile. Picking up his suitcase, he adds, "To do this, you'll need to put Brent at the very front of the line, just like Herbie in *The Goal*. Brent needs to be working at the earliest stages of the development process. Bill, you of all people should be able to figure this out."

"Good luck, guys," he says, and we all watch as he closes the door behind him.

Steve finally says, "Anyone have any suggestions or proposals?"

Chris replies first. "As I shared earlier, even minor Phoenix bug fix releases are so problematic that we can't afford to be doing them monthly. Despite what Erik said, I think we need to slow down our release schedule. I propose moving to one release every other month."

"Unacceptable," Steve says, shaking his head. "Last quarter, we missed almost every target we set by a mile. This will be our fifth consecutive quarterly miss—and that was after we lowered our expectations with Wall Street. All our hopes depend on completing Phoenix. You're telling me that we're going to have to wait even longer to get the features we need, while our competitors continue to pull away from us? Impossible."

"It may be 'impossible' to you, but look at it from my perspective," Chris says levelly. "I need my developers building new features. They can't be constantly tied up with Bill's team, dealing with deployment issues."

Steve replies, "This quarter is make or break. We promised the world that we'd get Phoenix out last month, but because of all the features we delayed, we're not getting the sales benefits that we hoped for. Now we're over a month through the quarter, with the holiday buying season in fewer than thirty days. We are out of time."

Thinking this through, I force myself to accept that Chris is stating the reality he sees, and that it is based on facts. And the same goes for Steve.

I say to Chris, "If you say that the Phoenix team needs to slow down, you won't get any argument from me. In the Marines, when you have a company of a hundred men with a man wounded, the first thing you lose is mobility.

"But we still need to figure out how to achieve what Steve needs," I continue. "As Erik suggested, if we can't do that inside the Phoenix framework, maybe we can do it outside of Phoenix. I propose we form a SWAT team by detaching a small squad from the main Phoenix team, telling them to figure out what features can help us hit our revenue goals as soon as possible. There's not a lot of time, so we'll need to select the features carefully. We'll tell them that they're allowed to break whatever rules required to get the job done."

Chris considers this for a moment and finally nods. "Phoenix is all about helping customers buy things from us, faster and in larger quantities. The last two releases have all been putting down the groundwork to make that happen, but the features to really increase sales are still bogged down. We need to focus on generating good customer recommendations and enable Marketing to create promotions to sell profitable products that we have in inventory."

"We have years of customer purchasing data and because of our branded credit cards, we know our customer demographics and preferences," Steve interjects, leaning forward. "Marketing assures me that we can create some really compelling offers to our customers, if we could only get those features shipped."

Chris, Wes, and Patty dive in to discuss this further, while John looks dubious. Eventually Wes says, "You know, this just may work." When everyone nods, including John, I feel there's a sense of excitement and possibility that was missing just minutes ago.

Part 3

CHAPTER 30

• *Monday, November 3*

An hour after the meeting with Steve adjourned, I'm still mulling over Erik's cryptic comments. I feel like we're on the verge of something big, but I have too many questions. I finally decide to call him.

"Yeah?" he answers.

"Bill here," I say. "I need some more clues about what the hell we're supposed to be doing…"

"Meet me outside the building," he says, hanging up.

When I get outside, the wind is gusty and fierce. I look around for a couple of moments, when I hear a horn honk. Erik is in an expensive-looking red BMW convertible, with the top down. "Come on in. Hurry!"

"Nice ride," I say, climbing into the passenger seat.

"Thanks," he says. "My friend insisted that I borrow this while I'm in town."

As he floors the accelerator, I grab the armrest and hurriedly buckle my seatbelt. I see a purse on the floor, and immediately wonder who this "friend" is.

"We're heading back to MRP-8," he says.

When I ask him to raise the convertible top, he looks over at me and says, "I thought there was no such thing as an 'ex-Marine.' Maybe they made you guys softer than in my day."

"You were in the service?" I ask, trying to hide my chattering teeth.

He laughs. "Over twenty years."

"You retired as an officer, I suppose?" I asked.

"Major, Special Forces, US Army," he replies, looking at me. I keep hoping he'll keep his eyes on the road, given how fast we're going. Instead, he continues, "Same branch as Steve, but he joined as an officer. I joined as an enlisted grunt, just like you."

He doesn't reveal any more, but he has already told me enough to understand his military career. He was obviously a senior NCO, like many I had to deal with on a daily basis, now recognizing his all-too-familiar demeanor and physical bearing. He must have been identified as one of those rare high-potential people by the higher-ups, who decided to invest in his future, sending him to college and Officer Candidate School, then rejoining the ranks as the oldest second lieutenant around, probably ten years older than everybody else.

It takes a special person to go through that.

We make it to the plant in record time and are now standing on the catwalk. He begins the speech that I've been expecting. "A manufacturing plant is a system. The raw materials start on one side, and a million things need to go just right in order for it to leave as finished goods as scheduled out the other side. Everything works together. If any work center is warring with the other work centers, especially if Manufacturing is at war with Engineering, every inch of progress will be a struggle."

Erik turns to me, pointing, "You've got to stop thinking like a work center supervisor. You need to think bigger, like a plant manager. Or better yet, think like the person who designed this manufacturing plant and all of the processes it relies upon. They look at the entire flow of work, identify where the constraints are, and use every possible technology and bit of process knowledge they have to ensure work is performed effectively and efficiently. They harness their 'inner-Allspaw.'"

I'm about to ask what he means by an "Allspaw," when he just waves my question away. "In manufacturing, we have a measure called *takt* time, which is the cycle time needed in order to keep up with customer demand. If any operation in the flow of work takes longer than the takt time, you will not be able to keep up with customer demand."

"So when you run around screaming, 'Oh no! We don't have environments for Phoenix ready! Help, help! Oh, no! We can't deploy, because someone broke the Phoenix environments again!'" he says in a high, girlish voice, "That means the cycle time of some critical operation in your area of responsibility is greater than the takt time. That is the reason you can't keep up with customer demand.

"As part of the Second Way, you need to create a feedback loop that goes all the way back to the earliest parts of product definition, design, and development," he says. "Given the conversations you're having with Dick, you may even be able to go earlier in the process."

Pointing at the floor, he says, "Look down at the long lane of equipment between the orange tape on the floor. That lane makes some of the highest profit items we have. But as fate would have it, that particular flow of work involves two operations that have the longest setup and process times: application of a paint powder coating and baking it in the heat treat oven."

He looks up, arms spread outward. "Back in the day, the cycle time for those two operations was so much larger than takt time, we were never able to keep up with customer demand. How can life be so unfair? The most profitable items used *both* of our constraints: the heat treat oven *and* the paint booths! What do we do?

"Customers were even offering to throw money at us, begging us for more of these widgets, but we had to turn them away. The setup time for each job took hours or even days. We had to use enormous batch sizes to meet demand. We had these huge trays to paint and would bake as many units at a time as possible. We knew we had to reduce batch sizes to improve throughput, but everyone said that it couldn't be done."

"How Toyota solved this problem is legendary," he says. "During the 1950s, they had a hood stamping process that had a change-over time of almost three days. It required moving huge, heavy dies that weighed many tons. Like us, the setup times were so long that they needed to use large batch sizes, which prevented them from using one stamping machine to manufacture multiple different car models simultaneously. You can't make one hood for a Prius and then one hood for a Camry if it takes you three days to do the changeovers, right?

"What did they do?" he asks rhetorically. "They closely observed all the steps required to do the changeover, and then put in a series of preparations and improvements that brought the changeover time down to under ten minutes. And that, of course, is where the legendary 'single-minute exchange of die' term comes from.

"We studied all the works of Sensei Taiichi Ohno, Steven Spear, and Mike Rother. We knew that we had to decrease our batch size, but we weren't dealing with hood stamping dies. We were dealing with painting and curing," he continues. "After weeks of brainstorming, investigation, and experimentation with Engineering, we had a crazy idea: Maybe we could do the painting and curing in a single machine. We cobbled together an oven that also applied the paint powder onto the parts, which were pulled through on a chain and gear that we took from a bicycle.

"We combined four work centers into one, eliminating over thirty manual, error-prone steps, completely automating the work cycle, achieving single-piece flow, and eliminating all that setup time. Throughput went through the roof.

"The benefits were enormous," he says with pride. "First, when defects were found, we fixed them immediately and we didn't have to scrap all the other parts in that batch. Second, WIP was brought down because each work center never overproduced product, only to sit in the queue of the next work center. But the most important benefit was that order lead times were cut from one month to less than a week. We could build and deliver whatever and however many the customer wanted and never had a warehouse full of crap that we'd need to liquidate at fire-sale prices.

"So, now it's your turn," he says sternly, poking a finger into my chest. "You've got to figure out how to decrease your changeover time and enable faster deployment cycle time.

"I think your target should be…" he says, pausing for a moment. "Ten deploys a day. Why not?"

My jaw drops. "That's impossible."

"Oh, really?" he says, deadpan. "Let me tell you a story. Back in 2009, I was a board director at a technology company, where one of our engineers went to the Velocity Conference and came back raving like a madman, full of dangerous, impossible ideas. He saw a presentation given by John Allspaw and his colleague Paul Hammond that flipped the world on its head. Allspaw and Hammond ran the IT Operations and Engineering groups at Flickr. Instead of fighting like cats and dogs, they talked about how they were working together to routinely do ten deploys a day! This is in a world when most IT organizations were mostly doing quarterly or annual deployments. Imagine that. He was doing deploys at a rate one thousand times faster than the previous state of the art.

"Let me tell you," he continues, "we all thought that this engineer had lost his marbles. But I learned that the practices that Allspaw and Hammond espoused are the inevitable outcome of applying the Three Ways to the IT value stream. It totally changed how we managed IT and it saved our company.

"How did they do it?" I ask, dumbfounded.

"Good question," he replies. "Allspaw taught us that Dev and Ops working together, along with QA and the business, are a super-tribe that can achieve amazing things. They also knew that until code is in production, no value is actually being generated, because it's merely WIP stuck in the system. He kept reducing the batch size, enabling fast feature flow. In part, he did this by ensuring environments were always available when they were needed. He automated the build and deployment process, recognizing that infrastructure could be treated as code, just like the application that Development ships. That enabled him to create a one-step environment creation and deploy procedure, just like we figured out a way to do one-step painting and curing.

"So, we now know that Allspaw and Hammond weren't so crazy after all. Jez Humble and Dave Farley independently came to the same conclusions, and then codified the practices and principles that enable multiple deployments per day in their seminal book *Continuous Delivery*. Eric Ries then showed us how this capability can help the business learn and win in his Lean Startup work."

As Erik talks, he is as animated as I've ever seen him. Shaking his head, he looks sternly at me.

"Your next step should be obvious by now, grasshopper. In order for you to keep up with customer demand, which includes your upstream comrades in Development," he says, "you need to create what Humble and Farley called a *deployment pipeline*. That's your entire value stream from code check-in to production. That's not an art. That's production. You need to get everything in version control. Everything. Not just the code, but everything required to build the environment. Then you need to automate the entire environment creation process. You need a deployment pipeline where you can create test and production environments, and then deploy code into them, entirely on-demand. That's how you reduce your setup times and eliminate errors, so you can finally match whatever rate of change Development sets the tempo at."

"Hold on," I say. "What is it exactly that I'm supposed to automate?"

Erik looks at me sternly. "Go ask Brent. Get him assigned to that new team, and make sure that he doesn't get distracted. Now more than ever, until you get your build process automated, he is your bottleneck. Get the things that are in his head encoded into the build procedures. Get humans out of the deployment business. Figure out how to get to ten deploys a day."

I can't get over my skepticism. "Ten deploys a day? I'm pretty sure that no one is asking for that. Aren't you setting a target that's higher than what the business needs?"

Erik sighs, rolling his eyes. "Stop focusing on the deployment target rate. Business agility is not just about raw speed. It's about how good you are at detecting and responding to changes in the market and being able to take larger and more calculated risks. It's about continual experimentation, like Scott Cook did at Intuit, where they did over forty experiments during the peak tax filing season to figure out how to maximize customer conversion rates. During the peak tax filing season!

"If you can't out-experiment and beat your competitors in time to market and agility, you are sunk. Features are always a gamble. If you're lucky, ten percent will get the desired benefits. So the faster you can get those features to market and test them, the better off you'll be. Incidentally, you also pay back the business faster for the use of capital, which means the business starts making money faster, too.

"Steve is betting his entire survival on your ability to execute and deploy capabilities faster. So, get to work with Chris to figure out how at every stage of the agile development process, you not only have shippable code, but a working environment it can deploy into!"

"Okay, okay," I say. "But why did you drag me all the way over here in the freezing cold? Wouldn't explaining it on a whiteboard have been enough?"

"You think IT Operations is rocket-science compared to manufacturing. What absolute baloney," he says dismissively. "From where I'm sitting, the people in *this* building have been far more creative and courageous than anything I've seen come from you IT guys so far."

CHAPTER 31

• *Monday, November 3*

It's 12:13 p.m. when I walk into the SWAT team kick-off meeting. My hair is dripping wet and my shirt is soaked from my ride back in Erik's convertible. Chris is talking. "—and so Steve has authorized this small team to deliver the promotion functionality and do whatever it takes to make a positive impact on the holiday shopping season."

Chris turns to me and points to the back of the room. "I went ahead and ordered lunch for everyone to kick this off. Go ahead and—what happened to you?"

I wave away his question. Looking at where he's pointing, I'm pleasantly surprised to see a turkey sandwich lunch box still at the back. Grabbing it, I take a seat and try to gauge the temperature of everyone in the room, especially Brent.

Brent responds, "Explain again why I'm here?"

"That's what we're here to figure out," Wes says earnestly. "You know as much as we do. One of the potential board members insisted that you be a part of this team. Quite frankly, he's been right enough times that I trust him, even if I have no freaking idea why."

Patty chimes in. "Well, he gave us a couple of clues. He said that the problems we need to focus on are the deployment process and the way we're building the environments. He seems to think we must be doing something fundamentally wrong because of all the chaos resulting from each Phoenix deployment."

As I unwrap my sandwich I say, "I just came back from a meeting with him. He showed me a bunch of stuff and explained how they do single-minute exchanges of die at Toyota. He thinks we need to build the capability to do ten deploys per day. He not only insists this is possible but also that it supports the feature deployment cycles the business needs, not just to survive, but to win in the marketplace."

Surprisingly, Chris speaks out the most fiercely. "*What*? Why in the world would we need to do ten deploys a day? Our sprint intervals are three weeks long. We don't have anything to deploy ten times a day!"

Patty shakes her head. "Are you sure? What about bug fixes? What about performance enhancements when the site grinds to a halt, like what's happened during the last two major launches? Wouldn't you love to do these types of changes in production routinely, without having to break all the rules to do some sort of emergency change?"

Chris thinks for a couple of moments before responding. "Interesting. I would normally call those types of fixes a patch or a minor release. But you're right—those are deployments, too. It would be great if we could roll out fixes more quickly, but come on, *ten deploys a day?*"

Thinking about what Erik said, I add, "How about enabling Marketing to make their own changes to content or business rules or enabling faster experimentation and A/B split testing, to see what offers work best?"

Wes puts both of his hands on the table. "Mark my words, folks. It can't be done. We're dealing with the laws of physics here. Forget about how long it currently takes, which requires over one week of preparation and over eight hours to do the actual deployment! You can only put bits down on the disk so fast."

That's exactly what I would have said before the plant tour with Erik. I say earnestly, "Look, maybe you're right, but humor me for a second: Just how many steps are there in the entire end-to-end deployment process? Are we talking about twenty steps, two hundred, or two thousand?"

Wes scratches his head for a moment before he says, "What do you think, Brent? I would have thought about a hundred steps…"

"Really?" Brent responds. "I would have thought it was more like twenty steps."

William interjects, "I'm not sure where you're starting to count, but if we begin at the point where Development commits code and we label it as a 'release candidate,' I can probably come up with a hundred steps, even before we hand it to IT Operations."

Uh-oh.

Wes interrupts, "No, no, no. Bill said 'deployment steps.' Let's not open up a can of—"

As Wes talks, I think about Erik challenging me to think like a plant manager as opposed to a work center supervisor. I suddenly realize that he probably meant that I needed to span the departmental boundaries of Development and IT Operations.

"You guys are both correct," I say, interrupting Wes and William. "William, would you mind writing down all the steps on the whiteboard? I'd suggest starting at 'code committed,' and keep going until the hand-off to our group."

He nods and walks to the whiteboard and starts drawing boxes, discussing the steps as he goes. Over the next ten minutes, he proves that there are likely over one hundred steps, including the automated tests run in the Dev environment, creating a QA environment that matches Dev, deploying code into it, running all the tests, deploying and migrating into a fresh staging environment that matches QA, load testing, and finally the baton being passed to IT Operations.

When William is finished, there are thirty boxes on the board.

Looking over at Wes, I see that rather than looking irritated, he actually appears deep in thought, rubbing his chin while looking at the diagram.

I indicate to Brent and Wes that one of them should continue where William left off.

Brent gets up and starts drawing boxes to indicate the packaging of the code for deployment; preparing new server instances; loading and configuring the operating system, databases, and applications; making all the changes to the networks, firewalls, and load balancers; and then testing to make sure the deployment completed successfully.

I contemplate the entirety of the diagram, which surprisingly reminds me of the plant floor. Each of these steps is like a work center, each with different machines, men, methods, and measures. IT work is probably *much more complex* than manufacturing work. Not only is the work invisible, making it more difficult to track, but there are far more things that could go wrong.

Countless configurations need to be set correctly, systems need enough memory, all the files need to be put in the right place, and all code and the entire environment need to be operating correctly.

Even one small mistake could take everything down. Surely this meant that we needed even *more* rigor and discipline and planning than in manufacturing.

I can't wait to tell Erik this.

Realizing the importance and enormity of the challenge in front of us, I walk to the whiteboard, and pick up the red marker. I say, "I'm going to put a big red star on each step where we had problems during previous launches."

Starting to make marks on the whiteboard, I explain, "Because a fresh QA environment wasn't available, we used an old version; because of all the test failures, we made code and environment changes to the QA environment, which never made it back into the Dev or Production environments; and because we never synchronized all the environments, we had the same problems the next time around, too."

Leaving a trail of red stars, I start marching into Brent's boxes. "Because we didn't have correct deployment instructions, it took us five turns to get the packaging and deployment scripts right. This blew up in production because the environment was incorrectly built, which I've already brought up."

Even though I didn't do it on purpose, by the time I'm done, almost all of William and Brent's boxes had red stars next to them.

Turning around, I see everyone's dispirited faces as they take in what I've done. Realizing my potential mistake, I hurriedly add, "Look, my goal isn't to blame anyone or say that we're doing a crappy job. I'm merely trying to get down on paper exactly what we're doing and get some objective measures of each step. Let's fight the problem that's on the whiteboard as a team and not blame one another, okay?"

Patty says, "You know, this reminds me of something that I've seen the plant floor guys use all the time. If one of them walked in, I'm guessing that they'd think we're building a 'value stream map.' Mind if I add a couple of elements?"

I pass the whiteboard marker to her and sit down.

For each of the boxes, she asks how long each of these operations typically takes then jots the number on top of the box. Next, she asks whether this step is typically where work has to wait then draws a triangle before the box, indicating work in process.

Holy crap. To Patty, the similarity between our deployments and a plant line isn't some academic question. She's treating our deployment as if it actually was a plant line!

She's using Lean tools and techniques that the manufacturing folks use to document and improve their processes.

Suddenly, I understand what Erik meant when he talked about the "deployment pipeline." Even though you can't see our work like in a manufacturing plant, it's still a value stream.

I correct myself. It's our value stream, and I'm confident that we're on the brink of figuring out how to dramatically increase the flow of work through it.

After Patty finishes recording the durations of the steps, she redraws the boxes, using short labels to describe the process steps. On a separate whiteboard, she writes down two bullet points: "environments" and "deployment."

Pointing to what she just wrote, she says, "With the current process, two issues keep coming up: At every stage of the deployment process, environments are never available when we need them, and even when they are, there's considerable rework required to get them all synchronized with one another. Yes?"

Wes snorts, saying, "No reward for stating something *that* obvious, but you're right."

She continues, "The other obvious source of rework and long setup time is in the code packaging process, where IT Operations takes what Development checks into version control and then generates the deployment packages. Although Chris and his team do their best to document the code and configurations, something always falls through the cracks, which are only exposed when the code fails to run in the environment after deployment. Correct?"

This time, Wes doesn't respond right away. Brent beats him, saying, "You've nailed it. William can probably relate to these problems: the release instructions are never up-to-date, so we're always scrambling, trying to futz with it, having to rewrite the installer scripts and install it over and over again…"

"Yep," William says, nodding adamantly.

"I'd suggest we focus on those two areas, then," she says, looking at the board and then grabbing her seat again. "Any ideas?"

Brent says, "Maybe William and I can work together to build a deployment run book, to capture all the lessons learned from our mistakes?"

I nod, listening to everyone's ideas, but none of them seem like the massive breakthrough we need. Erik had described the reduction of setup time for the door stamping process. He seemed to indicate that it was important. But why?

"Having each group cobble an environment together obviously isn't working. Whatever we do must take us a big step toward this 'ten deploys a day' target," I say. "This implies that we need a significant amount of automation. Brent, what would it take for us to be able to create a common environment creation process, so we can simultaneously build the Dev, QA, and Production environments at the same time, and keep them synchronized?"

"Interesting idea," Brent says, looking at the board. He stands up and draws three boxes labeled "Dev," "QA," and "Production." And then underneath them, he draws another box labeled "Build Procedure" with arrows into each of the boxes above.

"That's actually pretty brilliant, Bill," he says. "If we had a common build procedure, and everyone used these tools to create their environments, the developers would actually be writing code in an environment that at least resembles the Production environment. That alone would be a huge improvement."

He takes the marker cap out of his mouth. "To build the Phoenix environment, we use a bunch of scripts that we've written. With a bit of documentation and cleanup, I bet we could cobble together something usable in a couple of days."

Turning to Chris, I say, "This seems promising. If we could standardize the environments and get these in daily use by Development, QA, and IT Operations, we could eliminate the majority of variance that's causing so much grief in the deployment process."

Chris seems excited. "Brent, if it's okay with you and everyone else, I'd like to invite you to our team sprints, so that we can get environment creation integrated into the development process as early as possible. Right now, we focus mostly on having deployable code at the end of the project. I propose we change that requirement. At each three-week sprint interval, we not only need to have deployable code but also the exact environment that the code deploys into, and have that checked into version control, too."

Brent smiles widely at the suggestion. Before Wes can respond, I say, "I completely agree. But before we go further, can we investigate the other issue that Patty highlighted? Even if we adopted Chris' suggestions, there's still the issue of the deployment scripts. If we had a magic wand, whenever we have a fresh QA environment, how should we deploy the code? Every time we deploy, we constantly ping-pong code, scripts, and God knows what else among groups."

Patty chimes in. "On the manufacturing floor, whenever we see work go backward, that's rework. When that happens, you can bet that the amount of documentation and information flow is going to be pretty poor, which means nothing is reproducible and that it's going to get worse over time as we try to go faster. They call this 'non-value-add' activity or 'waste.'"

Looking at the first whiteboard with all the boxes, she says, "If we redesign the process, we need to have the right people involved upfront. This is like the manufacturing engineering group ensuring that all parts are designed so that they are optimized for manufacturing and that the manufacturing lines are optimized for the parts, ideally in single-piece flow."

I nod, smiling at the similarities between what Patty is recommending and what Erik suggested earlier today.

Turning to William and Brent, I say, "Okay, guys, you have the magic wand. You're at the front of the line. Tell me how you'd design the manufacturing line so that work never goes backward, and the flow is moving forward quickly and efficiently."

When they both give me a blank look, I say with some exasperation, "You have a *magic wand*. Use it!"

"How big is the magic wand?" William asks.

I repeat what I said to Maggie. "It's a *very* powerful magic wand. It can do anything."

William walks to the whiteboard and points at a box called "code commit." "If I could wave this magic wand, I would change this step. Instead of getting source code or compiled code from Dev through source control, I want packaged code that's ready to be deployed."

"And you know," he continues, "I want this so much, I'd happily volunteer to take over responsibility for package creation. I know exactly the person I'd assign, too. She would be responsible for the Dev handoff. When code is labeled 'ready to test,' we would then generate and commit the packaged code, which would trigger an automated deployment into the QA environment. And later, maybe even the Production environment, too."

"Wow. You'd really do that?" Wes asks. "That would be really great. Let's do it—unless Brent really wants to keep doing the packaging?"

"Are you kidding?" Brent asks, bursting out laughing. "I'll buy whoever this person is drinks for the rest of the year! I love this idea. And I want to help build the new deployment tools. Like I said, I've got a bunch of tools that I've written that we can use as a starting point."

I can feel the energy and excitement in the room. I'm amazed at how quickly we went from believing the 'ten deploys a day' target was a delusional fantasy, to wondering how close we can get.

Suddenly, Patty looks up and says, "Wait a second. This entire Phoenix module deals with customer purchase data, which has to be protected. Shouldn't someone from John's team be a part of this effort, as well?"

We all look at one another, agreeing that he needs to be involved. And once again, I marvel at how much we've changed as an organization.

CHAPTER 32

• *Monday, November 10*

The next two weeks fly by with the SWAT team activities taking up much of my time, as well as Wes' and Patty's.

It's been over a decade since I've had daily interactions with developers. I had forgotten how quirky they can be. To me, they seem more like indie musicians than engineers.

In my day, developers wore pocket protectors—not vintage T-shirts and sandals—and carried slide rules, not skateboards.

In many ways, most of these guys are my temperamental opposites. I like people who create and follow processes, people who value rigor and discipline. These guys shun process in favor of whim and whimsy.

But thank goodness they're here.

I know that stereotyping an entire profession isn't fair. I know that all these diverse skills are vital if we want to succeed. The challenge is how to pull all of us together, so that we're working toward the same goal.

The first challenge: to name the SWAT team project. We couldn't keep calling it "mini-Phoenix," so we eventually had to spend an hour debating names.

My guys wanted to call it "Cujo" or "Stiletto." But the developers wanted to call it "Unicorn."

Unicorn? Like rainbows and Care Bears?

And against all my expectations, "Unicorn" wins the vote.

Developers. I'll never understand them.

Regardless of my distaste for the name, Project Unicorn was shaping up amazingly well. With the objective of doing whatever it takes to deliver effective customer recommendations and promotions, we started with a clean code base that was completely decoupled from the Phoenix behemoth.

It was amazing to see how this team tackled obstacles. One of the first challenges was to start analyzing the customer purchase data, which was the first brick wall. Even touching the production databases meant linking to their libraries, and any changes to them would require convincing the architecture team to approve it.

Since the entire company could be out of business by that time, the developers and Brent decided to create a completely new database, using open source tools, with data copied from not only Phoenix but also the order entry and inventory management systems.

By doing this, we could develop, test, and even run in operations without impacting Phoenix or other business critical applications. And by decoupling ourselves from the other projects, we could make all the changes we needed to without putting other projects at risk. At the same time, we wouldn't get bogged down in the processes that we didn't need to be a part of.

I wholeheartedly approved and applauded this approach. However, a small part of me wondered how we're going to manage the inevitable sprawl, if every project could spawn a new database on a whim. I remind myself to ensure that we standardize what types of databases we can put into production to ensure that we have the right skills to support these long-term.

In the meantime, Brent worked with William's team to create the build procedures and automated mechanisms that could simultaneously create the Dev, QA, and Production environments. We were all astonished that within the three-week sprint, perhaps for the first time in memory, all the developers were using exactly the same operating system, library versions, databases, database settings, and so forth.

"This is unbelievable," one of the developers said at the sprint retrospective, held at the end of each sprint. "For Phoenix, it takes us three or four weeks for new developers to get builds running on their machine, because we've never assembled the complete list of the gazillion things you need installed in order for it to compile and run. But now all we have to do is check out the virtual machine that Brent and team built, and they're all ready to go."

Similarly, we were all amazed that we had a QA environment available that matched Dev so early in the project. That, too, was unprecedented. We needed to make a bunch of adjustments to reflect that the Dev systems had considerably less memory and storage than QA, and QA had less than those in Production. But the vast majority of the environments were identical and could be modified and spun up in minutes.

Automated code deployments weren't quite working yet, nor was the migration of code among the environments, but William's team had demoed enough of those capabilities that we all had confidence that they'd have it nailed down soon.

On top of that, the developers had hit their feature sprint goals ahead of schedule. They generated reports showing "customers who bought this product bought these other products." The reports were taking hundreds of times longer than expected, but they promised that they could improve performance.

Because of our rapid progress, we decided to shrink the sprint interval to two weeks. By doing this, we could reduce our planning horizon, to make and execute decisions more frequently, as opposed to sticking to a plan made almost a month ago.

Phoenix continues to operate on a plan written over three years ago. I try not to think about that too much.

Our progress seemed to be improving exponentially. We're planning and executing faster than ever, and the velocity gap between Unicorn and Phoenix keeps getting larger. The Phoenix teams are taking notice and starting to borrow practices left and right and getting results that we hadn't thought possible.

Unicorn momentum seems unstoppable and now has a life of its own. I doubt we could have made them stop and go back to the old way, even if we wanted to.

While I'm in the middle of a budgeting meeting, Wes calls. "We've got a big problem."

Stepping out of the room, I say, "What's up?"

"No one has been able to find Brent for the last two days. You have any idea where he is?" he asks.

"No," I reply. "Wait, what do you mean you can't find him? Is he okay? You've tried his cell phone, right?"

Wes doesn't bother hiding his exasperation. "Of course I called his cell phone! I've been leaving voicemails for him hourly. Everyone is trying to find him. We've got work up the wazoo, and his team mates are starting to freak out that—holy crap, it's Brent calling… Hang on…"

I hear him pick up his desk phone, saying, "Where the hell have you been? Everyone is looking for you! No… No… Des Moines? What are you doing there? Nobody told me… A secret mission for Dick and Sarah? What the fuck—"

I listen to him for a couple of moments with some amusement as Wes attempts to get to the bottom of the situation with Brent. Finally I hear him say, "Hang on a second. Let me find out what Bill wants to do…" as he picks up his cell phone again.

"Okay, you must have heard some of that, right?" he says to me.

"Tell him I'm calling him right now."

After I hang up, I dial up Brent, wondering what Sarah has done now.

"Hi, Bill," I hear him say.

"Mind telling me what's going on and why you're in Des Moines?" I ask politely.

"Nobody from Dick's office told you?" he asks. When I don't say anything, he continues, "Dick and the finance team rushed me out the door yesterday morning to be a part of a task force to create a plan to split up the company. Apparently, this is a top priority project, and they need to figure out what the implications to all the IT systems are."

"And why did Dick put you on the team?" I ask.

"I don't know," he replies. "Trust me, I don't want to be here. I hate airplanes. They should have one of their business analysts doing this, but maybe it's because I know the most about how the major systems connect to one another, where they all reside, all the services they depend on… By the way, I can tell you right now that splitting up the company will be a complete nightmare."

I remember when I led the acquisition integration team when we acquired the large retailer. That was a huge project. Splitting the company up may be even more difficult.

If this is going to impact every one of the hundreds of applications we support, Brent is probably right. It will take years.

IT is everywhere, so it's not like cutting off a limb. It's more like splitting up the nervous system of the company.

Remembering that Dick and Sarah yanked one of my key resources away from me without even asking, I say slowly and deliberately, "Brent, listen carefully: Your most important priority is to find out what your Unicorn teammates need and get it to them. Miss your flight if you have to. I'll make some phone calls, but there's a good chance that my assistant Ellen will book you a return flight home tonight. Do you understand?"

"You want me to deliberately miss my flight," he says.

"Yes."

"What will I tell Dick and Sarah?" he asks, uncertainly.

I think for a moment. "Tell them I need you on an emergency call, and that you'll catch up with them."

"Okay…" he says. "What's going on here?"

"It's simple, Brent," I explain. "Unicorn is the one last hope we have of hitting our quarterly number. One more blown quarter, and the board will surely split the company apart, and you'll be able to help the task force then. But if we hit our numbers, we have a shot at keeping the company together. That's why Unicorn is our absolute highest priority. Steve was very clear on this."

Brent says dubiously, "Okay. Just tell me where to go, and I'll be there. I'll leave you to argue with the mucky-mucks." He is clearly annoyed by the mixed signals being sent to him.

But not nearly as annoyed as I am.

I call Steve's assistant Stacy and tell her I'm on my way.

As I make my trek to Building 2 to find Steve, I call Wes.

"You did what?" he chortles. "Just great. You're now in the middle of a political battle with Steve on one side and Dick and Sarah on the other. And, quite frankly, I'm not sure you chose the winning side."

After a moment, he says, "You really think Steve is going to back us up on this one?"

I suppress a sigh. "I sure hope so. If we don't get Brent back full-time, Unicorn is sunk. And that probably means that we'll get a new CEO, get outsourced, and also figure out how to split up the company. That sound like a fun job to you?"

I hang up and walk into Steve's office. He smiles wanly and says, "Good morning. Stacy says you have some bad news for me."

As I tell him what I learned during my phone call with Brent, I'm surprised to see his face turn scarlet. I would have thought he knew about all of this, given that he's the CEO.

Obviously not.

After a moment, he finally says, "The board assured me that they wouldn't go further down the company breakup path until we see how this quarter turns out. I suppose they ran out of patience."

He continues, "So tell me what the impact is to Unicorn if Brent gets reassigned."

"I've talked with Chris, Wes, and Patty," I reply. "Project Unicorn would be completely sunk. I'm a skeptical guy by nature, but I really think Unicorn is going to work. With Thanksgiving only two weeks away, Brent owns a significant portion of getting the capabilities we need built. And by the way, many of the breakthroughs we're making are starting to be copied by the Phoenix team, which is fantastic."

To underscore my point, I say with finality, "Without Brent, we will not be able to hit any of the sales and profit goals that we've tied to Unicorn. No chance."

Pursing his lips, Steve asks, "And what happens if you backfill Brent with your next best guy?"

I relay to Steve what Wes told me, which mirrored my own thinking. "Brent is very unique. Unicorn needs someone who has the respect of the developers, has enough deep experience with almost every sort of IT infrastructure we have, and can describe what the developers need to build so that we can actually manage and operate in production. Those skills are rare, and we don't have anyone else that can rotate into this special role right now."

"And what if you assign your next best person to Dick's task force?" he asks.

"I'd guess that the breakup planning won't be as accurate but could still get completed just fine," I reply.

Steve leans back in his chair, saying nothing.

Finally he says, "Get Brent back here. I'll handle the rest."

CHAPTER 33

• *Tuesday , November 11*

By the next day, Brent is back on Unicorn, and one of the level 3 engineers has joined Dick's team somewhere in the snowy Midwest. Within hours, I get copied on an e-mail from Sarah:

> From: Sarah Moulton
> To: Bob Strauss
> Cc: Dick Landry, Steve Masters, Bill Palmer
> Date: November 11, 7:24 AM
> Subject: Someone is undermining Project Talon
>
> Bob, I've discovered that Bill Palmer, the acting VP of IT Operations, stole the critical resource for Project Talon.
>
> Bill, I'm deeply concerned with your recent actions. Please explain to us why you ordered Brent to return home? This is absolutely intolerable. The board has instructed us to explore strategic options.
>
> I demand that Brent rejoin the Talon team as soon as possible. Please confirm you understand this message.
>
> Sarah

Genuinely alarmed that I'm being called out on an e-mail to the company chairman, I call Steve, who is obviously furious at Sarah's apparent change in loyalties. After swearing under his breath, he assures me that he'll handle this and that I am to continue as planned.

At the daily Unicorn stand-up meeting, William doesn't look happy. "The good news is that as of last night, we've generated our first customer promotion report and it appears to be working correctly. But the code is running fifty times slower than we expected. One of the clustering algorithms isn't parallelizing like we thought it would, so the prediction runs are already taking more than twenty-four hours, even for our small customer data set test."

Grumbles and groans go around the room.

One of the developers says, "Can't we just use brute force? Just throw more hardware at the problem. With enough compute servers, we can bring the run times down."

"Are you kidding me?" Wes says, with exasperation. "We only budgeted for twenty of the fastest servers we could find. You'd need over a thousand servers to get the run times down to where we need. That's over $1 million in unbudgeted capital!"

I purse my lips. Wes is right. Phoenix is way over budget as it is, and we're talking about a large enough amount of money that it'll be impossible to get this approved, especially given our financial condition.

"We don't need any new hardware," the developer replies. "We've invested all this effort to create compute images that we can deploy. Why not send them out to the cloud? We could spin up hundreds or thousands of compute instances as we need them, tear them down when we're done, and just pay for the compute time we use."

Wes looks at Brent, who says, "It's possible. We're already using virtualization for most of our environments. It shouldn't be very difficult to convert them so that they run on a cloud computing provider."

After a moment, he adds, "You know, that would be fun. I've always wanted to try something like this."

Brent's excitement is contagious.

We start assigning tasks to investigate its feasibility. Brent teams up with the developer who had suggested the idea to do a quick prototype, to see whether it is even possible.

Maggie, who has taken such an interest in Unicorn that she's routinely attending the daily stand-ups, volunteers to look into pricing and will call her peers in the industry to see if any of them have done this before and to get any recommended vendors.

One of John's security engineers interrupts, "Sending our customer data to the cloud may have some risks like accidental disclosure of private data or someone unauthorized hacking into those compute servers."

"Good thinking," I say. "Can you list your top risks we should be thinking about, and prepare a list of potential countermeasures and controls?"

He smiles in response, happy to be asked. One of the developers volunteers to work with him.

By the end of the meeting, I'm surprised at the unanticipated payoffs of automating our deployment process. The developers can more quickly scale the application, and potentially few changes would be required from us.

Despite this, I'm extremely dubious of all this cloud computing hullabaloo. People treat it as if it's some sort of magical elixir that instantaneously reduces costs. In my mind, it's just another form of outsourcing.

But if it solves a problem we're having, I'm willing to give it a try. I remind Wes to keep an open mind, as well.

A week later, once again, it's demo time. We're all standing in the Unicorn team area. It's the end of the sprint, and the Development lead is eager to show off what the team has accomplished.

"I can hardly believe how much we got done," he starts off. "Because of all the deployment automation, getting compute instances running in the cloud wasn't as hard as we thought. In fact, it's working so well that we're considering turning all the in-house Unicorn production systems into test systems and using the cloud for all our production systems.

"We start the recommendations reporting run every evening and spin up hundreds of compute instances until we're done, and then we turn them off. We've been doing this for the past four days, and it's working well—really well."

Brent has a wide smile on this face, as does the rest of the team.

Next up is usually the product manager, but this time Maggie is presenting instead. She's obviously taking more than just casual interest in this project.

She pulls up a PowerPoint slide on the projector. "These are the Unicorn promotions generated for my customer account. As you can see, it's looked at my buying history and is letting me know that snow tires and batteries are fifteen percent off. I actually went to our website and purchased both, because I need them. The company just made money, because those are all items that we have excess inventory and high profit margins."

I smile. Now that's brilliant.

"And, here are the Unicorn promotions for Wes," she continues, going to the next slide, with a smile. "Looks like you got a discount on racing brake pads and fuel additives. That of any interest to you?"

Wes smiles. "Not bad!"

Maggie explains that all these offers are already in the Phoenix system, and it was just waiting for the promotion functionality to finally get them to the customers.

She continues, "Here's my proposal: I'd like to do an e-mail campaign to one percent of our customers, to see what happens. Thanksgiving is in one week. If we could do a couple of trials and everything goes well, we'd go full blast on Black Friday, which is the busiest shopping day of the year."

"Sounds like a good plan," I say. "Wes, is there any reason why we shouldn't do this?"

Wes shakes his head. "From an Ops perspective, I can't think of any. All the hard work has already been done. If Chris, William, and Marketing have confidence that the code is working, I say go for it."

Everyone agrees. There are some issues that come up, but Maggie says her team is willing to work all night to make it happen.

I smile inwardly. For once, it won't be just us staying up all night because something went really wrong. In fact, it's the exact opposite. People are staying up all night because everything was going right.

The following Monday, it's barely above freezing as I'm driving to work, but the sun is shining brightly. It looks like it's going to be a great week for the upcoming Thanksgiving holiday. Throughout the weekend, I'm a bit startled to see commercials with Santa Claus in them.

When I get to my office, I throw my heavy coat over my chair. I turn when I hear Patty walk into my office and see that she has a broad smile on her face. "Did you hear the amazing news from Marketing?"

When I shake my head, she merely says, "Read the e-mail that Maggie just sent out."

I flip open my laptop and read:

> From: Maggie Lee
> To: Chris Allers, Bill Palmer
> Cc: Steve Masters, Wes Davis, Sarah Moulton
> Date: November 24, 7:47 AM
> Subject: First Unicorn promotion campaign: UNBELIEVABLE!
>
> The Marketing team burned the midnight oil over the weekend and we were able to do a test campaign to one percent of our customers.
>
> The results were STELLAR! Over twenty percent of the respondents went to our website, and over six percent purchased. These are incredibly high conversion rates—probably over 5× higher than any campaign we've done before.
>
> We recommend doing a Unicorn promotion to all our customers on Thanksgiving Day. I'm working to get a dashboard up so everyone can see real-time results of the Unicorn campaigns.
>
> Also, remember that all the items being promoted are high margin items, so the effects on our bottom line will be excellent.
>
> PS: Bill, based on the results, we expect a huge surge in web traffic. Can we make sure the website won't fall over?
>
> Great work, all!
>
> Maggie

"I love it," I say to Patty. "Work with Wes to figure out what we need to do to handle the surge in traffic. We've only got three days to get this done, so we don't have much time. We don't want to screw this up and turn prospective customers into haters."

She nods and is about to respond when her phone vibrates. An instant later, my phone vibrates, too. She quickly looks down and says, "The dragon lady strikes again."

"I wish I had an 'unsubscribe' button for her e-mails," Patty says as she walks out.

A half hour later, Steve sent out a congratulatory note to the entire

Unicorn team, which everyone loved reading. More surprisingly, he also sent out a public reply to Sarah, demanding that she stop "stirring the pot and making trouble" and to "see me at your earliest convenience."

That still didn't stop all the public e-mails going back and forth among Sarah, Steve, and Bob. Seeing Sarah toadying up to our new chairman, Bob, was awkward and uncomfortable. It's like Sarah didn't even care how obvious she was being and all the bridges she was burning.

I walk into a meeting room to meet John about the resolution of all the sox-404 and Unicorn security issues. He's wearing a pin-striped Oxford shirt and a vest, complete with cufflinks. He looks like he just came out of a *Vanity Fair* photo shoot, and I guess he's continuing to shave his head daily.

"I'm amazed at how quickly the Unicorn security fixes are being integrated," he says. "Compared to the rest of Phoenix, fixing Unicorn security issues is a breeze. The cycle time is so short, we once put in a fix within an hour. More typically, we can get fixes in within a day or two. Compared to this, remediating Phoenix issues is like pulling our own teeth out, without any anesthesia. Normally, we'd have to wait for a quarter for any meaningful changes to be made, and jumping through all the hoops required to get an emergency change order through was almost not worth the trouble.

"Really," he continues, "patching is so easy, because we can rebuild anything in production with a touch of a button. If it breaks, we can build it again from scratch."

I nod. "I'm amazed at the what we can do with the fast Unicorn cycle times, too. With Phoenix, we only rehearsed and practiced doing the deployments once per quarter. Just in the last five weeks, we've done over twenty Unicorn code and environment deployments. It almost feels routine. As you said, it's the opposite of Phoenix."

John says, "Most of the reservations I had about Unicorn don't seem valid anymore. We've put in regular checks to make sure that the developers who have daily access to production only have read-only access, and we're making good progress on integrating our security tests into the build procedures. I'm pretty confident that any changes that could affect data security or the authentication modules will get caught quickly."

He leans back, crossing his arms behind his head. "I was scared shitless of how we'd gain any sort of assurance about securing Unicorn. It's partly because we're so used to taking a month to turn around application security review. In an emergency, like in response to a high-priority audit, we could sometimes turn things around in a week.

"But the notion of having to keep up with ten deploys a day?" he continues. "Complete lunacy! But after being forced to automate our security testing, and integrating it into the same process that William uses for his automated QA testing, we're testing every time a developer commits code. In many ways, we now have better visibility and code coverage than any of the other applications in the company!"

He adds, "You should know that we just closed out the last of the SOX-404 issues. We were able to prove to the auditors, thanks in large part to the new change control processes you put in, that all the current controls are sufficient, closing out the three-year repeat audit finding."

With a smile, he adds, "Congratulations, Bill. You've done what none of your predecessors have been able to do, which is to finally get the auditors off our back!"

Much to my surprise, the short week goes smoothly. Before everyone leaves on Wednesday for the Thanksgiving holiday, the big Unicorn campaign is ready. Code performance is still ten times slower than we need, but we're okay for now because we can just spin up hundreds of compute instances in the cloud.

We had a genuine showstopper when QA discovered that we were recommending items that were out of stock. That would have been disastrous, as customers would excitedly click on the promotion, only to find them listed as "backordered." Incredibly, Development developed a fix within a day, and it was deployed within an hour.

It's 6 p.m. and I pack up my stuff, looking forward to the long weekend. We've all earned it.

CHAPTER 34

• *Friday, November 28*

By midday Thursday, right in the middle of Thanksgiving, we knew we were in trouble. The overnight Unicorn e-mail promotion was an incredible success. The response rate was unprecedentedly high, with traffic to our website surging to record levels, which kept bringing down our e-commerce systems.

We initiated an emergency Sev 1 call, putting in all sorts of emergency measures to maintain our ability to take orders, including putting more servers into rotation and turning off computationally-intensive features.

Ironically, one of the developers suggested turning off all the real-time recommendations, which we had worked so hard to build. Why recommend more products to buy, he argued, if customers can't even complete a transaction?

Maggie quickly agreed, but it still took the developers two hours to change and deploy. Now, this feature can be disabled with a configuration setting, so we can do it in minutes next time around, instead of requiring a full code rollout.

Now that's what I call designing for IT Operations! It's getting easier and easier to manage the code in production.

We also kept optimizing database queries and moving the largest site graphics to a third-party content distribution network, offloading more traffic from our servers. By late Thanksgiving afternoon, the customer experience had improved to something tolerable.

The real trouble began the following morning. Although it is an official company holiday, I've called everyone one of my staff back into the office.

Wes, Patty, Brent, and Maggie are here for the noon meeting. Chris is here, but has apparently decided that being called in today demanded a different dress code. He's wearing a garish Hawaiian shirt and jeans and has brought in coffee and doughnuts for everyone.

Maggie convened the meeting a couple of minutes ago. "This morning, our store managers opened up their locations for Black Friday. From the moment they opened the doors, people poured in, waving around printouts of their Unicorn promotion e-mails. In-store traffic today is at record levels. The problem is that the promoted items are now almost completely gone. Our store managers started panicking because customers were leaving angry and empty-handed.

"When store managers try to issue rain checks or get an item shipped to the customer, they're having to manually key in the order from our warehouse. It's taking them at least fifteen minutes per order, which is resulting in long lines at the stores and more frustrated customers."

Just then, the speakerphone on the table beeps. "Sarah dialing in. Who's on the line?"

Maggie rolls her eyes, and several other people mutter to one another. Sarah's attempts to undermine Unicorn are well known now. Maggie has to take two minutes to announce everyone on the call and catch her up.

"Thank you," Sarah says. "I'll remain on the call. Please continue."

Maggie thanks her politely and begins brainstorming on how to solve the problems.

An hour later, we generated twenty actions we'll be tackling all weekend long. We'll be putting up a web page for store personnel where they can type in the coupon promotion code, which will automate the cross-shipment from our warehouses. In addition, we'll create a new form on the customer account web page where they can get items delivered directly to them.

It's a long list.

By Monday morning, the situation has stabilized. Which is good, because we have our weekly Unicorn meeting with Steve.

Chris, Wes, Patty, and John are here. Unlike our previous meetings, Sarah is here, too. She sits with her arms crossed, occasionally uncrossing them to tap out messages to someone on her iPhone.

Steve says to all of us with a wide smile, "I want to congratulate you for all your hard work. It has paid off beyond my wildest expectations. Thanks to Unicorn, both in-store and web sales are breaking records, resulting in record weekly revenue. At the current run rate, Marketing estimates that we'll hit profitability this quarter. It will be our first profitable quarter since the middle of last year.

"My heartiest congratulations to you all," he says.

Everyone except Sarah smiles at the news.

"That's only half the story, Steve," Chris says. "The Unicorn team is kicking butt. They've moved from doing deployments every two weeks to every week, and we're now experimenting with doing daily deployments. Because the batch size is so much smaller, we can make small changes very quickly. We're now doing A/B testing all the time. In short, we've never been able to respond to the market this quickly, and I'm sure there are more rabbits we can pull out of this hat."

I nod emphatically. "I suspect we'll want to follow the Unicorn model for any new applications we develop internally. It's easier to scale, as well as easier to manage, than any application we've supported in the past. We're setting up the processes and procedures so that we can deploy at whatever rate it takes to quickly respond to customers. In some cases, we're even enabling developers to deploy the code. The developer will be able to push a button and within several minutes, the code will be in the testing environment or in production."

"I can't believe how far we've come in such a short time. I'm proud of all of you," Steve says. "I want to commend you for truly working together and being worthy of one another's trust."

"Better late than never, I suppose," Sarah says. "If we're done congratulating ourselves, I've got a business wake-up call for you. Earlier this month, our largest retail competitor started partnering with their manufacturers to allow custom build-to-order kits. Sales of some our top selling items are already down twenty percent since they launched this offering."

Angrily, she adds, "For years, I've been trying to get IT to build out the infrastructure to enable this capability, but all we heard was, 'no, it can't be done.' Meanwhile, our competition has been able to work with any manufacturer who says yes."

She adds, "That's why Bob's idea of splitting up the company has so much merit. We're being shackled by the legacy manufacturing side of this business."

What? Buying the retail firm was her idea! Maybe life would have been easier for everyone if she had just gone to work for a retailer.

Steve frowns. "This is the next agenda item. As SVP of Retail Operations, it's Sarah's prerogative to bring business needs and risks to this team."

Wes snorts. To Sarah, he says, "You're kidding, right? Do you understand what we just achieved with Unicorn, and how fast we did it? What you're describing isn't that difficult, compared to what we just pulled off."

The next day, Wes walks in wearing an uncharacteristically glum face. "Uh, boss. I hate to say it, but I don't think it can be done."

When I ask him to explain, he says, "To do what our competitor is doing, we'd have to completely rewrite our manufacturing resource planning system that supports all the plants. It's an old mainframe application that we've used for decades. We outsourced it three years ago. Mostly because old people like you were going to retire soon.

"No offense," he adds. "We laid off many of our mainframe people years ago—they were making salaries way above the norm. Some outsourcer convinced our CIO at the time that they had the gray-haired workforce that could keep our application on life-support until we retired it. Our plan was that we would replace with a newer ERP system, but obviously, we never got around to it."

"Dammit, we're the customer and they're our supplier," I say. "Tell them that we're paying them not just to maintain the application but also to make any needed business changes. According to Sarah, we need this change. So find out how much they want to charge us and how long we'll have to wait."

"I did that," Wes says, pulling out a ream of paper from under his arm. "Here's the proposal they finally sent after I managed to get the stupid account manager out of the way so I could actually talk to one of the technical analysts.

"They want six months to gather the requirements, another nine months to develop and test, and if we're lucky, we might be able to put it into production one year from now," he continues. "The problem is, the resources we need aren't available until June. So, we're talking about eighteen months. Minimum. To even start the process, they would need $50K for the feasibility study and to secure a slot in their development schedule."

Wes is bright red now, shaking his head. "That worthless account manager keeps insisting that the contract just won't allow him to help us. Bastard. Obviously, his job is to make sure that everything that can be billed for is, and to dissuade us from doing anything not on the contract, like development."

I exhale loudly, thinking through the implications. The constraint preventing us from going where we need to go is now outside our organization. But if it's outside the organization, what can we possibly do? We can't convince an outsourcer to change their priorities or their management practices as we've done.

Suddenly, a glimmer of an idea hits me.

"How many people do they have allocated to our account?" I ask.

"I don't know," Wes says. "I think there are six people assigned at thirty percent allocation. It probably depends on their role."

"Get Patty in here, along with a copy of the contract, and let's work through the math. And see if you can grab someone from Purchasing, too. I have an audacious proposal that I'd like to explore."

"Who outsourced the MRP application?" Steve asks from behind his desk.

I'm sitting in Steve's office with Chris, Wes, and Patty, with Sarah standing off to the side, whom I try to ignore.

I explain our idea to Steve again. "Many years ago, we decided that this application wasn't a critical part of the business, so we outsourced it to cut costs. Obviously, they didn't view it as a core competency."

"Well, it's obviously a core competency now!" replies Steve. "Right now, that outsourcer is holding us hostage, preventing us from doing something that needs to be done. They're more than just a roadblock. They're now jeopardizing our future."

I nod. "In short, we'd like to break the outsourcing contract early, bringing those resources back into the company. We're talking about approximately six people, some of whom are still onsite. To buy out the remainder of the contract two years early would be almost one million dollars, and we would regain complete control of the MRP application and underlying infrastructure. Everyone on this team believes this is the right thing to do, and we've even got the initial blessing from Dick's team."

I hold my breath. I just threw out a very a big number. It's considerably bigger than the budget increase I asked for two months ago when I got thrown out of this office.

I quickly continue, "Chris believes that once this MRP application is back in-house, we could build an interface to Unicorn. We would then start building the manufacturing capability to move us from 'build to inventory' to 'build to order,' which would enable us to provide the custom kits as Sarah requested. If we execute everything flawlessly, and the integration with the order entry and inventory management systems goes as planned, we could match what our competitors are doing in about ninety days."

Out of the corner of my eye, I can see the wheels turning furiously in Sarah's head.

Steve doesn't shoot down the idea down right away. "Okay, you have my attention. What are the top risks?"

Chris takes this one. "The outsourcer may have made big changes to the code base that we don't know about, which would slow down the development schedule. But my personal belief is that this risk is minimal. Based on their behavior, I don't think they made any significant changes to functionality.

"I'm not worried about the technical challenges," he continues. "The MRP was not designed for large batch sizes and certainly not batch sizes of one that we're talking about here. But I'm sure we can make something work short-term and figure out a long-term strategy as we go."

When Chris finishes, Patty adds, "The outsourcer could also decide to make the transition back to us difficult, and there could be animosity from the affected engineers. There were a lot of hard feelings when we announced the contract—among other things, their pay was cut the instant they switched from being Parts Unlimited employees to being a vendor."

She continues. "We should get John involved right away, because we'll need to take away access from all the outsourcer staff that we're not bringing back in."

Wes laughs, saying, "I'd like to personally delete the login credentials of that jackass account manager. He's a jerk."

Steve is listening attentively. He then turns to Sarah and asks, "Your thoughts on the team's proposal?"

She says nothing for several moments but eventually says imperiously, "I think we need to check with Bob Strauss and get full board approval before we undertake a project this big and risky. Given the previous performance of IT, this could jeopardize all of our manufacturing operations, which is more risk than I think we should take on. In short, I personally do not support this proposal."

Steve studies Sarah, saying with a thin-lipped smile, "Remember that you work for me, not Bob. If you can't work within that arrangement, I will need your immediate resignation."

Sarah turns white, her jaw dropping, obviously realizing she's badly misplayed her hand.

Struggling to regain her composure, she laughs nervously at Steve's comment, but no one else joins in. I furtively look at my colleagues, and see that, like me, their eyes are wide, watching this drama unfold.

Steve continues, "On the contrary, thanks to IT, we may no longer need to consider all the onerous strategic options that you and Bob are preparing, but your point is well taken."

To the rest of us, Steve says, "I'm assigning you one of Dick's best people and our corporate counsel. They'll help you flawlessly execute this project and make sure we use every trick in the book to get what we need from the outsourcer. I'll make sure Dick gives this project his personal attention."

Sarah's eyes widen even further. "That's an excellent idea, Steve. That would significantly reduce our risk here. I think Bob will really like it."

The expression on Steve's face suggests that his patience for her theatrics is nearly at an end.

He asks us if there's anything else we need. When there isn't, he excuses everyone but asks Sarah to remain behind.

As we leave, I sneak a peek behind us. Sarah is sitting down where I previously sat, nervously watching everyone file out. Catching her eye, I smile at her and close the door.

CHAPTER 35

• *Friday, January 9*

I grip the steering wheel nervously as I drive to Steve's house. He's throwing a party for everyone who has worked so hard on Phoenix and Unicorn, inviting people from both the business and IT. The roads are uncharacteristically icy, with no melting even after weeks of sunshine. It was treacherous enough that Paige and I decided to stay at home for New Year's Eve instead of celebrating with her family as we usually do.

It's been over a month since that last meeting with Steve and Sarah. We haven't seen much of Sarah since then.

As I'm driving, I contemplate how quiet it's been. I keep expecting someone to call in another Sev 1 incident. Instead, my phone just sits in the cup holder, completely silent—like yesterday—and the day before that.

I can't say that I miss all of the excitement, but there are times now when I literally have nothing to do.

Thankfully, I'm now coaching all my managers through our two-week improvement cycles, according to the Improvement Kata, which keeps me from feeling totally useless. I'm especially proud that for an entire month, my group hit our target of spending fifteen percent of our time on preventive infrastructure projects. And it shows.

We're using the entire budget we've been allocated. We're closing our monitoring gaps, we've refactored or replaced our top ten fragile artifacts so that they're more stable, and the flow of planned work is faster than ever. Against my expectations, everyone jumped enthusiastically on Project Narwhal otherwise known as the "Simian Army Chaos Monkey" project. Like the legendary stories of the original Apple Mac os and Netflix cloud delivery infrastructure, we deployed code that routinely created large-scale faults, thus randomly killing processes or entire servers.

Of course, the result was all hell breaking loose for an entire week as our test, and occasionally, production infrastructure crashed like a house of cards. But, over the following weeks, as Development and IT Operations worked together to make our code and infrastructure more resilient to failures, we truly had IT services that were resilient, rugged, and durable.

John loved this, and started a new project called "Evil Chaos Monkey." Instead of generating operational faults in production, it would constantly try to exploit security holes, fuzz our applications with storms of malformed packets, try to install backdoors, gain access to confidential data, and all sorts of other nefarious attacks.

Of course, Wes tried to stop this. He insisted that we schedule penetration tests into predefined time frames. However, I convinced him this is the fastest means to institutionalize Erik's Third Way. We need to create a culture that reinforces the value of taking risks and learning from failure and the need for repetition and practice to create mastery.

I don't want posters about quality and security. I want improvement of our daily work showing up where it needs to be: in our daily work.

John's team developed tools that stress-tested every test and production environment with a continual barrage of attacks. And like when we first released the chaos monkey, immediately over half their time was spent fixing security holes and hardening the code. After several weeks, the developers were deservedly proud of their work, successfully fending off everything that John's team was able to throw at them.

These are the thoughts going through my head as I wind my way toward Steve's house. The sprawling grounds are all covered by snow, hiding the immaculately manicured lawns.

When I ring the doorbell an hour early, as Steve requested, I hear loud barking and then the sounds of a very large dog slipping on a hardwood floor, crashing into the door.

"Come on in, Bill. It's great seeing you again," Steve says, holding the dog's collar and gesturing toward the kitchen with a skewer of vegetables in the other hand. When we get to the kitchen, he points to the counter in front of him, where a large metal bucket of ice sits, full of bottles. "You want anything to drink? Beer? Soda? Scotch?" Looking around, he adds, "Margarita?"

I grab a beer out of the bucket, thank him, and then give him a quick summary of my somewhat boring day as he moves me to the living room.

Steve smiles. "Thanks for coming over early. We're going to have a record-breaking quarter. We couldn't have done it without you and Chris. For the first time in years, our market share is up! You know, I wish I could see the looks on our competitors' faces. They're probably scrambling, trying to figure out how we did it."

Steve is smiling broadly. "I actually saw Dick crack a smile the other day. Well, he showed his teeth, at least. Project Unicorn and that new project, Narwhal, are helping us understand what are customers actually want. Our average order size just hit a record last week, and Dick said that Unicorn had the fastest payback of any project we've done in recent memory."

He continues, "The analysts are starting to love us again. One told me last week that if we execute well, it'll be very difficult for our nonintegrated competitors to follow us. No doubt, they'll be raising our stock price targets, and Bob is finally withdrawing his support to split up the company."

"Really?" I say, raising my eyebrows in surprise. "I thought that Sarah was convinced that splitting up the company was the only way for us to survive."

"Ah, yes…" he says. "She's decided to look for other options elsewhere and is on a leave of absence."

My jaw drops. If I'm hearing this correctly, Sarah is being eased out of the company. I smile.

"By the way," Steve says. "Project Narwhal? Project Unicorn? Can't you guys come up with better names than that?"

I laugh. "No one is more upset about it than Maggie. She's convinced that all her product managers are laughing at her. She's told her husband that if the next project is called 'Hello Kitty,' she'll quit."

He laughs. "As you can guess, though, I didn't ask you to come early to critique your project names. Have a seat."

As I settle into a cushy armchair, he starts to explain. "We've had an open position for the CIO for months. You've been a part of that interview process. What have you thought of the candidates?"

"Honestly? I was disappointed," I say slowly. "They were all senior people with a lot more experience than me. They kept talking about tiny parts of the problem. They proposed only a fraction of what we've done in the past couple of months here at Parts Unlimited. I feel that if they signed on, we'd be at considerable risk of going back to all the bad old ways."

"I agree with you, Bill. Which is why I've decided that we should fill this position internally. You have any suggestions on who we should promote?"

I go through the possible candidates in my mind. It's not a long list. "I think Chris is the obvious choice. He was the driving force behind Unicorn, as well as Narwhal. If it weren't for his leadership, I'm pretty sure we'd still be stuck dead in the water."

He smiles. "You know, it's funny. Everyone thought you'd say that. However, I won't be following your recommendations."

He continues, "This is going to take a while to explain. You were everyone's unanimous choice to become CIO. But to be brutally candid, I don't want you there."

Reacting to my obvious distress, he says, "Hey, relax. Let me explain. My board holds me responsible for making the best use of company resources to achieve the goals that maximize shareholder value. My primary job is to lead my management team to make that happen."

He stands up, walking over to the window, looking out at the snow-covered yard. "You've helped me see that IT is not merely a department. Instead, it's pervasive, like electricity. It's a skill, like being able to read or do math. Here at Parts Unlimited, we don't have a centralized reading or math department—we expect everyone we hire to have some mastery of it. Understanding what technology can and can't do has become a core competency that every part of this business must have. If any of my business managers are leading a team or a project without that skill, they will fail."

He continues, "I need each and every one of my business managers to take calculated risks, without jeopardizing the entire enterprise. People everywhere in the business are using technology, so it's like the Wild West again—for better or for worse. Businesses that can't learn to compete in this new world will perish."

Turning back to me, he says, "In order for Parts Unlimited to survive, the business and IT can't make decisions exclusive of each other. I don't know where this is all going, but I know the way we're organized now, we're not firing on all cylinders.

"I've been discussing this with my board for the last couple of months," he says, sitting down, staring right at me. I know this expression. It's like my first meeting with him last year. This is what he looks like when he's trying to seduce someone. "I'm impressed with your performance and what you've done with IT. You used the same skills that I would expect anyone leading one of our large manufacturing divisions to use.

"Now I want to see you grow and learn, and build new skills to best help all of Parts Unlimited. If you're up to it, I am prepared to invest in you. I want to put you on a fast track, two-year plan. You'll do rotations in sales and marketing, manage a plant, get international experience, manage the relationships of our most critical suppliers, and manage our supply chain. Trust me, this will not be a vacation. You're going to need help—a lot of it. Erik has kindly agreed to mentor you, because we both believe this will be the most difficult thing you've ever done.

"But," he continues, "if you achieve each of fifteen specific performance targets we've laid out for you, we'll move you into a provisional Chief Operating Officer role in two years, where you'll work closely with Dick while he gets ready to retire. If you work hard, get results and play your cards right, you'll be the next COO of the company in three years."

I feel my jaw hanging open, my beer bottle dripping water onto my leg.

"You don't have to answer now," he says, obviously satisfied that his pitch is having the desired effect. "Half my board thinks I'm crazy. Maybe they're right, but I trust my instincts. I don't know how this is going to shape up, but I have confidence that this is what's best for the company. My gut tells me that in ten years, when we're mopping the last pieces of our competition off the floor, this is the gamble that will have made that possible.

"While we're dreaming big dreams here, let me say this," he continues. "In ten years, I'm certain every COO worth their salt will have come from

IT. Any COO who doesn't intimately understand the IT systems that actually run the business is just an empty suit, relying on someone else to do their job."

Steve's vision takes my breath away. He's right. Everything my team has learned, as well as what Chris and John have learned, shows that when IT fails, the business fails. It stands to reason that if IT is organized so that it can win, the business wins, too.

And Steve wants to put me on the vanguard of this movement.

Me. A technology operations guy.

Suddenly, I think of how one of Erik's higher ups decided to mustang him from a senior NCO to a lowly lieutenant, forcing him to climb the ladder again from the very bottom of the officer ranks. Obviously, Erik had the courage to do it, and the rewards for him (and his family, if he has one) seem pretty evident. He's living a life that seems to have transcended our mortal plane of existence.

As if Steve knows what I'm thinking, he says, "You know, when Erik and I first met, many months ago, he said that the relationship between IT and the business is like a dysfunctional marriage—both feel powerless and held hostage by the other. I've thought about this for months, and I finally figured something out.

"A dysfunctional marriage assumes that the business and IT are two separate entities. IT should either be embedded into business operations or into the business. Voilà! There you go. No tension. No marriage, and maybe no IT Department, either."

I just stare at Steve. In some Erik-like way, something about what he says seems inescapably true.

In that moment, I decide. I'll still have to talk with Paige, but I know with certainty that the journey Steve wants to send me on is important—both for me and my family and for my entire profession.

"I'll think about it," I say, solemnly.

Steve smiles broadly and stands up. When I grasp his outstretched hand, he clasps my shoulder firmly. "Good. This is going to be fun."

Just then, the doorbell rings, and within a few minutes, the whole gang is here—Wes, Patty, John, and Chris—so are Maggie, Brent, Ann, and, holy crap, even Dick and Ron.

As the party starts to get louder and louder, each of them congratulate me, drinks in hand. It's obvious that they knew everything already, including Steve's startling offer to go on a three-year training plan to become the next COO.

Dick approaches me, holding a glass of scotch. "Congratulations, Bill. I'm looking forward to working closely with you in the years to come."

Shortly, I find myself laughing with a bunch of other people, accepting their congratulations, and trading stories about the amazing journey we've been on.

Wes claps me on the shoulder. "Now that you're being promoted," he says, even more loudly and brashly than normal, "We all thought we should give you something that celebrates what we've accomplished. Something that you can take with you that will remind you not to forget about us, you know, little people."

As he reaches into the box at his feet, he says, "We argued for a long time about what it should be. But in the end, it was obvious…"

When I see what he pulls out from the box, I burst out laughing.

"Your old craptop!" he exclaims, holding it high in the air. "It was a shame to make it unusable by bronzing it, but you've got to admit, it's beautiful, isn't it?"

In disbelief, I gape at it as everyone laughs, clapping and cheering. It really is my old laptop. Taking it from Wes, I see the broken hinge and the duct tape I put on to hold the battery in. And now the entire laptop is covered in what looks like a thick layer of gold-colored paint, and it's mounted on a Mahogany pedestal.

At the bottom of the pedestal is a bronze label. I read aloud, "In fond memory of dearly departed Bill Palmer, VP of IT Operations," with the last year in parentheses.

"Holy crap, guys," I say, genuinely touched at their gesture. "You make it sound like I died!"

Everyone laughs, including Steve. The evening goes by quickly, and I find myself surprised that I'm having such a good time. I'm not usually a social person, but tonight, I feel like I'm in the company of friends and colleagues who I respect, trust, and genuinely like.

Sometime later, Erik arrives. He walks over to me, pausing to scrutinize the bronzed laptop. "You know, even though I give you a fifty-fifty chance of washing out, I still believe in you," he says, standing in front of me, taking a swig of beer. "Congratulations, kid. You deserve it."

"Thanks," I say, smiling broadly, genuinely touched at his faint praise.

"Yeah, well, don't let me down," he says gruffly. "I've never liked this town, and you'll be making me fly into that godforsaken airport for years to come. If you screw this up, it will all be for nothing."

"I'll do my best," I say with a surprising amount of confidence. "Wait a second. I thought you'd be coming into town anyway for our board meetings?"

"After what I've seen, I don't want any part of it!" Erik says, laughing loudly. "I think Parts Unlimited is going to make a lot of money. We'll see how good your competition really is, but my suspicion is that they'll have no idea what hit them. For me, this isn't just idle theory. If all goes according to plan, within a couple of weeks, I'll likely be one of the largest investors in this company. The last thing I want is a bunch of insider information that restricts my ability to buy and sell!"

I stare at Erik. He has enough money to become one of our largest investors but still dresses like a manufacturing line worker? I never would have guessed that he cared so much about money.

Eventually I ask dumbly, "What do you mean by 'insider information?'"

"I've long believed that to effectively manage IT is not only a critical competency but a significant predictor of company performance," he explains. "One of these days, I'd like to create a hedge fund that invests in companies, taking long positions on companies with great IT organizations that help the business win, and short the companies where IT lets everyone down. I think we'd make a killing. What better way is there to force the next generation of CEOs to give a shit about IT?"

He continues. "I can't do that if I'm tied up as a board director in all these companies. Bad optics. Too much potential jeopardy with the SEC, auditors, and all that."

"Ah," I say.

"Hey, sorry to interrupt," John interjects, "but I wanted to congratulate you and pay my respects." He then reaches out to shake Erik's hand, saying, "And to you, as well, sir."

Erik ignores his hand, staring at him up and down for a couple of moments. Then he laughs and shakes his extended hand. "You've come a long way, John. Well done. And by the way, I like the new look. Very Euro discotheque."

"Thanks, Erkel," he says, deadpan. "I couldn't have done it without you. I'm grateful."

"My pleasure," Erik says jovially. "Just don't hang out with auditors too much. It's not good for anyone."

John shakes his head agreeably, returning to the party. Erik turns to me and says conspiratorially, "Now *that* is a rather remarkable transformation, wouldn't you agree?"

I turn around to look at John. He's laughing and trading insults with Wes.

"So," Erik says, interrupting my train of thought. "What are your plans for the rest of the IT organization? Given this promotion, you've got some positions to fill."

I turn back to Erik. "You know, I could never have predicted this." Erik snorts dismissively, which I ignore. "Wes, Patty, and I have talked about this a lot. I'm sure I'm going to promote Patty to be VP of IT Operations. She's the closest we have to a plant manager for IT Operations, and she'll kick ass," I say with a smile.

"Good choice," he responds. "She certainly doesn't look like your typical IT Operations manager, though… And Wes?"

"Believe it or not, Wes made it very clear he doesn't want to be VP of IT Operations," I respond. With less certainty, I say, "If I'm supposed to vacate my role as CIO in two years, I think Wes will have a big decision to make. If I could wave a magic wand, he'd take over for Patty as head of IT Operations, and Patty will be become the next CIO. But how am I ever going to get everyone ready if Steve keeps heaping more responsibilities on me?"

Erik rolls his eyes. "Give me a break. You're bored in your current role. You're going to become a lot less bored. Fast. And remember that there are a lot of experienced people around you who've been on similar journeys, so don't be the idiot that fails because he didn't ask for help."

He turns to leave but then looks at me with a glint in his eye. "Speaking of helping other people, I think *you* owe *me* something."

"Of course," I respond sincerely, suddenly wondering if I've been set up from the very beginning. "Whatever you want, just say the word."

"I need you to help me elevate the state of the practice of how organizations manage technology. Let's face it. Life in IT is pretty shitty when it's so misunderstood and mismanaged. It becomes thankless and frustrating as people realize that they are powerless to change the outcome, like an endlessly repeating horror movie. If that's not damaging to our self-worth as human beings, I don't know what is. That's got to change," he says passionately. "I want to improve the lives of one million IT workers in the next five years. As someone wise once told me, 'Messiahs are good, but scripture is better.'"

He says, "I want you to write a book, describing the Three Ways and how other people can replicate the transformation you've made here at Parts Unlimited. Call it *The DevOps Handbook* and show how IT can regain the trust of the business and end decades of intertribal warfare. Can you do that for me?"

Write a book? He can't be serious.

I reply, "I'm not a writer. I've never written a book before. In fact, I haven't written anything longer than an e-mail in a decade."

Unamused, he says sternly, "Learn."

Shaking my head for a moment, I finally say, "Of course. It would be an honor and a privilege to write *The DevOps Handbook* for you while I embark on what will probably be the most challenging three years of my entire career."

"Very good. It'll be a great book," he says, smiling. Then he claps me again on the shoulder. "Go enjoy the evening. You deserve it."

Everywhere I look, I see people who are genuinely having fun and enjoying each other's company. With my drink in hand, I ponder how far we've come. During the Phoenix launch, I doubt anyone in this group could have imagined being part of a super-tribe that was bigger than just Dev or Ops or Security. There's a term that we're hearing more lately: something called "DevOps." Maybe everyone attending this party is a form of DevOps, but I suspect it's something much more than that. It's Product Management, Development, IT Operations, and even Information Security all working together and supporting one another. Even Steve is a part of this super-tribe.

In that moment, I let myself feel how incredibly proud I am of everyone in this room. What we've pulled off is remarkable, and even though my future is probably less certain than anytime in my career, I feel incredible excitement at the challenges the coming years are going to bring.

As I take another sip of beer, something catches my eye. A bunch of my people start to look at their phones. Moments later, on the other side of the room, one of the developers next to Brent is peering into his phone, too, with everyone huddled around him.

Old instincts kicking in, I urgently look around the room for Patty who is making a beeline toward me, her phone already in her hand.

"First off, congratulations, boss," she says, with a half smile on her face. "You want the bad news or the good news first?"

Turning to her, I say with a sense of calm and inner peace, "What have we got, Patty?"

AFTERWORD

THE PAST—AN HOMAGE TO THE GOAL

When Kevin Behr, George Spafford, and I first started writing *The Phoenix Project* we never suspected how quickly DevOps would be embraced by technology professionals within all types of organizations. When this book was first published in January 2013, DevOps was very much in its early years, less than four years after the famous "10+ Deploys Per Day: Dev and Ops Cooperation at Flickr" was presented by John Allspaw and Paul Hammond, and a little over two years after the first DevOpsDays conference in the United States.

However, virtually everyone in technology was already all too familiar with the problems commonly associated with Waterfall software delivery processes and large, complex, "big bang" production deployments. This dissatisfaction with the status quo was driving increased adoption of not just DevOps, but also Agile and Lean.

We knew from first-hand experience that these problems were being faced by almost every modern enterprise and across every industry vertical regardless of the size of the organization or whether it was for profit or non-profit!

This nearly universal problem led to chronic underperformance throughout the entire technology value stream, which included Development, Operations, and Information Security. But worst of all, it led to chronic underperformance of the organization these technologists all served.

With *The Phoenix Project*, we wanted to capture what the downward spiral looked and felt like, as well as what the surprising solutions felt like. So much about DevOps is counter intuitive, contrary to common practice, and even controversial. If production deployments are problematic, how on earth can deploying more frequently be a good idea? How can reducing the number of controls actually increase the security of our applications and environments? And can technology really learn anything from manufacturing? There are countless more examples of these difficult to believe claims.

Because we wanted to show both the problems and solutions in a recognizable and relatable form, we decided very early on that the only way we could describe with adequate fidelity the enormous complexity of this problem was in the form of novel, just like Dr. Eliyahu Goldratt did in *The Goal*, the seminal book he published in 1984.

The Goal helped many of us have a giant and meaningful "aha" moment. It has been credited for helping make Lean manufacturing principles become mainstream, and, since its publication, *The Goal* has been integrated into almost every mainstream MBA curriculum and operations management course, influencing our next generation of leaders.

When I first read *The Goal* around 2000, it was life changing. Even though I had never worked in manufacturing, certainly never as a plant manager, there was no doubt that this book contained lessons that were relevant to the work that we do every day in technology. For over a decade, my co-authors and I wanted to write a version of *The Goal* for the technology value stream—this book obviously became *The Phoenix Project*, the book you're holding right now.

Dr. Goldratt passed away in 2011 but left behind an incredible legacy. I'm particularly grateful for how he made time in 2004 to talk with Kevin Behr and me. It was amazing to see how he helped continually expand the Theory of Constraints body of knowledge.

I would recommend to any one who has interest in Dr. Goldratt's work to listen to his audiobook *Beyond the Goal*, which was released twenty-one years after *The Goal*. It brilliantly captures in one place his own lifetime of learnings, and synthesizes those learnings into a comprehensible and comprehensive whole.

In *Beyond the Goal*, Dr. Goldratt shares a story that was incredibly prescient for us. After *The Goal* was first published, Dr. Goldratt quickly started to receive letters in the mail about how people claimed that he must have been hiding in their manufacturing plants because he described all the problems they were facing in their daily work, as well as how the Theory of Constraints enabled them to solve their problem.

I can't think of a better or more persuasive testament to how well Dr. Goldratt understood the universality of the root cause of the problem, as well as the rules that described a generic direction for the solution.

Without a doubt, we wrote *The Phoenix Project* as an homage to *The Goal*, hoping to show that the same principles that Dr. Goldratt espoused originally for manufacturing could be used to improve technology work as well.

As another nod to both the work of Dr. Goldratt and the way he released it, simultaneous to the publication of this new edition, we are releasing *Beyond the Phoenix Project*, an audio series collaboration between John Willis (co-author of *The DevOps Handbook*) and me. The project will cover both the figures and philosophies that serve as the foundation for the DevOps movement, including a whole module on Dr. Goldratt.

I'm so pleased that *The Phoenix Project* is following in the footsteps of *The Goal*. *The Phoenix Project* has sold 400,000 copies, and like *The Goal*, it is being integrated into MIS programs, MBA curriculums, and even computer science programs.

Sometimes, the similarities to *The Goal* are downright uncanny. Shortly after the publication of *The Phoenix Project*, we started receiving emails. Many espoused sentiments like the following, "Holy cow, you are writing about our organization—It's like you've been hiding in our building. I know these characters. In fact, the application disaster in the book just happened to us." (And incredibly, in one case, the application being deployed was even called Project Phoenix!)

It has been particularly gratifying to see how this book has been used across technology organizations, often in a book club format to discuss how the current system can pit Development, Operations, and Information Security against each other, making it virtually impossible to achieve the most important organizational objectives, and more importantly, how this led to completely new types of interactions to explore a better way of working, with much improved outcomes.

I'm always amazed at stories where people have used *The Phoenix Project* to find each other: often a change agent will recommend or give out copies of *The Phoenix Project* to scores of people, paying careful attention to who comes back saying, "Wow, what's happening to Parts Unlimited is happening to us, isn't it?" Sometimes seeing a copy of the book prominently on someone's desk or bookshelf serves as a signal that this person is a fellow traveler, one who sees a common problem that spans functional domains and is potentially a fellow conspirator, a fellow risk-taker, who is willing to work together to create a coalition to overcome powerful, entrenched incumbent systems.

The Phoenix Project is ultimately a book about transformation, and so it is incredibly gratifying to see it being used as an instrument to create transformations in real life as well.

SURPRISES ON THE JOURNEY

There are so many surprises and learnings on this journey, and I wanted to share a couple that seemed fitting for this afterword.

One of the most delightful and startling blog posts I've read about *The Phoenix Project* was by Dave Lutz, famous for many things, including the server-room inspired cover song of "Imagine" by The Beatles that he performed at DevOpsDays Mountain View 2011. In this post, he ponders the role of Brent, an all too familiar character in Operations. He writes, "I find myself wondering what the outcome of the project would have been if Bill's first action was to fire Brent. Would the project have been finished earlier? (I don't have a moral problem firing a fictitious character in a thought experiment. I wouldn't do this in real life of course!)"

Mr. Lutz writes about how there are two types of Brents: hoarders and sharers. He writes:

I've also come across otherwise smart [people] who are of the mistaken belief that if they hold on to a task, something only they know how to do, it'll ensure job security. These people are knowledge Hoarders.

This doesn't work. Everyone is replaceable. No matter how talented they are. Sure it may take longer at first to find out how to do that special task, but it will happen without them.

For me, what Lutz wrote was fascinating for so many reason, like how *The Phoenix Project* has become shorthand to describe certain categories of problems and a safe way to discuss and conduct thought experiments, not just on the effects of processes, but on people.

And by the way, Mr. Lutz, I can state for the record that during the writing of this book we always knew that Brent was a sharer, not a hoarder; in fact, Brent is the only character whose name we didn't change. And without doubt, as you speculated, our real-life Brent always had the best interests of the organization at heart and was merely a victim of the system.

Another genuine surprise for me is how some people have written that we (the authors) must hate Information Security, and more specifically, that we hate Information Security people. One of the best examples actually came from a friend of mine, Paul Love, who was a co-author with me on *Visible Ops Security*.

In a blog post, I published an email that he wrote me: "When I first read *The Phoenix Project: A Novel About IT DevOps, and Helping Your Business Win*, John [the CISO character] made me angry. As a 20 year [sic] security veteran, John's totally selfish 'my way or the highway' attitude actually made me physically mad. Who did this guy think he was anyway? Why was Gene painting the infosec practitioner in such an unflattering light?"

He continued:

After finishing the book, I took a moment to look back on my career. Thinking of all of the people like John who I'd run into and worked with over the year I realized, with a little bit of terror, why I hated him so much.

Before I studied Visible Ops and DevOps, I was John.

I've sometimes received the same sort of reaction from people who don't know that I spent the majority of my career in the Information Security field as co-inventor of Tripwire, spending thirteen years as the founder and CTO of a company focusing on automating security and compliance.

As the saying goes, "We tease who we love." In many ways, John the CISO is my favorite character, and in many ways, his journey most closely mirrors my own. As my friend Jez Humble, co-author of *The DevOps Handbook*, observed, "[John] is a phoenix, too." Well put, Jez!

Whether we are a John, a Brent, a Wes, a Patty, or a Bill, when we're trapped in a system that prevents us from succeeding, our job becomes thankless, reinforces a feeling of powerlessness, and we feel like we are trapped in a system that preordains failure. And worse, the nature of technical debt that is not paid down ensures that the system gets worse over time, regardless of how hard we try.

We now know that DevOps principles and patterns are what allow us to turn this downward spiral into a virtuous spiral, through a combination of cultural norms, architecture, and technical practices.

As *The Phoenix Project* found it's way into the world, another group of us were working on *The DevOps Handbook* (Jez Humble, John Willis, Patrick DuBois, and me). One of the amazing moments during the creation of this book was when our editor, Anna, asked us each to describe our DevOps "aha" moment.

The amazing thing was that all of our answers were uncannily similar: We each described the incredible frustration of how difficult it was to do our work, whether it was the toil or the suffering. And we all shared the exhilaration of discovering the better way, under this broad umbrella of practices we call DevOps.

You can read about all of our "aha: moments in the first pages of the extended excerpt of *The DevOps Handbook* included in the back of this 5th Anniversary Edition of *The Phoenix Project*.

LOOKING INTO THE FUTURE

The problems that DevOps solve are at the center of what every modern organization is facing. Now more than ever, technology is not just the nervous system of an organization—it actually composes the majority of the muscle mass.

As Jeff Immelt, former CEO of GE, wrote, "Every industry and company that is not bringing software to the core of their business will be disrupted." Or as Jeffrey Snover, Technical Fellow at Microsoft, paraphrasing Dr. Nicholas Negroponte, wrote, "In previous economic eras, businesses created value by moving atoms. Now they create value by moving bits."

When *The Phoenix Project* was first published in 2013, DevOps was primarily used in Internet companies, commonly known as the FAANGs (Facebook, Amazon, Apple, Netflix, and Google). Of course, also in this category are Flickr, LinkedIn, Microsoft, Yahoo, Twitter, GitHub, and countless more.

Now, five years later, it has been amazing to see these principles and practices in large, complex organizations across every industry vertical. This is incredibly exciting, because this is undoubtedly where the majority of the economic value of DevOps will be created.

IDC, the analyst firm, says that there are about eleven million developers on the planet and seven million operations people on the planet. At the time of this writing, it would be wildly optimistic to project that one million of these engineers are already using DevOps principles and practices.

If that's the case, DevOps has 6.5% market share, leaving 93.5% of the market to go. The majority of these engineers are in large, complex organizations—these are the most well-known brands across every industry vertical or supporting our largest government agencies or military services.

The mission at hand is how we can elevate their productivity so that they're as productive as the high performers. We know through more than four years of *State of DevOps Reports* conducted by Puppet that high perfomers are two to three orders of magnitude more productive than their peers. In my mind, helping everyone reach this level of high performace will create trillions of dollars of economic value per year and is where the next surge of productivity will come from.

In 2016, I was talking with my friend Rob England, often known as his moniker The IT Skeptic. We were fellow travelers in the ITIL space ten years ago. We talked about how he famously and visibly changed his mind about DevOps. Initially, he believed, as many do, that anything that increases deployment frequency and enables developers more free-dom inevitably leads to disaster. But through many interactions, he eventually realized that DevOps can lead to far better outcomes. If you want to explore his journey more, you can read my full interview with him on CA.com, "Face-to-Face DevOps: To Protect and Serve."

In our conversations together, we talked about how DevOps is inev-itable, inexorable, and remorseless, and how DevOps is incredibly dis-ruptive to the technology sector, to the technology field, and for anyone in technology.

There's no doubt that DevOps is radically changing and transforming how we work in technology. Organizations that cannot adopt DevOps practices will be at a massive competitive disadvantage. As Dr. W. Edwards Deming is famously paraphrased, "Learning is not compul-sory...neither is survival."

Without a doubt, the best times for technology are ahead of us, not behind us. There's never been a better time to be in the technology field, and to be a lifelong learner.

On behalf of my co-authors, thanks to everyone who has made this journey so amazing and worthwhile!

—Gene Kim
Portland, OR
December 5, 2017

ACKNOWLEDGEMENTS

First and foremost, I want to acknowledge all the support from my loving wife, who put up with far more than I promised, Margueritte, and my sons, Reid, Parker, and Grant.

I want to thank Todd Sattersten, Tim Grahl, Merridawn Duckler, and Kate Sage for their incredible help and support throughout the development process of this book. Also, my profound thanks to the tireless contributions and scrutiny from Paul Muller from HP, Paul Proctor from Gartner, Branden Williams from RSA, Dr. Tom Longstaff at Johns Hopkins University, Julia Allen from SEI/CMU, Adrian Cockcroft from Netflix, Christopher Little from BMC, Bob McCarthy, Lisa Schwartz from ITSM Academy, Jennifer Bayuk, Ben Rockwood from Joyent, Josh Corman from Akamai, James Turnbull from Puppet Labs, Charlie Betz from Enterprise Management Associates, Dr. Gene Spafford from CERIAS at Purdue University, Dwayne Melancon from Tripwire, and Michael Krigsman from Asuret.

I also want to attribute the contributions of my fellow coauthors of *The DevOps Handbook*, Jez Humble, Patrick DeBois, and John Willis. Among others, they helped crystallize the practices that became *The Three Ways* that Erik talked about.

I want to acknowledge John Allspaw, Paul Hammond, and Jez

Humble for their groundbreaking and seminal contributions of showing how fast flow in the IT value stream is really done.

And thank you to all the other reviewers who helped shape the manuscript: David Allen, David Bills, Kip Boyle, Shane Carlson, Carlos Casanova, Scott Crawford, Iris Culpepper, Mike Dahn, Chris Eng, Paul Farrall, Daniel Francisco, Kevin Hood, Matt Hooper, Tom Howarth, Kevin Kenan, Paul Love, Norman Marks, Tom McAndrew, Ally Miller, David Mortman, Wendy Nather, Michael Nygard, John Pierce, Dennis Ravenelle, Sasha Romanosky, Susan Ryan, Fred Scholl, Lawrence "Butch" Sheets, Bill Shinn, Adam Shostack, Ariel Silverstone, Dan Swanson, Joe "Feech" Telafici, Jan Vromant, and Lenny Zeltser.

The methodology used to create, link, and compute Dick's organizational KPIs to IT activities is based on the Risk-Adjusted Value Management™ methodology, developed by Paul Proctor and Michael Smith at Gartner, Inc.

The tool used to scope the specific audit internal control objectives to specific IT controls is called GAIT, developed by the Institute of Internal Auditors.

And my heartiest thank you to my assistant, Hannah Concannon, who made it possible for me to focus on writing and finishing the book, as well as helping me do all the final edits.

I want to also acknowledge Tim Ferriss and the help of the other alumni of the Kimono group, who helped me understand the theory and practice of book launches.

Gene Kim
Portland, OR, June 10, 2012

I would like to thank my wife, Erica, and my daughters, Emily and Rachel, for their patience and understanding with my chosen profession, which requires so much travel. Special thanks to my joyfully subversive serial coconspirators, Gene Kim and George Spafford, for being highly adaptable and tolerating my loquacious rants.

I have been ridiculously fortunate to work with some of the most creative and brilliant CXOs in my practice over the years, such as Will "Prefontaine" Weider, CIO of Ministry Healthcare; Robert Slepin, CIO of John C. Lincoln Health Network; Oliver Eckel, CEO of Cognosec; Rob

Leahy, CFO of Transdermal Corporation; Jeff Hughes, VP of Radiant Systems; Paul O'Neil, CEO of Kerzner International; and Nana Palmer, COO of Kerzner International—you all have taught me so much about courage in experimentation and radically improving IT throughput.

Lastly, I would like to thank my friend and partner in crime for many of these improvement learnings, John Dennin, Senior Engagement Manager at Assemblage Pointe, Inc.

Kevin Behr
Lancaster, PA, June 1, 2012

The journey from Visible Ops to *When IT Fails* further cemented my utmost respect and appreciation for Gene and Kevin. The challenges and exchanges we've had in the course of writing this book tested our collective abilities to put in writing what we have encountered in reality in the IT industry.

Gentlemen, thank you very much!

Most importantly, thank you for the unwavering love, motivation, support, and patience of my better half, Rowena. Thank you to my children, Paolo, Alyssa, and Erika, who all unselfishly put up with my chaotic and time-consuming schedule, even when on vacation. To my parents, Carroll and Alpha, thank you for instilling in me a love of learning. You have been an instrumental part in my continued quest to keep improving in all aspects of my life.

George Spafford
Saint Joseph, MI, June 1, 2012

THE THREE WAYS

As excerpted from

THE DEVOPS HANDBOOK

How to Create World-Class Agility, Reliability, & Security in Technology Organizations

By Gene Kim, Jez Humble, Patrick Debois, and John Willis

TABLE OF CONTENTS
THE THREE WAYS

The journey to complete *The DevOps Handbook* has been a long one—it started with weekly working Skype calls between the co-authors in February of 2011, with the vision of creating a prescriptive guide that would serve as a companion to the as-yet unfinished book *The Phoenix Project: A Novel About IT, DevOps, and Helping Your Business Win.*

More than five years later, with over two thousand hours of work, *The DevOps Handbook* is finally here. Completing this book has been an extremely long process, although one that has been highly rewarding and full of incredible learning, with a scope that is much broader than we originally envisioned. Throughout the project, all the co-authors shared a belief that DevOps is genuinely important, formed in a personal "aha" moment much earlier in each of our professional careers, which I suspect many of our readers will resonate with.

Gene Kim

I've had the privilege of studying high-performing technology organizations since 1999, and one of the earliest findings was that boundary-spanning between the different functional groups of IT Operations, Information Security, and Development was critical to success. But I still remember the first time I saw the magnitude of the downward spiral that would result when these functions worked toward opposing goals.

It was 2006, and I had the opportunity to spend a week with the group who managed the outsourced IT Operations of a large airline reservation service. They described the downstream consequences of their large, annual software releases: each release would cause immense chaos and disruption for the outsourcer, as well as customers; there would be SLA (service level agreement) penalties, because of the customer-impacting outages; there would be layoffs of the most talented and experienced staff, because of the resulting profit short-falls; there would be much unplanned work and firefighting so that the remaining staff couldn't work on the ever-growing service request backlogs coming from customers; the contract would be held together by the heroics of middle management; and everyone felt that the contract would be doomed to be put out for re-bid in three years.

The sense of hopelessness and futility that resulted created for me the beginnings of a moral crusade. Development seemed to always be viewed as strategic, but IT Operations was viewed as tactical, often delegated away or outsourced entirely, only to return in five years in worse shape than it was first handed over.

For many years, many of us knew that there must be a better way. I remember seeing the talks coming out of the 2009 Velocity Confer-ence, describing amazing outcomes enabled by architecture, technical practices, and cultural norms that we now know as DevOps. I was so excited, because it clearly pointed to the better way that we had all been searching for. And helping spread that word was one of my personal motivations to co-author *The Phoenix Project*. You can imagine how incredibly rewarding it was to see the broader community react to that book, describing how it helped them achieve their own "aha" moments.

Jez Humble

My DevOps "aha" moment was at a start-up in 2000—my first job after graduating. For some time, I was one of two technical staff. I did everything: networking, programming, support, systems administra-tion. We deployed software to production by FTP directly from our workstations.

Then in 2004 I got a job at ThoughtWorks, a consultancy where my first gig was working on a project involving about seventy people. I was on a team of eight engineers whose full-time job was to deploy our software into a production-like environment. In the beginning, it was really stressful. But over a few months we went from manual deployments that took two weeks to an automated deployment that took one hour, where we could roll forward and back in milliseconds using the blue-green deployment pattern during normal business hours.

That project inspired a lot of the ideas in both the *Continuous Delivery* (Addison-Wesley, 2000) book and this one. A lot of what drives me and others working in this space is the knowledge that, whatever your constraints, we can always do better, and the desire to help people on their journey.

Patrick Debois

For me, it was a collection of moments. In 2007 I was working on a data center migration project with some Agile teams. I was jealous that they had such high productivity—able to get so much done in so little time.

For my next assignment, I started experimenting with Kanban in Operations and saw how the dynamic of the team changed. Later, at the Agile Toronto 2008 conference I presented my IEEE paper on this, but I felt it didn't resonate widely in the Agile community. We started an Agile system administration group, but I overlooked the human side of things.

After seeing the 2009 Velocity Conference presentation "10 Deploys per Day" by John Allspaw and Paul Hammond, I was convinced others were thinking in a similar way. So I decided to organize the first DevOpsDays, accidently coining the term DevOps.

The energy at the event was unique and contagious. When people started to thank me because it changed their life for the better, I understood the impact. I haven't stopped promoting DevOps since.

John Willis

In 2008, I had just sold a consulting business that focused on large-scale, legacy IT operations practices around configuration management and monitoring (Tivoli) when I first met Luke Kanies (the founder of Puppet Labs). Luke was giving a presentation on Puppet at an O'Reilly open source conference on configuration management (CM).

At first I was just hanging out at the back of the room killing time and thinking, "What could this twenty-year-old tell me about configuration management?" After all, I had literally been working my entire life at some of the largest enterprises in the world, helping them architect CM and other operations management solutions. However, about five minutes into his session, I moved up to the first row and realized everything I had been doing for the last twenty years was wrong. Luke was describing what I now call second generation CM.

After his session I had an opportunity to sit down and have coffee with him. I was totally sold on what we now call infrastructure as code. However, while we met for coffee, Luke started going even further, explaining his ideas. He started telling me he believed that operations was going to have to start behaving like software developers. They were going to have to keep their configurations in source control and adopt CI/CD delivery patterns for their workflow. Being the old IT Operations person at the time, I think I replied to him with something like, "That idea is going to sink like Led Zeppelin with Ops folk." (I was clearly wrong.)

Then about a year later in 2009 at another O'Reilly conference, Velocity, I saw Andrew Clay Shafer give a presentation on Agile Infrastructure. In his presentation, Andrew showed this iconic picture of a wall between developers and operations with a metaphorical depiction of work being thrown over the wall. He coined this "the wall of confusion." The ideas he expressed in that presentation codified what Luke was trying to tell me a year earlier. That was the light bulb for me. Later that year, I was the only American invited to the original DevOpsDays in Ghent. By the time that event was over, this thing we call DevOps was clearly in my blood.

Clearly, the co-authors of this book all came to a similar epiphany, even if they came there from very different directions. But there is now an overwhelming weight of evidence that the problems described above happen almost everywhere, and that the solutions associated with DevOps are nearly universally applicable.

The goal of writing this book is to describe how to replicate the DevOps transformations we've been a part of or have observed, as well as dispel many of the myths of why DevOps won't work in certain situations. Below are some of the most common myths we hear about DevOps.

Myth—*DevOps is Only for Startups:* While DevOps practices have been pioneered by the web-scale, Internet "unicorn" companies such as Google, Amazon, Netflix, and Etsy, each of these organizations has, at some point in their history, risked going out of business because of the problems associated with more traditional "horse" organizations: highly dangerous code releases that were prone to catastrophic failure, inability to release features fast enough to beat the competition, compliance concerns, an inability to scale, high levels of distrust between Development and Operations, and so forth.

However, each of these organizations was able to transform their architecture, technical practices, and culture to create the amazing outcomes that we associate with DevOps. As Dr. Branden Williams, an information security executive, quipped, "Let there be no more talk of DevOps unicorns or horses but only thoroughbreds and horses heading to the glue factory."

Myth—*DevOps Replaces Agile:* DevOps principles and practices are compatible with Agile, with many observing that DevOps is a logical continuation of the Agile journey that started in 2001. Agile often serves as an effective enabler of DevOps, because of its focus on small teams continually delivering high quality code to customers.

Many DevOps practices emerge if we continue to manage our work beyond the goal of "potentially shippable code" at the end of each iteration, extending it to having our code always in a deployable state, with developers checking into trunk daily, and that we demonstrate our features in production-like environments.

Myth—*DevOps is incompatible with ITIL:* Many view DevOps as a backlash to ITIL or ITSM (IT Service Management), which was originally published in 1989. ITIL has broadly influenced multiple generations of Ops practitioners, including one of the co-authors, and is an ever-evolving library of practices intended to codify the processes and practices that underpin world-class IT Operations, spanning service strategy, design, and support.

DevOps practices can be made compatible with ITIL process. However, to support the shorter lead times and higher deployment frequencies associated with DevOps, many areas of the ITIL processes become fully automated, solving many problems associated with the configuration and release management processes (e.g., keeping the configuration management database and definitive software libraries up to date). And because DevOps requires fast detection and recovery when service incidents occur, the ITIL disciplines of service design, incident, and problem management remain as relevant as ever.

Myth—*DevOps is Incompatible with Information Security and Compliance:* The absence of traditional controls (e.g., segregation of duty, change approval processes, manual security reviews at the end of the project) may dismay information security and compliance professionals.

However, that doesn't mean that DevOps organizations don't have effective controls. Instead of security and compliance activities only being performed at the end of the project, controls are integrated into every stage of daily work in the software development life cycle, resulting in better quality, security, and compliance outcomes.

Myth—*DevOps Means Eliminating IT Operations, or "NoOps:"* Many misinterpret DevOps as the complete elimination of the IT Operations function. However, this is rarely the case. While the nature of IT Operations work may change, it remains as important as ever. IT Operations collaborates far earlier in the software life cycle with Development, who continues to work with IT Operations long after the code has been deployed into production.

Instead of IT Operations doing manual work that comes from work tickets, it enables developer productivity through APIs and self-serviced platforms that create environments, test and deploy code, monitor and display production telemetry, and so forth. By doing this, IT Operations become more like Development (as do QA and Infosec), engaged in product development, where the product is the platform that developers use to safely, quickly, and securely test, deploy, and run their IT services in production.

Myth—*DevOps is Just "Infrastructure as Code" or Automation:* While many of the DevOps patterns shown in this book require automation, DevOps also requires cultural norms and an architecture that allows for the shared goals to be achieved throughout the IT value stream. This goes far beyond just automation. As Christopher Little, a technology executive and one of the earliest chroniclers of DevOps, wrote, "DevOps isn't about automation, just as astronomy isn't about telescopes."

Myth—*DevOps is Only for Open Source Software:* Although many DevOps success stories take place in organizations using software such as the LAMP stack (Linux, Apache, MySQL, PHP), achieving DevOps outcomes is independent of the technology being used. Successes have been achieved with applications written in Microsoft.NET, COBOL, and mainframe assembly code, as well as with SAP and even embedded systems (e.g., HP LaserJet firmware).

SPREADING THE AHA! MOMENT

Each of the authors has been inspired by the amazing innovations happening in the DevOps community and the outcomes they are creating: they are creating safe systems of work, and enabling small teams to quickly and independently develop and validate code that can be safely deployed to customers. Given our belief that DevOps is a manifestation of creating dynamic, learning organizations that continually reinforce high-trust cultural norms, it is inevitable that these organizations will continue to innovate and win in the marketplace.

It is our sincere hope that *The DevOps Handbook* will serve as a valuable resource for many people in different ways: a guide for planning and executing DevOps transformations, a set of case studies to research and learn from, a chronicle of the history of DevOps, a means to create a coalition that spans Product Owners, Architecture, Development, QA, IT Operations, and Information Security to achieve common goals, a way to get the highest levels of leadership support for DevOps initiatives, as well as a moral imperative to change the way we manage technology organizations to enable better effectiveness and efficiency, as well as enabling a happier and more humane work environment, helping everyone become lifelong learners—this not only helps everyone achieve their highest goals as human beings, but also helps their organizations win.

In the past, many fields of engineering have experienced a sort of notable evolution, continually "leveling-up" its understanding of its own work. While there are university curriculums and professional support organizations situated within specific disciplines of engineering (civil, mechanical, electrical, nuclear, etc.), the fact is, modern society needs all forms of engineering to recognize the benefits of and work in a multidisciplinary way.

Think about the design of a high-performance vehicle. Where does the work of a mechanical engineer end and the work of an electrical engineer begin? Where (and how, and when) should someone with domain knowledge of aerodynamics (who certainly would have well-formed opinions on the shape, size, and placement of windows) collaborate with an expert in passenger ergonomics? What about the chemical influences of fuel mixture and oil on the materials of the engine and transmission over the lifetime of the vehicle? There are other questions we can ask about the design of an automobile, but the end result is the same: success in modern technical endeavors absolutely requires multiple perspectives and expertise to collaborate.

In order for a field or discipline to progress and mature, it needs to reach a point where it can thoughtfully reflect on its origins, seek out a diverse set of perspectives on those reflections, and place that synthesis into a context that is useful for how the community pictures the future.

This book represents such a synthesis and should be seen as a seminal collection of perspectives on the (I will argue, still emerging and quickly evolving) field of software engineering and operations.

No matter what industry you are in, or what product or service your organization provides, this way of thinking is paramount and necessary for survival for every business and technology leader.

—John Allspaw, CTO, Etsy
Brooklyn, NY, August 2016

Imagine a world where product owners, Development, QA, IT Operations, and Infosec work together, not only to help each other, but also to ensure that the overall organization succeeds. By working toward a common goal, they enable the fast flow of planned work into production (e.g., performing tens, hundreds, or even thousands of code deploys per day), while achieving world-class stability, reliability, availability, and security.

In this world, cross-functional teams rigorously test their hypotheses of which features will most delight users and advance the organizational goals. They care not just about implementing user features, but also actively ensure their work flows smoothly and frequently through the entire value stream without causing chaos and disruption to IT Operations or any other internal or external customer.

Simultaneously, QA, IT Operations, and Infosec are always working on ways to reduce friction for the team, creating the work systems that enable developers to be more productive and get better outcomes. By adding the expertise of QA, IT Operations, and Infosec into delivery teams and automated self-service tools and platforms, teams are able to use that expertise in their daily work without being dependent on other teams.

This enables organizations to create a safe system of work, where small teams are able to quickly and independently develop, test, and deploy code and value quickly, safely, securely, and reliably to customers. This allows organizations to maximize developer productivity, enable organizational learning, create high employee satisfaction, and win in the marketplace.

These are the outcomes that result from DevOps. For most of us, this is not the world we live in. More often than not, the system we work in is broken, resulting in extremely poor outcomes that fall well short of our true potential. In our world, Development and IT Operations are adversaries; testing and Infosec activities happen only at the end of a project, too late to correct any problems found; and almost any critical activity requires too much manual effort and too many handoffs, leaving us to always be waiting. Not only does this contribute to extremely long lead times to get anything done, but the quality of our work, especially production deployments, is also problematic and chaotic, resulting in negative impacts to our customers and our business.

As a result, we fall far short of our goals, and the whole organization is dissatisfied with the performance of IT, resulting in budget reductions and frustrated, unhappy employees who feel powerless to change the process and its outcomes.[†] The solution? We need to change how we work; DevOps shows us the best way forward.

To better understand the potential of the DevOps revolution, let us look at the Manufacturing Revolution of the 1980s. By adopting Lean principles and practices, manufacturing organizations dramatically improved plant productivity, customer lead times, product quality, and customer satisfaction, enabling them to win in the marketplace.

Before the revolution, average manufacturing plant order lead times were six weeks, with fewer than 70% of orders being shipped on time. By 2005, with the widespread implementation of Lean practices, average product lead times had dropped to less than three weeks, and more than 95% of orders were being shipped on time. Organizations that did not implement Lean practices lost market share, and many went out of business entirely.

Similarly, the bar has been raised for delivering technology products and services—what was good enough in previous decades is not good enough now. For each of the last four decades, the cost and time required to develop and deploy strategic business capabilities and features has dropped by orders of magnitude. During the 1970s and 1980s, most new features required one to five years to develop and deploy, often costing tens of millions of dollars.

By the 2000's, because of advances in technology and the adoption of Agile principles and practices, the time required to develop new functionality had

---

† This is just a small sample of the problems found in typical IT organizations.

dropped to weeks or months, but deploying into production would still require weeks or months, often with catastrophic outcomes.

And by 2010, with the introduction of DevOps and the neverending commoditization of hardware, software, and now the cloud, features (and even entire startup companies) could be created in weeks, quickly being deployed into production in just hours or minutes—for these organizations, deployment finally became routine and low risk. These organizations are able to perform experiments to test business ideas, discovering which ideas create the most value for customers and the organization as a whole, which are then further developed into features that can be rapidly and safely deployed into production.

Table 1. *The ever accelerating trend toward faster, cheaper, low-risk delivery of software*

	1970s–1980s	1990s	2000s–Present
Era	Mainframes	Client/Server	Commoditization and Cloud
Representative technology of era	COBOL, DB2 on MVS, etc.	C++, Oracle, Solaris, etc.	Java, MySQL, Red Hat, Ruby on Rails, PHP, etc.
Cycle time	1–5 years	3–12 months	2–12 weeks
Cost	$1M–$100M	$100k–$10M	$10k–$1M
At risk	The whole company	A product line or division	A product feature
Cost of failure	Bankruptcy, sell the company, massive layoffs	Revenue miss, CIO's job	Negligible

(Source: Adrian Cockcroft, "Velocity and Volume (or Speed Wins)," presentation at FlowCon, San Francisco, CA, November 2013.)

Today, organizations adopting DevOps principles and practices often deploy changes hundreds or even thousands of times per day. In an age where competitive advantage requires fast time to market and relentless experimentation, organizations that are unable to replicate these outcomes are destined to lose in the marketplace to more nimble competitors and could potentially go out of business entirely, much like the manufacturing organizations that did not adopt Lean principles.

These days, regardless of what industry we are competing in, the way we acquire customers and deliver value to them is dependent on the technology value stream. Put even more succinctly, as Jeffrey Immelt, CEO of General Electric, stated, "Every industry and company that is not bringing software to the core of their business will be disrupted." Or as Jeffrey Snover, Technical Fellow at Microsoft, said, "In previous economic eras, businesses created value by moving atoms. Now they create value by moving bits."

It's difficult to overstate the enormity of this problem—it affects every organization, independent of the industry we operate in, the size of our organization, whether we are profit or non-profit. Now more than ever, how technology work is managed and performed predicts whether our organizations will win in the marketplace, or even survive. In many cases, we will need to adopt principles and practices that look very different from those that have successfully guided us over the past decades. (See Appendix 1.)

Now that we have established the urgency of the problem that DevOps solves, let us take some time to explore in more detail the symptomatology of the problem, why it occurs, and why, without dramatic intervention, the problem worsens over time.

THE PROBLEM: SOMETHING IN YOUR ORGANIZATION MUST NEED IMPROVEMENT (OR YOU WOULDN'T BE READING THIS BOOK)

Most organizations are not able to deploy production changes in minutes or hours, instead requiring weeks or months. Nor are they able to deploy hundreds or thousands of changes into production per day; instead, they struggle to deploy monthly or even quarterly. Nor are production deployments routine, instead involving outages and chronic firefighting and heroics.

In an age where competitive advantage requires fast time to market, high service levels, and relentless experimentation, these organizations are at a significant competitive disadvantage. This is in large part due to their inability to resolve a core, chronic conflict within their technology organization.

THE CORE, CHRONIC CONFLICT
In almost every IT organization, there is an inherent conflict between Development and IT Operations which creates a downward spiral, resulting in

ever-slower time to market for new products and features, reduced quality, increased outages, and, worst of all, an ever-increasing amount of technical debt.

The term "technical debt" was first coined by Ward Cunningham. Analogous to financial debt, technical debt describes how decisions we make lead to problems that get increasingly more difficult to fix over time, continually reducing our available options in the future—even when taken on judiciously, we still incur interest.

One factor that contributes to this is the often competing goals of Development and IT Operations. IT organizations are responsible for many things. Among them are the two following goals, which must be pursued simultaneously:

- Respond to the rapidly changing competitive landscape

- Provide stable, reliable, and secure service to the customer

Frequently, Development will take responsibility for responding to changes in the market, deploying features and changes into production as quickly as possible. IT Operations will take responsibility for providing customers with IT service that is stable, reliable, and secure, making it difficult or even impossible for anyone to introduce production changes that could jeopardize production. Configured this way, Development and IT Operations have diametrically opposed goals and incentives.

Dr. Eliyahu M. Goldratt, one of the founders of the manufacturing management movement, called these types of configuration "the core, chronic conflict"—when organizational measurements and incentives across different silos prevent the achievement of global, organizational goals.[†]

This conflict creates a downward spiral so powerful it prevents the achievement of desired business outcomes, both inside and outside the IT organization. These chronic conflicts often put technology workers into situations that lead to poor software and service quality, and bad customer outcomes, as well as a daily need for workarounds, firefighting, and heroics, whether in Product

---

† In the manufacturing realm, a similar core, chronic conflict existed: the need to simultaneously ensure on-time shipments to customers and control costs. How this core, chronic conflict was broken is described in Appendix 2.

Management, Development, QA, IT Operations, or Information Security. (See Appendix 2.)

DOWNWARD SPIRAL IN THREE ACTS

The downward spiral in IT has three acts that are likely familiar to most IT practitioners.

The first act begins in IT Operations, where our goal is to keep applications and infrastructure running so that our organization can deliver value to customers. In our daily work, many of our problems are due to applications and infrastructure that are complex, poorly documented, and incredibly fragile. This is the technical debt and daily workarounds that we live with constantly, always promising that we'll fix the mess when we have a little more time. But that time never comes.

Alarmingly, our most fragile artifacts support either our most important revenue-generating systems or our most critical projects. In other words, the systems most prone to failure are also our most important and are at the epicenter of our most urgent changes. When these changes fail, they jeopardize our most important organizational promises, such as availability to customers, revenue goals, security of customer data, accurate financial reporting, and so forth.

The second act begins when somebody has to compensate for the latest broken promise—it could be a product manager promising a bigger, bolder feature to dazzle customers with or a business executive setting an even larger revenue target. Then, oblivious to what technology can or can't do, or what factors led to missing our earlier commitment, they commit the technology organization to deliver upon this new promise.

As a result, Development is tasked with another urgent project that inevitably requires solving new technical challenges and cutting corners to meet the promised release date, further adding to our technical debt—made, of course, with the promise that we'll fix any resulting problems when we have a little more time.

This sets the stage for the third and final act, where everything becomes just a little more difficult, bit by bit—everybody gets a little busier, work takes a little more time, communications become a little slower, and work queues get a little longer. Our work becomes more tightly coupled, smaller actions cause bigger failures, and we become more fearful and less tolerant of making changes. Work requires more communication, coordination, and approvals; teams must wait just a little longer for their dependent work to get done; and our quality keeps getting worse. The wheels begin grinding slower and require more effort to keep turning. (See Appendix 3.)

Although it's difficult to see in the moment, the downward spiral is obvious when one takes a step back. We notice that production code deployments are taking ever-longer to complete, moving from minutes to hours to days to weeks. And worse, the deployment outcomes have become even more problematic, that resulting in an ever-increasing number of customer-impacting outages that require more heroics and firefighting in Operations, further depriving them of their ability to pay down technical debt.

As a result, our product delivery cycles continue to move slower and slower, fewer projects are undertaken, and those that are, are less ambitious. Furthermore, the feedback on everyone's work becomes slower and weaker, especially the feedback signals from our customers. And, regardless of what we try, things seem to get worse—we are no longer able to respond quickly to our changing competitive landscape, nor are we able to provide stable, reliable service to our customers. As a result, we ultimately lose in the marketplace.

Time and time again, we learn that when IT fails, the entire organization fails. As Steven J. Spear noted in his book *The High-Velocity Edge*, whether the damages "unfold slowly like a wasting disease" or rapidly "like a fiery crash… the destruction can be just as complete."

WHY DOES THIS DOWNWARD SPIRAL HAPPEN EVERYWHERE?

For over a decade, the authors of this book have observed this destructive spiral occur in countless organizations of all types and sizes. We understand better than ever why this downward spiral occurs and why it requires DevOps principles to mitigate. First, as described earlier, every IT organization has two opposing goals, and second, every company is a technology company, whether they know it or not.

As Christopher Little, a software executive and one of the earliest chroniclers of DevOps, said, "Every company is a technology company, regardless of what business they think they're in. A bank is just an IT company with a banking license."[†]

---

† In 2013, the European bank HSBC employed more software developers than Google.

To convince ourselves that this is the case, consider that the vast majority of capital projects have some reliance upon IT. As the saying goes, "It is virtually impossible to make any business decision that doesn't result in at least one IT change."

In the business and finance context, projects are critical because they serve as the primary mechanism for change inside organizations. Projects are typically what management needs to approve, budget for, and be held accountable for; therefore, they are the mechanism that achieve the goals and aspirations of the organization, whether it is to grow or even shrink.[†]

Projects are typically funded through capital spending (i.e., factories, equipment, and major projects, and expenditures are capitalized when payback is expected to take years), of which 50% is now technology related. This is even true in "low tech" industry verticals with the lowest historical spending on technology, such as energy, metal, resource extraction, automotive, and construction. In other words, business leaders are far more reliant upon the effective management of IT in order to achieve their goals than they think.[‡]

THE COSTS: HUMAN AND ECONOMIC

When people are trapped in this downward spiral for years, especially those who are downstream of Development, they often feel stuck in a system that pre-ordains failure and leaves them powerless to change the outcomes. This powerlessness is often followed by burnout, with the associated feelings of fatigue, cynicism, and even hopelessness and despair.

Many psychologists assert that creating systems that cause feelings of powerlessness is one of the most damaging things we can do to fellow human beings—we deprive other people of their ability to control their own outcomes and even create a culture where people are afraid to do the right thing because of fear of punishment, failure, or jeopardizing their livelihood. This can create

---

† For now, let us suspend the discussion of whether software should be funded as a "project" or a "product." This is discussed later in the book.

‡ For instance, Dr. Vernon Richardson and his colleagues published this astonishing finding. They studied the 10-K SEC filings of 184 public corporations and divided them into three groups: A) firms with material weaknesses with IT-related deficiencies, B) firms with material weaknesses with no IT-related deficiencies, and C) "clean firms" with no material weaknesses. Firms in Group A saw eight times higher CEO turnover than Group C, and there was four times higher CFO turnover in Group A than in Group C. Clearly, IT may matter far more than we typically think.

the conditions of *learned helplessness*, where people become unwilling or unable to act in a way that avoids the same problem in the future.

For our employees, it means long hours, working on weekends, and a decreased quality of life, not just for the employee, but for everyone who depends on them, including family and friends. It is not surprising that when this occurs, we lose our best people (except for those that feel like they can't leave, because of a sense of duty or obligation).

In addition to the human suffering that comes with the current way of working, the opportunity cost of the value that we could be creating is staggering—the authors believe that we are missing out on approximately $2.6 trillion of value creation per year, which is, at the time of this writing, equivalent to the annual economic output of France, the sixth largest economy in the world.

Consider the following calculation—both IDC and Gartner estimated that in 2011, approximately 5% of the worldwide gross domestic product($3.1 trillion) was spent on IT (hardware, services, and telecom). If we estimate that 50% of that $3.1 trillion was spent on operating costs and maintaining existing systems, and that one-third of that 50% was spent on urgent and unplanned work or rework, approximately $520 billion was wasted.

If adopting DevOps could enable us, through better management and increased operational excellence, to halve that waste and redeploy that human potential into something that's five times the value (a modest proposal), we could create $2.6 trillion of value per year.

THE ETHICS OF DEVOPS: THERE IS A BETTER WAY

In the previous sections, we described the problems and the negative consequences of the status quo due to the core, chronic conflict, from the inability to achieve organizational goals, to the damage we inflict on fellow human beings. By solving these problems, DevOps astonishingly enables us to simultaneously improve organizational performance, achieve the goals of all the various functional technology roles (e.g., Development, QA, IT Operations, Infosec), and improve the human condition.

This exciting and rare combination may explain why DevOps has generated so much excitement and enthusiasm in so many in such a short time, including technology leaders, engineers, and much of the software ecosystem we reside in.

Ideally, small teams of developers independently implement their features, validate their correctness in production-like environments, and have their code deployed into production quickly, safely and securely. Code deployments are routine and predictable. Instead of starting deployments at midnight on Friday and spending all weekend working to complete them, deployments occur throughout the business day when everyone is already in the office and without our customers even noticing—except when they see new features and bug fixes that delight them. And, by deploying code in the middle of the workday, for the first time in decades IT Operations is working during normal business hours like everyone else.

By creating fast feedback loops at every step of the process, everyone can immediately see the effects of their actions. Whenever changes are committed into version control, fast automated tests are run in production-like environments, giving continual assurance that the code and environments operate as designed and are always in a secure and deployable state.

Automated testing helps developers discover their mistakes quickly (usually within minutes), which enables faster fixes as well as genuine learning—learning that is impossible when mistakes are discovered six months later during integration testing, when memories and the link between cause and effect have long faded. Instead of accruing technical debt, problems are fixed as they are found, mobilizing the entire organization if needed, because global goals outweigh local goals.

Pervasive production telemetry in both our code and production environments ensure that problems are detected and corrected quickly, confirming that everything is working as intended and customers are getting value from the software we create.

In this scenario, everyone feels productive—the architecture allows small teams to work safely and architecturally decoupled from the work of other teams who use self-service platforms that leverage the collective experience of Operations and Information Security. Instead of everyone waiting all the time, with large amounts of late, urgent rework, teams work independently and productively in small batches, quickly and frequently delivering new value to customers.

Even high-profile product and feature releases become routine by using dark launch techniques. Long before the launch date, we put all the required code for the feature into production, invisible to everyone except internal employees and small cohorts of real users, allowing us to test and evolve the feature until it achieves the desired business goal.

And, instead of firefighting for days or weeks to make the new functionality work, we merely change a feature toggle or configuration setting. This small change makes the new feature visible to ever-larger segments of customers, automatically rolling back if something goes wrong. As a result, our releases are controlled, predictable, reversible, and low stress.

It's not just feature releases that are calmer—all sorts of problems are being found and fixed early, when they are smaller, cheaper, and easier to correct. With every fix, we also generate organizational learnings, enabling us to prevent the problem from recurring and enabling us to detect and correct similar problems faster in the future.

Furthermore, everyone is constantly learning, fostering a hypothesis-driven culture where the scientific method is used to ensure nothing is taken for granted—we do nothing without measuring and treating product develop-ment and process improvement as experiments.

Because we value everyone's time, we don't spend years building features that our customers don't want, deploying code that doesn't work, or fixing some-thing that isn't actually the cause of our problem.

Because we care about achieving goals, we create long-term teams that are responsible for meeting them. Instead of project teams where developers are reassigned and shuffled around after each release, never receiving feedback on their work, we keep teams intact so they can keep iterating and improving, using those learnings to better achieve their goals. This is equally true for the product teams who are solving problems for our external customers, as well as our internal platform teams who are helping other teams be more produc-tive, safe, and secure.

Instead of a culture of fear, we have a high-trust, collaborative culture, where people are rewarded for taking risks. They are able to fearlessly talk about problems as opposed to hiding them or putting them on the backburner—after all, we must see problems in order to solve them.

And, because everyone fully owns the quality of their work, everyone builds automated testing into their daily work and uses peer reviews to gain confi-dence that problems are addressed long before they can impact a customer. These processes mitigate risk, as opposed to approvals from distant authorities, allowing us to deliver value quickly, reliably, and securely—even proving to skeptical auditors that we have an effective system of internal controls.

And when something does go wrong, we conduct *blameless post-mortems*, not to punish anyone, but to better understand what caused the accident and how to prevent it. This ritual reinforces our culture of learning. We also hold internal technology conferences to elevate our skills and ensure that everyone is always teaching and learning.

Because we care about quality, we even inject faults into our production environment so we can learn how our system fails in a planned manner. We conduct planned exercises to practice large-scale failures, randomly kill processes and compute servers in production, and inject network latencies and other nefarious acts to ensure we grow ever more resilient. By doing this, we enable better resilience, as well as organizational learning and improvement.

In this world, everyone has ownership in their work, regardless of their role in the technology organization. They have confidence that their work matters and is meaningfully contributing to organizational goals, proven by their low-stress work environment and their organization's success in the marketplace. Their proof is that the organization is indeed winning in the marketplace.

THE BUSINESS VALUE OF DEVOPS

We have decisive evidence of the business value of DevOps. From 2013 through 2016, as part of Puppet Labs' *State Of DevOps Report*, to which authors Jez Humble and Gene Kim contributed, we collected data from over twenty-five thousand technology professionals, with the goal of better understanding the health and habits of organizations at all stages of DevOps adoption.

The first surprise this data revealed was how much high performing organizations using DevOps practices were outperforming their non–high performing peers in the following areas:

- Throughput metrics

- Code and change deployments (thirty times more frequent)

- Code and change deployment lead time (two hundred times faster)

- Reliability metrics

- Production deployments (sixty times higher change success rate)

- Mean time to restore service (168 times faster)

- Organizational performance metrics

- Productivity, market share, and profitability goals (two times more likely to exceed)

- Market capitalization growth (50% higher over three years)

In other words, high performers were both more agile and more reliable, providing empirical evidence that DevOps enables us to break the core, chronic conflict. High performers deployed code thirty times more frequently, and the time required to go from "code committed" to "successfully running in production" was two hundred times faster—high performers had lead times measured in minutes or hours, while low performers had lead times measured in weeks, months, or even quarters.

Furthermore, high performers were twice as likely to exceed profitability, market share, and productivity goals. And, for those organizations that provided a stock ticker symbol, we found that high performers had 50% higher market capitalization growth over three years. They also had higher employee job satisfaction, lower rates of employee burnout, and their employees were 2.2 times more likely to recommend their organization to friends as a great place to work.[†] High performers also had better information security outcomes. By integrating security objectives into all stages of the development and operations processes, they spent 50% less time remediating security issues.

DEVOPS HELPS SCALE DEVELOPER PRODUCTIVITY

When we increase the number of developers, individual developer productivity often significantly decreases due to communication, integration, and testing overhead. This is highlighted in the famous book by Frederick Brook, *The Mythical Man-Month*, where he explains that when projects are late, adding

---

[†] As measured by employee Net Promoter Score (eNPS). This is a significant finding, as research has shown that "companies with highly engaged workers grew revenues two and a half times as much as those with low engagement levels. And [publicly traded] stocks of companies with a high-trust work environment outperformed market indexes by a factor of three from 1997 through 2011."

more developers not only decreases individual developer productivity but also decreases overall productivity.

On the other hand, DevOps shows us that when we have the right architecture, the right technical practices, and the right cultural norms, small teams of developers are able to quickly, safely, and independently develop, integrate, test, and deploy changes into production. As Randy Shoup, formerly a director of engineering at Google, observed, large organizations using DevOps "have thousands of developers, but their architecture and practices enable small teams to still be incredibly productive, as if they were a startup."

The 2015 *State of DevOps Report* examined not only "deploys per day" but also "deploys per day per developer." We hypothesized that high performers would be able to scale their number of deployments as team sizes grew.

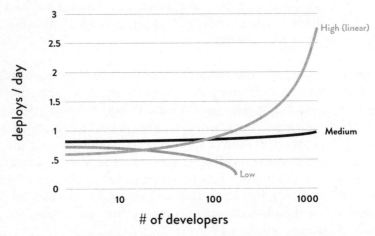

Figure 1. *Deployments/day vs. number of developers*
(Source: Puppet Labs, 2015 State Of DevOps Report.)[†]

Indeed, this is what we found. Figure 1 shows that in low performers, deploys per day per developer go down as team size increases, stays constant for medium performers, and increases linearly for high performers.

In other words, organizations adopting DevOps are able to linearly increase the number of deploys per day as they increase their number of developers, just as Google, Amazon, and Netflix have done.[‡]

---

† Only organizations that are deploying at least once per day are shown.

‡ Another more extreme example is Amazon. In 2011, Amazon was performing approximately seven thousand deploys per day. By 2015, they were performing 130,000 deploys per day.

THE UNIVERSALITY OF THE SOLUTION

One of the most influential books in the Lean manufacturing movement is *The Goal: A Process of Ongoing Improvement* written by Dr. Eliyahu M. Goldratt in 1984. It influenced an entire generation of professional plant managers around the world. It was a novel about a plant manager who had to fix his cost and product due date issues in ninety days, otherwise his plant would be shut down.

Later in his career, Dr. Goldratt described the letters he received in response to *The Goal*. These letters would typically read, "You have obviously been hiding in our factory, because you've described my life [as a plant manager] exactly..." Most importantly, these letters showed people were able to replicate the breakthroughs in performance that were described in the book in their own work environments.

The Phoenix Project: A Novel About IT, DevOps, and Helping Your Business Win, written by Gene Kim, Kevin Behr, and George Spafford in 2013, was closely modeled after *The Goal*. It is a novel that follows an IT leader who faces all the typical problems that are endemic in IT organizations: an over-budget, behind-schedule project that must get to market in order for the company to survive. He experiences catastrophic deployments; problems with availability, security, and compliance; and so forth. Ultimately, he and his team use DevOps principles and practices to overcome those challenges, helping their organization win in the marketplace. In addition, the novel shows how DevOps practices improved the workplace environment for the team, creating lower stress and higher satisfaction because of greater practitioner involvement throughout the process.

As with *The Goal*, there is tremendous evidence of the universality of the problems and solutions described in *The Phoenix Project*. Consider some of the statements found in the Amazon reviews: "I find myself relating to the characters in *The Phoenix Project*...I've probably met most of them over the course of my career," "If you have ever worked in any aspect of IT, DevOps, or Infosec you will definitely be able to relate to this book," or "There's not a character in *The Phoenix Project* that I don't identify with myself or someone I know in real life... not to mention the problems faced and overcome by those characters."

In the remainder of this book, we will describe how to replicate the transformation described in *The Phoenix Project*, as well provide many case studies of how other organizations have used DevOps principles and practices to replicate those outcomes.

THE DEVOPS HANDBOOK: AN ESSENTIAL GUIDE

The purpose of the *DevOps Handbook* is to give you the theory, principles, and practices you need to successfully start your DevOps initiative and achieve your desired outcomes. This guidance is based on decades of sound management theory, study of high performing technology organizations, work we have done helping organizations transform, and research that validates the effectiveness of the prescribed DevOps practices. As well as interviews with relevant subject matter experts and analyses of nearly one hundred case studies presented at the DevOps Enterprise Summit.

Broken into six parts, this book covers DevOps theories and principles using the Three Ways, a specific view of the underpinning theory originally introduced in *The Phoenix Project*. *The DevOps Handbook* is for everyone who performs or influences work in the technology value stream (which typically includes Product Management, Development, QA, IT Operations, and Information Security), as well as for business and marketing leadership, where most technology initiatives originate.

The reader is not expected to have extensive knowledge of any of these domains, or of DevOps, Agile, ITIL, Lean, or process improvement. Each of these topics is introduced and explained in the book as it becomes necessary.

Our intent is to create a working knowledge of the critical concepts in each of these domains, both to serve as a primer and to introduce the language necessary to help practitioners work with all their peers across the entire IT value stream, and to frame shared goals.

This book will be of value to business leaders and stakeholders who are increasingly reliant upon the technology organization for the achievement of their goals.

Furthermore, this book is intended for readers whose organizations might not be experiencing all the problems described in the book (e.g., long deployment lead times or painful deployments). Even readers in this fortunate position will benefit from understanding DevOps principles, especially those relating to shared goals, feedback, and continual learning.

In Part I, we present a brief history of DevOps and introduce the underpinning theory and key themes from relevant bodies of knowledge that span over decades. We then present the high level principles of the Three Ways: Flow, Feedback, and Continual Learning and Experimentaion.

Part II describes how and where to start, and presents concepts such as value streams, organizational design principles and patterns, organizational adoption patterns, and case studies.

Part III describes how to accelerate Flow by building the foundations of our deployment pipeline: enabling fast and effective automated testing, continuous integration, continuous delivery, and architecting for low-risk releases.

Part IV discusses how to accelerate and amplify Feedback by creating effective production telemetry to see and solve problems, better anticipate problems and achieve goals, enable feedback so that Dev and Ops can safely deploy changes, integrate A/B testing into our daily work, and create review and coordination processes to increase the quality of our work.

Part V describes how we accelerate Continual Learning by establishing a just culture, converting local discoveries into global improvements, and properly reserving time to create organizational learning and improvements.

Finally, in Part VI we describe how to properly integrate security and compliance into our daily work, by integrating preventative security controls into shared source code repositories and services, integrating security into our deployment pipeline, enhancing telemetry to better enable detection and recovery, protecting the deployment pipeline, and achieving change management objectives.

By codifying these practices, we hope to accelerate the adoption of DevOps practices, increase the success of DevOps initiatives, and lower the activation energy required for DevOps transformations.

Part **I**
Introduction

In Part I of *The DevOps Handbook*, we will explore how the convergence of several important movements in management and technology set the stage for the DevOps movement. We describe value streams, how DevOps is the result of applying Lean principles to the technology value stream, and the Three Ways: Flow, Feedback, and Continual Learning and Experimentation.

Primary focuses within these chapters include:

- The principles of Flow, which accelerate the delivery of work from Development to Operations to our customers

- The principles of Feedback, which enable us to create ever safer systems of work

- The principles of Continual Learning and Experimentation foster a high-trust culture and a scientific approach to organizational improvement risk-taking as part of our daily work

A BRIEF HISTORY

DevOps and its resulting technical, architectural, and cultural practices represent a convergence of many philosophical and management movements. While many organizations have developed these principles independently, understanding that DevOps resulted from a broad stroke of movements, a phenomenon described by John Willis (one of the co-authors of this book) as the "convergence of DevOps," shows an amazing progression of thinking and improbable connections. There are decades of lessons learned from manufacturing, high reliability organization, high-trust management models, and others that have brought us to the DevOps practices we know today.

DevOps is the outcome of applying the most trusted principles from the domain of physical manufacturing and leadership to the IT value stream. DevOps relies on bodies of knowledge from Lean, Theory of Constraints, the Toyota Production System, resilience engineering, learning organizations, safety culture, human factors, and many others. Other valuable contexts that DevOps draws from include high-trust management cultures, servant leadership, and organizational change management. The result is world-class quality, reliability, stability, and security at ever lower cost and effort; and accelerated flow and reliability throughout the technology value stream, including Product Management, Development, QA, IT Operations, and Infosec.

While the foundation of DevOps can be seen as being derived from Lean, the Theory of Constraints, and the Toyota Kata movement, many also view DevOps as the logical continuation of the Agile software journey that began in 2001.

THE LEAN MOVEMENT

Techniques such as Value Stream Mapping, Kanban Boards, and Total Productive Maintenance were codified for the Toyota Production System in the 1980s. In 1997, the Lean Enterprise Institute started researching applications of Lean to other value streams, such as the service industry and healthcare.

Two of Lean's major tenets include the deeply held belief that *manufacturing lead time* required to convert raw materials into finished goods was the best predictor of quality, customer satisfaction, and employee happiness, and that one of the best predictors of short lead times was small batch sizes of work.

Lean principles focus on how to create value for the customer through systems thinking by creating constancy of purpose, embracing scientific thinking, creating flow and pull (versus push), assuring quality at the source, leading with humility, and respecting every individual.

THE AGILE MANIFESTO

The Agile Manifesto was created in 2001 by seventeen of the leading thinkers in software development. They wanted to create a lightweight set of values and principles against heavyweight software development processes such as waterfall development, and methodologies such as the Rational Unified Process.

One key principle was to "deliver working software frequently, from a couple of weeks to a couple of months, with a preference to the shorter timescale," emphasizing the desire for small batch sizes, incremental releases instead of large, waterfall releases. Other principles emphasized the need for small, self-motivated teams, working in a high-trust management model.

Agile is credited for dramatically increasing the productivity of many development organizations. And interestingly, many of the key moments in DevOps history also occurred within the Agile community or at Agile conferences, as described below.

AGILE INFRASTRUCTURE AND VELOCITY MOVEMENT

At the 2008 Agile conference in Toronto, Canada, Patrick Debois and Andrew Schafer held a "birds of a feather" session on applying Agile principles to infrastructure as opposed to application code. Although they were the only people who showed up, they rapidly gained a following of like-minded thinkers, including co-author John Willis.

Later, at the 2009 Velocity conference, John Allspaw and Paul Hammond gave the seminal "10 Deploys per Day: Dev and Ops Cooperation at Flickr" presentation, where they described how they created shared goals between Dev and Ops and used continuous integration practices to make deployment part of everyone's daily work. According to first hand accounts, everyone attending the presentation immediately knew they were in the presence of something profound and of historic significance.

Patrick Debois was not there, but was so excited by Allspaw and Hammond's idea that he created the first DevOpsDays in Ghent, Belgium, (where he lived) in 2009. There the term "DevOps" was coined.

THE CONTINUOUS DELIVERY MOVEMENT

Building upon the development discipline of continuous build, test, and integration, Jez Humble and David Farley extended the concept to *continuous delivery*, which defined the role of a "deployment pipeline" to ensure that code and infrastructure are always in a deployable state, and that all code checked in to trunk can be safely deployed into production. This idea was first presented at the 2006 Agile conference, and was also independently developed in 2009 by Tim Fitz in a blog post on his website titled "Continuous Deployment."†

TOYOTA KATA

In 2009, Mike Rother wrote *Toyota Kata: Managing People for Improvement, Adaptiveness and Superior Results*, which framed his twenty-year journey to understand and codify the Toyota Production System. He had been one of the graduate students who flew with GM executives to visit Toyota plants and helped develop the Lean toolkit, but he was puzzled when none of the companies adopting these practices replicated the level of performance observed at the Toyota plants.

He concluded that the Lean community missed the most important practice of all, which he called the *improvement kata*. He explains that every organization has work routines, and the improvement kata requires creating structure for the daily, habitual practice of improvement work, because daily practice is what improves outcomes. The constant cycle of establishing desired future states, setting weekly target outcomes, and the continual improvement of daily work is what guided improvement at Toyota.

The above describes the history of DevOps and relevant movements that it draws upon. Throughout the rest of Part I, we look at value streams, how Lean principles can be applied to the technology value stream, and the Three Ways of Flow, Feedback, and Continual Learning and Experimentation.

---

† DevOps also extends and builds upon the practices of *infrastructure as code*, which was pioneered by Dr. Mark Burgess, Luke Kanies, and Adam Jacob. In infrastructure as code, the work of Operations is automated and treated like application code, so that modern development practices can be applied to the entire development stream. This further enabled fast deployment flow, including continuous integration (pioneered by Grady Booch and integrated as one of the key 12 practices of Extreme Programming), continuous delivery (pioneered by Jez Humble and David Farley), and continuous deployment (pioneered by Etsy, Wealthfront, and Eric Ries's work at IMVU).

1

Agile, Continuous Delivery, and the Three Ways

In this chapter, an introduction to the underpinning theory of Lean Manufacturing is presented, as well as the Three Ways, the principles from which all of the observed DevOps behaviors can be derived.

Our focus here is primarily on theory and principles, describing many decades of lessons learned from manufacturing, high-reliability organizations, high-trust management models, and others, from which DevOps practices have been derived. The resulting concrete principles and patterns, and their practical application to the technology value stream, are presented in the remaining chapters of the book.

THE MANUFACTURING VALUE STREAM

One of the fundamental concepts in Lean is the *value stream*. We will define it first in the context of manufacturing and then extrapolate how it applies to DevOps and the technology value stream.

Karen Martin and Mike Osterling define value stream in their book *Value Stream Mapping: How to Visualize Work and Align Leadership for Organizational Transformation* as "the sequence of activities an organization undertakes to deliver upon a customer request," or "the sequence of activities required to design, produce, and deliver a good or service to a customer, including the dual flows of information and material."

In manufacturing operations, the value stream is often easy to see and observe: it starts when a customer order is received and the raw materials are released onto the plant floor. To enable fast and predictable lead times in any value stream, there is usually a relentless focus on creating a smooth and even flow of work, using techniques such as small batch sizes, reducing work in process

(WIP), preventing rework to ensure we don't pass defects to downstream work centers, and constantly optimizing our system toward our global goals.

THE TECHNOLOGY VALUE STREAM

The same principles and patterns that enable the fast flow of work in physical processes are equally applicable to technology work (and, for that matter, for all knowledge work). In DevOps, we typically define our technology value stream as the process required to convert a business hypothesis into a technology-enabled service that delivers value to the customer.

The input to our process is the formulation of a business objective, concept, idea, or hypothesis, and starts when we accept the work in Development, adding it to our committed backlog of work.

From there, Development teams that follow a typical Agile or iterative process will likely transform that idea into user stories and some sort of feature specification, which is then implemented in code into the application or service being built. The code is then checked in to the version control repository, where each change is integrated and tested with the rest of the software system.

Because value is created only when our services are running in production, we must ensure that we are not only delivering fast flow, but that our deployments can also be performed without causing chaos and disruptions such as service outages, service impairments, or security or compliance failures.

FOCUS ON DEPLOYMENT LEAD TIME

For the remainder of this book, our attention will be on deployment lead time, a subset of the value stream described above. This value stream begins when any engineer[†] in our value stream (which includes Development, QA, IT Operations, and Infosec) checks a change into version control and ends when that change is successfully running in production, providing value to the customer and generating useful feedback and telemetry.

The first phase of work that includes Design and Development is akin to Lean Product Development and is highly variable and highly uncertain, often requiring high degrees of creativity and work that may never be performed again, resulting in high variability of process times. In contrast, the second

---

† Going forward, *engineer* refers to anyone working in our value stream, not just developers.

phase of work, which includes Testing and Operations, is akin to Lean Manufacturing. It requires creativity and expertise, and strives to be predictable and mechanistic, with the goal of achieving work outputs with minimized variability (e.g., short and predictable lead times, near zero defects).

Instead of large batches of work being processed sequentially through the design/development value stream and then through the test/operations value stream (such as when we have a large batch waterfall process or long-lived feature branches), our goal is to have testing and operations happening simultaneously with design/development, enabling fast flow and high quality. This method succeeds when we work in small batches and build quality into every part of our value stream.[†]

Defining Lead Time vs. Processing Time

In the Lean community, lead time is one of two measures commonly used to measure performance in value streams, with the other being processing time (sometimes known as touch time or task time).[‡]

Whereas the lead time clock starts when the request is made and ends when it is fulfilled, the process time clock starts only when we begin work on the customer request—specifically, it omits the time that the work is in queue, waiting to be processed (figure 2).

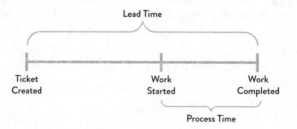

Figure 2. *Lead time vs. process time of a deployment operation*

Because lead time is what the customer experiences, we typically focus our process improvement attention there instead of on process time. However, the proportion of process time to lead time serves as an important measure

---

† In fact, with techniques such as test-driven development, testing occurs even before the first line of code is written.

‡ In this book, the term *process time* will be favored for the same reason Karen Martin and Mike Osterling cite: "To minimize confusion, we avoid using the term cycle time as it has several definitions synonymous with processing time and pace or frequency of output, to name a few."

of efficiency—achieving fast flow and short lead times almost always requires reducing the time our work is waiting in queues.

The Common Scenario: Deployment Lead Times Requiring Months

In business as usual, we often find ourselves in situations where our deployment lead times require months. This is especially common in large, complex organizations that are working with tightly-coupled, monolithic applications, often with scarce integration test environments, long test and production environment lead times, high reliance on manual testing, and multiple required approval processes. When this occurs, our value stream may look like figure 3:

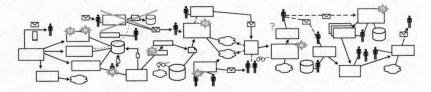

Figure 3: *A technology value stream with a deployment lead time of three months (Source: Damon Edwards, "DevOps Kaizen," 2015.)*

When we have long deployment lead times, heroics are required at almost every stage of the value stream. We may discover that nothing works at the end of the project when we merge all the development team's changes together, resulting in code that no longer builds correctly or passes any of our tests. Fixing each problem requires days or weeks of investigation to determine who broke the code and how it can be fixed, and still results in poor customer outcomes.

Our DevOps Ideal: Deployment Lead Times of Minutes

In the DevOps ideal, developers receive fast, constant feedback on their work, which enables them to quickly and independently implement, integrate, and validate their code, and have the code deployed into the production environment (either by deploying the code themselves or by others).

We achieve this by continually checking small code changes into our version control repository, performing automated and exploratory testing against it, and deploying it into production. This enables us to have a high degree of confidence that our changes will operate as designed in production and that any problems can be quickly detected and corrected.

This is most easily achieved when we have architecture that is modular, well encapsulated, and loosely-coupled so that small teams are able to work with high degrees of autonomy, with failures being small and contained, and without causing global disruptions.

In this scenario, our deployment lead time is measured in minutes, or, in the worst case, hours. Our resulting value stream map should look something like figure 4:

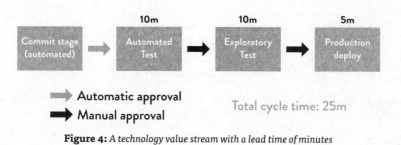

Figure 4: *A technology value stream with a lead time of minutes*

OBSERVING "%C/A" AS A MEASURE OF REWORK

In addition to lead times and process times, the third key metric in the technology value stream is percent complete and accurate (%C/A). This metric reflects the quality of the output of each step in our value stream. Karen Martin and Mike Osterling state that "the %C/A can be obtained by asking downstream customers what percentage of the time they receive work that is 'usable as is,' meaning that they can do their work without having to correct the information that was provided, add missing information that should have been supplied, or clarify information that should have and could have been clearer."

THE THREE WAYS: THE PRINCIPLES UNDERPINNING DEVOPS

The Phoenix Project presents the Three Ways as the set of underpinning principles from which all the observed DevOps behaviors and patterns are derived (figure 5).

The First Way enables fast left-to-right flow of work from Development to Operations to the customer. In order to maximize flow, we need to make work visible, reduce our batch sizes and intervals of work, build in quality by preventing defects from being passed to downstream work centers, and constantly optimize for the global goals.

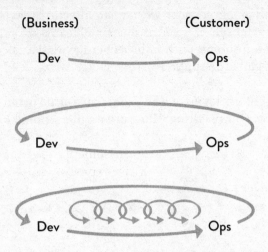

Figure 5: *The Three Ways (Source: Gene Kim, "The Three Ways: The Principles Underpinning DevOps," IT Revolution Press blog, accessed August 9, 2016, http://itrevolution.com/ the-three-ways-principles-underpinning-devops/.)*

By speeding up flow through the technology value stream, we reduce the lead time required to fulfill internal or customer requests, especially the time required to deploy code into the production environment. By doing this, we increase the quality of work as well as our throughput, and boost our ability to out-experiment the competition.

The resulting practices include continuous build, integration, test, and deployment processes; creating environments on demand; limiting work in process (WIP); and building systems and organizations that are safe to change.

The Second Way enables the fast and constant flow of feedback from right to left at all stages of our value stream. It requires that we amplify feedback to prevent problems from happening again, or enable faster detection and recovery. By doing this, we create quality at the source and generate or embed knowledge where it is needed—this allows us to create ever-safer systems of work where problems are found and fixed long before a catastrophic failure occurs.

By seeing problems as they occur and swarming them until effective countermeasures are in place, we continually shorten and amplify our feedback loops, a core tenet of virtually all modern process improvement methodologies. This maximizes the opportunities for our organization to learn and improve.

The Third Way enables the creation of a generative, high-trust culture that supports a dynamic, disciplined, and scientific approach to experimentation and risk-taking, facilitating the creation of organizational learning, both from our successes and failures. Furthermore, by continually shortening and amplifying our feedback loops, we create ever-safer systems of work and are better able to take risks and perform experiments that help us learn faster than our competition and win in the marketplace.

As part of the Third Way, we also design our system of work so that we can multiply the effects of new knowledge, transforming local discoveries into global improvements. Regardless of where someone performs work, they do so with the cumulative and collective experience of everyone in the organization.

CONCLUSION

In this chapter, we described the concepts of value streams, lead time as one of the key measures of the effectiveness for both manufacturing and technology value streams, and the high-level concepts behind each of the Three Ways, the principles that underpin DevOps.

In the following chapters, the principles for each of the Three Ways are described in greater detail. The first of these principles is Flow, which is focused on how we create the fast flow of work in any value stream, whether it's in manufacturing or technology work. The practices that enable fast flow are described in Part III.

2 The First Way:
The Principles of Flow

In the technology value stream, work typically flows from Development to Operations, the functional areas between our business and our customers. The First Way requires the fast and smooth flow of work from Development to Operations, to deliver value to customers quickly. We optimize for this global goal instead of local goals, such as Development feature completion rates, test find/fix ratios, or Ops availability measures.

We increase flow by making work visible, by reducing batch sizes and intervals of work, and by building quality in, preventing defects from being passed to downstream work centers. By speeding up the flow through the technology value stream, we reduce the lead time required to fulfill internal and external customer requests, further increasing the quality of our work while making us more agile and able to out-experiment the competition.

Our goal is to decrease the amount of time required for changes to be deployed into production and to increase the reliability and quality of those services. Clues on how we do this in the technology value stream can be gleaned from how the Lean principles were applied to the manufacturing value stream.

MAKE OUR WORK VISIBLE

A significant difference between technology and manufacturing value streams is that our work is invisible. Unlike physical processes, in the technology value stream we cannot easily see where flow is being impeded or when work is piling up in front of constrained work centers. Transferring work between work centers is usually highly visible and slow because inventory must be physically moved.

However, in technology work the move can be done with a click of a button, such as by re-assigning a work ticket to another team. Because it is so easy, work can bounce between teams endlessly due to incomplete information, or work can be passed onto downstream work centers with problems that remain completely invisible until we are late delivering what we promised to the customer or our application fails in the production environment.

To help us see where work is flowing well and where work is queued or stalled, we need to make our work as visible as possible. One of the best methods of doing this is using visual work boards, such as kanban boards or sprint planning boards, where we can represent work on physical or electronic cards. Work originates on the left (often being pulled from a backlog), is pulled from work center to work center (represented in columns), and finishes when it reaches the right side of the board, usually in a column labeled "done" or "in production."

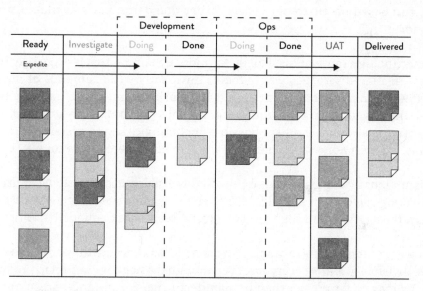

Figure 6: *An example kanban board, spanning Requirements, Dev, Test, Staging, and In Production (Source: David J. Andersen and Dominica DeGrandis, Kanban for ITOps, training materials for workshop, 2012.)*

Not only does our work become visible, we can also manage our work so that it flows from left to right as quickly as possible. Furthermore, we can measure lead time from when a card is placed on the board to when it is moved into the "Done" column.

Ideally, our kanban board will span the entire value stream, defining work as completed only when it reaches the right side of the board (figure 6). Work is not done when Development completes the implementation of a feature—

rather, it is only done when our application is running successfully in production, delivering value to the customer.

By putting all work for each work center in queues and making it visible, all stakeholders can more easily prioritize work in the context of global goals. Doing this enables each work center to single-task on the highest priority work until it is completed, increasing throughput.

LIMIT WORK IN PROCESS (WIP)

In manufacturing, daily work is typically dictated by a production schedule that is generated regularly (e.g., daily, weekly), establishing which jobs must be run based on customer orders, order due dates, parts available, and so forth.

In technology, our work is usually far more dynamic—this is especially the case in shared services, where teams must satisfy the demands of many different stakeholders. As a result, daily work becomes dominated by the priority *du jour*, often with requests for urgent work coming in through every communication mechanism possible, including ticketing systems, outage calls, emails, phone calls, chat rooms, and management escalations.

Disruptions in manufacturing are also highly visible and costly, often requiring breaking the current job and scrapping any incomplete work in process to start the new job. This high level of effort discourages frequent disruptions.

However, interrupting technology workers is easy, because the consequences are invisible to almost everyone, even though the negative impact to productivity may be far greater than in manufacturing. For instance, an engineer assigned to multiple projects must switch between tasks, incurring all the costs of having to re-establish context, as well as cognitive rules and goals.

Studies have shown that the time to complete even simple tasks, such as sorting geometric shapes, significantly degrades when multitasking. Of course, because our work in the technology value stream is far more cognitively complex than sorting geometric shapes, the effects of multitasking on process time is much worse.

We can limit multitasking when we use a kanban board to manage our work, such as by codifying and enforcing WIP (work in progress) limits for each column or work center that puts an upper limit on the number of cards that can be in a column.

For example, we may set a WIP limit of three cards for testing. When there are already three cards in the test lane, no new cards can be added to the lane unless a card is completed or removed from the "in work" column and put back into queue (i.e., putting the card back to the column to the left). Nothing can can be worked on until it is represented first in a work card, reinforcing that all work must be made visible.

Dominica DeGrandis, one of the leading experts on using kanbans in DevOps value streams, notes that "controlling queue size [WIP] is an extremely powerful management tool, as it is one of the few leading indicators of lead time—with most work items, we don't know how long it will take until it's actually completed."

Limiting WIP also makes it easier to see problems that prevent the completion of work.[†] For instance, when we limit WIP, we find that we may have nothing to do because we are waiting on someone else. Although it may be tempting to start new work (i.e., "It's better to be doing something than nothing"), a far better action would be to find out what is causing the delay and help fix that problem. Bad multitasking often occurs when people are assigned to multiple projects, resulting in many prioritization problems.

In other words, as David J. Andersen, author of *Kanban: Successful Evolutionary Change for Your Technology Business*, quipped, "Stop starting. Start finishing."

REDUCE BATCH SIZES

Another key component to creating smooth and fast flow is performing work in small batch sizes. Prior to the Lean manufacturing revolution, it was common practice to manufacture in large batch sizes (or lot sizes), especially for operations where job setup or switching between jobs was time-consuming or costly. For example, producing large car body panels requires setting large and heavy dies onto metal stamping machines, a process that could take days. When changeover cost is so expensive, we would often stamp as many panels at a time as possible, creating large batches in order to reduce the number of changeovers.

---

† Taiichi Ohno compared enforcing WIP limits to draining water from the river of inventory in order to reveal all the problems that obstruct fast flow.

However, large batch sizes result in skyrocketing levels of WIP and high levels of variability in flow that cascade through the entire manufacturing plant. The result is long lead times and poor quality—if a problem is found in one body panel, the entire batch has to be scrapped.

One of the key lessons in Lean is that in order to shrink lead times and increase quality, we must strive to continually shrink batch sizes. The theoretical lower limit for batch size is *single-piece flow*, where each operation is performed one unit at a time.[‡]

The dramatic differences between large and small batch sizes can be seen in the simple newsletter mailing simulation described in *Lean Thinking: Banish Waste and Create Wealth in Your Corporation* by James P. Womack and Daniel T. Jones.

Suppose in our own example we have ten brochures to send and mailing each brochure requires four steps: fold the paper, insert the paper into the envelope, seal the envelope, and stamp the envelope.

The large batch strategy (i.e., "mass production") would be to sequentially perform one operation on each of the ten brochures. In other words, we would first fold all ten sheets of paper, then insert each of them into envelopes, then seal all ten envelopes, and then stamp them.

On the other hand, in the small batch strategy (i.e., "single-piece flow"), all the steps required to complete each brochure are performed sequentially before starting on the next brochure. In other words, we fold one sheet of paper, insert it into the envelope, seal it, and stamp it—only then do we start the process over with the next sheet of paper.

The difference between using large and small batch sizes is dramatic (see figure 7). Suppose each of the four operations takes ten seconds for each of the ten envelopes. With the large batch size strategy, the first completed and stamped envelope is produced only after 310 seconds.

Worse, suppose we discover during the envelope sealing operation that we made an error in the first step of folding—in this case, the earliest we would discover the error is at two hundred seconds, and we have to refold and reinsert all ten brochures in our batch again.

[‡] Also known as "batch size of one" or "1x1 flow," terms that refer to batch size and a WIP limit of one.

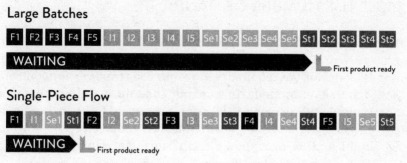

Figure 7: *Simulation of "envelope game" (fold, insert, seal, and stamp the envelope)*
(Source: Stefan Luyten, "Single Piece Flow: Why mass production isn't the most efficient way of doing 'stuff',"
Medium.com, August 8, 2014, https://medium.com/@stefanluyten/single-piece-flow-5d2c2bec845b#.907sn74ns.)

In contrast, in the small batch strategy the first completed stamped envelope is produced in only forty seconds, eight times faster than the large batch strategy. And, if we made an error in the first step, we only have to redo the one brochure in our batch. Small batch sizes result in less WIP, faster lead times, faster detection of errors, and less rework.

The negative outcomes associated with large batch sizes are just as relevant to the technology value stream as in manufacturing. Consider when we have an annual schedule for software releases, where an entire year's worth of code that Development has worked on is released to production deployment.

Like in manufacturing, this large batch release creates sudden, high levels of WIP and massive disruptions to all downstream work centers, resulting in poor flow and poor quality outcomes. This validates our common experience that the larger the change going into production, the more difficult the production errors are to diagnose and fix, and the longer they take to remediate.

In a post on *Startup Lessons Learned*, Eric Ries states, "The batch size is the unit at which work-products move between stages in a development [or DevOps] process. For software, the easiest batch to see is code. Every time an engineer checks in code, they are batching up a certain amount of work. There are many techniques for controlling these batches, ranging from the tiny batches needed for continuous deployment to more traditional branch-based development, where all of the code from multiple developers working for weeks or months is batched up and integrated together."

The equivalent to single piece flow in the technology value stream is realized with continuous deployment, where each change committed to version control is integrated, tested, and deployed into production. The practices that enable this are described in Part IV.

REDUCE THE NUMBER OF HANDOFFS

In the technology value stream, whenever we have long deployment lead times measured in months, it is often because there are hundreds (or even thousands) of operations required to move our code from version control into the production environment. To transmit code through the value stream requires multiple departments to work on a variety of tasks, including functional testing, integration testing, environment creation, server administration, storage administration, networking, load balancing, and information security.

Each time the work passes from team to team, we require all sorts of communication: requesting, specifying, signaling, coordinating, and often prioritizing, scheduling, deconflicting, testing, and verifying. This may require using different ticketing or project management systems; writing technical specification documents; communicating via meetings, emails, or phone calls; and using file system shares, FTP servers, and Wiki pages.

Each of these steps is a potential queue where work will wait when we rely on resources that are shared between different value streams (e.g., centralized operations). The lead times for these requests are often so long that there is constant escalation to have work performed within the needed timelines.

Even under the best circumstances, some knowledge is inevitably lost with each handoff. With enough handoffs, the work can completely lose the context of the problem being solved or the organizational goal being supported. For instance, a server administrator may see a newly created ticket requesting that user accounts be created, without knowing what application or service it's for, why it needs to be created, what all the dependencies are, or whether it's actually recurring work.

To mitigate these types of problems, we strive to reduce the number of handoffs, either by automating significant portions of the work or by reorganizing teams so they can deliver value to the customer themselves, instead of having to be constantly dependent on others. As a result, we increase flow by reducing the amount of time that our work spends waiting in queue, as well as the amount of non–value-added time. (See Appendix 4.)

CONTINUALLY IDENTIFY AND ELEVATE OUR CONSTRAINTS

To reduce lead times and increase throughput, we need to continually identify our system's constraints and improve its work capacity. In *Beyond the Goal*,

Dr. Goldratt states, "In any value stream, there is always a direction of flow, and there is always one and only constraint; any improvement not made at that constraint is an illusion." If we improve a work center that is positioned before the constraint, work will merely pile up at the bottleneck even faster, waiting for work to be performed by the bottlenecked work center.

On the other hand, if we improve a work center positioned *after* the bottleneck, it remains starved, waiting for work to clear the bottleneck. As a solution, Dr. Goldratt defined the "five focusing steps:"

- Identify the system's constraint.

- Decide how to exploit the system's constraint.

- Subordinate everything else to the above decisions.

- Elevate the system's constraint.

- If in the previous steps a constraint has been broken, go back to step one, but do not allow inertia to cause a system constraint.

In typical DevOps transformations, as we progress from deployment lead times measured in months or quarters to lead times measured in minutes, the constraint usually follows this progression:

- **Environment creation:** We cannot achieve deployments on-demand if we always have to wait weeks or months for production or test environments. The countermeasure is to create environments that are on demand and completely self-serviced, so that they are always available when we need them.

- **Code deployment:** We cannot achieve deployments on demand if each of our production code deployments take weeks or months to perform (i.e., each deployment requires 1,300 manual, error-prone steps, involving up to three hundred engineers). The countermeasure is to automate our deployments as much as possible, with the goal of being completely automated so they can be done self-service by any developer.

- **Test setup and run:** We cannot achieve deployments on demand if every code deployment requires two weeks to set up our test environments and data sets, and another four weeks to manually execute all our regression tests. The countermeasure is to automate our tests so we can execute deployments safely and to parallelize them so the test rate can keep up with our code development rate.

- **Overly tight architecture:** We cannot achieve deployments on demand if overly tight architecture means that every time we want to make a code change we have to send our engineers to scores of committee meetings in order to get permission to make our changes. Our countermeasure is to create more loosely coupled architecture so that changes can be made safely and with more autonomy, increasing developer productivity.

After all these constraints have been broken, our constraint will likely be Development or the product owners. Because our goal is to enable small teams of developers to independently develop, test, and deploy value to customers quickly and reliably, this is where we want our constraint to be. High performers, regardless of whether an engineer is in Development, QA, Ops, or Infosec, state that their goal is to help maximize developer productivity.

When the constraint is here, we are limited only by the number of good business hypotheses we create and our ability to develop the code necessary to test these hypotheses with real customers.

The progression of constraints listed above are generalizations of typical transformations—techniques to identify the constraint in actual value streams, such as through value stream mapping and measurements, are described later in this book.

ELIMINATE HARDSHIPS AND WASTE IN THE VALUE STREAM

Shigeo Shingo, one of the pioneers of the Toyota Production System, believed that waste constituted the largest threat to business viability—the commonly used definition in Lean is "the use of any material or resource beyond what the customer requires and is willing to pay for." He defined seven major types of manufacturing waste: inventory, overproduction, extra processing, transportation, waiting, motion, and defects.

More modern interpretations of Lean have noted that "eliminating waste" can have a demeaning and dehumanizing context; instead, the goal is reframed to reduce hardship and drudgery in our daily work through continual learning in order to achieve the organization's goals. For the remainder of this book, the term *waste* will imply this more modern definition, as it more closely matches the DevOps ideals and desired outcomes.

In the book *Implementing Lean Software Development: From Concept to Cash*, Mary and Tom Poppendieck describe waste and hardship in the software development stream as anything that causes delay for the customer, such as activities that can be bypassed without affecting the result.

The following categories of waste and hardship come from *Implementing Lean Software Development* unless otherwise noted:

- **Partially done work:** This includes any work in the value stream that has not been completed (e.g., requirement documents or change orders not yet reviewed) and work that is sitting in queue (e.g., waiting for QA review or server admin ticket). Partially done work becomes obsolete and loses value as time progresses.

- **Extra processes:** Any additional work that is being performed in a process that does not add value to the customer. This may include documentation not used in a downstream work center, or reviews or approvals that do not add value to the output. Extra processes add effort and increase lead times.

- **Extra features:** Features built into the service that are not needed by the organization or the customer (e.g., "gold plating"). Extra features add complexity and effort to testing and managing functionality.

- **Task switching:** When people are assigned to multiple projects and value streams, requiring them to context switch and manage dependencies between work, adding additional effort and time into the value stream.

- **Waiting:** Any delays between work requiring resources to wait until they can complete the current work. Delays increase cycle time and prevent the customer from getting value.

- **Motion:** The amount of effort to move information or materials from one work center to another. Motion waste can be created when people who need to communicate frequently are not colocated. Handoffs also create motion waste and often require additional communication to resolve ambiguities.

- **Defects:** Incorrect, missing, or unclear information, materials, or products create waste, as effort is needed to resolve these issues. The longer the time between defect creation and defect detection, the more difficult it is to resolve the defect.

- **Nonstandard or manual work:** Reliance on nonstandard or manual work from others, such as using non-rebuilding servers, test environments, and configurations. Ideally, any dependencies on Operations should be automated, self-serviced, and available on demand.

- **Heroics:** In order for an organization to achieve goals, individuals and teams are put in a position where they must perform unreasonable acts, which may even become a part of their daily work (e.g., nightly 2:00 a.m. problems in production, creating hundreds of work tickets as part of every software release).[†]

Our goal is to make these wastes and hardships—anywhere heroics become necessary—visible, and to systematically do what is needed to alleviate or eliminate these burdens and hardships to achieve our goal of fast flow.

CONCLUSION

Improving flow through the technology value stream is essential to achieving DevOps outcomes. We do this by making work visible, limiting WIP, reducing batch sizes and the number of handoffs, continually identifying and evaluating our constraints, and eliminating hardships in our daily work.

The specific practices that enable fast flow in the DevOps value stream are presented in Part IV. In the next chapter, we present The Second Way: The Principles of Feedback.

---

† Although heroics is not included in the Poppendieck categories of waste, it is included here because of how often it occurs, especially in Operation shared services.

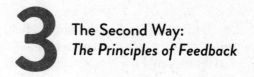

3 The Second Way:
The Principles of Feedback

While the First Way describes the principles that enable the fast flow of work from left to right, the Second Way describes the principles that enable the reciprocal fast and constant feedback from right to left at all stages of the value stream. Our goal is to create an ever safer and more resilient system of work.

This is especially important when working in complex systems, when the earliest opportunity to detect and correct errors is typically when a catastrophic event is underway, such as a manufacturing worker being hurt on the job or a nuclear reactor meltdown in progress.

In technology, our work happens almost entirely within complex systems with a high risk of catastrophic consequences. As in manufacturing, we often discover problems only when large failures are underway, such as a massive production outage or a security breach resulting in the theft of customer data.

We make our system of work safer by creating fast, frequent, high quality information flow throughout our value stream and our organization, which includes feedback and feedforward loops. This allows us to detect and remediate problems while they are smaller, cheaper, and easier to fix; avert problems before they cause catastrophe; and create organizational learning that we integrate into future work. When failures and accidents occur, we treat them as opportunities for learning, as opposed to a cause for punishment and blame. To achieve all of the above, let us first explore the nature of complex systems and how they can be made safer.

WORKING SAFELY WITHIN COMPLEX SYSTEMS

One of the defining characteristics of a complex system is that it defies any single person's ability to see the system as a whole and understand how all the pieces fit together. Complex systems typically have a high degree of interconnectedness of tightly coupled components, and system-level behavior cannot be explained merely in terms of the behavior of the system components.

Dr. Charles Perrow studied the Three Mile Island crisis and observed that it was impossible for anyone to understand how the reactor would behave in all circumstances and how it might fail. When a problem was underway in one component, it was difficult to isolate from the other components, quickly flowing through the paths of least resistance in unpredictable ways.

Dr. Sidney Dekker, who also codified some of the key elements of safety culture, observed another characteristic of complex systems: doing the same thing twice will not predictably or necessarily lead to the same result. It is this characteristic that makes static checklists and best practices, while valuable, insufficient to prevent catastrophes from occurring. (See Appendix 5.)

Therefore, because failure is inherent and inevitable in complex systems, we must design a safe system of work, whether in manufacturing or technology, where we can perform work without fear, confident that any errors will be detected quickly, long before they cause catastrophic outcomes, such as worker injury, product defects, or negative customer impact.

After he decoded the causal mechanism behind the Toyota Product System as part of his doctoral thesis at Harvard Business School, Dr. Steven Spear stated that designing perfectly safe systems is likely beyond our abilities, but we can make it safer to work in complex systems when the four following conditions are met:[†]

- Complex work is managed so that problems in design and operations are revealed

- Problems are swarmed and solved, resulting in quick construction of new knowledge

- New local knowledge is exploited globally throughout the organization

- Leaders create other leaders who continually grow these types of capabilities

---

† Dr. Spear extended his work to explain the long-lasting successes of other organizations, such as the Toyota supplier network, Alcoa, and the US Navy's Nuclear Power Propulsion Program.

Each of these capabilities are required to work safely in a complex system. In the next sections, the first two capabilities and their importance are described, as well as how they have been created in other domains and what practices enable them in the technology value stream. (The third and fourth capabilities are described in chapter 4.)

SEE PROBLEMS AS THEY OCCUR

In a safe system of work, we must constantly test our design and operating assumptions. Our goal is to increase information flow in our system from as many areas as possible, sooner, faster, cheaper, and with as much clarity between cause and effect as possible. The more assumptions we can invalidate, the faster we can find and fix problems, increasing our resilience, agility, and ability to learn and innovate.

We do this by creating feedback and feedforward loops into our system of work. Dr. Peter Senge in his book *The Fifth Discipline: The Art & Practice of the Learning Organization* described feedback loops as a critical part of learning organizations and systems thinking. Feedback and feedforward loops cause components within a system to reinforce or counteract each other.

In manufacturing, the absence of effective feedback often contribute to major quality and safety problems. In one well-documented case at the General Motors Fremont manufacturing plant, there were no effective procedures in place to detect problems during the assembly process, nor were there explicit procedures on what to do when problems were found. As a result, there were instances of engines being put in backward, cars missing steering wheels or tires, and cars even having to be towed off the assembly line because they wouldn't start.

In contrast, in high performing manufacturing operations there is fast, frequent, and high quality information flow throughout the entire value stream—every work operation is measured and monitored, and any defects or significant deviations are quickly found and acted upon. These are the foundation of what enables quality, safety, and continual learning and improvement.

In the technology value stream, we often get poor outcomes because of the absence of fast feedback. For instance, in a waterfall software project, we may develop code for an entire year and get no feedback on quality until we begin the testing phase—or worse, when we release our software to customers.

When feedback is this delayed and infrequent, it is too slow to enable us to prevent undesirable outcomes.

In contrast, our goal is to create fast feedback and fastforward loops wherever work is performed, at all stages of the technology value stream, encompassing Product Management, Development, QA, Infosec, and Operations. This includes the creation of automated build, integration, and test processes, so that we can immediately detect when a change has been introduced that takes us out of a correctly functioning and deployable state.

We also create pervasive telemetry so we can see how all our system components are operating in the production environment, so that we can quickly detect when they are not operating as expected. Telemetry also allows us to measure whether we are achieving our intended goals and, ideally, is radiated to the entire value stream so we can see how our actions affect other portions of the system as a whole.

Feedback loops not only enable quick detection and recovery of problems, but they also inform us on how to prevent these problems from occurring again in the future. Doing this increases the quality and safety of our system of work, and creates organizational learning.

As Elisabeth Hendrickson, VP of Engineering at Pivotal Software, Inc. and author of *Explore It!: Reduce Risk and Increase Confidence with Exploratory Testing*, said, "When I headed up quality engineering, I described my job as 'creating feedback cycles.' Feedback is critical because it is what allows us to steer. We must constantly validate between customer needs, our intentions and our implementations. Testing is merely one sort of feedback."

SWARM AND SOLVE PROBLEMS TO BUILD NEW KNOWLEDGE

Obviously, it is not sufficient to merely detect when the unexpected occurs. When problems occur, we must swarm them, mobilizing whoever is required to solve the problem.

According to Dr. Spear, the goal of swarming is to contain problems before they have a chance to spread, and to diagnose and treat the problem so that it cannot recur. "In doing so," he says, "they build ever-deeper knowledge about how to manage the systems for doing our work, converting inevitable up-front ignorance into knowledge."

The paragon of this principle is the Toyota *Andon cord*. In a Toyota manufacturing plant, above every work center is a cord that every worker and manager is trained to pull when something goes wrong; for example, when a part is defective, when a required part is not available, or even when work takes longer than documented.[†]

When the Andon cord is pulled, the team leader is alerted and immediately works to resolve the problem. If the problem cannot be resolved within a specified time (e.g., fifty-five seconds), the production line is halted so that the entire organization can be mobilized to assist with problem resolution until a successful countermeasure has been developed.

Instead of working around the problem or scheduling a fix "when we have more time," we swarm to fix it immediately—this is nearly the opposite of the behavior at the GM Fremont plant described earlier. Swarming is necessary for the following reasons:

- It prevents the problem from progressing downstream, where the cost and effort to repair it increases exponentially and technical debt is allowed to accumulate.

- It prevents the work center from starting new work, which will likely introduce new errors into the system.

- If the problem is not addressed, the work center could potentially have the same problem in the next operation (e.g., fifty-five seconds later), requiring more fixes and work. (See Appendix 6.)

This practice of swarming seems contrary to common management practice, as we are deliberately allowing a local problem to disrupt operations globally. However, swarming enables learning. It prevents the loss of critical information due to fading memories or changing circumstances. This is especially critical in complex systems, where many problems occur because of some unexpected, idiosyncratic interaction of people, processes, products, places, and circumstances—as time passes, it becomes impossible to reconstruct exactly what was going on when the problem occurred.

As Dr. Spear notes, swarming is part of the "disciplined cycle of real-time problem recognition, diagnosis,...and treatment (countermeasures or corrective measures in manufacturing vernacular). It [is] the discipline of the

---

† In some of its plants, Toyota has moved to using an Andon button.

Shewhart cycle—plan, do, check, act—popularized by W. Edwards Deming, but accelerated to warp speed."

It is only through the swarming of ever smaller problems discovered ever earlier in the life cycle that we can deflect problems before a catastrophe occurs. In other words, when the nuclear reactor melts down, it is already too late to avert worst outcomes.

To enable fast feedback in the technology value stream, we must create the equivalent of an Andon cord and the related swarming response. This requires that we also create the culture that makes it safe, and even encouraged, to pull the Andon cord when something goes wrong, whether it is when a production incident occurs or when errors occur earlier in the value stream, such as when someone introduces a change that breaks our continuous build or test processes.

When conditions trigger an Andon cord pull, we swarm to solve the problem and prevent the introduction of new work until the issue has been resolved.[†] This provides fast feedback for everyone in the value stream (especially the person who caused the system to fail), enables us to quickly isolate and diagnose the problem, and prevents further complicating factors that can obscure cause and effect.

Preventing the introduction of new work enables continuous integration and deployment, which is single-piece flow in the technology value stream. All changes that pass our continuous build and integration tests are deployed into production, and any changes that cause any tests to fail trigger our Andon cord and are swarmed until resolved.

KEEP PUSHING QUALITY CLOSER TO THE SOURCE

We may inadvertently perpetuate unsafe systems of work due to the way we respond to accidents and incidents. In complex systems, adding more inspection steps and approval processes actually increases the likelihood of future failures. The effectiveness of approval processes decreases as we push decision-making further away from where the work is performed. Doing so not only lowers the quality of decisions but also increases our cycle time, thus decreasing

---

† Astonishingly, when the number of Andon cord pulls drop, plant managers will actually decrease the tolerances to get an increase in the number of Andon cord pulls in order to continue to enable more learnings and improvements and to detect ever-weaker failure signals.

the strength of the feedback between cause and effect, and reducing our ability to learn from successes and failures.[‡]

This can be seen even in smaller and less complex systems. When top-down, bureaucratic command and control systems become ineffective, it is usually because the variance between "who should do something" and "who is actually doing something" is too large, due to insufficient clarity and timeliness.

Examples of ineffective quality controls include:

- Requiring another team to complete tedious, error-prone, and manual tasks that could be easily automated and run as needed by the team who needs the work performed

- Requiring approvals from busy people who are distant from the work, forcing them to make decisions without an adequate knowledge of the work or the potential implications, or to merely rubber stamp their approvals

- Creating large volumes of documentation of questionable detail which become obsolete shortly after they are written

- Pushing large batches of work to teams and special committees for approval and processing and then waiting for responses

Instead, we need everyone in our value stream to find and fix problems in their area of control as part of our daily work. By doing this, we push quality and safety responsibilities and decision-making to where the work is performed, instead of relying on approvals from distant executives.

We use peer reviews of our proposed changes to gain whatever assurance is needed that our changes will operate as designed. We automate as much of the quality checking typically performed by a QA or Information Security department as possible. Instead of developers needing to request or schedule a test to be run, these tests can be performed on demand, enabling developers

---

[‡] In the 1700s, the British government engaged in a spectacular example of top-down, bureaucratic command and control, which proved remarkably ineffective. At the time, Georgia was still a colony, and despite the fact that the British government was three thousand miles away and lacked firsthand knowledge of local land chemistry, rockiness, topography, accessibility to water, and other conditions, it tried to plan Georgia's entire agricultural economy. The results of the attempt were dismal and left Georgia with the lowest levels of prosperity and population in the thirteen colonies.

to quickly test their own code and even deploy those changes into production themselves.

By doing this, we truly make quality everyone's responsibility as opposed to it being the sole responsibility of a separate department. Information security is not just Information Security's job, just as availability isn't merely the job of Operations.

Having developers share responsibility for the quality of the systems they build not only improves outcomes but also accelerates learning. This is especially important for developers as they are typically the team that is furthest removed from the customer. As Gary Gruver observes, "It's impossible for a developer to learn anything when someone yells at them for something they broke six months ago—that's why we need to provide feedback to everyone as quickly as possible, in minutes, not months."

ENABLE OPTIMIZING FOR DOWNSTREAM WORK CENTERS

In the 1980s, Designing for Manufacturability principles sought to design parts and processes so that finished goods could be created with the lowest cost, highest quality, and fastest flow. Examples include designing parts that are wildly asymmetrical to prevent them from being put on backwards, and designing screw fasteners so that they are impossible to over-tighten.

This was a departure from how design was typically done, which focused on the external customers but overlooked internal stakeholders, such as the people performing the manufacturing.

Lean defines two types of customers that we must design for: the external customer (who most likely pays for the service we are delivering) and the internal customer (who receives and processes the work immediately after us). According to Lean, our most important customer is our next step downstream. Optimizing our work for them requires that we have empathy for their problems in order to better identify the design problems that prevent fast and smooth flow.

In the technology value stream, we optimize for downstream work centers by designing for operations, where operational non-functional requirements (e.g., architecture, performance, stability, testability, configurability, and security) are prioritized as highly as user features.

By doing this, we create quality at the source, likely resulting in a set of codified non-functional requirements that we can proactively integrate into every service we build.

CONCLUSION

Creating fast feedback is critical to achieving quality, reliability, and safety in the technology value stream. We do this by seeing problems as they occur, swarming and solving problems to build new knowledge, pushing quality closer to the source, and continually optimizing for downstream work centers.

The specific practices that enable fast flow in the DevOps value stream are presented in Part IV. In the next chapter, we present the Third Way, the Principles of Feedback.

4 The Third Way: *The Principles of Continual Learning and Experimentation*

While the First Way addresses work flow from left to right and the Second Way addresses the reciprocal fast and constant feedback from right to left, the Third Way focuses on creating a culture of continual learning and experimentation. These are the principles that enable constant creation of individual knowledge, which is then turned into team and organizational knowledge.

In manufacturing operations with systemic quality and safety problems, work is typically rigidly defined and enforced. For instance, in the GM Fremont plant described in the previous chapter, workers had little ability to integrate improvements and learnings into their daily work, with suggestions for improvement "apt to meet a brick wall of indifference."

In these environments, there is also often a culture of fear and low trust, where workers who make mistakes are punished, and those who make suggestions or point out problems are viewed as whistle-blowers and troublemakers. When this occurs, leadership is actively suppressing, even punishing, learning and improvement, perpetuating quality and safety problems.

In contrast, high-performing manufacturing operations require and actively promote learning—instead of work being rigidly defined, the system of work is dynamic, with line workers performing experiments in their daily work to generate new improvements, enabled by rigorous standardization of work procedures and documentation of the results.

In the technology value stream, our goal is to create a high-trust culture, reinforcing that we are all lifelong learners who must take risks in our daily work. By applying a scientific approach to both process improvement and product development, we learn from our successes and failures, identifying which ideas don't work and reinforcing those that do. Moreover, any local learnings are rapidly turned into global improvements, so that new techniques and practices can be used by the entire organization.

We reserve time for the improvement of daily work and to further accelerate and ensure learning. We consistently introduce stress into our systems to force continual improvement. We even simulate and inject failures in our production services under controlled conditions to increase our resilience.

By creating this continual and dynamic system of learning, we enable teams to rapidly and automatically adapt to an ever-changing environment, which ultimately helps us win in the marketplace.

ENABLING ORGANIZATIONAL LEARNING AND A SAFETY CULTURE

When we work within a complex system, by definition it is impossible for us to perfectly predict all the outcomes for any action we take. This is what contributes to unexpected, or even catastrophic, outcomes and accidents in our daily work, even when we take precautions and work carefully.

When these accidents affect our customers, we seek to understand why it happened. The root cause is often deemed to be human error, and the all too common management response is to "name, blame, and shame" the person who caused the problem.[†] And, either subtly or explicitly, management hints that the person guilty of committing the error will be punished. They then create more processes and approvals to prevent the error from happening again.

Dr. Sidney Dekker, who codified some of the key elements of safety culture and coined the term *just culture*, wrote, "Responses to incidents and accidents that are seen as unjust can impede safety investigations, promote fear rather than mindfulness in people who do safety-critical work, make organizations more bureaucratic rather than more careful, and cultivate professional secrecy, evasion, and self-protection."

These issues are especially problematic in the technology value stream—our work is almost always performed within a complex system, and how management chooses to react to failures and accidents leads to a culture of fear,

---

† The "name, blame, shame" pattern is part of the Bad Apple Theory criticized by Dr. Sydney Dekker and extensively discussed in his book *The Field Guide to Understanding Human Error*.

which then makes it unlikely that problems and failure signals are ever reported. The result is that problems remain hidden until a catastrophe occurs.

Dr. Ron Westrum was one of the first to observe the importance of organizational culture on safety and performance. He observed that in healthcare organizations, the presence of "generative" cultures was one of the top predictors of patient safety. Dr. Westrum defined three types of culture:

- Pathological organizations are characterized by large amounts of fear and threat. People often hoard information, withhold it for political reasons, or distort it to make themselves look better. Failure is often hidden.

- Bureaucratic organizations are characterized by rules and processes, often to help individual departments maintain their "turf." Failure is processed through a system of judgment, resulting in either punishment or justice and mercy.

- Generative organizations are characterized by actively seeking and sharing information to better enable the organization to achieve its mission. Responsibilities are shared throughout the value stream, and failure results in reflection and genuine inquiry.

Pathological	Bureaucratic	Generative
Information is hidden	Information may be ignored	Information is actively sought
Messengers are "shot"	Messengers are tolerated	Messengers are trained
Responsibilities are shirked	Responsibilities are compartmented	Responsibilities are shared
Bridging between teams is discouraged	Bridging between teams is allowed but discouraged	Bridging between teams is rewarded
Failure is covered up	Organization is just and merciful	Failure causes inquiry
New ideas are crushed	New ideas create problems	New ideas are welcomed

Figure 8: *The Westrum organizational typology model: how organizations process information (Source: Ron Westrum, "A typology of organisation culture," BMJ Quality & Safety 13, no. 2 (2004), doi:10.1136/qshc.2003.009522.)*

Just as Dr. Westrum found in healthcare organizations, a high-trust, generative culture also predicted IT and organizational performance in technology value streams.

In the technology value stream, we establish the foundations of a generative culture by striving to create a safe system of work. When accidents and failures occur, instead of looking for human error, we look for how we can redesign the system to prevent the accident from happening again.

For instance, we may conduct a blameless post-mortem after every incident to gain the best understanding of how the accident occurred and agree upon what the best countermeasures are to improve the system, ideally preventing the problem from occurring again and enabling faster detection and recovery.

By doing this, we create organizational learning. As Bethany Macri, an engineer at Etsy who led the creation of the Morgue tool to help with recording of post-mortems, stated, "By removing blame, you remove fear; by removing fear, you enable honesty; and honesty enables prevention."

Dr. Spear observes that the result of removing blame and putting organizational learning in its place is that "organizations become ever more self-diagnosing and self-improving, skilled at detecting problems [and] solving them."

Many of these attributes were also described by Dr. Senge as attributes of learning organizations. In *The Fifth Discipline,* he wrote that these characteristics help customers, ensure quality, create competitive advantage and an energized and committed workforce, and uncover the truth.

INSTITUTIONALIZE THE IMPROVEMENT OF DAILY WORK

Teams are often not able or not willing to improve the processes they operate within. The result is not only that they continue to suffer from their current problems, but their suffering also grows worse over time. Mike Rother observed in *Toyota Kata* that in the absence of improvements, processes don't stay the same—due to chaos and entropy, processes actually degrade over time.

In the technology value stream, when we avoid fixing our problems, relying on daily workarounds, our problems and technical debt accumulates until all we are doing is performing workarounds, trying to avoid disaster, with no cycles leftover for doing productive work. This is why Mike Orzen, author of

Lean IT, observed, "Even more important than daily work is the improvement of daily work."

We improve daily work by explicitly reserving time to pay down technical debt, fix defects, and refactor and improve problematic areas of our code and environments—we do this by reserving cycles in each development interval, or by scheduling *kaizen blitzes*, which are periods when engineers self-organize into teams to work on fixing any problem they want.

The result of these practices is that everyone finds and fixes problems in their area of control, all the time, as part of their daily work. When we finally fix the daily problems that we've worked around for months (or years), we can eradicate from our system the less obvious problems. By detecting and responding to these ever-weaker failure signals, we fix problems when it is not only easier and cheaper but also when the consequences are smaller.

Consider the following example that improved workplace safety at Alcoa, an aluminum manufacturer with $7.8 billion in revenue in 1987. Aluminum manufacturing requires extremely high heat, high pressures, and corrosive chemicals. In 1987, Alcoa had a frightening safety record, with 2% of the ninety thousand employee workforce being injured each year—that's seven injuries per day. When Paul O'Neill started as CEO, his first goal was to have zero injuries to employees, contractors, and visitors.

O'Neill wanted to be notified within twenty-four hours of anyone being injured on the job—not to punish, but to ensure and promote that learnings were being generated and incorporated to create a safer workplace. Over the course of ten years, Alcoa reduced their injury rate by 95%.

The reduction in injury rates allowed Alcoa to focus on smaller problems and weaker failure signals—instead of notifying O'Neill only when injuries occurred, they started reporting any close calls as well.[†] By doing this, they improved workplace safety over the subsequent twenty years and have one of the most enviable safety records in the industry.

As Dr. Spear writes, "Alcoans gradually stopped working around the difficulties, inconveniences, and impediments they experienced. Coping, fire fighting, and making do were gradually replaced throughout the organization by a

---

[†] It is astonishing, instructional, and truly moving to see the level of conviction and passion that Paul O'Neill has about the moral responsibility leaders have to create workplace safety.

dynamic of identifying opportunities for process and product improvement. As those opportunities were identified and the problems were investigated, the pockets of ignorance that they reflected were converted into nuggets of knowledge." This helped give the company a greater competitive advantage in the market.

Similarly, in the technology value stream, as we make our system of work safer, we find and fix problems from ever weaker failure signals. For example, we may initially perform blameless post-mortems only for customer-impacting incidents. Over time, we may perform them for lesser team-impacting incidents and near misses as well.

TRANSFORM LOCAL DISCOVERIES INTO GLOBAL IMPROVEMENTS

When new learnings are discovered locally, there must also be some mechanism to enable the rest of the organization to use and benefit from that knowledge. In other words, when teams or individuals have experiences that create expertise, our goal is to convert that tacit knowledge (i.e., knowledge that is difficult to transfer to another person by means of writing it down or verbalizing) into explicit, codified knowledge, which becomes someone else's expertise through practice.

This ensures that when anyone else does similar work, they do so with the cumulative and collective experience of everyone in the organization who has ever done the same work. A remarkable example of turning local knowledge into global knowledge is the US Navy's Nuclear Power Propulsion Program (also known as "NR" for "Naval Reactors"), which has over 5,700 reactor-years of operation without a single reactor-related casualty or escape of radiation.

The NR is known for their intense commitment to scripted procedures and standardized work, and the need for incident reports for any departure from procedure or normal operations to accumulate learnings, no matter how minor the failure signal—they constantly update procedures and system designs based on these learnings.

The result is that when a new crew sets out to sea on their first deployment, they and their officers benefit from the collective knowledge of 5,700 accident-free reactor-years. Equally impressive is that their own experiences at sea will be added to this collective knowledge, helping future crews safely achieve their own missions.

In the technology value stream, we must create similar mechanisms to create global knowledge, such as making all our blameless post-mortem reports searchable by teams trying to solve similar problems, and by creating shared source code repositories that span the entire organization, where shared code, libraries, and configurations that embody the best collective knowledge of the entire organization can be easily utilized. All these mechanisms help convert individual expertise into artifacts that the rest of the organization can use.

INJECT RESILIENCE PATTERNS INTO OUR DAILY WORK

Lower performing manufacturing organizations buffer themselves from disruptions in many ways—in other words, they bulk up or add flab. For instance, to reduce the risk of a work center being idle (due to inventory arriving late, inventory that had to be scrapped, etc.), managers may choose to stockpile more inventory at each work center. However, that inventory buffer also increases WIP, which has all sorts of undesired outcomes, as previously discussed.

Similarly, to reduce the risk of a work center going down due to machinery failure, managers may increase capacity by buying more capital equipment, hiring more people, or even increasing floor space. All these options increase costs.

In contrast, high performers achieve the same results (or better) by improving daily operations, continually introducing tension to elevate performance, as well as engineering more resilience into their system.

Consider a typical experiment at one of Aisin Seiki Global's mattress factories, one of Toyota's top suppliers. Suppose they had two production lines, each capable of producing one hundred units per day. On slow days, they would send all production onto one line, experimenting with ways to increase capacity and identify vulnerabilities in their process, knowing that if overloading the line caused it to fail, they could send all production to the second line.

By relentless and constant experimentation in their daily work, they were able to continually increase capacity, often without adding any new equipment or hiring more people. The emergent pattern that results from these types of improvement rituals not only improves performance but also improves resilience, because the organization is always in a state of tension and change. This process of applying stress to increase resilience was named *antifragility* by author and risk analyst Nassim Nicholas Taleb.

In the technology value stream, we can introduce the same type of tension into our systems by seeking to always reduce deployment lead times, increase test coverage, decrease test execution times, and even by re-architecting if necessary to increase developer productivity or increase reliability.

We may also perform *game day* exercises, where we rehearse large scale failures, such as turning off entire data centers. Or we may inject ever-larger scale faults into the production environment (such as the famous Netflix "Chaos Monkey" which randomly kills processes and compute servers in production) to ensure that we're as resilient as we want to be.

LEADERS REINFORCE A LEARNING CULTURE

Traditionally, leaders were expected to be responsible for setting objectives, allocating resources for achieving those objectives, and establishing the right combination of incentives. Leaders also establish the emotional tone for the organizations they lead. In other words, leaders lead by "making all the right decisions."

However, there is significant evidence that shows greatness is not achieved by leaders making all the right decisions—instead, the leader's role is to create the conditions so their team can discover greatness in their daily work. In other words, creating greatness requires both leaders and workers, each of whom are mutually dependent upon each other.

Jim Womack, author of *Gemba Walks,* described the complementary working relationship and mutual respect that must occur between leaders and frontline workers. According to Womack, this relationship is necessary because neither can solve problems alone—leaders are not close enough to the work, which is required to solve any problem, and frontline workers do not have the broader organizational context or the authority to make changes outside of their area of work.[†]

---

† Leaders are responsible for the design and operation of processes at a higher level of aggregation where others have less perspective and authority.

Leaders must elevate the value of learning and disciplined problem solving. Mike Rother formalized these methods in what he calls the *coaching kata*. The result is one that mirrors the scientific method, where we explicitly state our True North goals, such as "sustain zero accidents" in the case of Alcoa, or "double throughput within a year" in the case of Aisin.

These strategic goals then inform the creation of iterative, shorter term goals, which are cascaded and then executed by establishing target conditions at the value stream or work center level (e.g., "reduce lead time by 10% within the next two weeks").

These target conditions frame the scientific experiment: we explicitly state the problem we are seeking to solve, our hypothesis of how our proposed countermeasure will solve it, our methods for testing that hypothesis, our interpretation of the results, and our use of learnings to inform the next iteration.

The leader helps coach the person conducting the experiment with questions that may include:

- What was your last step and what happened?

- What did you learn?

- What is your condition now?

- What is your next target condition?

- What obstacle are you working on now?

- What is your next step?

- What is your expected outcome?

- When can we check?

This problem-solving approach in which leaders help workers see and solve problems in their daily work is at the core of the Toyota Production System, of learning organizations, the Improvement Kata, and high-reliability organizations. Mike Rother observes that he sees Toyota "as an organization defined primarily by the unique behavior routines it continually teaches to all its members."

In the technology value stream, this scientific approach and iterative method guides all of our internal improvement processes, but also how we perform experiments to ensure that the products we build actually help our internal and external customers achieve their goals.

CONCLUSION

The principles of the Third Way address the need for valuing organizational learning, enabling high trust and boundary-spanning between functions, accepting that failures will always occur in complex systems, and making it acceptable to talk about problems so we can create a safe system of work. It also requires institutionalizing the improvement of daily work, converting local learnings into global learnings that can be used by the entire organization, as well as continually injecting tension into our daily work.

Although fostering a culture of continual learning and experimentation is the principle of the Third Way, it is also interwoven into the First and Second Ways. In other words, improving flow and feedback requires an iterative and scientific approach that includes framing of a target condition, stating a hypothesis of what will help us get there, designing and conducting experiments, and evaluating the results.

The results are not only better performance but also increased resilience, higher job satisfaction, and improved organization adaptability.

PART I CONCLUSION

In Part I of *The DevOps Handbook* we looked back at several movements in history that helped lead to the development of DevOps. We also looked at the three main principles that form the foundation for successful DevOps organizations: the principles of Flow, Feedback, and Continual Learning and Experimentation. In Part II, we will begin to look at how to start a DevOps movement in your organization.

Endnotes

INTRODUCTION

366   *Before the revolution...* Eliyahu M. Goldratt, *Beyond the Goal: Eliyahu Goldratt Speaks on the Theory of Constraints (Your Coach in a Box)* (Prince Frederick, Maryland: Gildan Media, 2005), Audiobook.

368   *Put even more...* Jeff Immelt, "GE CEO Jeff Immelt: Let's Finally End the Debate over Whether We Are in a Tech Bubble," *Business Insider*, December 9, 2015, http://www.businessinsider.com/ceo-of-ge-lets-finally-end-the-debate-over-whether-we-are-in-a-tech-bubble-2015-12.

     Or as Jeffrey... "Weekly Top 10: Your DevOps Flavor," *Electric Cloud*, April 1, 2016, http://electric-cloud.com/blog/2016/04/weekly-top-10-devops-flavor/.

369   *Dr. Eliyahu M. Goldratt...* Goldratt, *Beyond the Goal.*

371   *As Christopher Little...* Christopher Little, personal correspondence with Gene Kim, 2010.

     As Steven J. Spear... Steven J. Spear, *The High-Velocity Edge: How Market Leaders Leverage Operational Excellence to Beat the Competition* (New York, NY: McGraw Hill Education), Kindle edition, chap. 3.

     In 2013, the... Chris Skinner, "Banks have bigger development shops than Microsoft," Chris Skinner's Blog, accessed July 28, 2016, http://thefinanser.com/2011/09/banks-have-bigger-development-shops-than-microsoft.html/.

372   *Projects are typically...* Nico Stehr and Reiner Grundmann, *Knowledge: Critical Concepts, Volume 3* (London: Routledge, 2005), 139.

     Dr. Vernon Richardson... A. Masli, V. Richardson, M. Widenmier, and R. Zmud, "Senior Executive's IT Management Responsibilities: Serious IT Deficiencies and CEO-CFO Turnover," *MIS Quaterly* (published electronically June 21, 2016).

373   *Consider the following...* "IDC Forecasts Worldwide IT Spending to Grow 6% in 2012, Despite Economic Uncertainty," *Business Wire*, September 10, 2012, http://www.businesswire.com/news/home /20120910005280/en/IDC-Forecasts-Worldwide-Spending-Grow -6-2012.

376   *The first surprise...* Nigel Kersten, IT Revolution, and PwC, *2015 State of DevOps Report* (Portland, OR: Puppet Labs, 2015), https://puppet .com/resources/white-paper/2015-state-of-devops-report?_ga=1.66 12658.168869.1464412647&link=blog.

377   *This is highlighted...* Frederick P. Brooks, Jr., *The Mythical Man-Month: Essays on Software Engineering, Anniversary Edition* (Upper Saddle River, NJ: Addison-Wesley, 1995).

378   *As Randy Shoup...* Gene Kim, Gary Gruver, Randy Shoup, and Andrew Phillips, "Exploring the Uncharted Territory of Microservices," XebiaLabs.com, webinar, February 20, 2015, https:// xebialabs.com/community/webinars/exploring-the-uncharted -territory-of-microservices/.

   The 2015 State... Kersten, IT Revolution, and PwC, *2015 State of DevOps Report*.

   Another more extreme... "Velocity 2011: Jon Jenkins, 'Velocity Culture'," YouTube video, 15:13, posted by O'Reilly, June 20, 2011, https://www.youtube.com/watch?v=dxk8b9rSKOo; "Transforming Software Development," YouTube video, 40:57, posted by Amazon Web Service, April 10, 2015, https://www .youtube.com/watch?v=YCrhemssYuI&feature=youtu.be.

379   *Later in his...* Eliyahu M. Goldratt, *Beyond the Goal*.

   As with The... JGFLL, review of *The Phoenix Project: A Novel About IT, DevOps, and Helping Your Business Win*, by Gene Kim, Kevin Behr, and George Spafford, Amazon.com review, March 4, 2013, http:// www.amazon.com/review/R1KSSPTEGLWJ23; Mark L Townsend, review of *The Phoenix Project: A Novel About IT, DevOps, and Helping Your Business Win*, by Gene Kim, Kevin Behr, and George Spafford, Amazon.com review, March 2, 2013, http://uedata.amazon.com/gp /customer-reviews/R1097DFODM12VD/ref=cm_cr_getr_d_rvw _ttl?ie=UTF8&ASIN=B00VATFAMI; Scott Van Den Elzen, review of *The Phoenix Project: A Novel About IT, DevOps, and Helping Your Business Win*, by Gene Kim, Kevin Behr, and George Spafford, Amazon.com review, March 13, 2013, http://uedata.amazon.com /gp/customer-reviews/R2K95XEH5OL3Q5/ref=cm_cr_getr_d_rvw_ ttl?ie=UTF8&ASIN=B00VATFAMI.

PART I INTRODUCTION

385   *One key principle...* Kent Beck, et al., "Twelve Principles of Agile Software," AgileManifesto.org, 2001, http://agilemanifesto.org/principles.html.

386   *He concluded that...* Mike Rother, *Toyota Kata: Managing People for Improvement, Adaptiveness and Superior Results* (New York: McGraw Hill, 2010), Kindle edition, Part III.

CHAPTER 1

387   *Karen Martin and...* Karen Martin and Mike Osterling, *Value Stream Mapping: How to Visualize Work and Align Leadership for Organizational Transformation* (New York: McGraw Hill, 2013), Kindle edition, chap 1.

389   *In this book...* Ibid., chap. 3.

391   *Karen Martin and...* Ibid.

CHAPTER 2

396   *Studies have shown...* Joshua S. Rubinstein, David E. Meyer, and Jeffrey E. Evans, "Executive Control of Cognitive Processes in Task Switching," *Journal of Experimental Psychology: Human Perception and Performance* 27, no. 4 (2001): 763-797, doi: 10.1037//0096-1523.27.4.763, http://www.umich.edu/~bcalab/documents/RubinsteinMeyerEvans2001.pdf.

397   *Dominica DeGrandis, one...* "DOES15—Dominica DeGrandis—The Shape of Uncertainty," YouTube video, 22:54, posted by DevOps Enterprise Summit, November 5, 2015, https://www.youtube.com/watch?v=Gp05i0d34gg.

       Taiichi Ohno compared... Sami Bahri, "Few Patients-In-Process and Less Safety Scheduling; Incoming Supplies are Secondary," The Deming Institute Blog, August 22, 2013, https://blog.deming.org/2013/08/fewer-patients-in-process-and-less-safety-scheduling-incoming-supplies-are-secondary/.

       In other words... Meeting between David J. Andersen and team at Motorola with Daniel S. Vacanti, February 24, 2004; story retold at USC CSSE Research Review with Barry Boehm in March 2004.

398   *The dramatic differences...* James P. Womack and Daniel T. Jones, *Lean Thinking: Banish Waste and Create Wealth in Your Corporation* (New York: Free Press, 2010), Kindle edition, chap. 1.

399   *There are many...* Eric Ries, "Work in small batches," StartupLessonsLearned.com, February 20, 2009, http://www .startuplessonslearned.com/2009/02/work-in-small-batches.html.

400   *In Beyond the...* Goldratt, *Beyond the Goal*.

401   *As a solution...* Eliyahu M. Goldratt, *The Goal: A Process of Ongoing Improvement* (Great Barrington, MA: North River Press, 2014), Kindle edition, "Five Focusing Steps."

402   *Shigeo Shingo, one...* Shigeo Shingo, *A Study of the Toyota Production System: From an Industrial Engineering Viewpoint* (London: Productivity Press, 1989); "The 7 Wastes (Seven forms of Muda)," BeyondLean.com, accessed July 28, 2016, http://www.beyondlean .com/7-wastes.html.

403   *In the book...* Mary Poppendieck and Tom Poppendieck, *Implementing Lean Software: From Concept to Cash*, (Upper Saddle River, NJ: Addison-Wesley, 2007), 74.

       The following categories... Adapted from Damon Edwards, "DevOps Kaizen: Find and Fix What Is Really Behind Your Problems," Slideshare.net, posted by dev2ops, May 4, 2015, http://www .slideshare.net/dev2ops/dev-ops-kaizen-damon-edwards.

CHAPTER 3

406   *Dr. Charles Perrow...* Charles Perrow, *Normal Accidents: Living with High Risk Technologies* (Princeton, NJ: Princeton University Press, 1999).

       Dr. Sidney Dekker... Dr. Sidney Dekker, *The Field Guide to Understanding Human Error* (Lund University, Sweden: Ashgate, 2006).

       After he decoded... Spear, *The High-Velocity Edge*, chap. 8.

       Dr. Spear extended... Ibid.

407   *Dr. Peter Senge...* Peter M. Senge, *The Fifth Discipline: The Art & Practice of the Learning Organization* (New York: Doubleday, 2006), Kindle edition, chap. 5.

       In one well-documented... "NUMMI," *This American Life*, March 26, 2010, http://www.thisamericanlife.org/radio-archives/episode /403/transcript.

408   *As Elisabeth Hendrickson...* "DOES15 - Elisabeth Hendrickson - Its All About Feedback," YouTube video, 34:47, posted by DevOps Enterprise Summit, November 5, 2015, https://www.youtube.com /watch?v=r2BFTXBundQ.

"In doings so… Spear, *The High-Velocity Edge,* chap. 1.

409   *As Dr. Spear…* Ibid., chap. 4.

411   *Examples of ineffective…* Jez Humble, Joanne Molesky, and Barry O'Reilly, *Lean Enterprise: How High Performance Organizations Innovate at Scale* (Sebastopol, CA: O'Reilly Media, 2015), Kindle edition, Part IV.

In the 1700s… Dr. Thomas Sowell, *Knowledge and Decisions* (New York: Basic Books, 1980), 222.

412   *As Gary Gruver…* Gary Gruver, personal correspondence with Gene Kim, 2014.

CHAPTER 4

414   *For instance, in…* Paul Adler, "Time-and-Motion Regained," *Harvard Business Review,* January-February 1993, https://hbr.org/1993/01/time-and-motion-regained.

415   *The "name, blame…* Dekker, *The Field Guide to Understanding Human Error,* chap. 1.

Dr. Sidney Dekker… "Just Culture: Balancing Safety and Accountability," Lund University, Human Factors & System Safety website, November 6, 2015, http://www.humanfactors.lth.se/sidney-dekker/books/just-culture/.

416   *He observed that…* Ron Westrum, "The study of information flow: A personal journey," *Proceedings of Safety Science* 67 (August 2014): 58-63, https://www.researchgate.net/publication/261186680_The_study_of_information_flow_A_personal_journey.

417   *Just as Dr. Westrum…* Nicole Forsgren Velasquez, Gene Kim, Nigel Kersten, and Jez Humble, *2014 State of DevOps Report* (Portland, OR: Puppet Labs, IT Revolution Press, and ThoughtWorks, 2014), http://puppetlabs.com/2014-devops-report.

As Bethany Macri… Bethany Macri, "Morgue: Helping Better Understand Events by Building a Post Mortem Tool - Bethany Macri," Vimeo video, 33:34, posted by info@devopsdays.org, October 18, 2013, http://vimeo.com/77206751.

Dr. Spear observes… Spear, *The High-Velocity Edge,* chap. 1.

In The Fifth… Senge, *The Fifth Discipline,* chap. 1.

Mike Rother observed… Mike Rother, *Toyota Kata,* 12.

This is why… Mike Orzen, personal correspondence with Gene Kim, 2012.

418   *Consider the following...* "Paul O'Neill," *Forbes*, October 11, 2001, http://www.forbes.com/2001/10/16/poneill.html.

         In 1987, Alcoa... Spear, *The High-Velocity Edge*, chap. 4.

         As Dr. Spear... Ibid.

419   *A remarkable example...* Ibid., chap. 5.

421   *This process of...* Nassim Nicholas Taleb, *Antifragile: Things That Gain from Disorder* (Incerto), (New York: Random House, 2012).

         According to Womack... Jim Womack, *Gemba Walks* (Cambridge, MA: Lean Enterprise Institute, 2011), Kindle edition, location 4113.

422   *Mike Rother formalized...* Rother, *Toyota Kata*, Part IV.

         Mike Rother observes... Ibid., Conclusion.

INTRODUCTION

339 *When this book was first...* John Allspaw and Paul Hammond, "10+ Deploys Per Day: Cooperation at Flikr," presentation at Velocity Conference, June 23, 2009.

341 *In Beyond the Goal, Dr. Goldratt shares...* Eliyahu M. Goldratt, Beyond the Goal: Eliyahu Goldratt Speaks on the Theory of Constraints (Your Coach in a Box) (Prince Frederick, Maryland: Gildan Media, 2005), Audiobook.

342 *One of the most delightful...* David Lutz, "Imagine DevOps," YouTube video, 3:05, posted March 21, 2011, https://www.youtube .com/watch?v=iYLxw6OsZug.

He writes, "I find myself... David Lutz, "The Phoenix Project," dlutzy blog, May 3, 2013, https://dlutzy.wordpress. com/?s=the+phoenix+project.

343 *I've also come across otherwise...* Ibid.

In a blog post, I published... Gene Kim, "Quote: 'I Used to Hate "The Phoenix Project" Until I Realized It Was About Me,'" ITRevolution .com blog, September 24, 2012, https://itrevolution. com/i-used-to-hate-when-it-fails-until-i-realized-it-was-about-me/.

After finishing the book... Ibid.

344 *As my friend Jez Humble...* Jez Humble, personal conversation with Gene Kim.

345 *As Jeff Immelt, former CEO...* Jeff Immelt, "GE CEO Jeff Immelt: Let's Finally End the Debate over Whether We Are in a Tech Bubble," Business Insider, December 9, 2015, http://www.businessinsider. com/ceo-of-ge-lets-finally-end-the-debate-over-whether-we-are- in-a-tech-bubble-2015-12.

Or as Jeffrey Snover... Electric Cloud, "Weekly Top 10: Your DevOps Flavor," Electric Cloud, April 1, 2016, http://electric-cloud.com /blog/2016/04/weekly-top-10-devops-flavor/.

IDC, the analyst firm, says… Abel Avram, "IDC Study: How Many Software Developers Are Out There?" InfoQ, https://www.infoq.com/news/2014/01/IDC-software-developers

In 2016, I was talking… Gene Kim, "Face-to-Face DevOps: Protect and Serve," CA.com, March 31, 2016, https://www.ca.com/us/rewrite/articles/devops/face-to-face-devops-to-protect-and-serve-.html.

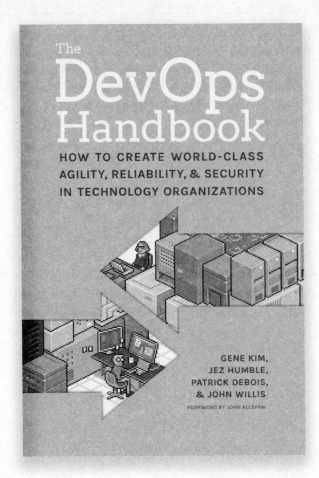

We hope you have enjoyed the first four chapters
of *The DevOps Handbook*, available now at all
fine booksellers around the world.

For information about special discounts for bulk purchases
or for information on booking authors for an event,
please visit our website at www.ITRevolution.com